RON CARTER
Finding The Right Notes

RON CARTER
Finding The Right Notes

Dan Ouellette

Foreword by Nat Hentoff

RON CARTER: FINDING THE RIGHT NOTES

© 2017 Retrac Productions

Third Retrac Productions edition 2017

This Retrac Productions edition of *Ron Carter: Finding The Right Notes* is a republication of the book first published by ArtistShare in 2008, with some revisions.

Published by Retrac Productions, Inc.
119 West 72nd Street, P.O. Box 218, New York, NY 10023

ISBN: 978-0-9899825-1-1

All rights reserved. No portion of this work may be reproduced or transmitted by any means, electronic or mechanical, including photocopying and recording, or by any information storage or retrieval system, without written permission from the copyright holder.

Front cover design: Myles Carter

"I think that the bassist is the quarterback in any group, and he must find a sound that he is willing to be responsible for."

—*Ron Carter*

Ron Carter: Finding the Right Notes

Contents

PRELUDE

Foreword *by Nat Hentoff*		3
Introduction		9
Chapter 1	The Grand Carnegie Jubilee	19

PART I - THE EARLY YEARS

Chapter 2	Early Years: Ferndale/Detroit	37
	Snapshot: Carter Family Reunion, 2006	47
Chapter 3	Early Years: Ron at Cass Tech	50
Chapter 4	Eastman/Rochester: Hope and Deferral	57
Chapter 5	Early Years: New York City	74

Photo Gallery 1   89

PART II - THE MILES YEARS

Chapter 6	The Miles Years, Part 1: Beginnings	99
Chapter 7	The Miles Years, Part 2: The Legacy	108
Chapter 8	The Miles Years, Part 3: After the Breakup	133
	Colloquy: Rudy Van Gelder on Ron Carter	147

PART III - RECORDING AS A LEADER

Chapter 9	The CTI Years: The Reign of Creed	153
Chapter 10	Milestone Records: The House of Keepnews	167
Chapter 11	EMI: Somethin' Else/Blue Note	175

Photo Gallery 2   185

PART IV - THE FREELANCE YEARS

Chapter 12	Sideman: The Carter Effect—Comfort and Provocation	195
	Snapshot: The Joey & Bill Show	213
Chapter 13	Jingles: A Different Kind of Session	218
Chapter 14	Film: Celluloid Jazz	222
	Snapshot: The Tales of Christian McBride	231
Chapter 15	Brazil: Bass Undulation	242
Chapter 16	Classical Meets Jazz	252
Chapter 17	Pedagogical Ron: A Retired Schoolteacher, Working on Weekends	258
	Snapshot: Sergio Larios on Pops	278

Photo Gallery 3 — 283

PART V - CONTEMPORARY RON

Chapter 18	The Art of Jazz Criticism	293
Chapter 19	The Ron Carter–Jim Hall Duo: Hugging Buddies	302
Chapter 20	The Striker Trio: Panning for Gold	315
Chapter 21	Quantum Quartets	327
	Colloquy: Q&A—The Quartet Questions Ron	340
Chapter 22	The Nonet	347
Chapter 23	The Commingling of Jazz and Hip-Hop	356
	Colloquy: Blindfold Test Live	363

PART VI - THE ART & SCIENCE OF THE BASS

Chapter 24	The Art of the Bass	377
	Colloquy: Bass Roundtable	386

PART VII - APPENDICES

Appendix 1	In Their Own Words: Anecdotes and Opinions	397
Appendix 2	Infrequently Asked Questions	409
Appendix 3	Selected Awards & Honors	413
Appendix 4	Selected Discography	415

Acknowledgments — 426
Index — 429

PRELUDE

Foreword

BY NAT HENTOFF

IF I WERE in charge of the Public Broadcasting System, I would schedule a regular weekly program, *Inside Jazz*, hosted by Ron Carter. Not only is he an internationally acknowledged master, bassist, composer and leader, but he's also deeply rooted in the history of the music and, in my experience, an especially lucid educator who brings newcomers and longtime jazz aficionados inside the music—and the musicians whose life stories are the music.

A musician's musician, Ron is described in the essential *Penguin Jazz Encyclopedia* (Richard Cook and Brian Morton) when he entered the world stage by joining Miles Davis:

"Carter's technique was fine enough to cope with any playing situation, but it was his ability to respond quickly and creatively to the high-level dialogues that Davis was instigating which set him apart—mixing and moving between different jazz bass methods so smoothly that he was able to transcend the obvious roles of timekeeper and harmonic floor. And it was all done so adroitly that he never drew unnecessary attention to himself."

But it's long past time that full attention be brought to the permanent contributions of Ron Carter to the music and the deeper illuminations of it in the interviews he has given. It's all there in Dan Ouellette's *Ron Carter: Finding the Right Notes*.

RON'S SKILL WITH words is equal to his resourcefulness with music notes. In a conversation with drummer Art Taylor in his *Notes and Tones* (Perigee Books), Ron teaches aspiring writers on jazz how to put the act of music into words: "Pound for pound, I'm not the strongest physical player, but I'll go out on a limb and say that I doubt there is another player who has more independence and coordination than I have. I dare say that if you could measure my sound vibration against the strongest player, his sound would not match mine in color, in length or in strength.

"It's a strong, penetrating sound. Miles was not a very strong player—not like some strong trumpet players we could think of—but his sound is so intense that it seems stronger than it is. It's incredible, man! That's my approach to the instrument—getting the most out of it by exerting the minimum physical effort."

When Ron pays tribute to his influences in jazz, you learn more about jazz from the inside. I once asked him why, as I'd heard, it was trombonist J.J. Johnson who especially influenced him at the start.

"The trombonists of J.J.'s time," Ron said, "were going as far out as they could go on their instruments for all the notes—as far as they were allowed to go. I worked opposite J.J. at a club for a week, and I noticed he never went much beyond the bell of his horn. Having studied trombone in school, I knew it's all right there—the overtone series and much else. J.J. had such a command of this series of notes and each range that it was not necessary for him to go all the way as the others tried to go. So I said to myself that it's possible to have the same kind of knowledge of the instrument on a string. I can play the same notes horizontally that I can play vertically."

ONE OF MY great kicks in writing about this music is getting to know the musicians off the stand as well. In my day job as a reporter for *The Village Voice*, *The Washington Times* and the National United Media Newspaper Syndicate, I've gotten to know members of Congress, a Supreme Court justice, human rights workers, Malcolm X, labor leaders, et al—but I've learned more about the world, and life itself, from some of the jazz musicians who became my friends, including Duke Ellington, Charles Mingus, Billie Holiday, Paul Desmond and Clark Terry.

And Ron, who has known so many more because they're part of his family, told me, "One of the things I've enjoyed as a member of the jazz community is I've met some great, great people who were musicians. I love all those guys, man. If they didn't play music, I wouldn't care. If I were to look to find an image to imitate, I would take some of each of the 30 or 40 guys I know who helped me to become a complete person."

I know what he means. When I was still in my early 20s, I was so lucky to have Duke Ellington as an occasional mentor. He taught me: "Don't get caught up in categories, like 'modern jazz' or 'cutting-edge music.' It's the individual!"

An individual like Ron Carter. And like many of these jazz individuals, Ron is knowledgeable about so much more than jazz and that knowledge becomes a part of his music.

He explained to me, "Another reason I'm happy to be a part of this career is that I've been able to see other people in their own environment, their own cultures—whether it's in Japan, China or the States. Each place has its own culture. To have the capacity to travel to all these cultural units has been an enlightenment for me. And the final happiness for me is I've been lucky to play with people who've allowed me—because they've trusted my musical judgment—to experiment with them and keep learning."

❖❖ ❖❖

IN OSCAR PETERSON'S book, *A Jazz Odyssey* (Continuum), he described his experience of transcendence while playing: "Creating an uninhibited, off-the-cuff musical composition in front of an audience is a daredevil enterprise—one that draws on everything about you, not just your musical talent. It requires you to collect all your senses, emotions, physical strength and mental power, and focus them totally onto the performance—utter dedication every time you play."

Oscar continued, "And if that is scary, it is also uniquely exciting. Once it's bitten you, you never get rid of it. Nor do you want to, for you come to believe that if you get it *all* right, you will be capable of virtually anything. That is what drives me, and I know it will always do so."

I asked Ron if anything came immediately to mind about that kind of transcendence, where everything is working—an experience he had on the stand that keeps resonating in him.

"There was a club in New York's Greenwich Village called Sweet Basil," Ron replied. "I was working there with a trio one night in the summer. As you now, the Village in the summer gets very active. People come from everywhere just to be there. I'm in this club, and we're supposed to start at 9 o'clock. It's now 9:15 and the pianist hasn't shown up. Well, the people are getting restless.

"They're starting to complain about there being no music, and the food isn't right. They're really getting antsy. It's Friday night, man, and the place is full.

"The club owner says, 'What do you want to do?' I went onstage and played for 45 minutes, solo bass. I think people were so stunned to see this guy do this that I had their attention. When everybody gets frustrated, finding the notes to play for them is some challenge. I found the notes that night, and ever since, when I'm not getting a particular audience's attention, I go back to that zone because I know it's possible to have that happen again."

Having been a friend of Miles Davis, I asked Ron what it had been like being in his zone of surprises. "As you know," he answered, "there are a lot of stories and rumors that are not complimentary about Miles. But in my five years with him, I never saw any of those events take place. Whatever his physical pain was, he came to work to play every night. I mean, every night.

"That kind of presence demanded the same kind of intensity from the remaining four of us. Miles seldom told us what to play or not to play. He trusted that we were bright enough and curious enough to know when it wasn't happening—and then make some adjustments. It was a great experience for me. And I would like to think that my playing with him was a great experience for *him*."

Listening to Miles's recordings from that period leaves no doubt about that.

Reading Dan's book, you'll find so much more about Ron's indispensable role in the history of this music.

I ASKED RON about the recurrent, premature obituaries about jazz, almost from the beginning of that word getting into our national conversation.

"Jazz will survive," he said. "One reason is that schools of higher education—colleges and universities—are teaching it."

I noted that the same is true with elementary, middle and high schools. I told Ron about second graders in Queens, New York, whose teacher plays a range of music for them, including John Coltrane. Those kids responded so deeply to the power of Coltrane's feelings and imagination. When their teacher told them that Coltrane's home, not far from the school, was about to be bought and destroyed by a real estate developer and that there was a campaign to save it and make it a national landmark, the kids held bake sales to join in and raise money.

Ron welcomed the news and added that he is further heartened by the continuance of jazz summer schools where kids who don't have exposure to jazz in their neighborhoods can go.

"There are some wonderful young players out there who are determined to make this music theirs," Ron said. "And as long as this remains a personal priority, we're going to be with this music for a very long time."

Ron also has a vision of how the audience for this music, across all age groups, can grow. "I'd try," he said, "to get a radio show, a weekly program showing the broad history of this music to make listeners aware of that broad history. I'd say, for instance, this is a Coltrane theme, but it's also over here in this hip-hop record and in this score from a movie. They'd see that this music, this jazz they're not allowed to hear anymore on most radio, is part of the whole big picture of music."

Warming to the effect such a lively education would have, Ron said, "I'm sure the audience would improve in size because in understanding how relevant this music is to all forms of musical expression, the listeners simultaneously would be finding a lot of music they like."

Ron's vision of such an awakening radio series ties in with my previous recommendation that he also would finally be able to get public television tuned into this country's most vital and regenerating gift to the world.

Referring to Ron's own permanent contribution to the life force of jazz, *The Penguin Guide to Jazz Recordings* (Cook and Morton) emphasizes that Ron "has such innate musicality that he has always been able to sustain progress as a leader in his own right."

I once asked Ron, "Now that you've accomplished so much, what, if anything, would you still like to do?"

He readily answered, "One of my phrases is, finding the best note. I'm still looking for the best set of notes."

And that's why this book is called *Finding the Right Notes*.

—NAT HENTOFF

Author of The Jazz Life, Listen to the Stories, American Music Is *and other books on jazz, including the forthcoming* At the Jazz Band Ball: Sixty Years on the Jazz Scene *(University of California Press). He also writes on jazz for* The Wall Street Journal *and* JazzTimes.

Introduction

A T SIX FEET, four inches, the bassist towers over the bandstand, no longer relegated to the back, in the shadows behind the frontline players.

And in a historical shift of jazz bass playing, he's no longer just a timekeeper, a rhythm man, a sidekick to the spotlight artist—but an architect of the highest order, an impromptu composer even when he's not taking solos.

Pliable yet powerful. The instigator. The catalyst. The shaper. The shepherd. The finest walker in the history of jazz. The risk-taker with an elegant streak. Refined.

The anchor of Miles Davis's classic '60s quintet. The most recorded jazz bassist of all time. National Endowment for the Arts Jazz Master.

If he were a character in a novel, he would be the protagonist.

That's Ron Carter, jazz legend—and icon, as his friend Herbie Hancock calls him.

"Ron's historical footprint is massive," said fellow bassist John Patitucci. "The historical statements he's made over the decades are phenomenal." John also recognizes that Ron's mystique and business-minded approach to jazz is renowned. "I've been fortunate to never be on the wrong side of Ron Carter. He is legendary about holding people accountable. He has very high standards."

Intimidating and perhaps gruff on the outside, Ron is funny, kind and personable to those he trusts and who have been granted the gift of knowing him.

In June 2004, Ron approached me at the Jazz Journalists Association's Jazz Awards show at B.B. King's in New York and started a conversation that concluded a couple of months later with me agreeing to write his biography, to chronicle his storied life.

Interested? Ron asked.

Most certainly, I replied. I'm honored.

Now, after hundreds of hours of interviews with Ron, his colleagues and his family, *Ron Carter: Finding the Right Notes* is born. It's not a tell-all, gossip-strewn account, but the tale of a sober musician who thrived in the Faustian world of many of his peers (unlike them, Ron did not drink or take drugs). Nor is this a Valentine card for a dedicated musician who enjoys his well-deserved celebrity. Rather, *Finding the Right Notes* captures an artist's journey that encompasses more than half of the history of jazz. Ron's biography tells the story of his musical life—from his early years as a cellist and his brilliant contributions in Miles Davis's '60s quintet to his days as a leader in his own right and his contemporary career where nightly he makes new strides in search of the right notes.

The finding of those right notes—notes that make the music magic and inspiring and fresh—has been Ron's lifelong quest. Countless times in our conversations, he returned to the search for this elusive jazz Holy Grail. In talking about his role in Miles's rhythm section, he said, "I had been to school and learned harmonic analysis. I knew the note choices already. I knew they existed, but I needed to find just the right ones. My job with Herbie and Tony [Williams] was to tell them that I was looking for something. Some nights I would only get close, and they were waiting for me to find what I was looking for. And they knew I would. I'd stick with it until I did. I searched every night and tried to find the most right of the right notes. It was an adventure. You know the path is available, but you have to keep the gate open."

In Howard Mandel's May 1996 *DownBeat* story on Ron, "The Anchor," the subject said, "I'm not sure I'm ever comfortable with my skill level. Technique's something you develop all the time. Intonation's a constant problem for bass players. Finding the right notes is a constant battle. To be able to play in tune with an out-of-tune piano is an ongoing fight. Satisfied is not always the word that applies to me. Looking for the best set of notes with the best pitch and best sound, yes—I still try to do that."

In an article on Ron by Brian Lonergan, he responded to the interviewer's comment that he has achieved a pinnacle in his playing: "Well, I'm kind of like Martin Luther King Jr., but I haven't been to the mountaintop yet. I'm trying to find out what the top of the mountain looks like, and the only way to get there is by playing every night like it's my last chance to get this right. I think I've come close several times, and the view [from the top], I would imagine, is spectacular. I'm about at the tree line right now, but I'm getting there."

JAZZ JEFE

IN GENERAL, BASS players are relegated to support status, even in jazz circles where appreciation and analysis of the multifarious elements of performance—melody, harmony, rhythm—reveal the idiom to be a fine art of the highest order. Though it is at the fulcrum of the music, the tall, four-string instrument too often gets short shrift. Figuratively and literally, the bass resides in the back of the band. "It's still back there," Ron said. "And it's unfortunate that the bass is viewed in that way. People call it the workhorse of the band, which to me is a left-handed compliment because bass players can do a whole lot more than that."

Ron recalls an early-evening performance he and his quartet gave at an open space in the Museum of Natural History in New York. An "indoor picnic" is how he described the setting. "We knew it wasn't going to be living-room silent because there was a bunch of 6-to-12-year-old kids running around, " he said. "But a lot of people made a ring around us and listened. Yet, what distressed me, when it was over, was how people came up to me and told me what a great solo I had performed. To me that's not the point of being a bass player. Solos are nice and interesting. But they don't show how the bass player conducts the band with his instrument—the notes he plays, where he plays them and how they determine the direction that the rest of the band will go."

The bass solo may be eight to 10 choruses long each night, Ron points out, but what about the thousands of choruses the bassist delivers throughout the evening? "I'd like to see people tune into the bassist who plays with a different mind-set, skill set, musical daring that affects everyone else in the band," he said. "But all too often there's the bass in the back, churning around in the background of the sound, hidden away behind the horns in the front. I'd like to see that view be put aside."

After catching Ron live dozens of times over the past few years, I can attest to his creative endeavors in schooling his audiences. No two sets are the same. No shows are mailed in, even after a grueling day of travel to get to a venue. As a jazz *jefe*, Ron makes certain that a high level of creativity is upheld. And, certainly, he makes sure that the bassist will never be invisible.

DEBUNKING MYTHS

IT'S ALMOST A given that when you talk to people who don't know Ron or haven't worked with him intimately, they say, "Ron Carter. You have to watch your step with him. He's intimidating. He's arrogant. All he ever did was get himself into Miles's band."

Hopefully, *Finding the Right Notes* will debunk these opinions and errant accusations about Ron. True, Ron is tall and imposing. He doesn't behave with the kind of backslapping faux friendliness that many entertainers possess. He's quiet and shy. Instead of being a beaming presence backstage, he's more inclined to be in a corner reading a mystery novel or poring over the box scores on a newspaper sports page.

Ron doesn't scowl. He doesn't burst into fits of rage. In fact, it's only on rare occasions that he loses control of his emotions. Drummer/vocalist Grady Tate has performed with Ron on many occasions over the years. "Ron's not loud about who he is," he said. "He just wants to play. People may think he's standoffish, but that's who Ron is. He's open to people, but not to idiots—who he will ignore. I've seen Ron angry, but that's the extent of it. I never saw him go off on anyone. It's Ron's coolness that prevails."

Drummer Lewis Nash agrees. A longtime collaborator in Ron's bands, he put it bluntly: "Ron has a low tolerance for bullshit. I hear what people—even other musicians—say about him, but all I can say is that they don't have a clue. It's disheartening. Ron is not appreciated in the way that he should be. You'd think that other musicians would recognize how much he has contributed to this music, without being flashy and top heavy."

Lewis says that Ron presents himself in a way that means business. He adheres to a high standard when it comes to the music and being professional. "Ron is very comfortable in his own skin, and he's very patient," Lewis said. "But if someone is being lackadaisical and unfocused, he'll be vocal about that. He's not afraid to express his opinion. It's not about sound and fury for Ron, but all about true substance."

New York bass-doctor David Gage, who has taken care of Ron's instrument needs for years, says that it's not easy for such a private man to be forthcoming off the stage. "Ron is so comfortable in front of a crowd when he's got his bass," he said. "He's very shy, but he has a wry sense of humor. People think he's aloof, but often it's all about them. They want to be liked by Ron, they want to have Ron say good things about them. If he doesn't, they say, 'He thinks I'm not good? Screw him.' Ron comes off hot and cold. He's a genuinely warm man, but he's also serious and strategic, always thinking about what to do next."

For many years, Ron has recognized that he's got a forbidding reputation. He makes no qualms about that. In Ed Williams's "Ron Carter: The Compleat Artist" article in the February 2, 1978 issue of *DownBeat*, he talked about the perception that he was arrogant. "I'm sure that's with a great deal of accuracy, and I don't back up from that," he said. "The fact is [black professional musicians] had to be arrogant because no one encouraged us. Everyone told us we were gonna be nothin.'"

To Ron, professionalism trumps all else. He continued, talking with Williams about his session work as a sideman: "I'm on time for the job. I am prepared musically and technically to meet the demands of the music. I will share my thoughts, as graciously as they will be allowed to be shared, with the leader, in terms of contributing a thought to the music that he has not considered." Ron said his goal was always to contribute to "a positive frame of reference in terms of expecting to be musically delighted" about the projects he's involved in. He added, "Humble is not the right word, but I try to downplay my level as graciously as I can, and just do the job and let what I play be my testimony to my arrogance."

The final myth about Ron in need of deconstruction is that his fame with Miles was his be-all and end-all. Bob Belden, who helped to produce the CD-box reissues of Miles's live and studio recording sessions at Columbia Records, scoffs at the idea. "That's always been the prejudiced image of Ron," he said. "But his association with Miles was just one-tenth of his career." He cited all of his work before the 1963–68 Miles era as well as after. "Ron is a serious cat. He's like Miles in that way. Hey, he's got a masters degree in music from a very tough school. He knows what he's doing. And he's not afraid to play all kinds of music."

THE RACIAL DIVIDE

ON NOVEMBER 4, 2008, as *Finding the Right Notes* was in its final stages of completion, Illinois Democratic Senator Barack Obama out-dueled, out-raced, out-finessed, out-graced, outwitted and outsmarted his Republican Party opponent, Arizona Senator John McCain, for the highest elected office in the United States. While Obama's quest for party nomination and then the presidency was deemed highly unlikely at all junctures throughout his two-year campaign, he became, against the odds, the first African-American president. On election night, his supporters celebrated him by transforming the rallying cry of his campaign, "Yes, we can!" to the gleeful shout of "Yes, we did!"

The next day the original "Yes, we can!" mantra was reawakened after President-elect Obama reminded his constituency that being elected to the presidency was only the first step—an act of affirmation that gave him the opportunity to make the dire shape-shifting changes the majority of the American public was thirsting for.

As I watched on TV Obama's victory speech at Chicago's Grant Park (which also serves as the main stage of Chicago's Labor Day weekend jazz festival), I couldn't help but think of Ron's life and how race factored so heavily into his career. Despite all the hurdles of racial discrimination thrust into his path on his way to becoming a master musician, Ron's commitment to his own yes-I-can, yes-I-will attitude was formidable.

Race was a factor for Ron, from his high school days in Detroit when he was not invited to perform at extracurricular functions (prompting him to switch his instrument from cello to bass) to his college days at Eastman School of Music when a world-class visiting conductor applauded his prowess on the bass but told him his own orchestra would never hire him because he was African American (prompting Ron to redirect his career aspirations from classical music to jazz).

Ron recalled his first road trip after he graduated from Eastman and joined Chico Hamilton's band. The tour bus stopped at a restaurant outside Washington, D.C., and the black musicians were forced to enter through the backdoor because they weren't allowed in the front. A few years later Ron experienced prejudice again while playing in Miles's band. They performed a show at the Left Bank Jazz Society in Baltimore, after which Ron and George Coleman drove back to New York. On the way home, they stopped at a restaurant in Maryland but were refused service because they didn't cater to blacks.

The year was 1963. A few months later, while on tour with Miles, Ron awoke on the morning of September 16 and was shocked to read in the newspapers about the Ku Klux Klan bombing of the 16th Street Baptist

Church in Birmingham, Alabama—the hub of the pro-integration movement in the city—that killed four teenaged black girls.

"I remember talking to Herbie and Tony about this that morning," Ron said. "We were dumbfounded. We were all still young, so we didn't know how to verbalize how stunned we were. We were astounded that some people were so afraid of integration that they would bomb a church without regard to its occupants. We couldn't grasp the physical hostility. Not getting waited on in a restaurant was one thing. But this was another level of hate."

The outrage at the bombing hastened the passage of the Civil Rights Bill of 1964. Yet, while integration was legally mandated by the act, racial discrimination raged on.

Even though Ron is recognized today as the dean of jazz bassists, race continues to be a theme. "It's there," he told me in one of our earliest conversations for this biography. "It cannot *not* be a part of any African American's life, especially in my age category. Most blacks who are in their 20s don't have the same kind of physical recollection of those days."

Even today, Ron says he has been pulled over in his car when driving home from a late-night gig. "It's two in the morning, and they ask me, where are you going and what's that in the back of your car?" Ron said. "That's why we call it being pulled over for a DWB—Driving While Black."

Ron recalled a few years ago being in a restaurant in Boston where waiters avoided serving him. Some years earlier, he was shopping in Bloomingdale's in New York, keenly aware that the store detectives were watching him, suspecting that he was there to shoplift. "After about a half hour, I walked up to them and told them that I knew what their job was," Ron said. "But I told them, while you were watching me, you didn't see that lady over there who just stole three ties."

And the discrimination may be subtle. "I was in line with my band, checking into a hotel in Paris," Ron said. "The guy before us put down his gold Visa card. Then I walked up with my platinum Visa, and the clerk called the manager. I said, 'You didn't do that to the guy with gold. And I've got platinum.'"

Does Ron feel that the racial divide has been bridged as a result of jazz—the mighty African-American-born art form that is widely embraced by white musicians and white concertgoers? "I don't think so," he said soberly. "People might get that perspective from outside the music, but they don't see inside the topic. We can talk about the integrated bands that we all play in today, and I haven't heard of a black musician not being allowed to play in front of an all-white audience. But without giving a lot of analytical thought on the subject, I don't see that racial divide being any smaller. I don't think it's happened yet."

Ron looks at the big picture. Certainly, there are mixed-race crowds at the clubs where he plays, but attendance at those shows is miniscule compared to the nation's population on the whole. "We'd like to think that even playing for 200 or even a thousand people every set is going to help fix the racial problem, but I still see huge obstacles ahead of us. White people sitting in a mixed audience may like the music, but when they leave, we're still black."

Ron paused and then added, "Psychologists would have a field day with me. Here I am, having reached what some people would call a pinnacle of success not normally allotted to African-American males. But they would also see that I'm not sure how to accept this level of accolades when my brothers and sisters haven't gotten this far."

Pianist Geri Allen, who, like Ron, graduated from Cass Tech in Detroit, sees hope in the image Ron has portrayed throughout his career. "Ron has advanced the African-American culture," she said. "He brings dignity to the music, which is helpful for other black musicians. The way he's carried himself through the years and the opinions he's expressed have been so important to us. Ron's persona may be misunderstood, but he personifies not the entertainer, but the artist. He may have offended people along the way, but he's held to his beliefs because that's who he is. He has been a spine for us black musicians."

While Ron's story throughout *Finding the Right Notes* does not focus on the topic of race, racial discrimination permeates it, which gives heft to the biography's title. In essence, in the midst of a culture that can't seem to make peace with the grace and puissance of racial diversity and social justice, throughout his life Ron has continually sought metaphorically to find the right notes for his personal journey.

RON'S CRIB

ON SEPTEMBER 1, 2005, I turned on my digital recorder for the first interview for this book, sitting at Ron's dining-room table. I had been to his Upper West Side apartment several times before on various assignments, including a cover story for *Strings* magazine, which prompted Ron to ask me to tell his story in writing.

The elevator to Ron's floor literally opens into his spacious, multiroom spread. The first thing you see upon entering is a tall, scuffed-up, hardplastic white case that transports his mainstay bass. It stands there in the foyer with a statuesque physicality—the perfect welcome into his home.

Once inside, you're immediately struck by the artwork throughout. It's as if you're in a museum. Most of the sculptures and paintings were purchased by Ron's late wife Janet, who collected a private gallery of African-American art. Prominently displayed are the dramatic brown/beige five-by-six-foot painting "Slave Ship" by Carole Byard, a bright orange and cerulean abstract wall sculpture that looks like a series of bass clefs in the shape of a chainsaw by Detroit artist Al Loving, and a gray-painted postmodern tapestry comprised of leather strips, paper punch-out holes and tiny knick-knacks by Howardina Pindell.

"Janet wanted her family to be surrounded by great art by African-American artists," Ron said, noting that while she was an English/Black Literature major at the University of Syracuse, she also minored in art. "So, she made her way around New York to find out who they were."

While working as a copyeditor for *Urbanite* magazine and later *Essence*, Janet became involved in the black arts community. She was not only one of the founding members of the Studio Museum in Harlem, which opened in 1967, but she also ran her own art gallery on Greene Street in SoHo from 1980 to 1982. She later collected and sold artwork out of their apartment.

"Janet was aware of the deficiencies of arts education for African-American children in the schools," Ron said. "So collecting the art was her way of trying to keep the scales better balanced. If art wasn't offered in the schools, our sons, Ron Jr. and Myles, would have top-shelf artwork in their home. And not only that, but they also got to meet artists like Carole Byard and Joe Overstreet, shake their hands, and know them as friends of the family."

HOW TO READ THIS BOOK

IN THE COURSE of writing *Finding the Right Notes*, I followed a sketchy outline of what I perceived to be the integral chapters of Ron's life, from his Ferndale/Detroit days as a child to his present-day musical contributions through the various bands he helms as well as through his frequent sideman gigs. But as I moved along, other chapters emerged, including, for example, his passion for the music of Brazil and his strong opinions on the role of music critics. That forced me to break from a chronological approach to storytelling while at the same time allowing me to fashion chapters that could stand on their own and be read in any order.

I also broke the standard biography mold by slipping in the equivalent of magazine sidebars or musical tangents. Interspersed throughout the book are Snapshots (four close-up portraits of Ron and his relationships with family and colleagues) and Colloquies (four Q&A-like sections, including full transcripts of two interview sessions that appeared in *DownBeat* in truncated form). These too can be read as stand-alones.

A word about two of the appendices: They serve to expand on the significance of Ron's career. The first, "In Their Own Words," is a roll call of artists weighing in on Ron's contributions as well as sharing anecdotes about his music and life.

And then there's the "Selected Discography" appendix. Anyone even remotely familiar with Ron's five-decades-plus work knows that he stands tall as jazz's reigning champion for making the greatest number of studio dates. Compiling a comprehensive discography is a daunting challenge, even for Ron, who is often surprised to be told of a date that he had totally forgotten about. Yet, ask him if he remembers a certain session, and he's spot-on with details and personnel. Every day that I researched and wrote this book I came across yet another reference to a record on which Ron appeared. So, with apologies, please accept a selected rundown of Ron's discography, gleaned from five different sources.

—DAN OUELLETTE

CHAPTER ONE

The Grand Carnegie Jubilee

THE OVERVIEW

On June 27, 2007, Ron Carter performed his first concert as a leader at Carnegie Hall in the Isaac Stern Auditorium, which seats 2,804 people. The show, titled "Ron Carter: The Master at 70," was part of the JVC Jazz Festival New York. It proved to be a triumphant concert commercially—sold-out except for a handful of seats that have obstructed views—and artistically as Ron presented four different bands: his trio, his quartet, his duo partnership with Jim Hall and a special quartet with former Miles Davis alums Herbie Hancock, Wayne Shorter and Billy Cobham. Afterwards, when asked what if a small crowd had attended instead of the full house, Ron replied, "I was never concerned about the number of people that showed up. I was concerned that I'd make a presentation worthy enough for those who did come."

A veteran of the jazz scene for more than a half-century, Ron has experienced times when the crowds weren't what he had hoped for. In 1977 he scored a week's stay at the Village Vanguard in New York with a new quartet he formed. "Some of my friends who knew me from working at the clubs uptown came to the Vanguard to the late show one night," he said. "After a full house for the first set, the house was maybe half full for the second. They asked me how I was doing. I told them that I was pretty disappointed and even despondent. They told me, 'Hey, you're still driving a Mercedes even if there's not a lot of gas in the car at the moment.' That's helped me through the times when I expected a larger turnout."

Full-capacity turnouts for anything to do with Ron was not an issue in 2007, the year in which he turned 70 (May 4) and released stateside one of his best albums, *Dear Miles*, on Blue Note (in June, right before the Carnegie Hall date). At my live *DownBeat* Blindfold Test with Ron at the International Association for Jazz Educators mega-conference in New York in January, he drew the largest crowd I'd seen for an audience-attended BFT (and I have done nearly 30 over the years at Monterey Jazz Festival, North Sea Jazz Festival and IAJE)—plus, no one left the auditorium to go sample another clinic or show.

Another example: when Monifa Brown, a DJ at the greater metropolitan jazz radio station in New Jersey, WBGO, interviewed Ron live at J&R Music in downtown New York. She wrote me an e-mail after the event:

"Just wanted to let you know that the Ron Carter performance/interview was superb. He was totally gracious with his time, conversation and performance. The jazz floor at J&R was absolutely mobbed. I think it was their biggest crowd ever. It was beautiful to see how many people came out to express their love and admiration of Ron Carter. He was a delight and made me feel instantly comfortable, choosing to share the same mic and do every interview segment with his arm around me. I am blessed to have had this rare opportunity that I will always cherish. Ron Carter is a living legend and should be deemed a national treasure!"

After his Carnegie show, I joked with Ron that this truly was his season. "You mean, that everything is falling in place?" he asked, then replied to his own question: "If you stay around long enough, I guess people acknowledge it."

True, but it was only a few short years before when he felt slighted by not having been acknowledged for what he considered to be a significant Carnegie event. On December 14, 2005, Ron and his trio partners, Russell Malone and Mulgrew Miller, performed at the music palace's 599-seat Zankel Hall, the revamped old Recital Hall of the original building that is housed underneath the Main Hall. It had opened for classical and jazz concerts in September 2003. This was Ron's first leader date in the heralded Carnegie complex that still has cachet as one of the world's premiere music performance spaces.

Zankel was not fully sold out, even though the crowd of some 575 thoroughly enjoyed the set. When the trio walked onstage, all in tuxedos, the audience gave it a standing ovation. After four tunes, Ron greeted the crowd and made the jocular but pointed comment, "I finally made it to Carnegie Hall—but we're in the basement."

Two days later, I arrived at Ron's apartment for an interview appointment and remarked to him, "The good news is that there's no transit strike this morning," referring to the 11th-hour negotiations that kept the New York City subways and buses in motion, thus avoiding a city-bustle stall and halt.

With *The New York Times* spread out on the table in front of him, Ron replied with a growl, "The bad news is that the trio didn't make *The Times*." He was visibly upset. He frowned and continued, "I expected to have some kind of coverage—a major concert in a major hall. But they reviewed some singer. Our show deserved some kind of interest other than from my fans and friends." He paused and said that this was his first major show as a leader at the Carnegie building. He had played there before as a sideman, though he couldn't recall exactly when and with whom. He added in an insulted tone of voice, "Plus, my first show there, and they made me play in the basement."

The jazz gentleman, who from afar looks as if no projectile can penetrate his sense of self, appeared flustered to the verge of being flabbergasted.

The more we talked, the more Ron fumed. "I thought this was a major enough event to command attention, to have editors assign a jazz writer to review this show in this hall and its specialized environment," he said. "Few jazz bands get to play there. The headline on the paper itself says, 'All the News That's Fit to Print.' It seems to me that what we did qualifies for that kind of interest." He thought for a few seconds and then added, "I'm of the mind-set as we speak to type a letter to *The Times*. I've done this before and got it published."

Two years later *The Times* did review a second Carnegie Hall showcase—the birthday concert—that Ron presented. While he got the coverage he desired then, he was not pleased with the critique.

Both Carnegie Hall events—the overdue recognition resulting in the first invite, an artistic triumph followed by the lack of media appreciation; and the second, more noteworthy appearance resulting in mixed local newspaper coverage—mirror Ron's career as a whole. In his early days, he strove mightily as a musician—an aspiring classical cellist, who switched to bass—with a vision of performing in a major orchestra, only to have his dream deferred. Jazz, by default, became his path, which proved to be his true calling—where his ability, his talent, his intellect, his soul as an artist became fully realized and recognized.

THE HERALDED HALL

BUILT ON THE corner of 57th Street and 7th Avenue in New York's rapid-paced midtown, Carnegie Hall opened in 1891 to provide the city with a grand venue to showcase the greatest soloists, ensembles and conductors of the world. Designed by architect and cellist William Burnett Tuthill, the primary performance space, called simply the Main Hall, has a curvilinear design with five levels of seating focused on the stage. Isaac Stern, the classical music violin virtuoso whose name now graces the hall, once noted, "It has been said that the hall itself is an instrument. It takes what you do and makes it larger than life."

Carnegie Hall also included the Recital Hall (now the Judy and Arthur Zankel Hall), underneath the Main Hall, and the third-floor 268-seat Chamber Music Hall (renamed the Joan and Sanford J. Weill Recital Hall in 1986). The Recital Hall was leased in 1895 to the American Academy of Dramatic Arts and later used by various theater groups until the early 1960s. After that, it was converted into a cinema. In 1997 Carnegie Hall reclaimed the space, began a major renovation project and reopened it as Zankel Hall in 2003.

While originally conceived as a majestic house of classical music, which later housed the esteemed New York Philharmonic, Carnegie Hall eventually opened its temple doors to the burgeoning jazz movement. The influx began on January 16, 1938 when the king of swing, Benny Goodman, escorted his music off the dance floor and onto the concert stage for the evening with a full array of jazz, including works performed by his orchestra as well as his small groups, including his interracial quartet comprising pianist Teddy Wilson, vibraphonist Lionel Hampton and drummer Gene Krupa. Sol Hurok, at the time one of the most prestigious impresarios in the U.S., booked the show, banking on Goodman's popularity at Hotel Pennsylvania's Manhattan Room and the Paramount Theatre, as well as that of his prime-time national radio program, *The Camel Caravan*. The Carnegie show was a sellout.

While the concert broke the seal, allowing jazz entry into the bastion of the mainstream European classical world, the recording of the Carnegie show was slow to emerge on disc. It wasn't until 1950, when the acetate tapes and aluminum studio masters were discovered on a shelf in Goodman's apartment by his sister-in-law, that the album *Benny Goodman Live at Carnegie Hall 1938* was released. (Today it's considered a classic, must-have jazz album.)

By then Carnegie Hall, though still largely a venue for the great classical music performers of the world, was regularly presenting jazz. It has continued to this day to be a forum for significant jazz events, featuring performances by such jazz titans as Miles Davis and Charles Mingus. Perhaps equally as significant as Goodman's debut there was the landmark 1957 concert by pianist Thelonious Monk and tenor saxophonist John Coltrane, which showcased the former's return to glory after losing his cabaret license in New York and launched the latter's comeback after kicking his heroin habit. That show too was recorded and the tapes shelved. They were discovered more than four decades later in an unmarked box at the Library of Congress and subsequently released in 2005 as the hugely successful CD, *Thelonious Monk Quartet With John Coltrane at Carnegie Hall*.

In 1992, impresario George Wein, who regularly featured jazz summits at Carnegie Hall as a part of his JVC New York Jazz Festival, founded the 17-piece Carnegie Hall Jazz Band, led by trumpeter Jon Faddis. In its 10-year existence, the orchestra performed more than 40 concerts, presenting more than 135 musicians (including 70 guest artists) and premiering new works by more than 35 composers and arrangers. It was lights out for the band in 2002 by decree of Carnegie Hall's new executive director, Robert J. Harth, who came on board in December 2001. At the time, the disgruntled Faddis told *The New York Times*, "Historically, jazz has always been looked down on. Jung used to talk about jazz being the ugly stepchild, and at one time our music was considered the music of the devil. Maybe we have not overcome that subconscious thought in the minds of the people who have the power to fund it."

In the article, Harth countered by saying that he applauded the band as a vital jazz orchestra but felt that Carnegie Hall would better serve the jazz community by reallocating its funds "to provide a wider variety [of jazz] as opposed to supporting just one band."

Since that time, Carnegie Hall has not only presented jazz in the Stern Auditorium (primarily jazz festival showcases by the likes of Sonny Rollins, Keith Jarrett, Diana Krall and Joshua Redman) but also features a regular season of shows at Zankel Hall. It was here that Ron's Striker Trio, with Mulgrew and Russell, made its Carnegie debut as a part of the hall's adventurous The Shape of Jazz 2005–2006 season, which also included performances by young drummer Matt Wilson with his Arts and Crafts quartet, pianist/vocalist Patricia Barber and pianist/composer Fred Hersch.

STRIKER AT ZANKEL

ZANKEL'S JAZZ LINEUP was programmed at the time by Festival Productions' artistic director Dan Melnick. "A lot of phenomenal jazz musicians never headlined Carnegie Hall," Dan said. "It has a lot to do with a musician's profile as a prominent leader as well as the expectations of the box office."

Dan noted that in the heyday of jazz, from the '40s through the '70s, it was easier for a musician to be recognized for his or her leadership credibility. Today, he said, it's a much harder hill to climb. "It's an uphill battle even for great artists. You have to have a record label, a manager and an agent all working together to insure that you get box-office cachet," he said. "All artists who are considered the greats have that struggle—from Dave Holland to Ahmad Jamal to the Heaths—to be concert hall attractions. You have to be so popular and have such a public face to a wide enough percentage of people to sell 2,600 seats at Carnegie Hall. The reality of jazz is that it doesn't have a lot of media exposure or radio airplay." Dan said that other than Krall, there isn't a modern female jazz singer, including Dianne Reeves and Cassandra Wilson, who could sell out a venue like Carnegie Hall, unless there's a double bill.

"Ron's in that same boat," Dan said. "He's one of the great names in the jazz world, but outside of that, most people don't know who Ron Carter is. They know the names of all the legends, from Tito Puente to Dizzy Gillespie to Miles Davis to Ray Charles, but they don't know Ron. And that's the battle Ron has always had—to get out from under the shadow of the predecessors."

Dan booked Ron's trio for the Zankel show after its appearance at the 2004 Newport Jazz Festival 50th anniversary weekend. The band was playing on a secondary stage, but Dan said the show was amazing. "The trio killed. It was acoustic, no drums and musically special. So a couple of months later when I was booking Zankel's next season, I felt Ron's trio would be perfect. The hall was built to hear bands like this. It's intimate and the perfect place to hear these three incredible musicians. Zankel is the perfect place to hear artists who have never had the opportunity to play upstairs as a leader."

Ron and Co. made good on Dan's bet. Backstage before the show, the leader was jovial and relaxed as were both Russell and Mulgrew. Onstage, that same spirit was intact as the threesome sculpted a show of refined elegance with Ron standing tall and stately, wearing a gray vest and a peach-colored kerchief in his jacket pocket. His fat, warm tone formed the foundation of the music that was performed in segue style, with the coda of one number leading into the prelude of another. Upbeat pieces with walking bass lines evolved into tender balladry with ponderous bass solos tinged with melancholy. Introduced as "one of my favorite songs," "My Funny Valentine" was given a lengthy meditation, followed by John Lewis's "The Golden Striker," delivered by the trio in a playful, skipping frolic. Then Ron blew the show wide open by going it solo on "Willow Weep for Me," playing his bass with a special brightness that brought the house to its feet.

Enjoying the crowd's response, Ron smiled, then shuffled through the sheet music to find a tune, remarking with his subtle sense of humor, "You can always tell who is the bandleader...he's the guy who doesn't have the right vest and he can never find the music on time." Maybe true, but he knew exactly what he was looking for. Ron closed the evening with a sumptuous version of "Autumn Leaves." Though appearing stoic for most of the evening, Ron flashed a smile to Russell and cracked a joke to him during the standing O at the end.

Dan marveled after the concert. "I loved it. It was brilliant," he gushed, admitting that he was nervous about the concert's length. "I fear that cats who do these concerts will go on too long, to go beyond the 70- to 95-minute set time. Ron played for more than two hours, but it was so musical, so sweet, and his bass solo was one of the most beautiful I've ever heard."

In his own reflection on the show, Ron said that he planned the set a couple of days before the concert: "I thought about what kind of story we could tell. I planned the show to be two 45-minute sets with an intermission in between, like we do at a club. But at soundcheck, I found out that we were playing 90 minutes straight through. At that point I decided to segue material, going from song A to song B and making a nice long paragraph. So, I had to change my original plan to adapt to this new set length. I figured, let's keep going in a certain direction until one of us in the band just gives up, then we'll go in another direction."

Another factor that figured into the set was that Ron didn't feel comfortable with the sound of the room once it had filled up with people. "It just didn't feel right," he explained, "but I thought, well, let's make this work. I changed the order of the tunes as Russell and Mulgrew were getting used to the sound of the room."

By following this tack, Ron admitted that he lost track of time during the set, stretching the show beyond the 90-minute length to 100 minutes, then eventually two hours. He may have lost his bearing on the time, but he was well aware of the audience. "Sometimes I judge these things by listening to the crowd," he said. "When you hear shuffling in the audience, hear paper rattling, people coughing, people leaving early to catch the subway, then you know the set is too long. In a small hall like Zankel, you can hear people walking out. But since no one was leaving at the one-hour-and-45-minute mark, we just kept going, taking it smooth and winding things down, which is why I took the solo where I did." He laughed and added, "That's also to let the audience know that I am the bandleader. Then I found the perfect song to end the show."

Ron's concert-giving philosophy is to make the first and last songs count the most. "People remember the first tune, an outstanding event in the middle and the last tune," he said. "All the other stuff may be happening onstage, but sometimes it doesn't stick. It's hard to remember all the songs in a set that starts at 8:30 and goes to, heaven forbid, 10:30, as it turned out."

Dan said that featuring a bass player as a leader is tricky. A pianist, a saxophonist, a singer is much more embraced by the public in a concert setting. Yet, bassists, as rare as they are at the helm, can make an impact, just as Ron did at Zankel. "Dave Holland is a good example," Dan noted. "He's worked hard in his adult life to be a leader, to keep a band together, to have a working ensemble. He made a decision to record and tour less as a sideman. Ron has done the same, while also balancing sideman and support dates. But he's very different from Dave in the sense that Ron is a legend."

As for Ron's frustration with the lack of coverage by *The Times*, Dan expressed sympathy for his hurt feelings, although he understands that with so much jazz activity in New York on any given night, it's difficult to get print coverage no matter who you are. But, he also feels there's something else at work. "I have a personal view," he said. "Every time Wynton Marsalis farts at Jazz at Lincoln Center, *The Times* covers it. And they're also writing a lot about cutting-edge and new artists. I can understand that, but the point is, they have an agenda and Ron Carter does not fit into that agenda. In fact, none of the Zankel Hall jazz shows fit. That's a huge problem and a total drag."

That said, less than two years later, Dan assembled a new Carter concert, this time for the large hall, and received prominent *New York Times* ink for his efforts.

CARNEGIE CARTER JUBILEE

I. The Set-Up

THE KEY TO sealing the deal to present the Ron show at Carnegie Hall in the Isaac Stern Auditorium, according to Melnick, was putting together the Miles Davis-related segment of the four-part concert. Given Herbie, Wayne and Billy's busy schedules, that piece of the program came together last, but guaranteed that the show would have a significant draw—again, the box office outweighs artistic merit, which, for better or worse, is an economic fact of life for the music industry.

With that quartet locked in, the date was firmed and the planning began, starting with Ron's vision. "JVC trusted my judgment," he said. "The only thing they insisted on was starting the show with the trio instead of the duo. They didn't want the latecomers disrupting the intimacy of the duo with Jim. It's true. The distractions of people settling in wouldn't affect the trio as much."

Otherwise, this was Ron's production from the get-go. He planned it out meticulously. He first plotted out the time frame: start at 8:05, finish at 10:50, with a 20-minute intermission. Two groups in the first half, two in the second. He considered what to present to represent his 50+ years of performance. Even though he and Jim Hall had only recently regrouped as a duo, their history stretched back more than 40 years, with three CDs to their credit. Then Ron thought of his current groups that he had been nurturing: the trio and the quartet.

Finally, he said, "No concert with me as the bandleader would be complete without some of my friends and colleagues from the Miles Davis days. I'm thankful they're all alive and well." As it turned out, the Herbie/Wayne/Billy grouping represented an "emotional reunion with friends I hadn't played with in a long time."

Other than the previous year's "Herbie's World" bash at Carnegie during the JVC festival when Ron played in a trio setting with Herbie and drummer Jack DeJohnette (and Michael Brecker making a special guest appearance in his last public appearance before passing away), Ron hadn't hooked up with his old rhythm-section mate since *Gershwin's World*, the 1998 album featuring an all-star cast commemorating songwriter George Gershwin's 100th birthday.

Ron couldn't remember the last time he had played with Wayne, and it had been four years since performing with Billy, on a tour in the drummer's band. (Ron recalled playing on Billy's first record as a leader, the post-Mahavishnu Orchestra *Spectrum*, in 1973, after the drummer's stint with Miles during his *Bitches Brew, A Tribute to Jack Johnson* and *Live–Evil* fusion days. Ron and Billy never performed together in Miles's employ.) "My hope was that they would be able to set aside their personal schedules," Ron said. "I was quite happy that no one had a problem."

As for the show prep, a few months earlier Ron and Jim played a week at the Blue Note in New York, getting reacquainted onstage for an extended period for the first time in quite awhile. "So, we already familiarized ourselves with the chores that we'd have to take on," Ron said. "I had just done a tour with Russell and Mulgrew, so we had our library prepared. Even though my quartet hadn't worked for a month or so, there was no surprise that it didn't sound that way. And I have so much faith in Herbie, Wayne and Billy's musicianship that I knew I could tell them what I wanted to do and they'd be able to do it. I'd only need to tell them once and they'd get it done, so the band came off sounding like we'd been together for awhile."

Due to a previous engagement, Herbie was flying in to New York the afternoon of the show, so that quartet's first gathering to discuss the repertoire came at the soundcheck. None of the other three sets required rehearsal time.

II. The Elegant Affair

STARTING PUNCTUALLY AT 8 p.m., Ron, decked out in a Japanese designer tuxedo, gracefully walked onstage alone and was met with a standing ovation—without playing a single note. Later, he said that he was surprised: "I expected a greeting because this was billed as a celebration of my 70th birthday with my friends. I expected the crowd to salute the event. I expected them to salute me as part of the event. But I didn't expect them to treat me as something separate from the event. That level of response was truly stunning. I don't think anyone expected that response. The guys backstage who had played at a lot of major events were surprised. Even the stagehands were stunned. They told me they had never heard a bass player get that kind of response at a Carnegie Hall event."

Obviously pleased, Ron made a grand attempt at modesty by saying that the legacy of the music was the reason for the greeting, but that evening you could tell that he felt loved, personally and professionally—and respected. "I try to look at it as a response to me and my career versus just being me," he said. "But I think the applause was 51 percent for me and 49 percent for the music. It's nice to know that I've been able to capture people's attention over the period of time in the history of the music, so much so that they wanted to salute me as a person, as a bass player, as a part of the music they love."

The welcome placed Ron at ease as he introduced Russell and Mulgrew and opened the trio's short three-song chamber jazz set ("Laverne Walk," "Eddie's Theme" and the Modern Jazz Quartet John Lewis tune "The Golden Striker") with a fat-grooved, blues-steeped bass line. The instrumental conversations among the three immediately followed, with the first tune featuring false endings that teemed with good-natured, instrumental inside jokes. There were smiles and laughs throughout as each trio member played with a touch of whimsy. The two other tunes were both crowd pleasers. Ron beamed as the crowd cheered, then handed Russell and Mulgrew parting gifts: each a silk handkerchief, or, as Ron calls them, "pocket squares."

"The first act of an evening like this is always difficult," Ron said later. "The sound of the room is different from soundcheck when no one's in the hall. So, the first band is the sacrificial lamb. The guys backstage are listening to the sound and making the proper adjustments. Russell and

Mulgrew had to go first, but they are so experienced they can make the adjustments in their playing as the music demands it—not because their egos are in the way."

While the crew was shuffling equipment onstage in preparation for Jim's appearance, a person in one of the balconies yelled out, "Happy birthday, Ron," which instigated another cheer from the hall.

Ron smiled, then introduced his guitar-playing duo partner: "We've been playing together for close to 40 years, back to a time when we both had more hair." Jim walked onstage, donning, in contrast to Ron's refined attire, a blue shirt, dark blue slacks, a brown vest and bright orange tie. The brief three-song set opened with Jim's angular chords on his original, "Careful," that developed into a lead-and-follow dance of single lines and chords, with Ron delivering dark, chocolaty tones. Arranged in a new geometric pattern, "Body and Soul" came next, with a slight blues flavor and an abundance of bent notes and lyrical dissonance. They concluded their intimate summit by sailing through Sonny Rollins's "St. Thomas," with Jim fx'ing a steel drum sound on his guitar and later strumming with a discordant swing. Jim's bright, sunny guitar lines contrasted magically with Ron's loamy runs teeming with glissando and hammer-on legato.

My biggest complaint was that the pair never totally warmed up. Two months earlier at the Blue Note in New York they required some 30 minutes to sync up in the first set of the first night of their weeklong gig. Just as they were catching a simpatico spirit at Carnegie Hall, the mini-set was over and Ron was bestowing Jim with a red silk handkerchief. "The duo is a fragile setting," said Ron later. "If I had my druthers, I'd have played another song but given the time constraints we couldn't."

As for the dynamics, Ron had his misgivings. "I would have liked Jim to be more present than he was," he said. "I avoid the term louder, instead of having more sound presence onstage. I have to be careful to not sonically overwhelm whomever I'm playing with. I have a pretty intense sound. If I'm not careful, I can wash people away with my bass. Jim's sound is more delicate than I would like, especially in such a big hall. But he plays with such finesse and with such great notes and lines that I'd take it even if it were down to zero-decibel level. You rarely get to play with an artist like Jim who has such good taste."

After intermission, Ron came back onstage alone, telling the audience that he had to scramble to three ATM machines to cobble together enough money to pay all the bands. It's a quip he often uses from the stage, both to show his naturally wry sense of humor but also to underscore that he makes good on his word to remunerate the supporting cast. No "it's in the mail" promises from Ron—after all, he was enlisted by Miles to be the payroll gatekeeper.

It was time for the former students of the Miles postgraduate school of music to gather. Ron hugged Herbie, Wayne and Billy as they walked from the wings. "You all know these songs already, so I won't bother introducing them," Ron said to the crowd as the quartet launched into an eerie, slurred bass-walking take on "So What," featuring a truncated Shorter solo. Ron soloed, then segued into a sprint through "Seven Steps to Heaven" that was slowed via bass pulse into a tender Ron-Herbie duet on "Stella by Starlight" that led to another *Kind of Blue* classic, "All Blues," which sped with Herbie's pianistic reaction to Ron's solo and Billy's energetic drive. It was all over too soon, as the group huddled and hugged, bowed to the house on its feet. Each member left with kerchief in hand.

Ron's bass served as the connective tissue between each musical transition, as he changed bass lines to cue the rest of the band that the music is ready to take another melodic turn. "Obviously the segue can't be more important than the song we're going to play," he said later. "It's a transition piece that goes on for however long it takes to go from song A to song B, and it's my job to make sure it doesn't turn into a song of its own. Yet, on certain nights if the segue isn't happening so that the next song won't sound right, I'll change the tune we play if the segue demands it."

Trusting the leader's judgment is essential to Ron. The Davis-driven quartet excelled at it. They listened to every note, every tempo modulation, every subtle hint Ron played. "If I thought Wayne was playing too many choruses in his solo, I'd play something to tell him to stop because we've got a long program here with another band yet to play," Ron explained. "If I wanted Herbie to play another chorus, I'd play a line that says, 'One more chorus. Let's see if I can fix this problem I'm having on the bass.'"

Ron's only regret was that Billy, who was set up on the right side of the stage separate from the rest of the rhythm section, was physically distant. "I wish I had had better contact with him," Ron said. "He was using a small drum set for the first time in quite awhile too. But Billy is so musical that wherever he's set up, it's going to be OK. I just wish we had been closer."

Ron made his musical intentions known to the group before the show. He gave the order of the tunes and felt free to make any adjustments on the fly. He talked with Herbie about playing "Stella," one of the smash tracks on the Miles live record they recorded at Lincoln Center in 1963. "Herbie didn't know what I was going to do, so we used the soundcheck to musically say hello," said Ron. "With Wayne, we talked about who was going to be first or second on soloing, so that there wouldn't be a delay. It was, 'Let's start now, not the day after tomorrow.' And for Billy, I told him that I wanted to get that fabulous cymbal sound that he always does. That was pretty much it."

Did playing with his former band mates Herbie and Wayne bring back memories of the Miles days? "Not specifically," Ron said. "It was just a onetime engagement. My focus was to make it sound as good as I could. If I reminisce during the course of a performance, I wouldn't be able to get it done. I can sit here and be esoteric and say, 'Yeah, I played this chorus and was thinking of being with Miles and Herbie and Wayne at the Plugged Nickel.' But that wasn't true. I had these three people beside me who were looking to me to lead them somewhere. I've got to lead them today, not on a 1965 record."

What about a feeling of alchemy? "When you're playing with artists like this, sure, you always feel that," Ron replied. "You don't *not* have that. The chemistry is still available to us, so we can just open the door and let it in."

The final set of the night featured Ron's quartet, comprised of pianist Stephen Scott, drummer Payton Crossley and percussionist Rolando Morales-Matos. As to why Ron decided to end the show with that group instead of the big-attraction all-star Miles-oriented band, he said, "My quartet was the marquee band. I wanted the audience to hear my current band and how we play from song to song in a unique way. First, they're all quality players and I wouldn't allow them to be intimidated by not having them close the show. Second, the music this quartet played was as valid as anything else on the program. Third, this band represents my current view of how to play music. There's not a jam-session mind-set at work, but a well-rehearsed band that works gigs and makes records. It's not that I was opposed to ending the show with a loud smash with Herbie, Wayne and Billy, but I thought that people would probably expect that. I was saying to the crowd, 'Check out my point of view versus your own point of view.'"

Ron's quartet opened with a Brazilian-tinged "Mr. Bow Tie," that led into two tunes associated with Miles—"Flamenco Sketches," which sped into a festive "Joshua"—then settled into an extended lyrical bass solo through "Willow Weep for Me," which was a charmed, spur-of-the-moment decision by the leader. He made the bass sing. "I felt that many people in the audience hadn't heard me play with the bass alone," he said. "So I thought this would be a nice way to salute their support of the music, to let them know that I can do something else besides playing time with a band."

After another standing O, Ron told the crowd, "It doesn't get any better than this for me," before launching into the show finale, the standard "You and the Night and the Music," which Ron recorded on his album *The Bass & I*. It proved to be a high-velocity, firecracker finish, with the crowd again on its feet and the quartet members taking their bows and each receiving their pocket-square thank-you gifts.

At the curtain call, all of the evening's guests except Jim came back onstage with their handkerchiefs in their lapel pockets.

III. Après Concert

JUST BECAUSE ALL the notes have been played doesn't mean the night is done. Backstage, usually reserved for a select few on a guest list, was packed as dozens of people flooded in, swept in a wave past two security guards who appeared unprepared for the rush. "It was a little chaotic for me," Ron admitted. "I was still hearing the concert in my head, trying to get some resolution to the music. I wished someone had a system in place that allowed me to thank those who were able to get backstage for their support in coming to this onetime concert. I wish I had known enough ahead of time to ask how the reception area would be handled. It was a little frantic for me. But that's a part of the process."

Ron's older sister Geneva flew in from Los Angeles for the show and was backstage to greet him. "She hadn't seen me play in a long time," Ron said. "It was a thrill for her to see her younger brother have this kind of acclaim thrust upon his shoulders."

Did Geneva realize how famous her brother was? Ron replied, "I'm her brother. I'm OK with that. She had a great time."

Towering above everyone in the large room was basketball Hall of Famer Kareem Abdul-Jabbar, an old friend. I spoke with him, craning my head upward to make eye contact with the seven-footer. He noted with pride that he had been on an outdoor Harlem basketball court shooting hoops with Ron years ago when he got word that his friend's wife Janet was ready to give birth to their first son, Ron Jr.

"I hadn't seen Kareem for a long time," said Ron. "He came on his own volition. I knew he had moved back to Harlem and had given a talk at a Harlem Jazz Society event that I couldn't make. I didn't know how to reach him. But we talked and we're planning to get together."

Ron was visibly pleased with the gathering, thanking people and signing old LPs and CDs, while smiling effusively the entire time. After leaving the hall, he returned home where his two sons, Ron Jr. and Myles, had decided to stay the night rather than drive back to Boston, which was the original plan. (Myles's twin sons slept comfortably in sleeping bags on the floor.) "By the time everyone settled down, I only had a moment to enjoy the concert, to put it back in place," said Ron, who got up early the next day in preparation for an evening flight to Paris for yet another show.

IV. The Critiques

IT WASN'T UNTIL Ron returned home a few days later that he read the reviews—one immensely positive by Will Friedwald in the *New York Sun*, with the headline, "Carter Is Miles Ahead," and the other couched in a snarky tone by Ben Ratliff in *The New York Times*, titled "At 70, Jazz's Ubiquitous Free Agent Still Has Miles to Go."

Friedwald opened his review by noting that if Ron were "recruited by NASA to be rocketed to Mars and became the first jazzman to perform on another planet, he would still be famous for one thing: having played with Miles Davis's 'second great quintet' of the 1960s." However, the scribe pointed out that the concert was not an event that looked back, but a statement of the present and future: "... rather than attempting a retrospective of all the different kinds of music he's made in his 50 years [of performing], the emphasis here was on three contemporary ensembles he leads today, in addition to the '60s Summit Reunion."

Will applauded Ron's decision to end the show with his own quartet that "was, unexpectedly, not an anticlimax," calling the group's music a "bass-centric chamber jazz of the first rank." He concluded his critique by noting: "Often, these tribute shows—particularly when the subject has reached an advanced age—have the feeling of a last hurrah. For a musician at the top of his game like Mr. Carter, the evening was a hurrah all right, but hardly a last one."

In *The Times*, Ratliff was decidedly lukewarm in his assessment of the concert. He labeled the trio set as the strongest, called the duo segment "bumpy but intermittently strong," and then panned the Miles-related quartet as not "quite [taking] flight," with "All Blues" suffering from "nice little ideas [that] grew stale in repetition" and Wayne's "thoughtful solo [that] brought no revelations." As for Ron's quartet, Ben deemed it "an adequate but low-key band" whose music "felt frustratingly distant, lacking a basic urgency."

Ratliff's article lede and kicker were both smarmily suspect. He started off his piece by lambasting the JVC Jazz Festival for what he called its formulaic programming. While noting that Ron "is important to jazz... at this point he can be given full-dress reconsideration without any excuse," he bundled this date with a Lee Konitz 80th-birthday show at Zankel two days earlier and the Nancy Wilson 70th-birthday party scheduled for the main hall two days later.

"I don't understand that complaint," said Ron. "I hate to use the classical music analogy, but they're always having these kinds of celebrations and no one seems to be bothered."

Without making reference to the several standing ovations, Ben enigmatically concluded his review by reporting that while Ron gave each member of his bands a handkerchief, he "gave the last one, bright red, to himself." Ron bristled at that statement: "The fact of the matter is that as I was leaving the stage, I gave that red handkerchief to a young man who was severely handicapped and who asked me if his friend could take a photo of the two of us."

But Ron took full umbrage at Ratliff's condescending tone and the headline ("At 70, Jazz's Ubiquitous Free Agent Still Has Miles to Go"). He quoted it and then said seriously, "The implication is that I'm competing with the musical track Miles Davis ventured on, instead of recognizing that this event features four of my favorite groups with nine of my favorite people. It's my birthday celebration and the only connection with Miles is that I played with him as did three other people. This wasn't about me adding 'mileage' to the Miles Davis legacy. The reason why we played the Miles tunes is that I wanted to present that music 38, 39 years after the fact—not compete with what we did then."

By the time we talked about Ratliff's critique, Ron said that he'd gotten over his "hostility toward him intellectually, but I'm still pretty far from getting to that same place emotionally. It's unfortunate that he didn't understand the gist of the concert, but used it to beat the JVC birthday concept into the ground when all the people there had a wonderful time musically."

Even though he laughed and said, "I've got to let this go before I get mad again," Ron's emotions flared once more. "It's unfortunate that Mr. Ratliff has a much wider forum to present his opinion than I do," he said. "Ideally, of course, I'd like to see a letter to the editor get published that can be read by the audience of readers who weren't there to hear for themselves to explain that this reviewer missed the boat."

As it turned out, his friend and onetime music-department colleague at The City College of New York, Barbara R. Hanning, did write a letter that read thusly: "The unfortunate headline ... is ambiguous at best. Given the whining tone of the review, it was probably intended as a put-down. I suggest, however, that it should be read another way: This indomitable force in the world of jazz, if Wednesday night's show is any indication, will be carrying on as 'jazz's ubiquitous free agent' for many more years, riding new crests on the waves of his brilliantly splashy career. In that case I, for one, hope to be around to continue to enjoy whatever spray reaches the shore."

The letter was never printed.

PART I
THE EARLY YEARS

CHAPTER TWO

Early Years: Ferndale / Detroit

IN 1943, RON was 6 years old, living with his family in Ferndale, an unincorporated Michigan town abutting Detroit. That year the city underwent a volatile race riot, one of the nation's bloodiest race-derived conflagrations of the time. The combatants were blacks, many of whom were relatively new to the area and eagerly sought by industrial plant owners for their labor, and whites, many also newly settled from the South and seeking employment. The two sides engaged in a festering series of violent confrontations that erupted over the course of a day and a half beginning on June 20.

With the riots taking place in the midst of World War II, the whole world was watching while the battles overseas were being fought. The tumult in Michigan proved rich fodder for the propaganda machine of the Axis Powers, which haughtily characterized the United States as a weak, hypocritical country that could not even manage its own affairs concerning social injustice, let alone wage a war outside its own boundaries.

The riots further forged Detroit's reputation as a northern city plagued by virulent racial intolerance and bigotry as a result of the massive influx of white and black workers. From 1933 to 1943, the black population had doubled to 200,000, with many forced to live in overcrowded and oppressive housing. To ease the housing crunch, the Detroit Housing Commission approved two sites for new projects—one for whites and one for blacks. By a shortsighted federal government mandate, the black housing project, called Sojourner Truth, was built adjacent to an all-white neighborhood, which heightened the racial tension. In 1942, the Ku Klux Klan, active in Detroit since the '20s and surging in popularity due to the arrival of white workers from the South, burned crosses in the African-American project.

In August 1942, *Life* magazine had featured an article, "Detroit Is Dynamite," which warned that the city "can either blow up Hitler or it can blow up the U.S." During this time, roving gangs waged turf wars that broke out in street-corner skirmishes. Shortly before the riots had begun, 25,000 white workers at Packard Motor Car Company, which made engines for bombers and PT boats, staged a work stoppage in protest of the promotion of three black workers. So the pump was primed for Detroit, then the fourth largest city in the country, to explode.

Within 24 hours of the initial combustion in Detroit, the U.S. found itself enmeshed in another conflict much different from those in the European and Pacific theaters of war. In response to the pleas of Mayor Edward Jeffries Jr. and Michigan Governor Harry Kelly, President Franklin Roosevelt dispatched more than 1,000 federal troops to quell the escalating violence in Detroit with three more battalions arriving soon after from Wisconsin. Soldiers, armed with automatic weapons, patrolled the battle zones in armored cars and jeeps. Even though order was soon restored, the U.S. Army occupied the city for six months.

Officially, during the 36 hours of rioting and looting, the death toll totaled 34 (25 of them black—of those, 17 were killed by white policemen), with 676 injured and nearly 2,000 people arrested. One of the most vital U.S. cities engaged in manufacturing war machinery, Detroit was temporarily forced to halt production. (The United Auto Workers union president R.J. Thomas helped to ease the tension by presenting a war-plant "peace plan," which included a provision that black workers would be treated equally, commensurate with their skill level and seniority.)

In 1943, the National Association for the Advancement of Colored People held an emergency meeting in the city not only to condemn the response of the white Detroit police department and city officials, but also to decry the nation as a whole for fostering discrimination and segregation.

Only a youngster at the time and living a distance from ground zero, Ron remembers hearing about the riots. "I was aware of the violence most of which took place downtown, but it didn't directly impact me," he said. "My parents didn't talk about it in front of us. They weren't making an issue of the issues."

Even so, Ron's life had already been marked by racial discrimination and segregation that would continue to exert influence on him during his Ferndale and Detroit years. "In Ferndale, it was white only and black only," he said. "I never even learned the national anthem until I went to Lincoln High School in Ferndale. Until then I thought it was 'Lift Ev'ry Voice and Sing.'" The song, written as a poem in 1900 by James Weldon Johnson and set to music in 1905 by his brother John Rosamond Johnson, was adopted by the NAACP as "The Negro National Anthem" in 1919 and became an African-American church standard.

"I always thought that other song was a ballgame tune that got played every time I listened to baseball games on the radio," said Ron.

EARLY FERNDALE YEARS

RONALD LEVIN CARTER was born in Ferndale on May 4, 1937, deep in the heart of the Depression. He was the son of Lutheran and Willie Otis Howard Carter. Ron's dad originally hailed from Terre Haute, Indiana, his mom from Birmingham, Alabama.

Ron was the fifth oldest child of eight, all of whom played a musical instrument. Geneva was the oldest (she played piano), followed by Lutheran Jr. (trumpet), Judy (piano), Wilma (viola) and Ron (whose first instrument was cello). Born a little over a year after Ron (in July 1938), Sandy played the bass and piano. Pat played the violin and piano, and Dail, the youngest, played the piano and French horn. Even though Ron's sister Sandy continues to take piano classes and plays in the amateur Culver City Flute Choir that has performed in downtown Los Angeles's Skid Row, none of Ron's siblings pursued music professionally. (Sandy said that she never considered having a career in classical music because "unless you knew someone, there was no place for a black girl.")

Ron's mother was an only child who grew up in an all-white neighborhood in Birmingham but went to an all-black grade school. "The white school was two blocks away," Willie said. "But I had to walk eight blocks to the black school. I was from the deep South, where we had no privilege."

Willie spent part of her time living in Terre Haute with her grandmother, who worked as a traveling midwife and took care of young babies born to wealthy white women. "My grandmother would tell the people that her granddaughter would be visiting so that the family would know I was coming," she said. "The cook would let me in the backdoor, but my grandmother, whenever I would leave to go out, always had me leave by the front door."

Willie met Lutheran, who had eight siblings, in Terre Haute when they were both in high school. "I met him when I asked him to sharpen my pencil," she said. "You didn't get to go into study hall unless you had business to do. I went with my girlfriend. She went inside, but I realized that my pencil lead was broken. I saw a young man coming upstairs, so I asked him to sharpen my pencil so I could go in and study." She laughed and added, "After that we talked for the next 59 years, three months and six days." (Lutheran died in April 1988 at the age of 78.)

Even though Lutheran's mother never forgave him for marrying Willie, the couple, both 18 and born in 1910, began to plan their life together. "She wanted Lutheran to be a teacher, but he wanted to work in the post office," Willie recalled. "He had an aunt who lived in Ferndale, so he went to stay with her to try to find work. One month to the day later, he traveled to Birmingham to pick me up and bring me to Ferndale. He didn't get to work in the post office. You had to know someone to get that kind of job."

Instead, Lutheran took on a number of odd handyman's jobs, including shoe polishing and sweeping up barbershop floors. He finally got work at the post office, but it was only temporary—sorting mail during the Christmas holidays. He and a friend worked at a factory cleaning engine parts with strong solvents, which Willie blames for the respiratory problems that he suffered later in his life. "He always had more than one job," she said.

"At the time, fire departments weren't hiring blacks, police departments weren't hiring blacks," Ron told writer Ed Williams in a 1977 *DownBeat* article. "Bright, young black people weren't being encouraged to develop their talents. Man, my father is a great mathematician, but in the '30s it was unheard of for a black person to be encouraged to bring out a great genius in math."

Willie didn't work until she and Lutheran began to raise a family. Initially, it was agreed that she would be a stay-at-home mother, but, she said, "I broke my promise and took on my own day work, washing other people's clothes and scrubbing dirty floors for $2.50 a day. I had an elderly lady sit with the children while I was off working and would get home before Lutheran. I saved up every penny so we could buy a house one day."

The all-black, rural Ferndale neighborhood Ron lived in was close to the border of Detroit and, he estimates, 20 blocks long and 15 blocks wide. The streets were unpaved, the lanes dusty. He recalls all the families in the neighborhood being large, with lots of kids. Everyone used to gather together to listen to the radio. Ron recalls once being in the street and hearing every household listening to a Joe Louis boxing match. "Joe Louis was big in the boxing world then," he told *Stop Smiling* magazine writer Peter Relic. "It was African-American pride that Louis was beating up a white guy."

The Carter household had a garden and shared the produce with the neighbors. "Everybody's neighbor looked out for their neighbor and their neighbor's neighbor," said Ron. "When I was there, my job was to get my snow shovel and shovel three houses down to the left and three houses down to the right.... It was all about community giving. We didn't expect a return or a paycheck."

For *DownBeat*'s Williams, Ron recalled an early incident in his life that fired up his parents. Even though the schools were segregated, one year the junior high graduation ceremony was shared by both white and black students. Ron attended the graduation of one of his older sisters, where the school principal prepared two speeches, one for the whites, one for the blacks. He encouraged the white students to continue their education to high school and college. "The black kids—well, he seemed to think that they were lucky just to be in the eighth grade," Ron recalled. "He couldn't conceive of the black students being able to spell, let alone have higher goals.... The principal had the audacity to say that all you white kids are prepared for high school and all you black kids got to dig ditches."

The speech riled Ron's parents up so much that they resolved to make sure their children would not only graduate from high school, but also college. "While I'm sure that my parents did not need any outside inspiration to see to it that we were successful in our educational careers, this principal only made the spark bigger in my house," Ron said. "This situation gave me an early sense of the kind of value society placed on our worth, and it gave me the chance to understand that those values certainly did not hold true. Furthermore, with the kind of discipline and sacrifice my parents instilled in us, we were destined to 'overachieve,' at least according to the expectations society had for us."

Willie says that she and Lutheran decided to work and save so that each of the children would have the money to attend college for two years. She noted that there was only one stipulation: If they got married, they forfeited the right to the funds. "I had heard of families doing more for one child than others," said Willie. "But we never did that. Each Carter kid got exactly what the others got. We wanted to give each kid the same opportunity as the others."

FATHER KNOWS BEST

RON'S FATHER SERVED as his role model. "There it was the Depression and he was doing all that he could to raise eight kids," Ron said. "I never saw him pulling his hair out because of how hard that was."

In a 1987 interview with Ken Franckling in the *Newport (R.I.) Daily News*, Ron listed Lutheran as one of the major influences of his life. "My father was not a musician per se, but he knew if you played real hard and worked real hard and had talent, you could succeed in the long run. He taught me tenacity, and the unwillingness to accept something short of yourself."

"Lutheran was such an idol to Ron," said Mary Ann Topper, a jazz-musician manager who, though she never managed Ron, knew him well. "He admired him so much for how he took care of his family." She recalls seeing Ron perform in New York at Fat Tuesday's, on 17th Street and 3rd Avenue, in 1988 on the day that his father passed away in Los Angeles, where Lutheran and Willie moved when he retired.

"Ron is such a sensitive person," she said. "That night in memory of his father, he played 'Just a Closer Walk With Thee,' which is the first time I heard him play a hymn." But, she said, like his hard-working father who never missed a day at work, Ron didn't take a break from the weeklong gig. "Lutheran died on a Tuesday night, which was Ron's opening night, and the family waited until he was done for the week before having the funeral in California so that he could attend."

After attending the funeral, Ron was so moved by the people who shared their memories that he wrote a song entitled "Friends," which was the title of his 1992 Blue Note album. Originally composed for his four-cello Nonet group, the song was inspired by the people at the service who heralded Lutheran for his friendship. "They talked about him seeing a need and getting something done, whether it was mowing someone's lawn or fixing a screen door," Ron said. "The word everyone kept returning to was 'friend,' which was the word that connected all the dots in their stories. I wanted to write a composition so that people who knew him would be reminded of him if they heard it."

A pipe- and cigar-smoking man who was an avid reader of newspapers, magazines and books, Lutheran was also a key factor in encouraging all the "Carter kids," as they were known in the Ferndale neighborhood, to play musical instruments. While not a trained musician, he loved music and, Ron recalls, had a good ear for accurate pitch. He also remembers his dad making banjos out of cigar boxes and rubber bands.

Willie was involved in the PTA at Grant School where the Carter kids attended and had heard from the principal that a truckload of instruments was being delivered for the school's music education program. "I told the kids to get down there and pick out an instrument," said Willie. "I didn't care which one, just get an instrument. So Ronald came home with a cello, and Sandy was the one who got a bass."

The Carter household also had a piano (Willie had taken lessons on piano until she was 18), which some of the children played in addition to their other instruments. Sandy remembers the family sitting down for dinner, and Ron getting up in the middle of the meal and picking out some music on the piano. "Ronald wasn't being obnoxious. He was just hearing some music in his head that he wanted to figure out. My folks thought that that was OK."

Ron was 10 when he first started out on the cello that he practiced faithfully. "It just struck me as a good instrument," he said. "It wasn't like I heard voices in my head that said I should choose it, or I didn't close my eyes and imagine myself on a concert stage playing it. It was just a kid's curiosity. It had a nice sound, so I thought, what can I do with this? It's like giving a kid a hammer and a nail, and wondering, how does this work and what can be done with it?"

Ron remembers that his first cello was aluminum, which he said had a "nice mellow sound that could also be aggressive if necessary. I was always reserved and shy so that sound seemed to work for me as a voice."

"Ronald would hibernate and practice all the time in his room," Sandy recalled. "It was all about woodshedding for him."

A straight-A student, Ron started taking lessons from a teacher at school, who soon called Willie and told her that he had outgrown her. The teacher suggested calling a cellist who played for the Detroit Symphony, but the cellist eventually decided to give him up too because of his maturing prowess on the instrument.

While Ron's growth in music was, at least by his teachers' estimates, particularly astounding, he couldn't rely on his parents, both struggling to raise a family of eight, to pay for his lessons. He got his first regular job: a paper route that had some 300 customers to whom he delivered afternoon newspapers seven days a week for three years. He worked the route in junior high and up through his first year in high school. "I rode my bicycle when the weather was good and used a sled when it was winter," he said. "I had to pay for lessons and buy charts. I figured that was part of the process for being responsible. The paper route was a way to do what I had to do and not rely on my parents' financial support."

Sandy remembers Ron finishing his paper route, then retreating into his room to practice. "When Ronald had the door closed, you knew not to enter," she said. "He was very quiet and serious. He didn't discuss things with me. His issues with excellence were high. He didn't have bad habits like drinking, which was not part of our family to begin with. And Ronald was never influenced by people around him. He was always his own person."

Sandy does recall one of Ron's weaknesses: sweets, particularly Fig Newtons, which he used to buy with money from his paper-route earnings. "He had a secret stash," said Sandy, who sneaked into his room once and found the cookies. "His room was always tidy. He didn't put pictures or things on his wall. There was a bed and dresser and a music stand. I would sneak in and eat some of the Fig Newtons. I'm sure he knew who the culprit was. But as kids growing up, we were always told to share whatever each of us had with the rest of the family. I guess Ronald never said anything to me because he would have gotten in trouble."

When the Carter kids were young, they formed a makeshift string ensemble to play for Lutheran. "Our dad loved for us to entertain him," said Sandy. "He had a fondness for hearing classical music. We had a radio but not a record player."

"We had our own string quartet that my father wanted to hear a couple of times a week," said Ron. "We played classical, but also a library of arranged songs from Broadway plays that were popular then, shows like *South Pacific*. We'd play for him for a couple of hours and then I'd go back to my room and continue to practice." On average during this time, he practiced eight hours a day.

Outside the home, Ron participated in the school district's weekend competitions that took place in towns such as East Lansing and Ann Arbor. He recalled this during a conversation with fellow bassist and friend Milt Hinton in an interview in *Jazz Magazine* in 1977. He said that the best players of a district would "perform solo pieces with piano accompaniment, or in string ensembles. There would also be an orchestra. A medal would be awarded for the best performance. My family was the black representative of our [community]. We always came back with gold and silver-plated medals."

Ron won several awards including the Southeastern Michigan Music festival's top rating and the Michigan School Band and Orchestra Association Solo Ensemble festival award.

Being so close in age, Ron and Sandy played cello-bass duos at PTA meetings, women's afternoon teas or other events in town. Sandy has a photocopy of a photocopy of a newspaper clip with a picture of her and Ron posing for the camera after a performance at the Ferndale Rotary Club.

She and her brother were the only black performers in an ensemble of nine players.

DETROIT TRANSPLANT

WHEN RON WAS 14, his family moved to Detroit because Lutheran was hired by the Detroit Street and Railways Company to work as a bus driver. The hiring of black workers in the racially tense city was still rare in the early '50s, so when Lutheran was offered the job that required relocating to Motor City, the Carters leaped at the opportunity.

Lutheran built the house the Carter family lived in, on 15744 Princeton. Both he and Willie had saved up money and bought a vacant lot. Having lived with her grandmother in a number of wealthy, well-styled houses when she was younger, Willie had a design for their house already in mind. "I wanted a [cinder] block bottom with shingles on top and a living room all across the downstairs," she said. "There would be a master bedroom upstairs and three other bedrooms upstairs. I didn't want the kids to be sleeping together, so I wanted bunk beds if necessary."

Willie recalls them being one of the first black families in the area to get a Federal Housing Administration loan to build. She also remembers the building of the house to be a community event as several neighborhoods had skills such as bricklaying and plumbing. "A lot of people came together and helped us," she said.

In a 1987 *JazzTimes* article, Ron reflected back on his father's work ethic, citing his commitment for keeping his "shoulder to the grindstone. It was a matter of not giving up on what you believe in. My father built a house all by himself. That, to this day, still amazes me. Putting rooms on the house, foundations, fences and gardens. He did it without using all the available books and schools you can go to. All I'm trying to do is play the bass.... If I can do it in the spirit [that he lived his life], hey, man, that's it!"

The move to Detroit took place halfway through Ron's ninth grade year at Lincoln High School in Ferndale. He continued to go to that school, walking a mile and a half from their new home, until he finished the school year.

It was during that year that Ron first went to the Masonic Temple Auditorium to hear the Detroit Symphony Orchestra perform with French cellist Pierre Fournier as a guest musician playing Dvorak's Cello Concerto in B Minor. "That was my first time in a big orchestra hall," Ron said. "The size was stunning. You have to remember, I was from Ferndale."

Still, by then Ron had already realized what his life calling was: playing music. He auditioned for the orchestra at Lincoln and earned first chair cello. "Once I realized I could advance in my peer group, that I could be recognized as better than others playing the same instrument, I knew that playing music was what I wanted to do. Playing first chair was just desserts for all the practice and dedication, all the terrible notes and all the good notes I had played."

Ron was also a member of the Youth Symphony Orchestra from Ann Arbor. At Lincoln he came under the tutelage of Mildred Batchelor, who recommended him to the Detroit Fiddlers' Band, a string orchestra for young musicians. A local newspaper ran an article on the group's new cello-section member with the headline "Ronald Carter—A Cellist With a Future" and the lede read, "Ronald Carter is a 14-year-old lad with a bright musical future, and he has made a remarkable start toward its realization." The article ran a class photo of Ron and another staged photo of him with three other members of the band looking at sheet music on a piano.

The band's musical director, Taras Hubicki, praised Ron for his musical talent and ambition, noting that he even showed up for rehearsals on crutches after having been in an automobile accident. The article also said, "Ronald has his heart set on the day when he will be ready to solo with the Fiddlers' Band. He feels that then he shall have arrived on a top rung of the ladder which leads to great musical accomplishment."

Ron also attended the Interlochen Center for the Arts national summer music camp in Interlochen, Michigan. He was the first black student to play in the camp's orchestra. From a postcard of the wooded camp that he sent home, he wrote in pencil, "Hi. After having tryouts on Tuesday, I'm playing the solo line in the cello section. Am having fun, good food and practice. Tell the kids hello. See you soon."

Ron dabbled in basketball and baseball, but neither sport was "emotionally active enough for me versus playing an instrument where you have to be physically, technically and emotionally active all the time. I'm not saying it's an easy sport, but with baseball you're out in the field watching the clouds go by, waiting for the ball to come. In basketball, you don't touch the ball until someone throws it to you. You're inert until someone hits the ball to you or throws you a pass. Being first chair in cello, I'm the guy who has to count the 24 bars. I'm in control of that."

Ron said that he thrived on this performance behavior especially given that he was only one of a couple guys in the orchestra who were black. "There was a lot of internal pressure," he said. "I could feel the pressure. That's when I started to understand racism. But I remembered what my father told me. You've got to be good, and this for me was what being good means. I'm responsible for those 24 bars. I'm going to do it. I think I'm right; prove me wrong."

When he finished Lincoln in the ninth grade, Ron made his entry into Detroit complete by auditioning on cello to be accepted into Cass Technical High School, an innovative school for grades 10 through 12. It not only had an impressive and forward-thinking art and music program, but also offered advanced classes in auto mechanics, sewing, engineering and architectural drafting. Ron passed his audition and entrance exam and started Cass Tech in 1952. "By and large there was an open society there,"

Ron said. "It was not so segregated as the general high schools in Detroit because this school was more focused on finding talented students."

Cass Tech became Ron's proving ground, first on cello and then, in January 1955, as a bass player.

SNAPSHOT

A Carter Family Reunion, 2006

Photograph by Dan Ouellette

A few hours before Ron played at the 28th Annual Playboy Jazz Festival at Hollywood Bowl on Saturday, June 17, 2006, he decided to break bread with his family, all of whom left Detroit many years earlier for warmer climes in California. He arranged to meet as many Carters as he could at the Renaissance Hotel restaurant in Hollywood for noon brunch. Ron had just flown from New York for the day with his Striker Trio, comprising guitarist Russell Malone and pianist Mulgrew Miller. He planned to make a hasty retreat back to New York right after his set.

At the Renaissance, family members arrived first—his nephew Stuart (son of Ron's late sister Wilma Huggins, who died in 2000) and his male partner, York. Then Ron's sister Geneva, at 76 the oldest of the Carter siblings, showed up with Ron's mother, Willie, who was proudly using a new walker with phosphorescent green tennis balls sliced in half and placed underneath each leg to keep it from slipping. She wore a stylish white bonnet and Sunday dress clothes for the gathering. She warmly welcomed me, even though that was the first time we met, and told me that she was 96-and-a-half-years-old ("I was born on January 19, so that makes me close to a half," she said).

I could see Ron's resemblance in her eyes. She spoke at a whispery level and listened with her right ear. I asked her if she was proud of Ron's accomplishments. She smiled sweetly and responded, "I'm proud of all my children." Then she added, "It's too bad what happened to him in the classical world." She talked about the slight in Ron's career more than a half-century earlier as if it were yesterday. That's how deep the wound goes.

Other family members arrived, including Ron's siblings Sandy (14 months younger than Ron) and Pat (the second to the youngest child, at 66). Among the missing in the Carter clan: two other deceased siblings, Lutheran Carter Jr. (the second to the oldest) who passed in 2004, and Judy Coleman, who was born in 1932 and died in 1996. Also missing: the "baby" of the family, Dail Paramore. He was born in 1941 and lives in Desert Hot Springs, California. In fact, all the living siblings reside in Southern California.

"That's right, we all moved to Los Angeles," said the ebullient Sandy. "It's the weather. I didn't want to shovel snow anymore."

Others in attendance at this mini-family reunion: Ron's 44-year-old son, Ron Jr. who lives in Boston and plays electric bass in a blues band. Ron's other son, Myles, had planned to attend, but the day before he was in a bicycle accident and suffered a shoulder injury. He was scheduled for an MRI on Monday and in no shape to make a cross-country flight back and forth in one day. However, Myles, who also lives in Boston, sent photos of his identical twin sons, which were passed around the table.

Sandy's three children also attended: the oldest, Leon (who, at 43, worked for the LAX airport police department and said, "I'm about the only one in this entire family who doesn't play an instrument"); Noel (who worked as a salesman and explained, "I'm always on the road"); and daughter Lesleigh, who was there with her husband Michael.

The party of 12 was low-key, and the brunch was uneventful. Willie sat at the head of the table next to Ron, who dressed casually for the occasion, in a long green khaki jacket. The family said a prayer before they ate.

Sitting to Ron's right side was Sandy, who was the source of much of the subtle joking. "You have a great sense of humor," I told her.

She smiled broadly and nodded. "You know, I was the one who started playing the bass first," she said, "because Ron was playing the cello. I have a photo of Ron and me playing a recital together. I'm going to send it to you."

Sandy added, "Now I play the piano. And I'm still taking lessons." She then asked me for a piece of paper and hit Ron up for an autograph. "I'm a notary public," she explained, "and this is for a real estate agent friend who asked me to get Ron's signature when I told him we were meeting up today."

Ron was happy to oblige.

Willie died in 2009 at the age of 99.

CHAPTER THREE

Early Years: Ron at Cass Tech

Cass Technical High School was a model school in Detroit as well as an innovator in education in the country as a whole. Founded in 1861 as Cass Union School, it was built on a triangle of land—on 2nd Avenue, Grand River Avenue and High Street West—that had belonged to Lewis Cass. He had been a military officer and onetime governor of Michigan—when it was still a territory—from 1813–1831, Michigan's senator in Congress after it became a state from 1845–1857, and the secretary of state in President James Buchanan's cabinet from 1857–1860. The public school originally offered training in woodworking and metal trades for young men, but expanded its curriculum in other vocational areas. These included industrial training, when in 1918 the burgeoning Ford Motor Company convinced the school to open its classrooms after hours for training its workers, and music education, a program started in 1919 by Clarence Byrn who felt that the arts should be recognized and nurtured as well as industry.

Until 1977, Cass Tech was the city's only magnet school and the only school to accept non-neighborhood enrollment. To gain entrance, students had to prove excellence by their junior high grades and pass the school's exam. The music program was started so that Cass graduates could join the ranks of musicians working in orchestras, concert ensembles, radio bands and dance groups. In 1954, for example, 14 Cass alumni were in the Detroit Symphony Orchestra.

Jazz, however, was not taught and in some circles frowned upon.

In an article by John Deak in the April 1991 issue of *American Visions* magazine, Ron talked about his classical education, reflecting back on his days at Cass. "[Classical music training] was all there was. There were no jazz schools, and I wasn't a jazz player then anyway. Classical training is important in that it gives you a level of discipline. It deals with strict forms and styles, and it's important to know all that."

Ron had some familiarity with jazz, mostly through the Saturday morning TV show, *The Soupy Sales Show*, that debuted as a local program in Detroit in 1953. "I remember watching it sometimes, and guys like Bud Powell and Max Roach played," he said. "But I never gave any thought to participating in playing jazz. How could I? I had a classical library to learn. There weren't enough hours in a day."

BEGINNING CASS

So, WITH HIS hopes of securing a prominent chair in an orchestra in the future as a means of earning a living, Ron entered Cass in the fall of 1952 and began to study harmony and theory in the music program that was located on the seventh floor of the building. He had retired his aluminum cello and owned one of his own. He gave up his paper route and concentrated on finding alternative sources of income so that he could buy what he needed to continue his music education. He worked weekends simonizing cars at a Detroit auto dealer at one point and did other "odds-and-ends jobs." Ron said, "There was always something. I never had a major job like being a cashier or clerk. But I did have the opportunity to play at socials every once in a while."

However, Ron began to notice that those extracurricular gigs were rare for him compared to other Cass classmates. The wheels began to turn about the disparity even while he was focusing on getting the music education he felt he needed to succeed as a working musician.

At Cass, there were nine periods a day, with each period being 45 minutes long, which was unusual at a time when most schools had one-hour classes. But the philosophy of the music program was to work efficiently in each class so that in addition to all the general-education requirements like English, social sciences, biology and mathematics, students could take three music classes a day and play in the band, the orchestra or sing in the choir.

Classmate Arthur Lieb, who was a year behind Ron and played bass and tuba at the school, remembers him as a well-liked student who dressed meticulously. "Back then we all wore suits to school every day," he recalled.

Arthur remembers the racial climate in Detroit at the time as still being tense. "Detroit was segregated by neighborhoods—Irish, Italian, Polish," he said. "Everyone knew where the black area was. People would say things like, 'They never take care of their homes,' when in reality the housing in the black neighborhood was largely owned by white slum landlords."

He recalls the race riots when he was young, when his father used to listen to police calls on the radio. Prejudice pervaded Arthur's home. "Jews and blacks had a bad name at our dinner table," he said. "Yet, I went to a black dentist through my sophomore year in college, and my father insisted that I wear clothes from a Jewish store."

When he arrived at Cass Tech, Arthur says the racial divide in the school was different from the outside world. That was the first time he got to know Jews and blacks. "With the musicians, it didn't matter what color your skin was," he said. "It was more about how you played your horn. As students, we were accepted to Cass for our musical talent, although there was more prejudice among the faculty members, all of whom were white. I remember after Ron left, I auditioned for the principal bass chair that he had occupied. My competition was a black bassist named Bob Friday. He was a better player than me, but I got the position."

"We never thought about black and white at Cass Tech," said Harry Begian, who taught there when Ron attended. "People ask me stupid questions like, how many blacks did you have in your band at Cass? Hell, I don't know. I never counted. All I know is that they were the greatest kids in the world and they played like hell—because they were fearless and committed to do what they were doing, and they were hungry to play music. That's all I know."

In Ron's first year at the school, Harry was his homeroom teacher. "I was only 28 when I started," he recalled. "So I had the biggest homeroom, which met between the third and fourth periods for 15 or 20 minutes. Sixty students, and it was pandemonium. They tore the place up until they went back to their classes. One day I quieted them all down and told them that I couldn't stand the noise anymore. I asked them, can we institute something to keep the class quiet so people can get some of their assignments done?"

Harry suggested the "rule of the paddle," which meant that an offending student would get hit with a thick paddle like the one that the school coach or assistant principal would use to restore order in the rest of the school. But Harry's idea was to have the students do the whacking and not him. "The students thought it was funny, but agreed to go along with it," he said. Soon, the department head noticed that Harry's homeroom class, once the most unruly at the school, had become the most orderly. He asked him how he had done it. Harry replied, "That's a secret I won't tell you."

One day a student came in late to homeroom, and another student named Walter was the person responsible for the rule of the paddle. Walter wasn't popular in the class, but he became even more unpopular when he gave the offending student an undeserved hard whack. However, the tables were turned when it came time for Walter to be hit with the paddle for an infraction he had committed in the class. The handler of the paddle was Ron.

Ron wound up but Harry stopped him. "There's Ron, over six feet tall and he took the paddle like a baseball bat up to his shoulder as if he were going to swing at a pitch," Harry recalled. "I told him that it wasn't a bat but a paddle."

"OK, Mr. Begian," Ron said, but then proceeded to teach Walter a lesson.

"Ron wound up and gave him one hell of a smackeroo on his rear end," Harry said. "I can still visualize Walter. For the rest of the week, he would come into the homeroom and not be able to sit down."

In remembering the incident, Ron laughs and says that episode was so out of character for him. "I was embarrassed," he said. "But I think I surprised everyone that I was so forceful."

Harry says that Ron was one of his favorite students. His first educational contact with Ron came in the woodwinds classes he taught on the eighth floor. Even though Ron was a cellist, at Cass he was required to learn a wind instrument and take a year of classes, Winds 1 and Winds 2. "I asked Ron which instrument he wanted to learn," Harry said. "He asked for a clarinet and he became the best student in the class in terms of developing facility on the instrument. During the second course, Ron asked me if I thought he could play in the top band I was teaching. He evidently had watched a rehearsal or two and maybe heard us do a concert. Well, I had noticed how serious a young man he was and how he approached playing the cello in the school orchestra. What a wonderful bow arm he had. So, I said, we'll see."

At the end of the term, Ron asked Harry again. "I told him that I've only got one vacant seat in the band," Harry said. "I think you can handle it, but not on soprano clarinet but alto clarinet."

Ron said, "I'll take it."

He passed the audition and was invited to play in the group. "And Ron carried his weight on the second instrument," said Harry.

Harry said that Ron was "a gentleman all the way around. He was refined, he spoke well, he was a fine student who stood out academically, and musically he had all the smarts. I have a photo of Ron playing the alto clarinet in the band, looking serious as could be. He was always serious—no goofing around, no horseplay. He was very direct. He didn't waste any words. He was one of the best students I ever taught."

Ron played the alto clarinet in Harry's Concert Band while playing cello in the Cass Symphony Orchestra, directed by Michael Bistritzky. (During Ron's first year, the bass chair was held by Paul Chambers, the bassist whom Ron succeeded a little over a decade later in Miles Davis's group.) Harry's group performed concerts that included an eclectic range of classical music by Rossini, Ravel, Schumann, Sousa, Stravinsky and Bach, while the orchestra performed music by Bach, Handel, Mozart, Brahms, Puccini, Beethoven and Mendelssohn. Ron also sang in the Cass Tech Choir, led by Glenn L. Klepinger.

Even though Ron was active in school and excelled in both music and academic subjects (he received scholarship certificates each semester and was inducted into the National Honor Society upon graduation), he wasn't satisfied, which led him to change course, instrument-wise, from cello to bass.

Cass was often asked to send its best students to teacher conventions, PTA meetings and socials. Ron rarely got the call. "I thought my talent level was equal to the guys who kept getting these jobs," he said. That desire to be recognized for his talent as well as make some money on the side combined with the bass chair opening in the school orchestra after Paul left led Ron to switch instruments—a midstream change that he thought would be effortless. "I knew the cello so well, and the bass was close enough to it, that I thought I'd be able to learn in a hurry," he said, then added, "What a mistake that was."

Nevertheless, Ron sold his cello to a classmate named Beverly Adams (who later married a man named Ron Carter), bought a bass by making payments on the instrument and began to woodshed intensively. Just as he worked to become proficient at playing the alto clarinet, Ron sought to master the bass. He thought he'd be able to dogpaddle into it ("How hard could it be?" he figured), but it proved to be a deep dive ("I quickly became amazingly aware of this deep hole I stepped into that I wasn't about to step out of").

So, how hard could it be? Hard! said Ron, who practiced five hours a day not only to learn the instrument but also to understand how the bass worked in relationship to all the other instruments in the orchestra. "The bass is bigger in size, right off. And as a result, it makes a whole different sound. Fingering the strings was completely different because the fingerboard was longer. I had to adjust my hearing to the lower pitch, where the notes appear way below the staff I'd been playing."

But Ron's biggest lesson was in discovering the different harmonic space the bass occupied in an orchestra. "With the cello, you played the melody and harmony. But playing the bass was a whole new harmonic revelation to me—to know what this bass note does to a chord. I learned that the bass had its own line to play, and how I could take musical cues from different parts of the orchestra when I played those notes. I was learning the library from the bottom up."

Did it seem like a risk at the time to be making such a big change? "Never. Not once. It never occurred to me to ask myself, what have I done? I had a goal in mind, and that was to get these gigs that the other guys were getting, As long as I was focused on the goal, the challenge didn't seem like a risk. I disciplined myself to maximize my time when I was practicing, figuring out what my peak hours were outside of school. I took bass lessons from a guy at the symphony, and focused on graduating from high school and trying to get into a good college where I could further my goals of having a classical music career."

Not only did Ron demonstrate his newfound prowess in bass at school, but playing the instrument opened up a new world to him: jazz. Ron told *Frets Magazine* (August 1979), "Detroit seemed to be a hotbed of good players, including Paul Chambers, Doug Watkins and Donald Byrd. We all went to the same high school—although we didn't play together at the time because they were two or three years older and were able to get into the clubs earlier."

Ron also noted in *Jazz Magazine* (Winter 1978) in a conversation with Milt Hinton that he was younger than many of the rising-star Detroit jazz musicians at the time, including Yusef Lateef, Kenny Burrell, Curtis Fuller, Louis Hayes, Pepper Adams, Wilbur Harden, Hugh Lawson and Barry Harris. "I'm 13. I can't be going to any jam session, get home at four o'clock in the morning and go to school at seven."

Ron recalls that Paul, while an accomplished classical player, took to the local jazz scene when he was young, playing bass choruses on occasion with touring jazz stars, such as Max Roach. "Paul was a very good classical-type player who was interested in making the gigs, meeting all the guys and playing with them," said Ron in the 1978 *DownBeat* "The Compleat Artist" interview by Ed Williams. He noted that because Paul was into the nightclub scene he often missed the eight o'clock morning orchestra class at Cass.

However, Ron did dip into jazz as a senior at Cass. A friend down the street from where he lived put together a jazz band that sometimes played parties at fraternity and sorority houses in Detroit. They needed a bass player, so they asked Ron. "The guy who led the band was a big Paul Desmond fan, the piano player loved Dave Brubeck and the drummer liked Max Roach," said Ron. "I told them I didn't know the tunes they wanted to play. There I was playing Beethoven every day, and he was kicking my ass, so how could I do anything else? But I took the songbooks they had, went to some rehearsals in my friend's basement, and I said, let's see what happens."

This gig proved to be an alternative school for Ron outside of Cass Tech. Not only did he have to learn a new library that included Brubeck, Bud Powell and Stan Getz tunes, but he also had to come to an understanding of how the bass worked in this new setting. "The first thing I learned was how important it was for the bass to play the pulse," Ron said. "Then I learned that a jazz player needs to play pizzicato that sounds more pronounced and personal than a classical musician. In an orchestra, you may have 12 bass players playing the same notes, so the sound is great and big. In jazz, there's just one guy who needs to make the volume of the pulse be audible enough."

As for improvisation, that didn't seem like a big deal at the time for Ron. "I'd been practicing classical my whole life, so I understood scales. I studied harmony and theory at Cass, so I wasn't a stranger to how a jazz band played harmonically." The biggest difference, Ron says, was speed. "I played Bach chorales for orchestra, but we played those in half the speed as a jazz tune. I had to acquire a language for playing faster tempos with jazz. The bass lines themselves weren't complicated but because they came faster than I was used to I couldn't think quickly enough to play the right notes that would work."

That would take time, Ron recognized, but it didn't feel like a priority. "I saw this as an increase in my income," he said. "But I was determined to be a classical musician, getting a little better each week and receiving encouragement from my teachers."

Ron graduated from Cass Tech in May 1955.

In its music program history, Cass Tech boasts an impressive roster of graduates who went on to significant success in the jazz world as well as in pop, including Diana Ross and The White Stripes duo, Jack White and Meg White. In addition to Ron, jazz hall of famers from Cass Tech include trumpeter/big band arranger Gerald Wilson; trumpeter Donald Byrd; guitarist Kenny Burrell; pianists Kirk Lightsey, Sir Roland Hanna and Geri Allen; bassists Doug Watkins and Paul Chambers; violinist Regina Carter; and vocalist Carla Cook.

After graduation, true to his wishes and determination, Ron was accepted to the Eastman School of Music in Rochester, New York. Even though he got a scholarship, he still had to work to pay for room, board and expenses. Jazz gigs in that city, one of the main stops in the regional jazz circuit at the time, would come in handy.

CHAPTER FOUR

Eastman / Rochester: Hope and Deferral

FOR FOUR YEARS from 1955 to 1959, Ron continued his education in the mastery of the bass in a classical setting at the prestigious Eastman School of Music in the small city of Rochester in northwestern New York. At the same time, Ron was also gaining more experience as a jazz artist, working with an impressive cast of local musicians (including Pee Wee Ellis, Roy McCurdy, and Chuck and Gap Mangione) as well as meeting the national jazz elite as they toured through Rochester on the Northeast-to-Midwest club circuit or on their way back into the States from Canada.

But those undergraduate years weren't easy for Ron. He arrived at Eastman with the goal of eventually gaining a seat in a major symphony orchestra somewhere in the U.S. and left four years later, his dreams deferred, to plunge, by default, into the jazz scene in New York.

In the "Marathon Man: Ron Carter Returns" article in the 2001 Rochester alternative weekly newspaper, *City*, writer Ron Netsky asked Ron what he took away from his years at the Eastman School of Music. "One of the things I got out of it was man's insensitivity to man," he answered, then added, "Does the answer surprise you?"

Netsky asked if race were a factor? Ron replied that Eastman was a musical institution with such a competitive spirit that being African American made it even more difficult. "It's not enough to be talented," he said and then noted, "I'm sure you expected a more positive answer, but that's positive—I learned at an early age what kind of world we're living in. I also made some great relationships and met some great friends who I hold dear as we speak."

Likewise, when asked by the Webzine *JazzWax* what was the most important lesson he learned at Eastman, Ron replied, "Don't let discouragement be your focus...I felt I wasn't getting the kind of interest I should have been getting. I thought there were opportunities that should have been presented to me that weren't because I was an African American."

Ron estimates that of a student body of 700 at the time, there were only six blacks, including himself. He felt a subtle sense of discrimination, noting that he believed he was the best undergraduate student player there. Ron was acknowledged as such when the school formed the Eastman Philharmonic, a student-professional orchestra. He earned first chair on bass. But he was also kept out of the loop on employment opportunities beyond the school campus.

"Sometimes they'd put notices up on the board for auditions for major orchestras," Ron said. "It seemed to be common knowledge around the school that the openings were available and that auditions were taking place. But somehow no one got around to telling me to look at the bulletin board or that there was something there that I might be interested in. It wasn't a fair thing to do to me…. At the time, it seemed that everyone knew about the major opportunities but me, and I didn't think that was OK."

JazzWax asked Ron, how did he keep this prejudice from overwhelming him? He answered, "I thought I played well, and I didn't care what they thought. I mean, of course I cared, and it did matter. But I wasn't going to let their view of my talent and my viability as a fulltime classical player affect me….I was comfortable with my view of myself, and I was making a few jazz gigs so I wasn't actually starving. I just felt that their way of looking at me was their view, not mine."

ROCHESTER BACKGROUNDER

THE CITY OF Rochester was highly segregated at the time of Ron's Eastman tenure. "Life was rough back then," said jazz drummer and Rochester jazz historian Noal Cohen, who was born and raised in the city. "White guys weren't open to black guys, so it wasn't easy for African Americans to move around there." Even though he was brought up in a left wing, FDR-adoring family, Noal's parents didn't know any blacks in their social circle, and he didn't have much contact because he went to a segregated school.

Noal remembers a gig he once led at a Jewish country club in the city where he assembled a band that included Pee Wee Ellis on saxophone. "The organizer pulled me aside during the show and told me not to bring a black guy there again. It was a really derogatory remark."

In his work documenting the city's jazz history, Cohen has traced the jazz activity in clubs and at concerts by scanning microfilm of Rochester newspapers at the city's main library. He has been looking for reviews, listings and advertisements in the papers. Unfortunately, The Pythodd, one of the hot club spots for jazz that regularly booked acts like the Three Sounds, Jack McDuff, Johnny Hammond Smith, Les McCann and Ray Bryant, was not covered. "The action there wasn't documented," Noal said. "It was partly because the club didn't advertise in the newspapers, but I also think it had a lot to do with the fact that it was located in what people called the black ghetto."

Five years after Ron left for New York, Rochester went through its own race riot in 1964. Due to the increase of the African-American population in the '50s, whites became fearful even though jobs for blacks were low skilled, wages were poor and housing was substandard. The disturbance took place over a period of three days beginning on July 24, and peace was restored only when Governor Nelson Rockefeller dispatched the New York National Guard. Four people were killed, 350 were injured, more than a thousand were arrested and more than 200 stores were looted or damaged.

Noal recalled a story that ran in *The New Republic* magazine after the riots: "The author described Rochester as a Southern plantation transplanted up north."

EASTMAN BACKGROUNDER

ESTABLISHED IN 1921 by George Eastman, the founder of the Eastman Kodak Company, the Eastman School of Music became the first professional constituent college of the University of Rochester. Expressing his love for music, the industrialist/philanthropist espoused that the life of a community thrives on its cultural passion. "I am interested personally in music, and I am led thereby to want to share my pleasure with others," Eastman said. "It is impossible to buy an appreciation of music. Yet, without appreciation, without the presence of a large body of people who understand music and get enjoyment out of it, any attempt to develop the musical resources of any city is doomed."

Eastman first approached University of Rochester president Rush Rhees in 1918 about his ideas, then bought property as well as the corporate rights of Rochester's D.K.G. Institute of Musical Art, which had been established in 1913. Ground was broken for the new school in 1920.

In September 1921, with a charter faculty of 32 teachers, 104 music students began taking classes at Eastman School. The following year the Eastman Theater opened, featuring the Rochester Philharmonic Orchestra, also founded by George Eastman. In 1924 a five-floor annex was built that connected the school to the theater. The Sibley Music Library, housed within the school, moved to a new building in 1937. (It relocated again in 1989 to a new edifice and became the largest academic music library in the world. In 2001, the library established the Ron Carter Archive Audio Archive and Collection, consisting of more than 700 recordings of his leader and sideman dates that he bequeathed to the school.)

With Eastman's financial backing and the leadership of the school's director, Howard Hanson, who served from 1924–1964, Eastman became a well-respected college that graduated students who went on to careers in the classical and opera worlds, with a strong connection to the Boston Symphony Orchestra and New York's Metropolitan Opera Orchestra. Eastman School was built on a strong foundation of artistry and scholarship in classical music. It wasn't until well after Ron graduated in 1959 that jazz became a part of the curriculum there. In fact, during Ron's time there, performing jazz was frowned upon.

The classical violinist Sanford Allen, a good friend of Ron's and a collaborator with Cass Tech grad Roland Hanna, recalls the pianist's experience at Eastman in 1954. "Roland was studying classical music, but to support himself he would play jazz gigs on the weekend," Sanford said. "One Saturday night he was playing at a club and some Eastman faculty members came in. They waved to Roland and chatted amiably with him after the show. However, on Monday, Roland was called to the faculty offices and told that his conduct was unacceptable. He was told, 'We don't have jazz weekends at Eastman.' Roland packed his belongings, moved to New York and continued his schooling at Juilliard."

Even so, because Rochester was a hub of jazz activity in the '50s—both touring acts and locals—Eastman students enriched the scene. A student at the University of Rochester, Noal Cohen recalls the clandestine jazz action at Eastman during the mid- to late '50s. At his attictoys.com Web site dedicated to Rochester's jazz history, he wrote: "I can well remember jam sessions held in the tiny Eastman practice rooms with a dozen or so musicians packed in so tightly that there was barely enough air to breathe."

While Ron focused on his academic classical life (he studied with renowned bassist Oscar Zimmerman, who taught at Eastman while also serving as the principal bassist in the Rochester Philharmonic Orchestra), he worked weekends in the jazz clubs. Did he suffer the same fate as Hanna for moonlighting? "I never had to contend with that vibe," he said. "Roland was five years older than me. He was gone from Eastman when I started so maybe things had changed. But I never hid playing jazz at the local clubs. Maybe because I was such a good classical music player, they decided not to make an issue of it. Or maybe they just didn't know."

In the August 1979 issue of *Frets Magazine*, Ron said that most of the other students at Eastman looked unfavorably at jazz. "There were those who didn't acknowledge it, those who didn't know what it was, those who wished to play but couldn't," he said, then added, "and those who could play and did. Jazz was a part of the city, and it was certainly part of my musical line of thought."

ENTRY INTO EASTMAN

BASED ON HIS achievements at Cass Tech, Ron was offered a full scholarship, plus room and board, to major in bass at Eastman, but that didn't include money for books and other necessities. So, as he did in Detroit in his senior year, he sought work in the area jazz clubs, mostly on the weekends, given his rigorous academic life during the week. He took classes during the day, but also developed an eight-hour practice routine. He told *The Black Collegian* writer Kalamu ya Salaam in the publication's March/April 1978 issue that being at Eastman fostered in him the importance of "discipline of practice, discipline of getting the maximum amount out of whatever time you have."

Ron went on to recommend the importance of musicians going to school, "although I wouldn't necessarily say a classically oriented school." He added, "But some form of formal music education is essential to be a quality player because you can't learn enough on your own and not enough guys on the street have the time to show you."

At Eastman, Ron said that even though the college did not offer jazz classes, he was getting his schooling in that genre elsewhere. He told *Frets*, "I was working around town with a quartet, a trio, or whatever the job could handle. I was part of the house rhythm section in a club where everybody used to play when they came through Rochester. Carmen McRae, Sonny Stitt and Max Roach were there pretty frequently, and when an act came without a band, I would get to play with them."

In *All About Jazz* in 2006, Ron told writer Brian P. Lonergan that he met such bassists as Sam Jones and Ike Isaacs when they came through town, and they assured him good bass players were high in demand in New York. Ron said, "I had no specific focus on being a 'famous jazz player,' but I felt I had a great classical background, I knew the literature, I was learning the jazz library by working these gigs and I felt that if I could be a complete bass player, I could find work and support a family."

One of Ron's earliest friends at Eastman was Ned Corman, a clarinet player who grew up on his family's farm in Bellafonte, Pennsylvania, about 200 miles south of Rochester. While their careers in music diverged after college (Ned went into teaching as well as performing with such leaders as choral maestro/hitmaker Fred Waring and the Pennsylvanians and British entertainer Tommy Steele of *Half a Sixpence* Broadway fame), the two became close at school. In fact, many years later, out of the blue Ron sent Ned an autographed photo with the inscription on it, "The best way to spell friend is Ned."

It wasn't an issue for Ron that Ned was white. Color didn't matter. "I knew the other African-American students at Eastman—three men, two women—but we never socialized," Ron said. "Then there wasn't that kind of camaraderie that developed during the '60s and '70s when blacks organized together to retain the African-American identity. At Eastman we didn't have a sense of group support or desire to do something once a week like meet to talk about grievances because of race. We were all so busy. I was practicing every hour on the bass to get ahead. Eastman wasn't a setting that allowed for having a survivor group. For me, my friends at the school were people like Ned. We shared classes, and we shared cookies."

One of Ned's funny memories of Ron in the early days was about his sweet tooth. "My mother would send a pound of cookies to me in the mail each week," Ned said. "It was uncanny that Ron would be in the mailroom when the cookies arrived."

Ron laughed at the reminder of "Grace's chocolate chip cookies" that Ned shared with him. "We'd always share what our parents would send us. We received breakfast and dinner as a part of our schooling, but we had to scuffle for lunch. So it was cookies and milk in between our main meals."

Ned and Ron not only had an interest in music but also sports. "Ron and I spent more time hanging out with sports than we did with music," Ned said. "We had physical education classes together, and we played touch football on the large lawn in front of our dorm." They also played basketball, favoring one-on-one contests.

"We had a wonderfully competitive relationship," said Ron. "Ned was a good pool player. He beat me all the time. I figured the only way to even the score was to play basketball with him. Ned was six-foot tall, but I was six foot, four inches. I always beat him at hoop."

Ron was so good at basketball that he even tried out for the University of Rochester's freshman basketball team and scored a position on the team. "During orientation week, both the university and Eastman campuses had a get-together," Ron said. "It took place at the University of Rochester campus which was about two miles away from Eastman. It was partly a welcome to the school and an introduction to the university's facilities such as the bookstore and library. Well, I picked up this feeling from the university students that all musicians were fruits, that they were only interested in music and nothing else. I was insulted."

Ron figured that the only way to counter this prejudice was to try out for the basketball team. "After three days of scrimmages, I made the second team," he said. "I wanted to show guys that not all musicians were fruits. You don't have to believe what other people's views of you are. If you're determined enough and good enough, you can change viewpoints without screaming."

Ron bicycled back and forth from Eastman to the university gym and played in seven or eight games, averaging seven to eight minutes each game. He was a decent shooter, but an even stronger rebounder ("I was playing against guys who were six foot seven, had wide bodies and big thighs, but I knew where the rebound was going to come down"). However, he was only able to make two of four practices each week because he had conflicts with his classical studies.

"But I made a point," Ron said.

When asked if he had ever fantasized about having a career in sports versus music, he pointed to the times, when a black athlete didn't have many options to pursue professional athletics in the main arena. "Jackie Robinson joined the Dodgers in 1947 when I was 10, and he didn't really make a big dent in baseball till the '50s," he said. "By then I already had a view of what I wanted to do with my life. By the time Jackie impacted baseball, I figured I could tell a story through music instead."

THE JAZZ SCENE

WHEN NOAL COHEN, who graduated from Rochester in 1959, first met Ron on the jazz scene, he admits that he was not only in "awe of this cool six-foot-something black guy" but also intimidated. They played together in several bands. "I don't think I ever met a more single-minded person than Ron during that time," Noal said. "He was absolutely determined, in a quiet way, to do what it took to succeed in life. He never drank; he didn't do drugs. He was a guy who people would look at it and know that he had his shit together."

Noal says that he and Ron were never close. "I wasn't that great a drummer and I wasn't going anywhere," he said. "Plus, I always felt that Ron had a shield around him to protect himself. He didn't get tight with a lot of people."

During that time Ron was regularly playing in clubs like Mardi Gras and Golden Grill in the Don Manning Trio, as well as taking an active interest in getting to know the touring musicians, Noal said. "Ron would go out of his way to meet these guys. He was a young guy clearly looking ahead. He was positioning himself I believe to move to New York someday."

Noal recalls going to Ron's place in his senior year to pick him up for a gig. "There was Ike Isaacs visiting Ron," he recalled. "Ike was touring with Lambert, Hendricks and Ross at the time. It impressed me that Ron had the foresight and self-confidence to be talking about the music with people from New York. So, we all piled into my car, with Ron's bass and Ike, who I drove back to his hotel downtown."

Even then, Ron had a knack for straightforwardness when it came to the music. Noal remembers getting ready for one gig he had with Ron at Sodus, New York, on the shore of Lake Ontario. "When I picked him up, I told him about a cymbal I was going to use for the gig," he said. "I asked him what he thought about this old cymbal that I found at my parents' house. He looked at the cymbal, then looked at me and told me, 'Put it back.'"

Pianist Jerry Moors, who says he was known as "Lenny" during his Eastman years and today serves as the bandmaster for Princess Cruises, recalls doing a local jazz gig with Ron and flubbing a take on "All the Things You Are." He said, "I didn't know the bridge very well and kind of faked through it. Afterwards, Ron called me aside and asked me what was going on in the bridge. I said I didn't know it very well, and he said, 'Never play a tune unless you know it.' Of course, he was right. A good lesson."

MANGIONE PASTA

ONE OF THE key associations Ron made on the Rochester jazz scene was with two brothers, pianist Gap and trumpeter Chuck Mangione (who Ron always called Charlie). Their grocer father was a passionate jazz fan who not only went to the club shows in town but also invited the musicians over to his house for a home-cooked meal later. "My father was dedicated to taking me and Chuck to hear some of the greatest jazz players who ever lived," Gap said. "He was never a shy person. I remember him dragging Chuck and me up to Dizzy Gillespie after a set and saying, 'My name is Frank Mangione. Here's my kids. They play too.' I was trying to find a place to hide."

Chuck recalls the same incident that took place at the Ridgecrest Inn, where touring groups would perform six nights each week, with a Sunday matinee. "Gap and I were avid fans of an album Dizzy had put out with Art Blakey," he said. "We knew the tunes inside out." So, in the next set Diz invited the brothers to sit in. After the show he came to Pappa Mangione's house for an Italian dinner that Nancy Mangione cooked.

Gap remembers seeing Louis Armstrong, Duke Ellington, Count Basie—all regulars in Rochester clubs—as well as Max Roach, Sonny Rollins and Clifford Brown (two months before he died). Oftentimes musicians would come to the Mangione house, sit down for a pasta meal and then jam afterwards in the dining room. "My mom loved to cook for people," Chuck said. "Both my parents loved to have people come over. Our house became a pit stop for the touring bands."

Gap (born in 1938) often joined the jams as did his younger brother Chuck (born in 1940). The two later formed their own band called the Jazz Brothers and in the late '50s and early '60s recorded three albums for Riverside Records. Chuck, of course, soared to fame later on with his hit "Feels So Good."

A year younger than Ron, Gap had heard about this bassist from Eastman who had a good reputation. He needed a bass player for a gig in 1957 at a club in Batavia, New York, some 30 miles outside of Rochester. He asked Ron to work in his quintet that also had two saxophonists and a drummer. "I called him up and Ron said fine. I didn't have much of an impression of him. He seemed taciturn. It was not a voluble conversation."

Gap recalls the gig as uneventful, but notes that Ron was still learning how to play jazz. "He could read, he had great time, but he hadn't yet developed his bass lines. I wrote some bass lines for him, and he put in the changes he wanted, which made it a lot more fun for him."

They stayed in touch, with Ron on occasion coming to the Mangione house across town to engage in the impromptu jams. Occasionally he would be there when the jazz royalty arrived. He and the Mangione brothers also played more gigs in town before Gap moved to Syracuse to attend the University of Syracuse.

At Syracuse, Gap organized informal gatherings of musicians to try to put together a big band. He also played at little clubs in town, including a bar called Frank's, and at the university student union. "I'd invite Ron and Chuck to come to Syracuse to play in a small band I had," Gap said.

While Gap went off to school, Chuck continued to play in Rochester. Three years younger than Ron, Chuck remembers him as being a person "who had a vision or a plan or a direction for his life. He was slim, tall and handsome and was serious in his approach to the music. He was more sophisticated than your average musician. I don't remember hanging out with Ron except when we played together."

The Ridgecrest was a club where white patrons would go to hear jazz; at The Pythodd a mixed crowd of whites and blacks gathered. When Chuck first started playing there, he was still in high school and between sets he retreated backstage to do his homework while Ron drank tea and smoked his pipe.

"The Pythodd was a small club with a huge bar and a small bandstand," Chuck said. "It was a neighborhood club in the black section of Rochester and served outrageous fried chicken and great pies. I played dates there with Ron a couple of nights a week and oftentimes Pee Wee Ellis would also play with us. By that time it was obvious that Ron was the leader of what was happening on the bandstand."

Onstage Ron would push Chuck all in the name of having fun playing jazz. "We'd play some of the latest jazz hits, which Ron always made an educational experience," Chuck said. "He would play something, and then accelerate into a ridiculous tempo which made my eyes bigger than my head. It was like he was saying, hey, do you want to go along for this ride? Or he'd play a blues, not in B flat or F, but a blues in B, which was a challenge. He didn't do this in a mean way but as a way of trying to grow musically."

Chuck, who started Eastman in Ron's senior year, said, "Ron was like a gentle giant. He never raised his voice or came down on me. I'd see him at school in the hallway, but we never played together in the orchestra or ensembles. He was way beyond me, and he was really together."

During this time, Ron came into contact with another Rochester native, drummer Roy McCurdy, who for most of Ron's experience at Eastman was in the Air Force. "I was stationed in Alaska, so I'd get three to four weeks of leave which is when I'd come home to play with Chuck and Gap," Roy said. "That's when I played with Ron. By the time I was discharged Ron had already gone to New York. Before that, I remember both of us discussing who was going to be the first to go there."

Ron won, but Roy soon followed, joining the Art Farmer-Benny Golson Jazztet band in 1960. Two years later, Ron and Roy were reunited in Sonny Rollins's trio, which set up shop at the Five Spot in New York for an eight-week stretch. "That started when Sonny called me to join him in Chicago for a gig at McKee's Lounge on the Southside of the city," Ron said. "When we played the Five Spot, it had just moved from 4th Street and 3rd Avenue to 8th Street and 3rd Avenue. The club was still unfinished so they only had plastic sheeting over the windows, which made for a lot of chilly nights on the bandstand."

BIG BROTHER

BORN IN FLORIDA in 1941 and raised in Texas, Pee Wee Ellis moved with his family to Rochester in 1955. He had already played saxophone on a stage in Texas, so he gravitated quickly to the jazz scene in his new city. "I was 14 and playing at The Pythodd," he said. "I knew Chuck and guys like [trumpeter] Waymon Reed who was a year older than me. I played in a band with Ron on bass, and he was so solid. He was into playing jazz standards in different tempos. It was his way of having a lot of fun."

Pee Wee says that Ron always looked out for him. "He was like a big brother to me," he said. "We played a lot of gigs in upstate New York. I remember him packing us up in his '52 Ford and driving to Syracuse with his bass, drums, horns and everything. I don't know how we all fit in his car."

Pee Wee also knew Ron from Madison High School in Rochester, where the youngster attended and the elder did his student teaching. "I used to get on his case for being late," Ron said.

During his time at the high school, Ron picked up the tuba to perform in the marching band. He had already learned clarinet from his Cass Tech days—a Selmer clarinet with a green Lucite mouthpiece that he clung onto until he got to New York when he had to sell it to pay some bills—so tuba came next due to its association with the string bass. "It was so cold playing the tuba for football games where the band would be up in the bleachers in the winter with the wind blowing," Ron said. "But I figured it would be good to play the tuba because once I got to New York I could double on that. I could play the instrument well enough to get by, but not for being in the pit for a Broadway show."

Pee Wee and Ron became friends during this period. In fact, they went to New York together for the first time during Easter break in 1957. "Pee Wee had an aunt and uncle who lived there at 162nd and Broadway, so we drove to New York in my car," Ron said. "The first time we went we actually walked all the way from his aunt's house to Birdland, which was at 52nd and Broadway [a distance of approximately five and a half miles]. It was packed and you could hardly see the stage because there was so much smoke. We hung out near the kitchen because neither of us drank, and we saw John Coltrane, Johnny Griffin and Thelonious Monk."

The pair ended up going back uptown on the subway, but Pee Wee's aunt had forgotten to give him the house keys. So teacher and student crashed in the car, got up the next morning and headed back to Rochester where Pee Wee had to go back to school and Ron to his early-morning class at Eastman.

"On the way while driving on the throughway, we got stopped by a state trooper," Ron said. "He made me open up everything in the trunk and in our duffle bags. He even told me to take off the hubcaps. He searched everywhere, but couldn't find anything. He ended up giving me a ticket for not registering my car, which had Michigan plates, in New York. I got to Eastman one hour late for a rehearsal. My teacher asked me what happened and I told him the whole story. He got me a lawyer, and the ticket was thrown out of court."

In 1957 Pee Wee moved to New York to attend Manhattan School of Music and took lessons with Sonny Rollins. In 1965, he began his four-year stint with James Brown, co-writing the hits "Cold Sweat" and "Say It Loud—I'm Black and Proud." In 1969, he became the arranger and musical director for CTI's Kudu Records imprint, which is where he reunited with Ron. When he decided to record Esther Phillips, he enlisted Ron.

"There were a lot of bass giants then, but Ron was my first call," Pee Wee said. "If he had any ideas, I was ready to take his advice. Ron was always a mentor to me. He was a sensible guy, and he had his head on straight. Ron was such a solid player. I knew he'd provide the foundation that Esther needed."

AN O.P. MOMENT

WHEN RON BECAME established years later, he always told interviewers that he had a short list of musicians who he had never played with but wished he had. One was Oscar Peterson. When Oscar read one story on Ron, he called him to play a date so that he "could get off that list." However, Ron didn't tell scribes that he had already joined the piano titan onstage in 1957 at Strong Auditorium on the River Campus of the University of Rochester.

Noal Cohen recalls the event where O.P. was playing with his trio of Herb Ellis on guitar and Ray Brown on bass in a smaller venue one flight below the main house. "The place was loaded," Noal said. "Jazz was big on college campuses then, which was the Dave Brubeck era. One of the school's fraternities hosted a jam session at the show where young talent were invited to play with Oscar."

Ellis and Brown took a break and O.P. held court with a group of youngsters that included Chuck Mangione and Waymon Reed on trumpets, Benny Salzano on tenor saxophone, Ron on bass and Noal on drums. "It was a disaster in so many ways," said Noal. "We went onstage and the place was filled. We decided to play a blues. Chuck counted, 1-2-3-4 at medium tempo, but Oscar played it 1-2, a slow blues. The only thing that's harder than playing fast is playing slow. It was very tense during the tune. It wasn't happening. Then we played 'Groovin' High,' which was a little better."

Ellis and Brown came back onstage and dismissed the rookies as if saying to the upstarts, "Now, we're going to show you how to do it." Noal recalled, "I think Ray even said something like that, that they were going to put us in our proper places. It was humiliating. It was like a football player dancing in the end zone after a touchdown."

MEETING JANET

It was during one of Ron's visits to Syracuse in March 1958 to play with Gap that he met Janet Hasbrouck, an English major and a member of the Syracuse Jazz Society, an informal group that supported the local jazz scene. "A group of students who had an affinity for jazz would go to the shows kind of like how people subscribe to cultural events by getting season tickets," said Ron. "At one concert, Gap, who knew most of the people in love with jazz in Syracuse, introduced me to Janet. We talked a little, but I had to go back to school the next day so we didn't talk long."

Ron returned the following weekend to visit again and then asked Janet for her phone number. After that, they established a telephone relationship. They met up a couple of more times when Ron drove to Syracuse to play with Gap.

Was it love at first sight? "I'm not sure," Ron said. "But it didn't take us long to figure out that we should spend more time together."

At the time, Janet was finishing her B.A. studies in English, with a minor in art, while also working fulltime doing office clerical work for the Niagara Mohawk Power Company. She and Ron married on June 7, 1958.

When reminded that the courting period was relatively short—less than three months—Ron said with a laugh, "Ah, you have to remember that was the atomic age."

Ron and Janet tied the knot at a short ceremony in a Rochester Episcopal church, only attended by Janet's sister as maid of honor and Ron's friend Peter Gibson, a Rochester native who frequented the jazz clubs, as best man. "It was a small affair," said Peter who had been impressed by Ron's playing in the area clubs.

After the marriage vows were exchanged, Ron and Janet drove to the Mangione grocery store. "It was a Saturday, so it was hectic," said Gap. "But there they were, in their finery, just wanting to stop by and say hi on their wedding day."

Ron's parents, who were not invited to the wedding, worried that their son, now married, would quit school. But Ron would have none of that. He was on a mission.

Ron still had his senior year to finish, so, since the college did not have co-ed housing for married students, he and Janet moved off campus. Their first apartment was on the second floor of a duplex. After three weeks, the landlady-owner, who lived on the first floor, asked them to move. "She was very nice about it," Ron said. "She told me I practiced too much. I was practicing all the time to get better. But she didn't like hearing the bass playing all day and all night with me patting the floor with my foot to the beat."

So, Ron and Janet moved into married housing at Rochester's Colgate Divinity School a couple of miles away from Eastman in Highland Park. "I really enjoyed living there," said Ron. "It was out of the pressure cooker. I miss the seclusion there, away from the school environment and the pressures of living in a dorm where guys would always be knocking on your door. That place provided for a nice breath of fresh air."

Janet got a job at the local power company, and Ron not only continued his studies, but went into overdrive performing, both in the local jazz clubs as well as with the Eastman-Rochester Philharmonic, which paid $60 a week. While he was the first black musician to be in the orchestra, Ron raised the ire of some of the subscribers by sporting a beard.

"There was a big brouhaha over that in my senior year," Ron said. "People were complaining. I heard about it from one of my Eastman teachers. They offered to buy me out of playing there, but I said I wasn't interested unless they bought me out for the entire year." The complaints ceased. However, that indignity was minor compared to the next one that occurred.

STOKOWSKI SNUB LEADS TO STUPOR

WHILE RON WAS in the Philharmonic, many top-tier conductors visited as guests. Ron saw that as getting exposure to the movers and shakers of the classical music world that he hoped would lead to a career. He loved playing jazz, but he was focused on gaining entry into the elite classical world. "You play good, you get the job," Ron said. "But I found out in my senior year that that was not the case at all. It still had to do with the color of your skin."

One of the guest conductors was Leopold Stokowski, the world-renowned orchestra maestro who at the time was the musical director of the Houston Symphony Orchestra (a post he held from 1955–1961). Ron's bass playing made a deep impression on Stokowski, who one day pulled him aside. "Young man, you play wonderful bass," he said. "But I'm in Houston, and I know that the board of directors is not ready for a colored man to be in its orchestra."

"I didn't know what to do," Ron said. "Here I had invested half my life to prepare myself for a career in classical music, but one of the world's top conductors tells me his orchestra wouldn't hire a 'colored' person. I was stunned—here I am a handsome African-American man who switched to bass because when I was a cellist, I couldn't get a job that a white cellist could. That no matter how good I play, I can't make it because I'm black? The only word I could think of was disillusioned. Are 10 of my 20 years shot? Is what happened to me in high school still the case? Well, I thanked Mr. Stokowski for his honesty, then walked away. I tried to live with that and not strangle myself."

Ron confided his disappointment only in Janet, who tried to pick up his spirits by saying that he'd have to put his talent elsewhere for it to be appreciated. "I was walking around in a stupor for a couple of hours," Ron said. "Janet suggested teaching, but I didn't practice all those hours just to be a teacher."

The sting of the rejection continues to ruffle Ron's feathers. "Go to the library and look up the five major orchestras to see if there are any black musicians in them," he said. "Tell me if the faces have changed, from 1985 to 1995 to 2005. The reality is they haven't."

Ron's response is "quite reasonable," said Sanford Allen, the first African American to be in the New York Philharmonic Orchestra. "In the last 46 years, the Philharmonic has had two blacks who played regularly. I left in 1977, and the other black was French horn player Jerome Ashby, who joined two years after I left."

Ashby, who died in 2007, became an associate principal horn member in 1979 and made his Philharmonic solo debut in 1982. "And that's the history of the orchestra," said Sanford. "And this is still very much an issue on a national level."

Another pioneer who sought to break down the racial barriers in classical music was bassist Art Davis, who played jazz in the employ of Dizzy Gillespie in the late '50s and John Coltrane in the latter years of his life in the '60s. He too faced prejudice, most notably by the New York Philharmonic. He filed a racial discrimination case against the orchestra for not holding a "blind audition," wherein a performer would be heard but not seen. As a result of his case, Davis was blacklisted, which made it difficult for him to secure any work in the classical world. He eventually waved the white flag, went back to school to get a doctorate in clinical practice and spent the rest of his life primarily as a therapist. He died in 2007.

TRIUMPHANT RETURN TO EASTMAN

WHILE CLASSICALLY ORIENTED Eastman vocally celebrated its alumni who had made significant statements in the classical music world, it was slow to also honor its graduates who went on to shine in other musical genres.

"I don't know the reason, but Eastman did not maintain a relationship with Ron after he graduated," said Jeff Campbell, associate professor of jazz studies and contemporary media, and instructor of such classes as Jazz Double Bass and Jazz Combo and Improvisation. "It felt like there was an estrangement."

Jeff speculates that Ron didn't feel that he was treated well when he was asked to apply for a job at Eastman several years after he graduated. Somehow the request was delayed, so that by the time Ron received it, the position had already been filled. "I think Ron felt that he hadn't been treated very well." Jeff noted that Ron did come back to the campus to do a master class clinic. However, that was the one and only invite he received to be involved with Eastman as an alum.

In the early part of this decade, Jeff went to the school director and dean of Eastman, Jim Undercofler (who later became the CEO of the Philadelphia Orchestra), and recommended that he reach out to Ron. "I suggested that Jim write him a letter telling him that we respect him and we want to honor him, but we would need cooperation from him to make it happen," Jeff said. "Ron replied immediately: 'How soon can you be here?' So we went to New York and had a wonderful visit with him. All hard feelings were gone, and he was extremely open to working with us."

A bass player who released the CD, *West End Avenue* (named after the street Ron lives on in New York), Jeff grew up listening to Ron's music and tracked down any article he could find on him. "I became aware of how he spoke in print, how he could be so outspoken and have strong opinions on things," he said, then noted that as he got to know Ron better years later the gentle and caring parts of his personality emerged.

Jeff received his Bachelor's degree in music from Brigham Young University and then went to Eastman to get both his masters and doctorate. For his master's dissertation, Jeff wrote a paper on Duke Ellington's bassist Jimmy Blanton. For his doctorate, he decided to expand his reach by taking on seven or eight jazz bassists who had made significant advances in playing the bass. He made a list that included Blanton, Oscar Pettiford, Ray Brown, Paul Chambers, Scott LaFaro and Ron.

"To do the work with thoroughness, I chose to write about the bookends, Jimmy and Ron." Jeff said. "Plus, Ron was the only living person on the list." That offered him the opportunity to meet with Ron and talk about the bass. It also afforded him the opportunity to become friends with Ron (he was one of the select guests at Ron's 70th birthday celebration in Central Park in 2007).

Through Jeff's intervention, Ron began to become involved with Eastman. He donated his 700-plus LP and CD collection to the school's Sibley Music Library in 2001 (see discography appendix). That same year Eastman invited Ron and his quartet to perform at the school in Kilbourn Hall as well as hold a master class and present a lecture titled, "Where Is the Music Played?" In a press release about the event, Undercofler said, "Ron Carter's multifaceted engagement with music exemplifies one of the primary goals of an Eastman education. We are delighted to welcome 'home' one of our most distinguished alumni."

In 2002, Ron was invited back to Eastman to be the commencement speaker. At the ceremony Ron received the University of Rochester's most prestigious award and highest honor for alumni, the Hutchison Medal, which recognizes outstanding achievement and service to community, state and nation.

In his acceptance speech, Ron detailed his own curriculum vitae with his characteristic wit and pride about why he felt he got the award. He rhetorically asked, when his name is read along with the list of the others who received the Hutchison Medal, what will "be some thoughts that go with it?"

Ron's response: "The most recorded jazz bassist of the century, or the person who gave private lessons to literally hundreds of bassists for the past 40 years? A distinguished professor of music emeritus at The City College of New York, or a father who would come home from a nightclub performance at three a.m. and proceed to play with his kids, much to his wife's chagrin? One of the bassists who helped to move the bass to a new level, or a lover of cactus and sports cars? Someone who was truly a student of Music with a capital 'M,' or one of eight children raised by two loving and concerned parents? A tall, handsome and elegant African-American male, or a tall, handsome and elegant African-American male?"

Ron's son, Ron Jr., delivered the medal to Ron's mother, who attended the commencement, just as she had, in the company of her husband, Lutheran, 43 years earlier when Ron graduated from the school.

REVVING UP FOR NEW YORK

WITH PROSPECTS FOR a classical career dashed, Ron's only option was to dive headlong into the jazz world—and that meant heading to New York City, the home of so many of the jazz musicians he met during his years in Rochester. Not only were the job opportunities brighter, but also the racial intolerance would be far less than where he had been living the past four years. "There wasn't much to do in Rochester," Ron said. "It wasn't a big town then, and while it wasn't overt when I lived there, the racial discrimination was clearly on the scene. Housing was limited and I thought job options were limited. Clearly, four years there had been enough. There was nothing wrong with living in a small town, but I knew there were other things out there based on my broad feeling of finding another level to reach."

Ron had already made contacts with drummer Chico Hamilton and saxophonist Benny Golson, both of whom told Ron to look them up if he decided to make the move to New York. Ron didn't have guaranteed work, and even had to contend with Janet's surprise that he was going to make a go at finding job security as a jazz bassist.

"Janet was hoping that I'd become a college professor and maybe do jazz on the weekend as a hobby," Ron said. "I don't think she was prepared to see this as a livelihood, and for good reason. Jazz musicians that she knew in Syracuse all had day jobs, and they weren't making money from playing music. Plus, there was that perception of jazz musician, the literary history of a person playing jazz. It was not encouraging. It focused on reputed drug habits, difficulty in finding work, dealing with lousy working conditions."

Reluctantly trusting in Ron's confidence, Janet left Rochester to find a place for them to live in New York, 350 miles away. Gap and Chuck helped Ron load up a U-Haul van and traveled with him to New York to unload at a studio apartment in Harlem, at 139th and Lenox Avenue, in Delano Village, a new seven-building residential complex. They unloaded the van and returned the U-Haul. Not long after their arrival, Ron's car broke down, and he sold it for $100.

With Janet securing a job as a reservationist with American Airlines, Ron started to explore the jazz life in late-night New York, carrying his bass to the subway in Harlem and making the trip downtown to clubs in Greenwich Village.

The year was 1959, arguably the most seminal year in jazz history. Orrin Keepnews, co-owner of and producer at the legendary independent label Riverside Records, recalls the year as a time when a lot of important music was being recorded. He said, "1959 was one of those years when people weren't saying that jazz is dying."

"I arrived at the right time," said Ron. "After all, it's all about timing."

CHAPTER FIVE

Early Years: New York City

BY ALL ACCOUNTS, 1959 proved to be an alchemic year for jazz recordings, yielding a bumper crop of seminal LPs. Charles Mingus belted out *Mingus Ah Um*, John Coltrane leaped forward with *Giant Steps*, Duke Ellington played his subtone cards on the *Anatomy of a Murder* film soundtrack, the Dave Brubeck Quartet turned 4/4 swing on his head with *Time Out* (delivering the classic odd-metered tracks "Take Five" and "Blue Rondo à la Turk"), Cannonball Adderley broke new soul-jazz ground with the live album *Cannonball Adderley Quintet in San Francisco* (with its huge nighttime jazz radio hit of Bobby Timmons's "This Here") and Ornette Coleman opened ears with his topsy-turvy, prophetic *The Shape of Jazz to Come*.

Then there was Miles Davis—employing two of the above rising stars, Trane and Cannonball—who conjured up, with the help of Bill Evans, what became the biggest-selling jazz album of all time, *Kind of Blue*. According to RIAA, the album is four times platinum (representing three million in sales), and Nielsen SoundScan, which began tracking album sales in 1991, calculated 2.9 million in the fall of 2008, which means that the true sales figures could well be far north of four million.

The so-called "new music," of course, was met by derision in some circles, yet in others was heralded as a harbinger of more jazz insurgency, which in truth arose in the next decade with a number of shape-shifting blasts.

There couldn't have been a riper and more stimulating time for Ron to arrive at the center of the jazz universe. From 1959 to 1963, when he joined Miles for five years in his band (April 1963 to June 1968), Ron was ready and eager for action. It came quickly.

He joined the bands of Chico Hamilton, Randy Weston and later Bobby Timmons, as well as became one of the top go-to bassists for session work and gigs—all the while getting his masters in bass on scholarship from the Manhattan School of Music (enrolling in January 1960 and graduating in 1961). Carter performed a balancing act, working with relative mainstreamers such as Betty Carter (no relation, except they both hailed from Detroit), Kenny Burrell and Eddie Heyward while also keeping company with freethinkers like Don Ellis, Jaki Byard and Eric Dolphy, who was in Chico's band.

As soon as he arrived, Ron began to make himself comfortable in his new home. What better way than to begin haunting the clubs in the city, from the mainstays in midtown and in the Village to smaller houses uptown. Ron caught many of the top-drawer artists of the day with whom he would later play, including J.J. Johnson, Tommy Flanagan and Nat Adderley

CHICO AND MANNERABLE RON

ONE OF RON'S first job offers came from Mercer Ellington who had heard of Ron from the Rochester scene. He said that Duke Ellington was looking for a new bassist. "Janet and I had no money, and Duke was offering such a low wage—almost nothing—that I couldn't even consider it," said Ron. Instead, he went to see drummer-bandleader Chico Hamilton, who was playing a double bill with Miles Davis at Birdland.

While he was still at Eastman, Ron had auditioned with Chico, whose cellist, Nat Gershon, was thinking of leaving the band. "Chico was on the Jazz for Moderns tour that also included Maynard Ferguson's and Dave Brubeck's bands. "I played the book for Chico, but I still had another semester to go," said Ron. "So he told me to call him when I got to New York."

By then, Gershon had decided to stay with Chico's band, but the bass seat was open. Chico had already been auditioning bassists for a couple of weeks and, remembering Ron from Eastman, offered him the opportunity to try out. "I can't exactly recall who turned me on to him, but Ron made the audition and I was impressed," said Chico. "He could read, which was important at the time because two-thirds of the book I was playing was written out. We had charts. Ron also played good time. He got the pulse going. I was used to having George Duvivier play with me, but I could see the potential in Ron. Plus, he was mannerable and cool which I felt was important because we were getting ready to go on the road for a long tour."

"I played the book on the stage and Chico told me I could have the gig if I wanted it," Ron said. The drummer offered to pay a good salary, so Ron signed on.

With Ron and young reeds player Eric Dolphy in tow, Chico embarked on the Jazz for Moderns package tour, with Ferguson, Brubeck, and Lambert, Hendricks and Ross. It was a five-month gig of one-nighters with all the members of the bands—some 60 people—packed into a bus. The first gig was in Virginia, which was Ron's first experience being in the South. They drove all night and pulled up to a restaurant at 2 a.m. Everyone in the bus got out to eat, but the African-American musicians were stopped at the front door and told they could only enter by the back.

"I'd been discriminated against, but not like that at a restaurant," Ron said. "Here we were, all these black and white musicians traveling and performing together, and we could only be served around back." In an interview with Milt Hinton in *Jazz Magazine* in 1978, Ron said, "That was my first rude awakening to the fact that the 'Star Spangled Banner' is not all that the lyrics say it's supposed to be."

"I was the first person to take Ron to Los Angeles," said Chico. "He was like another Paul Chambers, you dig? Ron was very professional. And I remember him being carried away by Eric's playing. I had always been very fortunate to have such good players in my bands, musicians who developed into giants. Being in my band gave Ron good exposure. He had a good foundation."

Chico ended up disbanding the group in early 1960 and moving to California. "I got to a point where I felt that I was starting to imitate myself," he said. "That's when it's important to do something different."

STUDIES AND SELECTED SESSIONS—1960—PART 1

RON RETURNED TO New York, starting his program at Manhattan School of Music one month late. He told the Webzine *JazzWax*, "I didn't know much about Juilliard at the time. I thought it was an upper-class, classical school. I knew from the Manhattan School of Music's brochure that its format was less rigid. Continuing my education at that school seemed to be the best choice."

While Ron was scraping up jazz gigs at night, during the day he was taking classes, including Music Theory 1, which he was forced to take because the school differed from Eastman in that it "used different symbols and a different language to recognize various chords and progressions." While he admits that being told he had to take a remedial class was a downer ("it was a sock to the head"), Ron figured that if learning a new vocabulary was the only way to get his masters, he'd play by Manhattan's rules.

Meanwhile, Ron was finding steady work. He joined Randy Weston's band that included Cecil Payne at the Five Spot for an eight-week stint (including one stretch where the band worked opposite Ornette Coleman's big-buzz quartet). Ron later went to Chicago with Randy for dates and still later played with the pianist in a trio at a restaurant in Lenox, Massachusetts, not far from the School of Jazz that John Lewis had established. "I had already heard that Ron was an outstanding bassist," Randy said. "When I started playing with him, I realized that he had the quality to interpret whatever I played. He had a natural way of listening to the music, and he gave me that bottom, space, rhythm. He made it perfect."

Randy had found his way to the jazz camp in the '50s. While he had made inroads on the New York jazz scene during that time, the gigs were infrequent at best. He had been a restaurateur before devoting his life fulltime to music. But the Brooklyn native got so ground down and discouraged by the pressures of making a living that he wanted out of New York—and jazz. A friend recommended the Berkshires in Western Massachusetts for a sabbatical. Randy made his way to the Music Inn, working as a second cook and playing the piano at night. In his Web site biography, Randy said, "I met a lot of people who encouraged me to stay with my music."

Even while gigging with Randy, Ron estimates that he also played with a dizzying array of bands—as many as 20—as he began to fortify his bass presence in the city. He quickly became a valuable session man for recording dates. One of his earliest sessions was with tenor saxophonist Ernie Wilkins (who was the staff arranger for the Harry James band from 1958 to 1960) on his debut, *The Big New Band of the '60s*. The Swingin' Ernie Wilkins Orchestra included Clark Terry, Zoot Sims, Charlie Persip, and two ex-Detroit musicians, Kenny Burrell and Yusef Lateef. The big band recorded in March and April.

Ron told *JazzWax*, "I look back at that record, and I'm quite surprised that given all the status of those players around me, they decided that this person new to New York could have an impact on this session."

That date led to Ron recording Charlie's debut album, *Charles Persip and the Jazz Statesmen* (on Bethlehem Records), which also featured the young trumpeter Freddie Hubbard and drumming giant Art Blakey. In May, Ron played on Yusef's Riverside album, *The Three Faces of Yusef Lateef*. In June, he recorded Randy's tune "Saucer Eyes" with Randy, Cecil and drummer Roy Haynes for Roulette Records. The number was issued on *The Roulette Jazz Sampler*.

That summer Ron joined Randy in Lenox for several dates while also attending the School of Jazz. Part of the Music Inn—a musical experiment started in the McCarthy era that convened innovative artists of all races, from Dave Brubeck and Gunther Schuller to Billy Taylor and Ornette Coleman—the school served to integrate the white jazz audiences with the black players. In its final years, from 1957–'60, it was directed by John Lewis and his band, the Modern Jazz Quartet, which helped to foster the atmosphere of creativity.

One of the instructors at the school was Eastman grad Ed Summerlin, a tenor saxophonist who was part of the avant-garde jazz scene in New York as well as a pioneer in combining liturgical music with jazz. At the time he was best known for his 1959 liturgical jazz composition, "Requiem for Mary Jo" (other works included "Episcopal Evensong," "Jazz Vespers Service" and "Liturgy of the Holy Spirit"), as well as music he wrote for such '50s network Christian television shows as *Lamp Unto My Feet* and *Life Is Worth Living*, the latter hosted by Bishop Fulton J. Sheen.

"I met Ron when he was playing with Randy," said Ed, who later started the jazz program at The City College and was responsible for bringing Ron into the school in 1983 after John Lewis left. "I got to know Ron. I was really impressed by the way he played. He complemented Randy by playing the right notes. He wasn't just thumping away. You could tell he was different than most of the bass players of the early '60s. There weren't many virtuoso bass players then."

Longtime *Los Angeles Times* jazz critic Don Heckman, then a New Yorker, was an alto saxophonist who was also heavily influenced by the new horizons for expanding jazz beyond bebop. He too went to Lenox that summer and recalled Ed as being "an instructor who had to face such hot shots as me and Gary McFarland who were into this weird stuff like Stockhausen."

Back in New York, Ed kept in contact with his former pupils. "I started to call them to do concerts of my music in churches," he said. "And I formed a band with Ron, Don and pianist Steve Kuhn. We were playing experimental music that I knew had no commercial value, but it was still a great group." (They eventually recorded an album in 1967, with Steve Swallow on one track in place of Ron, called *Improvisational Jazz Workshop* on Ictus Records. It garnered a four-and-half-star rating in *DownBeat*.)

"Ron was one of the few guys who could read difficult music," said Ed (who passed away in 2006 at the age of 78). "I wrote the parts out, and Ron read them. He was also great at improvising. It was so easy to play with him. That's why he got to be my favorite."

"Ed wrote a lot interesting pieces that had a lot of room to play free," Don said. "And so Ron played free. Yet there was always a sense of coherence and structure to what he was playing. A soloist may go free, but you could always hear Ron. He wasn't imposing, but he would take what the soloist was doing and give it logic and a place to go."

In reflecting back on those times, Ed said, "Most people feel that Ron is such a straight-ahead player. But he's actually done all kinds of music, from very conservative jazz to contemporary classical to experimental music that goes pretty far out."

SELECTED SESSIONS—1960—PART 2

DURING THE SUMMER session at the Music Inn, Ron got a call from Dolphy, who was ready to record his second album, *Out There*, for Prestige imprint New Jazz (his debut, *Outward Bound*, had been recorded five months earlier). Those tracks were recorded in August at Rudy Van Gelder's studio in New Jersey. It solidified the out-leaning reputation of Eric, who was already turning heads and opening ears around town, to the greater jazz world. On the album Eric played alto saxophone, clarinet, bass clarinet and flute. Ron was enlisted to play cello (bowed to perfection). The rest of the group included George Duvivier on bass and Roy Haynes on drums. The album is one of the highlights of Eric's short-lived career (he died four years later).

In October, Ron played bass on trumpeting explorer Don Ellis's debut album, *How Time Passes* (Candid Records). A feast of time and tempo in flux, the album also featured Jaki Byard on piano and Charlie Persip on drums. (Ron also appeared on Don's 1961 *New Ideas* album for Prestige with Jaki and Charlie.)

In an interview by Don Williamson in *All About Jazz*, Ron said that while Ellis had an intriguing approach to jazz, he wasn't interested in following that musical vein. "[Don] had another way of looking at music. For him 4/4 wasn't the only way to play it. It was interesting to hear what the other possibilities were, and he spent a lot of time developing these other possibilities that were successful for him. As a bass player, I'm always aware of the various approaches."

When asked if Don had given him his first exposure to odd-metered music, Ron replied, "It was always available in classical music, but working with Don was the first time I explored it as a jazz musician."

In November Ron went into the studio again with Randy for his groundbreaking album, *Uhuru Afrika* (Roulette), which featured a 24-piece jazz orchestra negotiating the complex music that showcased the groundbreaking and sophisticated melding of jazz with African music. The all-star cast included Clark Terry, Freddie Hubbard, Slide Hampton, Gigi Gryce, Yusef Lateef, Cecil Payne, Kenny Burrell, Max Roach, Charlie Persip, Candido, Babatunde Olatunji and Armando Peraza. The first movement, "Uhuru Kwansa," ended with a beautiful two-bass conversation between Ron and Duvivier.

Also in November and December Ron appeared on Gil Evans's classic Verve disc, *Out of the Cool* (see CTI chapter), as well as reunited with Eric for his *Far Cry* date with trumpeter Booker Little, Jaki and Roy.

While 1960 was a breakthrough year for Ron, he wasn't as busy as he was in the following years when his career began to snowball. "I remembered what I had been told in Rochester—that there was always a need for good bass players in New York," Ron said. "But guys like George Duvivier, Milt Hinton, Richard Davis and Paul Chambers came before me. They set the standards for bass performance—getting to a date early, having the bass in great shape, reading the music beforehand. Those guys got the gigs first, but I was also being considered."

In the meantime, though, Ron was hustling work, realizing that he still had some dues to pay. "I saw people playing in different bands whose skill levels were the same as mine," Ron said. "But I knew that I had to wait. I didn't play much in the main clubs like Birdland. That was where the money was."

So, to make ends meet, Ron signed up for substitute teaching at Roosevelt Junior High School in Roosevelt, a town in Long Island's Nassau County. "I used to work two days a week or so," he said. "The kids were nice and I taught math, geography and physical education. I like those subjects. That meant I couldn't practice as much as I wanted, which was still paramount. But that was OK because the job helped to pay the bills."

THE DOWNS & UPS

NOT EVERYTHING CAME easy on the music front. In the early '60s, when pianist Cedar Walton was playing with Art Blakey and the Jazz Messengers, he recalls Ron being asked to audition for the band to replace Jymie Merritt, who had served as Blakey's bassist since 1958. The drummer was scouting for a replacement and since Ron was relatively new in town he called him up. "I remember Ron trying out at one gig, but I don't remember why he didn't join," said Cedar. "We ended up with Reggie Workman. But it was a good thing Ron didn't come into the band because he ended up making history a few years later."

Cedar doesn't know exactly why the Blakey-Carter rhythm combination didn't work, but he surmised, "Art didn't need a virtuoso bass player. He was looking for an equal, someone who he could play against. Maybe Ron didn't fit that equation. I can't tell you, but I do know that Ron became much more effective where he ended up."

Ron also did another audition, this time with Benny Golson, who he had met in Rochester. Benny and Art Farmer were looking for a new bass player for their co-led Jazztet band. Benny called Ron and asked him to come to his Upper West Side apartment on 92nd Street between Columbus and Central Park West. He played the piano while Ron played the band's book.

"Many bass players play with a thump, and the notes decay too soon," Benny said. "But Ron's notes lingered like they didn't want to leave. I also noticed the choice of notes he made. He had a great sense of rhythm and knew how to accompany in the moment. What made Ron special was his combination of talent and ear and empathy."

Benny knew he had found the band's new bassist. "Ron, you're the one. Fantastic. Can you make our next gigs?"

Ron asked when the rehearsals were. "Right away," Benny replied, noting that the band was ready to start a tour.

Ron wondered if Benny would consider delaying the beginning of rehearsals. "Why wait?" Benny said.

"I'm in school and I've got finals," Ron said.

"Well, how were you planning to play with the Jazztet?" Benny asked.

"I'll quit school," Ron replied.

"No you won't," Benny said. "I'm not going to destroy your education. You'll spend two to three months with us on the road, and then what will you do?"

Today, Benny looks back at that conversation with pride. "I was so heartbroken not to be able to work with Ron because he was so good," he said. "But I'm happy that I made him stay in school. Look at the marvelous job he did with students later on when he taught at City College. That wouldn't have been possible if he had quit Manhattan School of Music to go on the road with me."

But Benny didn't forget Ron. He recommended him to TV commercial producers who were looking for studio musicians. And Benny also tapped Ron to perform on three of his 1962 albums. The two albums he recorded for Audio Fidelity Records over three days of sessions in April were *Just Jazz!* and *Pop + Jazz = Swing*, both of which featured a big band that included Freddie Hubbard, Curtis Fuller, Wayne Shorter, Bill Evans, Charlie Persip and others. Ron was also on Benny's hit album, *Free*, on Argo Records, that included the tune "Shades of Stein."

Benny wrote that song in tribute to Gertrude Stein, who had written the "Rose is a rose is a rose is a rose" line in her 1913 poem "Sacred Emily" from her 1922 book of verse, *Geography and Plays*. "I wanted to make a melody like that," Benny said. "It was tricky, but Ron just walked on through."

Today, Benny continues to admire Ron's ability to play the bass and move the music. "Ron soars above the circle of the earth in unoccupied space," he said, then paused, searching for an even more over-the-top metaphor. He laughed and said, "How's this? Ron climbs atop his neutron star and travels musically to anywhere he chooses."

Another experience soon after Ron arrived in New York firmed up his determination to be a jazz musician committed to both integrity and adventure. It took place in a studio session with pianist Harold Mabern. "I talked with Harold about the changes in a tune he wanted to record," Ron said. "He was insisting there was only one way to play it. I said that there could be other ways to play it. I wanted him to look at some other choices, but he was unwilling to accept the possibility of another choice."

The conversation got heated over whose point of view regarding the changes was right.

"I was so angry that I offered to take the matter outside and deal with it physically," Ron said. "That's when I realized that music meant so much to me that I'd be willing to fight about it. That was the first really clear indication to me of how committed and dedicated I was to playing this music."

Ron added, "You can stick a pin in that incident for me. It was a turning point." And then he hastened to note that today he and Harold are dear friends and have often recorded together since that youthful exchange. (Case in point: saxophonist Eric Alexander's 2002 *Nightlife in Tokyo* CD that featured Ron, Harold and drummer Joe Farnsworth.)

SELECTED SESSIONS & GIGS—1961

IN THE LATE '60s, pianist Bobby Timmons left Cannonball Adderley's employ (and also ended a short return stint with Art Blakey's Jazz Messengers) and began his solo career with a trio comprising Ron and drummer Albert "Tootie" Heath. Bobby sought to bank on his own burgeoning fame as a composer (he had contributed "Moanin'" to Blakey's book and wrote the hits "This Here" and "Dat Dere" for Cannonball).

Orrin Keepnews, who was the co-owner/producer at Riverside Records, which had signed Cannonball and Bobby, recalls the latter taking flight as a bandleader. "Bobby wanted to go out on his own, and Ron and Tootie, neither of whom really had a 'name' yet, agreed to be his sidemen. The trio went on the road and had a certain amount of trouble because Bobby turned out to be one of those people who thought it was a good idea to clean up his life by using alcohol as a substitute for junk."

Ron recalls the trio's first gig, at the Jazz Workshop in San Francisco's North Beach. "Tootie and I went to the club and at nine o'clock there was no Bobby," he said. "No Bobby at 9:30, no Bobby at 9:45. The place was packed. We thought about trying to find a piano player so we could do the trio set. But finally, it was 11:45 and Tootie and I thought, 'Let's just do a duo.'"

So the bassist and drummer did the whole set alone. As for Bobby's absence, Ron said, "He was sick. And in the six months we toured together, he'd get really sick." Still, when Timmons was on, Ron loved it.

"Ron always says to me that that was one of the best trios he's ever been in," said Tootie, who started to call his bass-playing friend Mr. Carter while Ron called him Prince Albert, monikers they continue to use when seeing each other today. "I've been in some good trios since that time too, but that was my favorite. Ron and I connected. It was such a pleasure to play together. We both really liked Bobby. I had grown up with him in Philly."

While Timmons played with another trio (that included Sam Jones on bass), this particular band's highpoint came when Orrin booked it at the Village Vanguard and rolled the tapes in October 1961, which yielded *Bobby Timmons Trio in Person*. The album was released by Riverside. Soon after, Bobby decided to quit touring, which broke up the band. (Ron recorded another trio album with Bobby in 1963 for Riverside, *Born to Be Blue!*, with Modern Jazz Quartet drummer Connie Kay.)

The abovementioned Sam Jones figured in a couple of other gigs Ron had during this time. The first occurred in April 1961 when Ron hit the road to Europe in Cannonball's band that included his brother Nat on cornet, Victor Feldman on piano, Sam on bass and Louis Hayes on drums. Sam played cello in one of the group's songs each night, so Ron filled in on bass. The band returned from Europe and on May 16, 1961 went into the studio for Riverside with Orrin to record *The Cannonball Adderley Quintet Plus*. Wynton Kelly spelled Victor on some tracks (during which time Victor played vibes) and Ron was invited to play bass on the track "P.C."

"We played a lot of shows, doing Sunday and Monday matinees," Ron recalled. "During the course of the tour, Sam's hands began to hurt so he asked me to play bass on the last set, which he sat out." (Ron was attending school at the time and asked permission to go on the road. Going on tour was OK'd, but upon return Ron learned that he had been pegged to give a bass recital in two weeks, performing a Mozart concerto and some etudes with his professor, classical pianist Stanley Bednar. Ron was forced to cram. "I had to transcribe the material for string bass," he said. "In the end, it worked out really well.")

Ron filled in for Sam again one night at Circle in the Square, a venue across from the Village Gate in New York. The occasion? A Thelonious Monk show. "Sam got the flu and asked me to play for him," Ron said. That was followed by a week in Philadelphia at a club named Pep's. He and Monk traveled to Philadelphia and back to New York each day, driven by Monk's patron, the Baroness Pannonica "Nica" de Koenigswarter (a member of the Rothschild international financial dynasty and British bebop aficionado). "The Baroness picked me up at around five or six in the evening in her Bentley, and drove two hours to Pep's," Ron said. "We played three sets each night, finished at one a.m. then drove back so that I could make it to my eight o'clock class at school."

Not much was said during the car trips or onstage, Ron said. "The only thing Monk told me was not to pat my feet when I played. He felt that that slowed the time." For the gigs, Monk didn't let anyone know what the tunes were going to be or what keys and tempo to play in. "Monk didn't have a program order," Ron said. "He just started and trusted that we all knew the tunes. He never said anything to me. He just went to the bandstand and expected me to get to work."

Ron was familiar with Monk's music, having seen him many nights in clubs in New York and had heard most of his songs, which were staples on the jazz radio stations at the time.

Beyond getting to play with Monk, the dates showed Ron that he was becoming known in his new home. "The fact that Sam called me to sub was almost enough for me," he said. "When you recommend someone to step in, it's perilous. You hope the person you call will be able to bring enough stability. Sam knew that Monk and I were strangers, but he felt that I was adult enough to stand up to this giant and not fall over. With this responsibility that Sam laid on me, I wanted to make him feel like he had made the right choice—and that if he needed someone to fill in again with anybody else, he'd feel comfortable enough to call me."

While Ron had many gigs in 1961, none was more important than his August date with star guitarist Wes Montgomery on his classic album *So Much Guitar!* on Riverside. "Ron pulled me aside many years later and thanked me for getting him on that session which he considered to be his most consequential gig up to that point," Orrin said. The quintet session also included Hank Jones on piano, Lex Humphries on drums and Ray Barretto on congas.

Orrin had seen Ron play in some sessions and first encountered him live at the Half Note in New York. His impression was that Ron had full command of himself and whatever situation he was in. "I couldn't tell if that was for real or a persona," he said. "But here's this new bass player who's got his shit together and he knows what he's doing. He knows how to get from A to B. Plus Ron's attitude was good."

While Orrin had been enlisting Sam for a lot of sessions, he became increasingly impressed by Ron. "He had worked his way into being one of a handful of young bass players in New York who were dominating the scene," Orrin said. "Ron became one of my first-call people. I knew he was someone to count on, especially in underrehearsed and relatively spontaneous dates. You could give him the music, he'd read it and play it with the proper jazz expression."

Orrin paused, and then added how Ron's towering presence was also a plus: "There are two kinds of tall. There are those who fight their height and those who take advantage of it. I never saw Ron bow his shoulders."

(Orrin recalled a session years later, in 1989, where Ron used his height to his advantage during a rather tense recording session with alto saxophonist Frank Morgan. The album was *Frank Morgan All-Stars* and consisted of Charlie Parker material performed by Orrin's handpicked group that also included Joe Henderson on tenor saxophone, Bobby Hutcherson on vibes and Mulgrew Miller on piano. "I do a lot of pacing around the studio when I work," Orrin said. "At one point Frank went off and got all emotional because I reminded him of the guards in the prison where he had been incarcerated for his drug problems. I was the only white guy there with a band of black musicians. When Frank blew up, Ron stepped in to get the session under control. He just stood over Frank, and that's when you're aware of how tall Ron is. It's like six-nine looking down on you. He froze Frank, calmed him down and we went on to finish the record.")

Regarding the Wes *So Much Guitar!* date, Ron says that it was a milestone moment for him. "At the time I was still in the process of growing up musically and getting into any kind of environment to accelerate growth," he said. "I look back at that and there were all these wonderful bass players on the scene—George Duvivier, Paul Chambers, Sam Jones, Doug Watkins, Percy Heath. Orrin would have had no problem getting one of those guys, but he picked me for the session. That was quite a tribute to Orrin's ability to forecast the future, and to my playing enough over my head to earn the right to be there."

Orrin was so impressed with Ron's playing that he signed him to be in the Riverside Jazz Stars, who recorded *A Jazz Version of Kean* in October and November 1961. He was in pretty impressive company, including trumpeters Clark Terry and Blue Mitchell, trombonist/arranger Melba Liston, tenor saxophonist Jimmy Heath, Bobby Timmons, Tootie Heath and Ernie Wilkins arranging and conducting.

WHERE?—1961

GIVEN THAT JAZZ'S popularity was bursting at the seams with new expressions across a wide swath of styles, Prestige Records—one of jazz's most esteemed independent labels—decided to tap into the new music font. So, the company formed the appropriately named New Jazz imprint.

It was the brainchild of Esmond Edwards who, while originally hired by Prestige as a photographer, later graduated to engineer and producer. (Edwards, who passed away on January 20, 2007, went on to become one of the first and most influential African-American recording industry execs, with a resume that included Verve and Chess.)

"Esmond was looking for new talent in New York," Ron said. "He haunted the clubs every night, and he was at the forefront of the Loft Scene." One of Edwards's early signs was Dolphy, who had already been in Prestige's stable. His debut New Jazz album in 1960, *Out There*, gave Ron important exposure. "During the making of that album, Esmond felt that I'd be a good candidate as a leader on New Jazz," he said. "He wanted me to play cello primarily and also bass. We talked about personnel because I didn't know very many people in New York at that point, and then he told me I'd need to choose some material and make up the arrangements. I thought, I can do that."

And he did. Ron's debut album as a leader, *Where?*, was born on June 20, 1961 in the Englewood Cliffs, New Jersey studio of Rudy Van Gelder. For the recording (six tunes recorded as first takes), Eric played alto saxophone, bass clarinet and flute. The rest of the band was comprised of pianist Mal Waldron (Carter's first face-to-face with him), Duvivier and Persip.

Ron knew full well and appreciated Eric's penchant for playing his horns angular and out, but was surprised at Mal's adventurous approach to the piano. "When we were rehearsing the tunes, I heard Mal playing these out-there chords," Ron said. "This was Billie Holiday's accompanist? What's he doing? But what he was playing was right for the times. I got a free lesson from Mal. Everyone in the band was playing free and in the spur of the moment. Even Charlie was beating his drums differently, playing in that Roy Haynes style. It was great being in that environment."

As for working with George, who sat out two numbers, Carter said it was essential to have a top-flight bassist for the album because he was focusing on playing the cello. (*Where?* is the first jazz album with the cello played in proper tuning as opposed to bassists like Oscar Pettiford and Ray Brown who played the cello in bass tuning.) "I had seen George play with Lena Horne as well as with Chico, so I knew I could trust his sense of the music just like I hope people today trust me when I do studio sessions," Ron said. "George had a great sound, a great fiddle and he played wonderful notes."

Where? opened with Ron's rowdy composition "Rally," an edgy and upbeat tune featuring Eric's dark-brewed bass clarinet gusts, Mal's dancing runs and the leader's gripping arco leads played in unison in stretches with Eric. Another Ron original, "Bass Duet," featured him and George conversing, soloing with bluesy intonation and supportively comping in a relaxed, graceful swing. Side A of the album ended with a swinging cover of the Hammerstein-Romberg standard, "Softly As in a Morning Sunrise," which had been Ron's featured number in Bobby Timmons's trio. Ron walked and bowed the bass with lyrical grace while Eric soared with his alto in his singular oblique style.

Side B featured a three-pack of pieces that Ron said were "tunes that you play and have a great time with. For my first record, I didn't want to make everything feel so weighty, like having to worry about playing the flat 9s, sharp 13s and tri-tones just right." Two of the songs came from Randy Weston's songbook: the title track with Ron bowing the melody line on cello and the skipping "Saucer Eyes," with Eric on flute and Ron setting up solid walking support.

"I had been working with Randy for something like 30 weeks a year at the time, and I got to know his library," Ron said. "I had the chance to study his songs, analyze them as to how they work. He's one of the great unsung songwriters. Playing his music was like getting a lesson in composition every night."

In between Randy's tunes was a happy-go-lucky, sunny take on Sy Oliver's "Yes, Indeed," with Eric trilling high notes on the flute and Ron delivering a staccato pizzicato cello solo. "I was fascinated by Sy Oliver from his Jimmy Lunceford period," Ron said. "I like that band sound. It's not self-conscious or pretentious."

The next day Ron, Eric, Charlie and Mal reconvened in Rudy's studio to record the pianist's New Jazz album, *The Quest*. Then they all went their separate ways, as befitting in-demand jazz musicians, so these dates are the only documentation of their collaboration. "It's too bad that we didn't have an opportunity to gig around town at all," Ron said. "What we did might have had more of an impact."

Ron didn't record as a leader for another eight years (*Uptown Conversation* for Atlantic came out in 1969), but he had plenty of good excuses, most noticeably pioneering new territory with his rhythm partners Herbie Hancock and Tony Williams in Miles Davis's '60s quintet, arguably the greatest jazz band ever.

In reflecting back to the beginning of his discography, Ron says that he learned a lot, but he was confident, even with a band whose members were all older and more experienced than he was. "I didn't have any time to be excited or worried," he said. "All I remember was that there was a weight of responsibility on my shoulders. Here's a producer who's taken a chance on me to make a decent record, and I was concerned about letting these four people down who trusted me to do the job."

In the original liner notes to *Where?*, Ron told writer Joe Goldberg, "Music is changing and the instruments have to change with it. You can't get away with doing the same thing anymore. There's a new era in music, and I'd like to feel that I'm a part of it."

CHANGES IN 1962 & 1963

AFTER EARNING HIS masters from Manhattan School of Music the year before, 1962 saw Ron continue his whirlwind of recording-session work.

For Riverside, he appeared on the soul-jazz Johnny Griffin album, *Kerry Dancers*, and Modern Jazz Quartet vibraphonist Milt Jackson's *Big Bags* and *Invitation*. For New Jazz, Ron recorded Jaki Byard's *Hi-Fly* (he had also appeared the previous year on the pianist's Prestige recording, *Here's Jaki!*, with Roy Haynes) and British trumpeter Dizzy Reece's *Asia Minor* album with Joe Farrell, Hank Jones and Charlie Persip. For Atlantic Ron recorded with alto saxophonist Leo Wright on his *Suddenly the Blues* LP that also featured Kenny Burrell. While 1961 had been a year of "hanging in there" for Ron, 1962 upped the ante for him in making his stand as an important, rising-star jazz figure in New York.

"I was beginning to find my way," Ron said. "And I was finding that it was going to be possible to earn a living by playing music. With Janet working and me playing gigs, our two salaries were allowing us to make it through the week. But because she worked during the day and I was working at night, I'd go weeks without seeing her awake."

That was soon to change as Ron and Janet welcomed their first child, Ron Jr., into the world on April 18, 1962. Did the couple ever talk about raising a family? "No, it didn't occur to me," Ron said. "I was fighting to stay in school and working at nights, then getting up at eight in the morning to go to a theory class. I was more concerned with graduating."

Ron said that since they had both come from large families (the Carters had eight children, the Hasbroucks six) raising their own family seemed inevitable. "It just happened. There was no plan. Janet told me she was pregnant and I said that works for me."

After Ron Jr. was born, did dad feel the pressure to push even harder in his line of business? "No. I never felt that weight. I saw my father raise eight kids during the Great Depression and I never saw him pulling his hair out. It never occurred to us that there might be a problem with having a family. It's not a new concept. It's just what families do. They raise families, hopefully successfully. So when our turn came, we never adjusted the program."

That held true when Ron and Janet's second son, Myles, was born on December 14, 1965. "Ron Jr. and Myles just became part of the program," he casually said.

Janet stopped working and Ron became the breadwinner, scrimping on meals and hotel expenses when he was on the road so that he could send money home to her. While Janet had originally been disappointed that Ron hadn't taken the secure professional route of teaching music, she understood that her husband's different plan had merit. "Once Janet recognized that playing jazz was what I wanted to do, and that I was working enough so that she didn't have to work while raising the family, things were all right," said Ron.

They moved from their Harlem studio to a two-bedroom apartment at River Terrace, a rental complex at 158th Street and Riverside Drive, which is where the Carter family lived until 1973, when they moved to West End Avenue.

By 1963, Ron was a bass fixture on the New York jazz scene. Not only were gigs and recording sessions popping, but New York was also buzzing with the commercial jingle market. (Ron and several bass players formed the New York City Bass Club to buy amplifiers that they left in studios so they wouldn't have to do so much heavy lifting for the sessions.) "I realized then that you didn't necessarily have to go out of town to make a living," Ron said. "There were seven or eight jazz labels, and jazz radio was really big with DJs like Symphony Sid on the air. The clubs were booming, with eight-week gigs for bands. Johnny Carson and Merv Griffin had their TV shows here that had big bands, and the film industry was really growing."

In March 1963, Ron was hired by trumpeter/flugelhornist Art Farmer for an extended club date at the Half Note. Art's co-led Jazztet with Benny Golson had broken up in 1962, so he was leading a new band that included guitarist Jim Hall. It was during this date that Miles Davis came downtown for a visit.

It's unknown if Miles had been hearing stories about Ron from his ex-bassist Paul Chambers (who had left Miles's employ along with rhythm-team members drummer Jimmy Cobb and pianist Wynton Kelly to form a trio) or his friend Gil Evans (who knew Ron's work from his *Out of the Cool* sessions). But when Miles arrived at the Half Note, he was on a mission to sign Ron as the first member of his new band, a sextet that had a six-week West Coast tour lined up.

However, when Miles asked Ron to jump Art's ship and board his, he was stopped in his tracks. Any other musician would have jumped at the chance to pack up and hit the road with one of jazz's marquee players, but not Ron. "I had a lot of work then," Ron said. "And I had a great gig with Art. I was learning some wonderful new tunes. I thanked Miles for the opportunity and said I'd love to play for him, but I was in the middle of a gig and I couldn't leave just like that."

With all due respect, Ron asked Miles to do something that the jazz star was not used to doing—and that, Ron figures, made all the difference in their professional and personal relationship during the next five years.

Ron (on bass) in a practice room at Eastman School of Music, circa 1958 (*Paul Hoeffler; courtesy of Claire Hoeffler*)

Top: Ron at Eastman School of Music, circa 1956 (Freshman class officers: Ron, far right, Student Association Representative; Ron's good friend Ned Corman, far left, treasurer) (*Courtesy of Ron Carter*)

Bottom: Cass Tech Choir, 1954, from the school yearbook; Ron, front row, third from the left; future New York City Opera member Muriel Costa-Greenspon, second row, sixth from the left (*Courtesy of Arthur J. Lieb—front row, first on the left*)

Above: Ron (on cello) in a practice room at Eastman School of Music, circa 1958 (*Paul Hoeffler; courtesy of Claire Hoeffler*)

Below Left: Ron on graduation day at Eastman School of Music, June 1959, with his father Lutheran (*Courtesy of Sandy Nixon*)

Below Right: Ron at Eastman, June 1959 (*Courtesy of Sandy Nixon*)

No dancing at the Pythodd, 1958: Ron and tenor saxophonist Pee Wee Ellis were regular performers at the Pythodd Club in Rochester, New York. The Pythodd, which Chuck Mangione described as having "a huge bar and a small bandstand," booked popular jazz acts and catered to a racially mixed clientele. (*Paul Hoeffler; courtesy of Claire Hoeffler*)

Above: Ron in a rehearsal hall at Eastman School of Music, circa 1958 (*Paul Hoeffler; courtesy of Claire Hoeffler*)

Below: Ron with his wife Janet Hasbrouck Carter, Rochester, New York; an inscription on the back of the photograph reads "August 28, 1959," (*Courtesy of Sandy Nixon*)

Above: Details from a collage of Ron's performance clippings, by Willie Carter, on the wall of her apartment (*Dan Ouellette*)

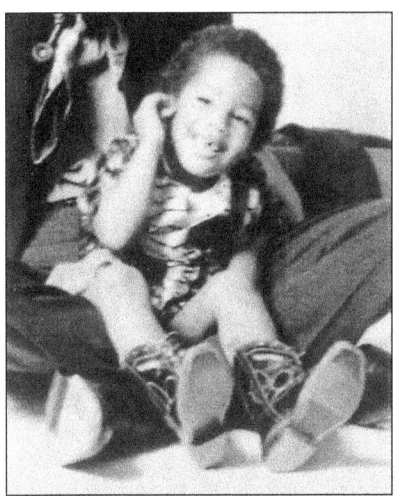

Above and Left: Photo shoot with sons Ron Jr. (top left) and Myles (middle left) for the 1969 album *Uptown Conversation* (Atlantic Records), Ron's second date as leader (*Chuck Stewart; courtesy of Ron Carter*)

Below: A sheet of proofs documenting another photo session (*Bernie Block; courtesy of Ron Carter*)

The photograph below shows the left hand position. Notice that the fingers are all curved, that the finger_tips_ are used and the thumb is placed directly under the second finger.

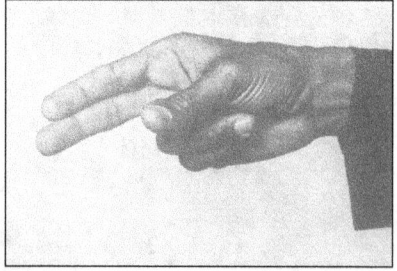

Two images from *Building a Jazz Bassline*, Ron's self-published instructional booklet from 1966, demonstrate the positions of the bassist's left and right hands. The publication included sample basslines juxtaposed against the melody and chords for two original compositions, "Little Waltz" and "P.J." (*Courtesy of Ron Carter*)

PART II
THE MILES YEARS

CHAPTER SIX

The Miles Years, Part 1: Beginnings

WHEN HE WAS 3 years old, Miles Dewey Davis had an indelible experience that remained with him the rest of his life. In his life story, *Miles: The Autobiography*, co-authored by poet Quincy Troupe, Miles recalled playing around the gas stove in his kitchen and "being shocked by the whoosh of the blue flame jumping off the burner."

The sudden flash, he said, sparked his restless passion to explore. "I saw that flame and felt that hotness of it close to my face," he told Troupe. "I felt fear, real fear, for the first time in my life. But I remember it like some kind of adventure, some kind of weird joy, too. I guess that experience took me someplace in my head I hadn't been to before. To some frontier, the edge, maybe, of anything possible.... The fear I had was almost like an invitation, a challenge to go forward into something I knew nothing about."

That childhood incident epitomized the course of Miles's life as a trumpeter, composer and bandleader—and jazz shape-shifter. Throughout his category-defying career, he kept returning to that blue flame of adventure—mystified as well as inspired by it. He forged ahead, relentlessly at times, making triumphant personal strides as well as helping to revitalize jazz by not allowing his audiences to get too comfortable in their listening habits. Miles not only helped to blaze new stylistic trails—cool jazz, modal jazz, electric jazz-pop fusion—but he also became the leading authority on the fine art and magical alchemy of improvisation while exploring bebop, hard bop and even, in his later years, hip-hop.

Even though he died at the age of 65 in 1991, his genius still lives, both in his oeuvre —including such defining moments as *Birth of the Cool, Kind of Blue*, his entire '60s quintet recordings, *Bitches Brew, On the Corner*— and in his enduring influence.

In recent years alone, Miles's 1959 masterwork, *Kind of Blue*, has sold well over a million copies in the U.S., reports Bob Belden who helped to spearhead the production end of Columbia/Legacy's vast and impressive Davis reissue program. Why the continuous appeal to all things Miles? Why, almost two decades after his death, is it still Miles in roses? "Why? Because people miss him," Bob said. "As different generations come of age, a new group of listeners, whether they're punkers or art rap guys, come to appreciate him. Miles played a joke on the jazz audience. He was a smart cat, a well-rounded musician who knew that people would eventually come to him for the beauty of the music. True art does win."

Ron, who anchored Miles's seminal quintet from 1963 to '68, concurs. "No one else is doing anything of depth that commands attention," he said. "No one—not rappers, jazz rappers or new age musicians—has formed a music that gets people interested in it enough to stand up and pay attention, to track it down."

First enlisted by Miles for a sextet he toured on the West Coast in 1963, Ron says that no one knew what direction the bandleader was going in with the music. "Miles was always looking," he said. "You never knew what door he would try to open. When he formed our quintet, he was looking for a group that would freely exchange ideas to take the music in new directions. My only disappointment was that we only played live a small number of the tunes we recorded. In that sense the material was never fully developed."

To put Ron's regret into context, consider Columbia/Legacy's eight-CD box, *Miles Davis: The Complete Plugged Nickel Sessions*, seven superlative live sets the quintet recorded over the course of two evenings in December 1965 at the Plugged Nickel nightclub in Chicago. Not only is the playing inspired, but the collection also provides an illuminating sonic snapshot of the trumpeter leading his youthful quintet through performances bursting with creative spontaneity and collective originality.

In his autobiography, Davis reflected on the band: "If I was the inspiration and wisdom and link for this band, Tony [Williams] was the fire, the creative spark; Wayne [Shorter] was the idea person, the conceptualizer of a lot of things we did; and Ron and Herbie [Hancock] were the anchors. I was just the leader who put us all together. Those were all young guys and although they were learning from me, I was learning from them too."

THE FIRST ENCOUNTERS

RON MET MILES for the first time when he was still a student at Eastman. In 1958, Miles's '50s quintet with John Coltrane was traveling with the all-star Jazz for Moderns tour that also included Dave Brubeck, Maynard Ferguson, Chico Hamilton, and vocalese trio (Dave) Lambert, (Jon) Hendricks & (Annie) Ross. "They were traveling by train from Toronto, so the band had no way to get from the Eastman Theatre to the train station for their next stop after the show," recalled Ron, who had attended the concert and knew Miles's bassist, Paul Chambers. He was a fellow Detroiter and Cass Tech alum whose father worked with Ron's dad at the Detroit Street and Railways Company. "I had an old car at the time, so Paul asked if I could give them a ride. So he, Miles and Trane got in, and I took them to the train station."

Though the meeting was fleeting, Ron walked away impressed with the man and his impact on the music. "I never thought I'd play with Miles because at the time my focus was on being a classical soloist. But even though I wasn't into jazz fulltime, I appreciated his music and understood where Miles was taking it. All those Prestige albums he had recorded at that time showed that he was clearly making the move. In fact, Miles was the move. To be in his band, you had to be the best."

At the concert Ron recalls Brubeck playing his hits and Ferguson hitting all the impossible high notes on his trumpet, but he was most moved by Miles's performance. "His band served as the most vivid example of what swing feels like," Ron said. "He was the essence of swing. It all sounded wonderful. All you had to do with that band was add water and stir."

What also impressed Ron was Miles's ability to assemble a top-drawer band. "That group was at the top of its game when I saw them in Rochester," Ron said. "Everyone wanted to play piano like Red Garland and be a drummer like Philly Joe Jones. Paul didn't have a lot of followers then, but he was great, and Trane was just starting to get his following. Miles always had that Pied Piper relationship with musicians."

Ron says that the major jazz bands of the day were Brubeck, Count Basie's group, and Lambert, Hendricks & Ross. "But the group that everyone wanted to be a part of was Miles's band," he said. "Everyone knew the records, the hits, the tunes, the changes. When you went to jam sessions, you needed to know what note was correct for each particular figure. The rhythm fit, and the ensemble play was great."

The next time Ron saw Miles was in Toronto in 1959. He and Chuck Mangione drove there from Rochester to see the same quintet. He remembers the band playing the new material fresh from the *Kind of Blue* sessions. "We came expecting to hear 'Bye Bye Blackbird' and tunes like that, so we were taken aback by the new material he was playing. I had studied modes in school related to classical harmony, but it was something new to hear modal playing in jazz. Chuck and I were both listening and had question marks over our heads. What are they doing?"

Ron didn't go backstage to see Miles, which he felt would have been an intrusion. He said, "What do you say? Mr. Davis, I love your music?" (Yet, in Miles's autobiography, the trumpeter recalled meeting Ron there.)

Ron's next encounter with Miles came four years later in New York at the Half Note club on the second night of a two-week engagement he was playing with Art Farmer. "I had never seen Miles at another gig that I played," Ron said. "He was not invisible when he showed up in clubs. You knew when he was there, as he walked around in his little cape. And everyone knew that he was a leader who was on the top shelf of the top shelves of jazz."

Miles approached Ron to join his band; Ron cordially referred his request to Art. Miles had been sitting in the corner and, after the first set, he called Ron over and told him he was putting a new band together and was looking for a new bass player because Paul had left to join Wynton Kelly's trio. Jimmy Cobb was still Miles's drummer, but he too was going to join Wynton during the trumpeter's West Coast tour. Of course Ron was interested, but he was committed to Art's gig.

Ron said, "Mr. Davis, I have a job working with Art Farmer. If you want me to join, you have to ask him because I'm determined to be committed to playing with him unless he says I don't have to."

"Are you serious?" Miles asked Ron.

"Yeah, man, I'm working. I have a job and I'm happy with this job."

Miles said OK and then approached Art after the second set. "Miles asked and Art graciously said yes," Ron said. "I think that set the tone for me and Miles. He understood from that point on that I had priorities. He saw that I loved and respected Art, which to me was normal. Plus, he saw how I put the music first. At the time, drugs were prevalent on the scene and some guys had drug problems. But that was not my scene and Miles knew that somehow. He knew he wouldn't have to worry about me showing up late or nodding on the bandstand during the last set. Miles saw me differently."

Art told Ron, "This is your time," and let him join Miles's employ.

Next stop for Ron: the West Coast with Miles, in a sextet setting, with five weeklong gigs, including a stint at San Francisco's Blackhawk club and the-end-of-tour two weeks at Shelly's Manne-Hole in Hollywood, during which time Miles recorded part of his first studio album in two years, *Seven Steps to Heaven*.

MILES IN TRANSITION

RON HAD BIG shoes to fill when he joined Miles. He recalls hearing groans sometimes from the audiences on those early gigs on the West Coast when he took the bandstand and not Paul Chambers. Plus, he had to endure the criticisms of other musicians on the scene who questioned why he got the gig. "My first real exposure to the jazz community when I came to New York was with Randy Weston, and that was wonderful because there was no sense of competition," Ron said. "Playing in that band, which had a noncombative stance, was not about ego. But when I went to play with Miles, people turned up the competitive heat because that was the band you had to be in. I'd hear stories about musicians saying, 'That guy doesn't belong there.' My view was, well, why don't you tell Miles that, that this should be your job? Those guys never had the nerve to say that."

A prime factor in Ron entering Miles's world was that the leader's band was in transition mode. Since 1961 the group had been in flux, with Trane fully launching his solo career and the rhythm section threatening to take flight. J.J. Johnson and Hank Mobley joined Miles's band and left. Meanwhile, Miles's ill health and drug use caused him to miss gigs, including an abruptly canceled eight-day run at the Uptown Theater in Philadelphia in late December 1962—which resulted in his being forced to pay damages to the venue.

Early the next year, Miles was poised to create a new group to rise from the ashes of the old one. The band that left for the West Coast was comprised of Jimmy on drums and a trio of Memphis-bred musicians: tenor saxophonist George Coleman (late of Max Roach's band), alto saxophonist Frank Strozier and pianist Harold Mabern. By the time the tour ended in Hollywood, Jimmy had left, Strozier was pink-slipped and Mabern was replaced by British-born, Los Angeles-based Victor Feldman. Miles hired Frank Butler on drums and kept George and Ron in the band.

"We all knew Jimmy was there just doing time because he was going to open up another door and settle in with Wynton Kelly's trio," Ron said. "In a general sense, no one felt any permanence in the personnel of Miles's band. The tenor of the gig was that it was temporary. No one knew who was going to be replaced at any given moment. The doorknob was there, but the door wasn't opened yet."

Jimmy recalls that Paul and Wynton had quit Miles's employ because of a misunderstanding over being paid. "So Miles hired Ron, George, Frank and Harold to do this tour he had planned," Jimmy said. "I decided to stick with Miles, but only for three or four weeks. So I got to play with Ron for the first time. I could tell that he had a lot of talent and was on his way to becoming one of the best bass players in the world. But during that tour I could tell he was a little nervous, just like everyone in that band. You're learning new music, you're joining a new group. Sure, you get the jitters."

As for Strozier, George told John Szwed who wrote *So What—The Life of Miles Davis*, that he felt Miles wanted a quintet versus a sextet. He said Miles would complain about the length of solos during the band's live dates. "... What he would do, he'd say (in a whisper), 'Hey, Frank, go tell George he's playin' too long,' and then he'd come to me and say the same thing—'Tell Frank he's playin' too long.'"

At first, Ron felt like he was the odd man out when the band hit the road. "Jimmy and Miles had a long-term relationship, and the other three guys all grew up in Memphis and knew each other—their individual whims and personalities. I didn't have a pre-established relationship with anyone in the band." He did establish friendships during the course of the tour, but when there was down time, the band mates were all off on their own.

Everyone, that is, except Miles, who often called Ron to hang out, whether it was going to lunch or to the driving range to hit golf balls—a habit Ron had acquired during his Rochester days at the insistence of his wife Janet, who sought an activity they could share that had nothing to do with the intensity of his studies.

"I'd always outdrive Miles," Ron said with a laugh and then added, "From that point, when Miles began extending invitations to me, I felt that I was going to stay in the band. I didn't know who else would, but I could feel that Miles felt comfortable enough with me off the bandstand."

SEVEN STEPS TO HEAVEN

WRITING IN THE liner notes of *Seven Steps to Heaven*, Bob Belden picked up on the comfort level of Ron playing with Miles, noting that the bandleader was "relaxed, pensive and tempered" during the Los Angeles sessions. Bob wrote, "Ron Carter's bass is a welcome sound for Miles as you can hear Miles 'play off' of Ron's time and harmony on 'Basin Street Blues.' There is an understated counterpoint that, if examined closely, would reveal much of what would become a refined element to any Miles Davis recording or performance with Ron Carter."

The West Coast quintet recorded several songs for the album, but the session proved to be a struggle for Miles because of the material as well as the new group he assembled. Upon returning to New York, he hired new members—first, 17-year-old drummer Tony Williams, whom he had seen perform with Jackie McLean a couple of months earlier, and then 23-year-old pianist Herbie Hancock, who had come to Miles's attention on the recommendation of Donald Byrd and who was making jazz waves with his hit tune, "Watermelon Man."

Unsure of how the chemistry would work, Miles asked Ron, then 27, to come to his apartment on 77th Street between West End Avenue and Riverside Drive to hook up with Herbie and Tony. Herbie, who had come to New York in 1961 to work with Byrd, recalls that his audition for Miles's group was both odd and fun. "I didn't find this out until many years later, but Miles had me, Tony and Ron play together in the recreation room downstairs while he was upstairs listening to us over the intercom," Herbie said. "He came in when we first got there, played a few notes on his horn, then said, 'Ah, shit, I'll be right back' and that's the last we saw of him. Ron led the audition, but not in a traditional sense. He was essentially functioning as a musical director. Miles had left sheets of music on the piano, so Ron took the lead, and said, 'Let's play this' or 'Do you want to try this?' At the end of the session, Miles returned and asked us all to return the next day."

Herbie remembers the informal sessions lasting for three days, around four hours a day, again with Miles largely not visibly present. "Miles probably felt that we'd be too intimidated if he were there," Herbie said. "He had the wisdom to know this was the only way to let us get loose. He wanted to get the truth from us." On the second day of the audition, after an hour of the rhythm section finding its identity with the music, Miles arrived in the rec room with Gil Evans and Philly Joe Jones.

"They sat there for a half hour or hour, and then left," Herbie said. "Later on I heard that Miles had asked Gil and Philly Joe, who were his two closest friends, to come to his place to listen to his new band."

On the last day of the audition, Miles entered the basement room and played a few pieces with his new rhythm section. In his autobiography, Miles said, "I knew right away that this was going to be a motherfucker of a group. For the first time in a while I found myself feeling excited inside, because if they were playing that good in a few days, what would they be playing like in a few months?"

In a 1996 conversation with Tony Williams for *SF Weekly*, the drummer told me, "It was one of my goals to play with Miles. It was great. When he called to ask me to join, the heavens opened and there was light."

After that initial rapturous thrill, was Tony petrified to be playing with Miles, who was 37 at the time—20 years older than he was? "No, it wasn't scary at all. Hey, Miles wanted me for the job, so I figured he knew what I could do. It was just like any job you go on. You're concerned with getting the job done, not making mistakes and having a good time. When you're young, there are very few things that scare you. There's more fear later in your life when you learn more and you understand what could go wrong. But when you're young, you're enthusiastic about everything. You can't expect a 17-year-old to be intimidated. Kids are more cocky than intimidated."

As for Ron, he was thrilled. It quickly became apparent to him that a new kind of alchemy was ready to make itself known to the jazz world. Crucial to the rhythm section's interaction, Ron says, is the absolute trust each member committed to the team. "I call that group a laboratory band. Miles had the lab and the tunes were the chemicals. He allowed us to go in, take our different test tubes and then make our combinations of changes and rhythms. We boiled them up to see if together they had a validity."

Everyone's input was essential to make the rhythm section work. Selfishness was left at the session-room door and commonality of purpose took over. "Over a period of time, we evolved," Ron said. "There was smoke, dust and sparks. Whenever anyone wanted to know where we were in a tune, they came to trust me that what I played would get us back to the top of the tune. In Miles's apartment, we began to set up that comfort zone."

On May 14, Miles, with his new rhythm team and George Coleman in tow, entered the Columbia 30th Street Studio and rerecorded three tunes from the *Seven Steps to Heaven* session in Los Angeles: two Victor Feldman-composed tunes (the title track and "Joshua") and the Bennie Green number "So Near, So Far" (which was the original title of the album based on the Los Angeles sessions). Miles was so enthused that he contacted his agent, Jack Whittemore, and instructed him to book the band solid.

The earliest gig was in Philadelphia at the Showboat. Jimmy Heath, who attended the show, pulled Miles aside after he had played a solo and slipped into the audience. Jimmy told him to watch out because his new rhythm section was bound to set everyone onstage on fire every night.

With tempos speeding and Miles's horn playing inspired, *Seven Steps to Heaven* ushered in a period of ensemble playing that proved to be revolutionary. With several live concert albums (most of which Miles neglected to tell the band about in addition to conveniently "forgetting" to pay them) and six studio dates, the Miles Davis Quintet of the '60s (with Wayne Shorter joining in 1964 after Coleman quit) launched into the jazz stratosphere, destined to be the genre's greatest band of all time.

NEW DIRECTIONS

SZWED WROTE IN his Miles biography, "The recording [the band] did for the second half of *Seven Steps to Heaven* shows this new group at work, still taking shape, but their effect on Miles is already clear: he is energized, and his solos are louder, higher, faster, and full of risk."

This new Miles sound excited listeners, including aspiring musicians. Chick Corea was highly influenced by the Quintet while he was growing up in Boston. He and his friends would hang out and be mesmerized by the records the band made. He recalled the first time he heard *Seven Steps to Heaven*: "The rhythm section played so transparently. We were just glued to Tony's drumming. Tony and Herbie could go real free because Ron was pinning the whole thing down with his bass. Ron didn't play in a pedestrian way. He held it all together, and it was easy to tune into what he was playing and see what a creative part of the music he was. It was inspiring."

As a result of those listening experiences, Chick says that he considers Ron to be one of his mentors, even though they're only four years apart in age. He said, "Ron is in that category of amazing trendsetters who all set a high level of artistry and creativity in their music."

In 1998 Columbia/Legacy delivered the boxed set, *The Miles Davis Quintet: The Complete Columbia Studio Recordings 1965–1968*, one of several multidisc collections from Miles's lengthy tenure at Columbia. These recordings, compiled for the first time by reissue co-producers Michael Cuscuna and Belden, exhibit Miles's gifted ensemble largely creating new acoustic material.

During these sessions, Miles's abstract, deeply personal playing commanded center stage as he sketched around the fringes of the melodies—yearning, wailing, musing, lamenting and singing on his trumpet—and painted moods that ranged from smoky blue melancholy to vermilion exuberance. But equally captivating were the contributions of all the Quintet members—especially the rhythm section trio—who thrived in the highly creative studio settings.

What's particularly noteworthy about this boxed set is how well it opens a window onto one of Miles's most fertile periods, a time when his music was evolving from the acoustic sphere into free-form fusion. Well known for his refusal to stand pat, Miles is documented here at his ingenious best while on the threshold of yet another new adventure.

In talking about the Quintet, Ron likes to use the metaphor of scientists concocting new serums of music. Belden uses several metaphors—including likening the band to a basketball squad that operates as a team—to get to the essence of the band and the way it broke new sound barriers. "It's impossible to explain to people who don't know about music what was happening with this band," Bob said. "You end up using clichés to fit a narrative. That band operated like a social network or a club where entry is earned, not inherited.

"When that group performed, the bandstand became like a living soul, with each member speaking the same language but with different accents," Bob said. "Ron was one-fifth of a human organism. He never had to think about playing because they were all one organism. It wasn't about being overtly conscious. It had a level of confidence you can't imagine. All you have to do is listen to the Miles session tapes. Those explain it all."

Writing in the jazz textbook, *Jazz Styles—History and Analysis*, Mark C. Gridley devoted a section to the Miles 1963–'68 rhythm section. He wrote, "These musicians created a new jazz idiom. Though moments in their music resembled the sounds of hard bop and free jazz, their music did not truly belong to either of those classifications....The innovations of this band were performed so smoothly that many listeners, especially journalists, failed to recognize its historical significance. This music disappointed so many fans who expected extensive repetition of brief rhythms, recycled jazz phrases, and funky melodies that it ranked as one of the least popular phases in the Davis recording career."

Cuscuna, who worked on all the Columbia/Legacy box sets, agrees. "The music of Miles's quintet was layered, complex, challenging," he said. "And that music still holds up today. But that band made albums that sold the least number of copies than at any other point in Miles's career."

But that didn't faze Miles. He knew he had assembled a team that was going to expand the boundaries of jazz with a freshness and surprise that would be fueled by startlingly collective originality.

CHAPTER SEVEN

The Miles Years, Part 2: The Legacy

THE '60s MILES Davis Quintet lasted a mere six years, from 1963 to 1968 (with Wayne taking over for George in 1964), but continues to be heralded as one of the best ensembles—if not the best—in the history of jazz. Bookending that period, Miles scored two revolutionary megahits a decade apart: 1959's *Kind of Blue* and 1969's *Bitches Brew*.

Writing in the liner notes of Columbia/Legacy's 50th anniversary collector's edition of *Kind of Blue*, Gerald Early, Washington University (St. Louis) professor and editor of the book *Miles Davis and American Culture*, surmised that it was that record, along with Dave Brubeck's *Time Out* "that made jazz a middlebrow music, a respectable music for middle-class, educated people who felt they had refined taste. This was enormously important to Davis both commercially and artistically for the rest of his career. As jazz ceased to be dance music, it needed middlebrow status in order to survive as art music. Davis was essential in making this transformation possible."

Ron counts down the reasons why he thinks *Kind of Blue* was so successful for Miles: "First, it doesn't have the fanaticism that many people associate with jazz—that screaming and falling-over-oneself expression. Second, the melodies are wonderful. Third, there's that aura of Miles and later Trane's own aura. People who came late to the scene gravitated to Miles and Trane—they became important to the Jazz 101 class. Fourth, *Kind of Blue* was so far removed from the jazz at the time that people were immediately attuned to it as something different. That sentiment continued. Fifth, it's a great record. How perfect is that?"

Perfect, perhaps, but Miles was restless, as is evidenced by his next major period—the Quintet, the most long-lived, stable group of his career—which led him to the threshold of his decision to plug in and usher in the era of fusion, steeped in *Brew*'s electric gumbo of Jimi Hendrix-inspired rock, Sly Stone- and James Brown-grooved soul, and expansive free-form jazz. But during those middle years, Miles and Co. were stretching beyond what anyone could have imagined, even if the music was commercially impaired.

In an interview with Marc Myers's online *JazzWax*, Ron said that he didn't like to reflect on what made the quintet so special. "I never go there. That's for historians. Being in the sound, you don't analyze the speakers. You just enjoy what's going on. You just hope that historians will be honest enough, and put their biases aside about Miles's later years, or what they feel about me personally, or Herbie's success. I hope historians will put all that aside and look at the group as a literal scientific experiment and analyze it on that basis."

In Miles's autobiography, he praised his Quintet for its energy, commitment and innovation: "I learned something new every night with that group." He added, "I loved that band, man, because if we played a song for a whole year and you heard it at the beginning of the year, you wouldn't recognize it at the end of the year." Calling Tony a "little genius," Miles said he had to react to the drummer's every move in his own playing. "And this goes for the whole band. So the way we all played together changed what we were playing each and every night during that time."

In Brigid Bergin's *Bass Player* interview with Ron, she asked him what he learned musically in the Quintet. First, he said, he discovered that one note he played could affect everyone in the band, whether it was Tony's rhythm, Herbie's piano voicing, Wayne's saxophone reaction or Miles deciding to lay out to listen. "The next thing was to convince those guys that I really meant that note," Ron said. "The third thing I learned was that if you want to have an experimental group, you need players who know their instruments." Ron added that all the quintet musicians understood the big picture of music as well as how notes are related to each other.

That all translated onto the stage each night. Ron gave Brigid a scenario of the creative process at work: "Wayne would play a phrase that Herbie would play in a different part of the tune, and Tony would play that phrase's rhythm in a different part of the tune, and I would find a note to match this rhythm. And Miles would just be kind of stunned by this development taking place around him. He'd just step back and raise his eyebrows because he couldn't believe that this just took place. And it happened most nights, just like that."

To put the Quintet's era in context socially, politically and culturally, the ensemble rose to prominence during a time of upheaval in the United States. Change was in the air. The Quintet's impact on jazz mirrored that of the Beatles in the pop-rock world. (They, too, gained widespread popularity in the United States in 1963 and disbanded in 1969.) Like Miles's group, the Beatles morphed into a powerhouse of exploration, beginning with *Rubber Soul* (1965) and *Revolver* (1966). Unlike Miles's group, the Beatles were commercial stars who eclipsed acoustic jazz's popularity and hastened its dormancy in the '70s.

Miles's Quintet was born six months before the assassination of President John F. Kennedy (November 1963), which unsettled the country after a burst of enthusiasm following his 1960 election, and a little more than a year before the landmark Civil Rights Act of 1964 (July 1964), legislation that outlawed racial segregation in schools and employment and buoyed hopes for racial equality and justice. It was a time of mourning and anticipation, but most importantly a period of American history during which authority was questioned, new perspectives increasingly trumped the old ways and youth led the charge to explore new musical vistas as fervently as the U.S. government sought to put a man on the moon.

THE STUDIO RECORDINGS

THE QUINTET, INCLUDING Wayne, appeared on seven of Miles's studio albums over the course of its history, revealing the leader's quest for free collaboration:

- *E.S.P.* (1965) — The Quintet's debut was tracked after nearly a half-year's worth of tours and shortly before Miles was sidelined for 10 months with an arthritic hip that required surgery; it features three Ron compositions: "R.J." (named after his son) and two that list Miles as co-writer, "Mood" and "Eighty-One," which represent his complete compositional contribution to the band. Full-band extrasensory perception is on display.

- *Miles Smiles* (1966) — Recorded several months after the group's historic December 1965 appearances at the Plugged Nickel nightclub in Chicago, the sophomore Quintet disc features one of Wayne's best-known tunes, "Footprints." Miles was proud of the band's growth, noting that on the album "you can really hear us pulling away, stretching out." A young jazz fan at the time, producer Michael Cuscuna remembers hanging out in New York in the late '60s with avant-garde drummer Barry Altschul. "Barry put *Miles Smiles* on his record player and said, 'Block everything out and just listen to Ron Carter.' I loved it because it taught me the way the album was recorded and why everybody in the band was playing what he did. It was one of the most sublime performances of that time."

- *Sorcerer* (1967) — Even though the title tune was penned by Herbie (he described Miles as a sorcerer), Wayne's works are featured (four of the seven tracks, including the concert staple "Masqualero"); the nonquintet track "Nothing Like You," recorded in 1962 with Bob Dorough on vocals and Wayne on tenor sax, is oddly tacked onto the album, probably to document Miles's first recording date with him.

- *Nefertiti* (1967) — The last of the Quintet's all-acoustic recordings, the album is again dominated by Wayne's compositions, including the title track and "Pinocchio," and exhibits even deeper band-member telepathy.

- *Water Babies* (1967–68) — Unreleased until 1976, during Miles's "retirement" period, the album is a two-headed creature. The first part features the acoustic Quintet while the second half leans electric with Chick Corea and Dave Holland replacing Herbie and Ron, respectively.
- *Miles in the Sky* (1968) — This is a transformational album with touches of electricity (on the Miles composition, "Stuff," Herbie plays electric piano while Ron plays electric bass) and even a guest: George Benson on electric guitar on Wayne's tune "Paraphernalia." There are four tracks in all, with Tony's "Black Comedy" the shortest at 7:25; the rest are extended polyrhythmic, adventurously harmonic excursions that range from about 13 to 17 minutes.
- *Filles de Kilimanjaro* (1968) — One step further into fusion land, Ron's finale with Miles features him on electric bass on three of the five tracks on which he appeared, and Herbie on Fender Rhodes (recorded in June). Both were replaced by Dave and Chick, respectively, on two tracks recorded in September, five months before Miles's fusion breakthrough, *In a Silent Way*, and less than a year before *Bitches Brew*.

THE LIVE RECORDINGS

THE QUINTET, WHICH never played a tune the same way from set to set, was widely captured live, beginning in 1963 with George in the tenor saxophone chair, continuing with Sam Rivers briefly in 1964 and shortly thereafter featuring Wayne—marking the band's personnel completion as a forward-thinking ensemble that re-imagined the jazz potential and re-invigorated the leader's thirst for the daring blue flame. A selected discography of seven Quintet live recordings reveals the full depth of the Miles muse and the ESP of the rhythm section that fueled the proceedings as well as intuitively and spontaneously changed the flow of the music:

- *Miles in Europe* (recorded in 1963) — The first live recording of Miles's new band, this album was captured in July at the Juan-Les-Pins Jazz Festival on the Côte d'Azur in Antibes, France, and released on Columbia.
- *Live at the Monterey Jazz Festival* (1963) — Recorded in September and issued in 2007 by Monterey Jazz Festival Records (an imprint of the Concord Music Group), this performance from the festival's audio archives reveals the rapid growth of the rhythm section's synergy.
- *My Funny Valentine* (1964) — Recorded at Lincoln Center's Philharmonic Hall, appropriately two days before Valentine's Day, this album of ballads put Miles's new band on full display. Ron wrote in the Columbia/Legacy 2004 reissue liner notes: "Thanks to this

concert being recorded (unbeknownst to four of us!), we have a rare opportunity to hear five men in a jazz laboratory (four wearing tuxedos, forsaking white lab coats) experimenting with known elements (melody and chords) and freely adding other ingredients (rhythm, alternate chords, dynamics, different combos and textures). The results were not too shabby!"

- *Four and More* (1964) — From that same *My Funny Valentine* concert and later reissued with it as *The Complete Concert: 1964* (Columbia), this album featured the uptempo tunes from the show.
- *Miles in Tokyo* (1964) — After George left the quintet, Miles enlisted Sam to accompany the band to Tokyo, on Tony's recommendation. It proved to be a short-lived experiment, with the front line never quite jelling to Miles's satisfaction. (Columbia)
- *Miles in Berlin* (1964) — This album captures Wayne for the first time as an official member of the band. The chemistry was finally right, which resulted in Miles taking the new, complete band into the studio as soon as he possibly could to fully document it with new tunes instead of his standard repertoire. Ron didn't know this album existed until Rahsaan Roland Kirk turned him on to it. (Columbia)
- *The Complete Live at the Plugged Nickel* (recorded in 1965, released in 1995, now out of print) — This eight-CD package is one of the defining moments in Miles's live recording career. It features seven Quintet sets recorded over the course of two nights in December at the Plugged Nickel in Chicago. While excerpts of this engagement were released in various configurations over the years—including a double-album sampling domestically released in 1982 and a seven-CD Japanese box issued in 1993—Columbia/Legacy's definitive version represented the first time all seven sets of the ensemble interplay were compiled in their entirety, thanks to a discovery of the original master tapes that included 30 extra minutes of music previously unavailable. (Each disc contained a full set—complete with background talk and telephone and cash register rings—except for the second set of the first night which clocked in at 81 minutes and fit on two CDs.)

Not only is the playing of Miles's standards-oriented repertoire inspired—from the opening notes of "If I Were A Bell" in the first of three sessions on December 22 (the noisier of the two evenings, crowd-wise) to the final bars of the set-closing tune, "The Theme," in the fourth set of December 23—but this box also provides an illuminating sonic snapshot of the trumpeter's genius and his equally brilliant band.

Listening to the performances is a study—conceivably a semester's worth—in the fine art and magical alchemy of jazz improvisation. What's so remarkable about this gig was the myriad ways in which the band interpreted the tunes, many of them repeated over the course of the two evenings. Even though the ballad, "I Fall in Love Too Easily," was performed four times, the varying colors, shades and textures of each rendition refreshed and transformed the standard. The same held true for the two blazing versions of "Walkin'," which on the second take was highlighted by even greater tension-and-release tempo undulations than the previous evening's reading.

Rather than play by the numbers, Davis and company used the melodies as skeletons and shaped them according to the whims and passions of the moment, listening intensely to each other and responding with a variety of strategies. They engaged in fertile instrumental dialogues; effortlessly shifted rhythms; heated up the tempos and cooled them down; launched into ideas that steered a piece in new directions; or even laid low for a stretch while the rest of the band determined the course.

Individually, each member of the rhythm section played to the top of his game, with Ron's supple bass lines undergirding the entire proceedings, Herbie's delicate single-note runs and chunky, even angular chords providing a melodic beauty to the tunes, and Tony's volcanic eruptions of polyrhythms propelling many of Miles's favorite performance pieces from that period into a sprint (i.e., "So What," which flew as compared to its original version on *Kind of Blue*).

Likewise, Shorter was masterful on tenor sax, surging on the uptempo tunes to the point of being jettisoned, untethered, into the free zone while displaying lyrical fluidity on the ballads.

Miles was pleasantly surprised by his reunited band (because of his surgery in April, he didn't return to live performing until November at the Village Vanguard, at which time Reggie Workman took over on bass for Ron, who had committed to a gig elsewhere). "Everybody played liked we hadn't been separated at all," Miles said in his autobiography. "I have always believed not playing with each other for a while is good for a band, if they are good musicians and like playing with each other. It just makes the music fresher, and that's what happened at the Plugged Nickel, even though we were playing the same book as we had always played...[but] it seemed like everyone was playing out."

Cuscuna, who produced *The Complete Live at the Plugged Nickel* for reissue, said that the live performances provide a good example "of a band taking chances with each member trusting the others." He noted that that kind of freedom is something a band would never try in a studio setting. "This is Jazz Ensemble 101," he said. "It's about guys going out on the limb and the others sticking with them. It's the quintessential example of trust, expertise, and the willingness to take risks to try to break new ground."

MILES ON RON

IN HIS AUTOBIOGRAPHY, Miles expressed great fondness for Ron, even while voicing disappointment that his first-call bassist wasn't always available for his gigs out of town, which required him to enlist such subs as Gary Peacock, Richard Davis and Buster Williams. "On a personal level, I was probably closest to Ron because he was the paymaster for the band and he used to ride with me when we drove places, and sometimes he would drive," Miles recalled. "We'd drive down to St. Louis when we would be playing in the area, and I think he was the only one in the band [who] had met my mother before she died. He met all my friends from high school, some of whom had become big gangsters."

When they were on the bandstand, Miles always stood next to Ron to hear what he was playing because back then there were no bass amplifiers. He used to stand near the drummer, but hearing Tony from anywhere on stage was easy because of his hard-driving, loud playing. Plus, Miles noted, "I stood next to [Ron] to give him my support because everyone was talking about me and Wayne and Herbie and Tony and not talking about Ron too much, and this used to upset him."

Miles was also impressed by how Ron, Tony and Herbie would have late-hour conferences in their hotel rooms about that evening's performance. "Every night they would come back and play something different. And every night I would have to react," Miles said. He added, "Man, it was something how the shit changed from night to night after a while. Even we didn't know where it was all going. But we did know it was going somewhere else and that it was probably going to be hip, and that was enough to keep everyone excited while it lasted."

RON ON MILES

"MILES FELT FROM the beginning that I could fit into his band," Ron said. "Not only for my musical ability, but also because I was a complete person. I knew things other than his tunes. I was bright—I had two degrees. I didn't drink, didn't do drugs. I had a focus. I feel that Miles saw those things in me. I think he enjoyed being around someone who wasn't afraid of him, but would converse with him intellectually about a broad range of topics. He appreciated that off the bandstand. We didn't have gossip sessions and didn't talk about women."

Only rarely did Ron and Miles talk about music when they were away from the stage. They never talked about Miles's time playing and hanging out with Charlie Parker, although sometimes Miles would reflect on the days with his '50s quintet. "I remember Miles talking about Paul Chambers," said Ron. "He told me that some nights Paul would be so on that he played the bass like a guitar. But on other gigs Paul would be so messed up that he could hardly get through the night. That, Miles told me, really discouraged him."

Ron got to know Miles when they would travel together to gigs. Once, the band was scheduled to perform on the West Coast, and Miles wanted to drive to St. Louis on the way in his Maserati. "He asked me if I had a driver's license, then let me drive. George Coleman took my bass on the plane for me. Once Miles and I got to St. Louis, he shipped the car the rest of the way to California. We did that again with his Ferrari a couple of times."

What were their conversations like? "When Miles wasn't asleep, we talked about the stock market and sports. He loved boxing. I knew who the boxers were, but Miles knew them personally. We talked about the news, stuff like corruption in high places. We talked about politics—black politicians and black health programs they were starting uptown. He was encouraged by that, though he was dismayed that more people in the African-American communities weren't actively involved in making their neighborhoods better places to live."

Just as Bird used to do benefit concerts for socially active groups, Ron says Miles would do a benefit in a heartbeat for a cause he believed in. While Ron admired him for that, he also experienced problems, such as when the Quintet, with Coleman, played at Lincoln Center's Philharmonic Hall on February 12, 1964—the evening that yielded the two live albums, *My Funny Valentine* and *Four and More*.

"We had been off for awhile because Miles was sick, so we were all excited to see each other again," Ron said. "But then Miles informed us that he was doing the show as a benefit for CORE [the Congress of Racial Equality civil rights organization], and he was donating all the proceeds of our performance to the cause. I agreed with the cause, but Miles making the decision without talking to us about it beforehand didn't sit well with me. So, I told him, 'You can't give my money without my permission.'"

Miles replied, "Well, what are you going to do?"

Ron packed up his bass and began to leave.

Miles asked, "Where are you going?"

"Home!"

When Miles asked him why, Ron replied that he thought it was unfair to not get paid especially on the first night they were back together after the band had been on hiatus for so long.

Miles asked Ron how much he wanted and then had checks written out for each band member. In the liner notes to the 2004 reissue of *My Funny Valentine*, Ron wrote, "But for me it wasn't about the money; it was the principle of the thing. He agreed to pay us—no one asked how much—and we waited for the introduction to go on stage to a full house."

Original liner note writer Nat Hentoff pointed out that the show was a benefit concert for voter registration in Mississippi and Louisiana, and that in addition to CORE the event was co-sponsored by the NAACP Legal Defense Fund and the Student Non-Violent Coordinating Committee.

Nat called the album "an important 'live' addition to the Davis discography" and heralded Ron on the tune "I Thought About You" that focused on "the subtly inflected Davis wit." He noted: "And listen, too, to Ron Carter behind George Coleman's solo. He is a bassist of formidable technique who has long since learned the power of selection among his resources. And his beat is as alive as his breathing. As in the case of Tony Williams, the feeling for time is so basic to Carter's work that he can build on that assurance to make time both accurate and pliable."

Ron's insistence on being treated fairly and openly prompted Miles to ask him to take on an added responsibility within the band.

"I ended up being the paymaster, or straw boss," Ron said. "I had to make sure the hotel reservations were all set up, and then at the end of each night he gave me a bunch of money to be split up four ways. There was no tour manager back then. I was older than Herbie and Tony, and I had gained Miles's respect from the beginning. He felt that as honest as I had been with him about not leaving Art Farmer's band I would be responsible to take care of the money. He knew I wouldn't be shortchanging the other guys."

Ron says that when the band went on the road they didn't know how much they were going to get paid before they left. And, back then, each band member was responsible for paying for his hotel fees. The promoters weren't concerned with that. "So, we had to hope that we would make enough money to get a decent hotel, and, for me, to have enough money left over to send money back home to Janet to pay the bills," Ron said. "I can't remember ever asking Miles how much we were going to get when we went on tour. But today my groups don't ask me that either. They don't know how much they're getting paid until the end of the gig. They trust my sense of honesty."

Ron remembers the first time he played with Miles in Chicago at the Sutherland Lounge on the city's South Side. The plan was for the band to stay upstairs in the club's hotel. "We got in late to Chicago, with just enough time to get onstage," he said. "Afterwards we checked out our rooms but they were awful—run down and dirty. So at three in the morning we were driving all around Chicago with Herbie's friend to try to find a place to stay." Ron ended up staying at Janet's uncle's house for two weeks, and Herbie stayed at home because his parents lived there. Ron added, "Fortunately, I was always able to find a decent place when I went on the road, which was better than staying up all night long or sleeping on a park bench."

Even though Ron was responsible for paying the band, he says that Miles tested him along the way. He cites the specific example of when the Quintet played in Montreal. Usually the band got paid after a week's gig, but in this case the promoter wrote Miles a check. Miles told Ron to come by his house on Monday to get paid. Ron did so, only to find that Miles didn't have the money as he had promised. "He gave the money to the guy who was working on renovating his apartment," Ron said. "So I said, what about me? What about us?" The band was scheduled to go to California on tour the next day, so Ron said, "You're going to California? Well, I'm not going."

Miles exclaimed, "What?"

Ron said, "I worked last week, and you didn't pay me. I'm going to California to have that happen again? No."

Ron left Miles's place, but then got a call a half hour later. Miles had made arrangements to have the cash at a local liquor store that he did business with. Ron went and got paid. "It was a test to check on my moral fiber to see how far he could go with me," Ron said.

In the "Ron Carter Talks With Milt Hinton" article in *Jazz Magazine* in 1978, Ron recalled Miles going around the bandstand during a show to make suggestions to Herbie about chord voicing or Tony about which drum to play. "But in the six years I was with the band, [Miles] never made one comment to me on how to play or what to play," Ron said. "Not once, and we worked on a lot of gigs. I guess he felt that if it wasn't right I'd fix it on my own."

He added, "Once when we were playing 'Autumn Leaves,' *again*, I didn't want to end the chorus with a G-minor chord even though we were playing in G minor. I played a B natural at the bottom of the chord. After the chorus, Miles asked me, 'What note was that?' I told him G with B in the bass to make a G-major seventh. He said, 'Oh,' and that was it. He trusted that we were the right guys and that if he left us alone we'd find the right zone on our own without him having to direct us."

Even though Miles was infamous for his fiery personality, he never snapped at Ron, even when he stepped on his trumpet one night after a show in 1965. "We were playing at the Sutherland Lounge, where the bandstand was in the center with a bar around it," Ron said. "After one evening's sets, Miles was talking and he put his trumpet down. I was always the last guy off the stage because I had to take care of my bass. So as I was leaving the stage which required walking down eight or nine steep steps, I stepped right on his trumpet."

Miles's reaction? He raised his eyebrows. Ron told him that he didn't see the trumpet on the floor. "Miles wasn't upset or accusatory," Ron said. "He didn't dock my pay or punch me out. He never related to me in a vindictive manner. Of course, he was different if he was dealing with a club owner or a promoter or even a writer that he didn't like." Miles simply called the Martin company, which sent him a new trumpet the next day.

(Years later, when Ron's son Ron Jr. was learning to play the trumpet, Miles gave him the dented instrument, mouthpiece and all. Years after that, Wallace Roney got the trumpet repaired for Ron, who would bring it to his classes at City College and let his trumpet-playing students use it.)

Ron bristled at one of the criticisms jazz journalists liked to make of Miles: playing his shows with his back to the audience. He said, "Have they ever been to a classical concert with someone like Leonard Bernstein conducting? You ever see his face? You only see his back and arms. Hello? When you think of all the great notes Miles played, all the changes he made, all the people in his bands over the years, and he's singled out for this...well, I think it's a waste of time and energy and ink. The more Miles stepped into the band on the stage, the better he could hear what was going on. Before the days of amps and pickups, Miles stopped by the bass, which is naturally the softest instrument of the band. Think of Miles as a scientist interested in hearing."

During the course of the Quintet's road history, Ron would at times be missing in action, which led some to speculate that either Miles or he wasn't happy. That wasn't true, Ron maintains. "Sometimes Miles would call on Monday for a gig on Tuesday," Ron said. "Sometimes he would have shows booked 10 days in advance, but he never got around to telling us. By that time, I had already taken on some other gigs. I go back to that first meeting with Miles, where he knew that I had that level of respect for my word. When I wasn't able to make a show because I had already taken on another gig, I put him on notice that I still honored my word."

One bone of contention Ron had with Miles was his cavalier attitude about recording live sets without telling the rest of the band. "I can understand if he didn't want to influence us in any way by telling us he was recording," Ron said. "But it pissed me off that Miles didn't tell us later." For all of the live albums, the band found out after the fact by seeing the albums being sold in record stores.

So, rather than confront Miles, Ron hired a lawyer and went to the musicians' union, which forced Columbia Records to pay each member of the band scale for their performances on those albums. "I never looked around for a reason to accept that as OK," Ron said. "I never delved into why. But to me there was no legitimacy for that kind of financial irresponsibility."

In Fred Jung's "Fireside Chat With Ron Carter," he asked Ron why the Quintet's music went to a higher plateau than other jazz bands. Ron replied, "Miles knew how to program songs. He knew how to make them shorter or longer as he thought the music would tolerate. He accepted experimentation. He was always fair and honest with me. He always came to work to play with whatever physical pain he was feeling. I came away believing that I was a really good player."

HERBIE ON RON AND THE QUINTET

RON WAS ON Herbie's radar before he moved from his hometown of Chicago to New York. Herbie can't remember exactly how or when he knew about him, but he surmises it must have been from Ron's early appearances on various albums as a sideman. After Herbie came to New York in 1961, he met Ron but never recorded with him. But he was well aware of Ron getting the call from Miles in 1963: "We knew that he was a young lion bass player who was next in line with Miles after Paul Chambers," he said. "But the first time I played with him was at the audition at Miles's apartment."

Herbie's first impression of Ron was that he was "really the top, hot, modern bass player who had new, fresh ideas. He was the first-choice bass player." Herbie had already played some with Tony, who had moved to New York early in 1963 from Boston, so they had a friendship. "Tony was the best drummer I had ever heard," Herbie said. "He was young, but he turned me on to all kinds of new music: jazz, classical, electronic, avant-garde."

When Herbie got the Miles gig, he was thrilled. "Miles was like Zeus," he said. "I dreamed of playing with a lot of bands, but I never dreamed of playing with Miles. That was beyond my wildest dreams. That was the top of the line, like getting a Ferrari. I couldn't help but feel great playing with all these musicians of the highest caliber. But then I experienced that 'special chemistry' when the band began to evolve."

It took Herbie some time to find his pianistic identity for the chemistry to churn. "When I first joined the band, I figured the safest route was to play what Miles was used to hearing to make him feel comfortable. I listened to his records with all the piano players who had come before me. But as long as I was approaching the music that way, I wasn't open to letting that special chemistry come in. My mind was closed."

After a couple of months on the road with the band, Herbie began to feel frustrated. He was copying all the other pianists but not allowing himself to come out from hiding. Finally that frustration came to a head. "I thought, I've just got to play, to really play," Herbie said. "If that conflicts with Miles, I'll just have to bear the consequences. So at the Sutherford Lounge in Chicago one night, I let it loose. I figured that Miles was going to fire me after the set, but he leaned over to me and said, 'Why didn't you play like that before?' That shocked me. Then it dawned on me that a copy is never as good as the original. Miles wanted to hear *me*. And so did Ron and Tony."

It was at this time that Herbie was "free" enough to start hearing the rhythmic possibilities that Ron and Tony had already been experimenting with. "Then that chemistry we began to develop spread to the rest of the band," he said. "When Wayne came aboard, he totally fit the direction the band was going in."

Herbie recalls the conversations he, Ron and Tony would have about how to support the horn soloing. "We talked a lot about that," he said. "For example, Ron would lay a pattern that was different from a straight walking bass line. It was hip. Tony picked up the pattern and then played something in reaction before it was time for Miles to solo, which would cause him to play notes he hadn't thought to play. All this happened automatically with the rhythm section after a while."

Ron was a unique bassist who caused Herbie to redirect his playing. "It was all about Ron's intelligence of playing and the note choices he made," he said. "It wasn't about soloing but about the rhythm. It required me to be a better listener in a way I wasn't accustomed to. Beforehand, with bass players, I could anticipate what they would play. But Ron was more creative, more adventurous, more interesting in his approach to the bass line. Whereas before I didn't listen to much of what the bass player was doing, with Ron, it was a whole different ballgame. I had to pay attention. I knew that from the first time we played together. And it made a difference in my piano playing. It forced me to respond in a way that reflected his influence. From moment to moment, it made me shift and develop in a very personal way. There was nothing cookie-cutter about it."

Arguably, the most out-leaning, atraditional live experience the band had was when they performed the 1965 Plugged Nickel date. "We had never played like that before," Herbie said. "The band at that time had been constantly developing, reaching new plateaus every three months or so. The communication among us was so solid that it was like telepathy. We knew what to expect each other to do. Everything was working."

However, while traveling to the Chicago date, Tony told Herbie that things were getting too easy. Herbie agreed, and the two hatched a plan to break out of what they had been doing and conjure up new challenges. "Tony and I made a pact that we'd go to opposite extremes," Herbie said. "Instead of playing with expectation, we'd play the opposite of what was expected. We decided to call it anti-music—purposefully destroying the music to put it together in a new way. We were willing to sacrifice the audience even if what we played sounded like crap. We figured they'd be victimized for the greater good."

Before they got to the club, they discussed the plan with Ron and Wayne, who both agreed to convert the Plugged Nickel into a laboratory for transforming the warhorse repertoire Miles was playing. However, when they arrived at the club, they saw the professional tape recorders Columbia had brought in to record the sets. "I looked at Tony and said, oh oh," Herbie remarked. "But we had made the pact and we went ahead with our plan. So during the set we built up to a point where there would typically be a big explosion, but I left it open and Tony did the same, essentially doing the opposite of what was expected. Miles seemed to enjoy it and went along with it."

After the first set of the first night of recording (December 22), they asked the Columbia team if they could hear the playback. They were refused, so the band, still intent on anti-music, never heard any of the material. Herbie figured that the Columbia guys thought it was "too weird for any of us to listen to." He held that opinion for years until a two-album set of the material was finally released, first in Japan in 1976 and later in the U.S. in 1982 (a third album, *Cookin' at the Plugged Nickel*, was released in 1987).

"Somebody called me on the phone and told me that the Plugged Nickel stuff was amazing," Herbie said. "I said, what? I didn't even know that it had been released. This guy told me that Wayne was killing, that he had never heard him sound so real, so raw, so adventurous. We all thought that what we had done was horrible. When I finally got a copy of the record, I was amazed. It opened a doorway to the sound that became the classic sound of that band that was experimental and partially avant-garde. There were so many dimensions to it. No one tried to copy it for years. The jazz fans loved it, even if they didn't quite understand what we were doing."

As for Ron the man, Herbie says that Ron has always exhibited a sense of inner drive (both in his commitment to music but also literally—he loved to go long distances in his fast cars). "There are a lot of physical challenges you confront in playing jazz, but Ron always plowed right through," he said. "He had a lot of determination. If it meant not getting enough sleep, that was OK. He still played top-shelf."

As for hanging while the Quintet was on the road, Herbie says that Ron pretty much kept to himself. "Tony and I were young, unmarried, and we were into checking out the chicks. Maybe we were a little bit irresponsible. We were always into exploring things, going to jam sessions, staying up all night long. Ron was married and had kids, and was a lot stricter. He always went to bed early. It's in Ron's nature to be more ordered and organized. I think it was about how he was raised. Ron was the type of person for whom duty was a very big thing—to be responsible, on time, totally prepared, to do things a certain way according to certain rules of ethics and etiquette."

While Ron was socially conventional, Herbie says he always sought adventure on the bandstand—as well as dependability. "Ron was the perfect bass player. He was the anchor. He didn't have a lead foot, and he always kept me from going too far astray. He knew how far to let me go before pulling me back in. I'd play and get lost. Ron knew that and knew when to play the right notes as cues to bring me back in."

RON ON HERBIE

RON'S RECOLLECTION OF his first time playing with Herbie was in Miles's basement room. He hastens to add that those get-togethers were not an audition, but rehearsals. "I felt we *were* the band and that's why we were there," he said. "There was only one piano player, one drummer and one bass player, so I was assuming we were going to be the rhythm section. Maybe Miles was a little insecure about his decision, which may explain why he invited Gil and Philly Joe to visit, to make sure he had made the right choices."

As for the Sutherland breakout gig that Herbie talked about, Ron doesn't remember the specifics, only that by then the band was changing. "We were all more comfortable with the library and with each other, and we weren't concerned with imitating history," he said. "We could acknowledge it, but we didn't need to read the same page. We could play all the styles of Miles's old bands, and we knew the history of the music well enough to assimilate the sound, the rhythms, the order of changes and the bass lines that served as a jumping-off point to work our way into a new place."

Beyond taking the evidence of the Plugged Nickel records to the union to have it contact Columbia for payment for the live sessions, Ron was indifferent about the music on the albums when they finally came out. At that time his career as a leader and sideman was buzzing. He filed the LPs in his collection with the wrappers still on. Several years later when driving with Jack DeJohnette to a recording session at Rudy Van Gelder's studio, a song from one of the live albums came on the radio.

Jack said, "Ron, have you heard this whole record?"

"No, but I have it at home."

"You've got to listen to it."

"Why?"

"Man, the music being developed here is really quite amazing."

"C'mon, Jack, you're kidding."

"No, you have to listen to this record."

When Ron got home, he took the cellophane off the LPs and played them. He rarely checked out other live albums of the band, preferring instead to give them only a cursory listen. But for the Plugged Nickel tracks, he dug in. He was surprised by what he heard. "When you're in that space at the time, you don't hear how you're playing," he said. "But I could hear then that we were understanding the music at a deeper level and starting to see the possibilities open for us. We weren't playing the music. We *were* the music."

What struck Ron most about the live sets was that everyone was fully immersed in the music. "The intergroup response was with all five of us, not just the three rhythm players," he said. "This seemed to be the first recording, the first evidence that it wasn't just three guys plus two others. Miles and Wayne were responding to the background rhythm almost in spite of it. Five artists were responding to the same stimuli. It wasn't cake and icing; it was all cake."

Ron focused on how the band was functioning—how a chord Herbie played made Miles play something out of the ordinary, how Tony's drumming would create the same dynamic with Wayne, how one note he played would set Herbie and Tony off in a new direction.

As for the anti-music aspect of the date, Ron chalks that up to the youthful enthusiasm Herbie and Tony had for the points of view they were hearing in avant-garde circles. "I had already been there a few years earlier playing with guys like Don Ellis," he said. "I'd go hear guys like Henry Grimes and listen to the sounds that he was getting out of the bass that had never occurred to me. I never found a place for that in my own music, but I was curious about the possibilities. That appealed to me. I played with a lot of the avant-garde guys. Herbie and Tony never did. So these dates at the Plugged Nickel are the first tangible proof that they were experimenting with that point of view by using Miles's music."

Ron figures that because he, Herbie, Tony and Wayne were committed to exploring the music they all became good friends who continued to work together sporadically after their tenure with Miles. Again, Ron used the scientist metaphor, this time describing the band members as chemists who worked for the head chemist. "Miles would give us his chemistry set. If something didn't work and blew up, we always knew we would be able to put the foam on the fire in the next chorus." Because ego wasn't a factor in their quest to find the right notes night in and night out, Ron said that they became "as close as we could get to being blood brothers."

WAYNE ON RON

MILES HAD CALLED Wayne two or three times in 1961 and 1962 while the saxophonist was the musical director for Art Blakey's Jazz Messengers. Wayne turned him down. However, by 1964, after five years with Art, he was feeling restless in a jazz-ensemble context where individual expression was confined to the tune's solos. He yearned to stretch further.

Meanwhile, the young rhythm section in Miles's band was pushing the tempo, increasing the sound volume, dissecting melodies and putting the fragments back together, and rushing full speed into risky territory where solid footing was scarce. George Coleman starred on *My Funny Valentine*, but soon after was not only becoming disgruntled with the new direction but was also losing favor with the rest of the band, particularly Tony. George was quoted in John Szwed's biography of Miles as saying, "[Tony] was always complaining to Miles that I wasn't hip enough for him."

At the time, Miles was overindulging in alcohol, drugs and women, which irked George, who often had to front the band when Miles either didn't show for a gig or left early. Shortly before the band was supposed to play in Japan, George quit. Sam Rivers filled in, but Miles still had Wayne on his mind.

Wayne began to express interest in the saxophone chair. "Ron and Herbie called me, then Tony called," he said. "They all urged me to join. We want you, they said." Wayne's only hesitation was that he was contemplating forming his own quartet. But since he was still young, he was warned off doing so because, when push came to shove, club owners would more likely book a "guarantee" like Dizzy Gillespie.

When Wayne talked to Ron, he could discern the dry humor in his personality and his commitment to the growing camaraderie in the burgeoning band. Miles on a few occasions had already told him, in his sandpapery voice, "Let me know when you're ready."

"It was destiny that we came together," Wayne said. "The whole thing was formulating. I couldn't destroy that by not joining. When I left Art, it was like leaving a family. But when I joined Miles, they all welcomed me like family. Of course, it also meant that I had to go beyond the streets and clubs into graduate and doctorate work."

In Michelle Mercer's biography of Wayne, *Footprints: The Life and Music of Wayne Shorter*, the saxophonist said that instead of the "bish-bash, sock'em dead routine" of the Blakey band, with the Miles group "I felt like a cello, I felt the viola, I felt liquid, dot-dash and colors started really coming."

Wayne joined in September 1964 and stayed in Miles's band until early 1970. His first gig with the group was at the Hollywood Bowl. The first time Wayne played with the band he experienced the "rhythmic motor." He said, "How can they switch so fast with nuance? I went from Art's hard bop to Miles's streamlining. In that band you had to be ready. And it was all about truth and honesty. I realized I wasn't there to play hard tones, but to paint."

Wayne soon discovered how learned Ron was in classical music—which he appreciated—and the two would check out the scores Miles kept on his kitchen table. On the road, Miles discouraged the practicing of exploration offstage. "He was all about doing it for real, on stage, mistakes and all," Wayne said. "We were going into uncharted waters. I remember once Herbie, in all humility, said that he didn't know what to play with his left hand on a particular tune. And Miles just said, 'Don't play nothing.'"

Wayne was impressed with Ron's openness to playing pedal tones, which was rare for a jazz bassist to do. Those are sustained tones, played typically by the bass, with nonchord notes that have a strong tonal effect in that they pull the harmony back to its root.

(Ron explains it as a common note among different chords that becomes the focal point of the sounds of the various chords. It is not the root note of the chord, but typically the dominant, the fifth note of the scale. "That kind of playing makes the rest of the band realize that I'm not playing roots all the time, which is the first note of the chord, and making them hear the chord with a different sound," he said. "And the bass is dictating what this chord must sound like. I like expressing the power and authority that the bass can have. Before, bass players were only interested in giving their lines various shapes, but I wanted to do more, to find a way to tie all the chords together. I'm still finding ways to do that today.")

On the road, Wayne remembers Ron doing a lot of reading, especially newspapers to keep up on the events of the day. "He was studious-minded," he said. "He was interested in world politics as much as New York's education system."

Wayne also recalled Ron's height when they traveled. "Ron is a tall person, and a tall person is very easily visible. Ron was always so visible, and visibility is all about what you do. A lot of people can hide and not be easily seen, but there was always a light of visibility on Ron. And he wanted that shining light to reflect a well-heeled person who was a family man who took care of himself and his family. I noticed that some tall people stand straight while others are curved, hunched over. Ron was always straight."

As for Ron's periodic absence from the band, Wayne says he knew it was only temporary. "It was never long-term, until the end when Miles brought Dave Holland in. Ron had aspirations too, and he did a lot of sessions. He recorded with a lot of people. But he was also taking care of his family. The subs were OK. We managed. And it was a chance for them to learn something from Miles."

In noting that Ron was in charge of the payroll, Wayne said that Ron was also responsible in other ways on the road. He recalls an event that took place when the Quintet played in Detroit at 20 Grand, a club that was often frequented by gangsters and their entourage. "Ron saved Miles's life one night," he said. "Miles was at the bar talking to a woman and drinking a combination of cognac and champagne. He got into an argument and raised the champagne bottle above his head in slow motion. Someone tried to grab the bottle from him, but Miles went after him. The bartender had a gun under the bar and there was an opening below where he had it pointed at Miles. Ron grabbed Miles and pulled him away."

Wayne said that when the band appeared in these kinds of clubs, they would arrive and people would pay attention immediately as they walked to the stage. "It was like here comes the royalty. And we knew that the high rollers who were there with their women were feeling a streak of jealousy. So we all watched our backs. I had been in the army, so I was ready to kick ass. From my basic training, I had a feeling of invincibility. When Ron walked in, he had a definite stride. You couldn't miss his confidence. I never saw him make a move without that confidence."

Wayne added, "Ron was always about taking care of business. He was always prepared. He never had questions. He had the answers."

RON ON WAYNE

IN MICHELLE'S BOOK on Wayne, she asked Ron about the trust among the band members. "Wayne seemed to have a sense of curiosity as to what it would take to make the music different. Wayne left the counter space that would allow us to help him help us."

In the *JazzWax* interview, Ron was asked how important Wayne was to the quintet. "He brought a width and breadth of compositions to the band that we hadn't played before," he replied. "It made me feel that I could take a little more risk than I could take with someone else. That's not to speak of George Coleman pejoratively at all. It's just that Wayne plays different and in a way that let me try things that were different from the norm."

Ron liked to call him Doctor. "That's what he was," Ron said. "He was the doctor who could see a cure on the horizon. And he keeps going that way until he sees what it is. He's a bright, amazing guy." Ron remembers Wayne going to bookstores in airports while they were waiting to catch a flight. "Part of my job was to make sure he didn't buy so many that he couldn't carry them all home. Wayne was a film collector who was always looking for literature related to his films. I was always telling him, let's wait until the next airport to see if they have a better book, or write the title down and we can get it when we get to New York."

Even though Wayne was the true elder among Miles's sidemen, Ron sometimes took the role of band spokesman. "Wayne is even less outgoing than I am," Ron said. "When people wanted to interview us, Wayne would often talk in ethereal terms, using $25 words. And interviewers didn't follow what he was saying. They'd come to me and I'd say three words and give them what they needed."

On the topic of 20 Grand, which was a popular club that had a bowling alley and a fireplace lounge on the first floor, where the jazz room was also located, Ron remembers the incident well. "Miles did have too much to drink and he did pick up a champagne bottle ready to whack someone," he said. "Miles would get himself into these situations because he was who he was. He seemed to always get out of trouble because of who he was or because he could outpunch people or he had guys willing to protect him because he was Miles. But at 20 Grand, he had no chance."

Everyone knew Ron and knew he was levelheaded because he didn't drink or do drugs. "People were comfortable with me in the clubs. So that night the bartender trusted me to take care of Miles, to get him outside for some air and that tomorrow night he'd be fine. The bartender told me, OK, because if you don't, he'll be dead. Miles probably never even remembered that incident or acknowledged how close he was to getting killed because we were going from town to town, from eye blink to eye blink."

What was Miles's reaction to Ron taking him outside? He can't remember, but said, "He was probably telling me that he could beat this guy up, and why was I getting in his way? So I probably told him that I didn't think he could, and that getting outside would help everyone get another point of view."

Not all the club scenes were as dicey. The Quintet played jazz clubs that were the hangouts for popular entertainers and sports stars. "There was glamour and glitter back then," Ron said. He met Tony Curtis on one occasion and four of the five Boston Celtics basketball starters at another. "Those clubs were grand places to be, and like Wayne said, we were the royals. Everyone had respect for us, even the thugs. Some people may not have fully understood the music, but they recognized its magnetic force and saw the power of Miles and the music."

TONY ON RON

ONLY 17 WHEN Miles signed him for the quintet, Tony posed a problem for the band on tour. He was under the drinking age and therefore presented a possible liability. Ron became his guardian of sorts, making sure the youngster was protected while the group played the seedy jazz venues. While Tony hooked up with Herbie, who was closer in age, he always appreciated Ron's watchful eye. And he savored Ron's bass playing, even giving him the moniker "Checkpoint Charlie" for his steady monitoring of the sometimes-raucous rhythm section playground.

Tony died in 1997 at the age of 51, after a routine gallbladder surgery was botched, which resulted in a life-snuffing heart attack. On the last day of February, his friends, colleagues, fans and family gathered together to pay their respects to the late drummer at a Roman Catholic funeral mass at St. Ignatius Church in San Francisco. (I reported on this for *DownBeat*.) Herbie and Ron served as pallbearers along with Max Roach, Ginger Baker, Bobby Hutcherson, Stanley Clarke and Wallace Roney. In addition, several locally based musicians, including Carlos Santana, John Handy, Joe Henderson, Eddie Marshall and Jeff Chambers, attended the somber memorial service.

During the service, Tony's wife Colleen Williams spoke to the gathering about how he "showed up in life with a bang" and went on to live with a passion and exuberance. "Just before he died, Tony got three speeding tickets within two weeks," she said. "He loved velocity."

Wayne expounded on the same theme when reflecting about him. "I remember when we played with Miles. Whenever Miles wanted to play something with velocity, he'd call the tune 'Joshua,' and Tony would say, 'Yeah!' Tony was a soldier like [the biblical] Joshua. He used velocity to make things right. Tony's velocity right now is eternal."

Max recalled Tony's greatness as a drummer and how fellow musicians were so impressed with his footwork that they used to call him "a four-legged monster." Ron reminisced about being Tony's guardian. "As it turned out," Ron said, "he became my guardian. I'll miss Tony."

Herbie remembered his early days with Tony: "I met Tony when he was 16 years old. From day one he was like a brother to me, even though I was five years his senior. I thought of him like a little kid until I heard him play the drums. You have no idea how much I learned from him—not just about rhythms, but about conquering fears."

At the conclusion of the service, four-fifths of the Miles Davis tribute band that Tony had been a part of in 1992—Herbie, Wayne, Ron and Wallace Roney on trumpet—bid the drummer farewell with an exquisite rendering of "Sister Cheryl." Played with heartfelt emotion, the piece served as a solemn prayer—mournful and chilling, yet beautifully joyous.

Colleen harks back to the days when Tony played with Ron. "Ron was a central person in Tony's life," she said. "Ron was the elder in that group. There was an age gap, but Tony was precocious. He was not one to sign over any rights on his life, but he did so with Ron; primarily Ron was a friend who looked at the whole person, the whole situation. Tony respected Ron. He admired Ron's authenticity as well as his commitment to his family and his young children."

Like Ron, Tony saw the opportunity of playing with Miles as a way of connecting with jazz history in a rarefied setting that required a rhythmic center with strong personalities. Also, Tony shared Ron's demand for punctuality.

Colleen says that from Tony's perspective bands came and went on the music scene, but Miles's group was special. "Tony always talked about it as a familial band that held a special place in time," she said. "It was a significant band in his mind, where the right people showed up and played at such a deep level. It was a unique constellation. When they played, they jelled like a family. Miles, Herbie, Wayne and Ron were like a family to him. It went beyond friendship."

Like all the other band members, Tony played for the music. Colleen points out that the last studio project Tony worked on in his life was titled *Wilderness* (released in 1996 on Ark 21). "Tony was a *Star Trek* fan who saw that each person's life is a wilderness and an infinite frontier. That's how he felt about music, which is why he never wanted to be formulaic. That's what all of the guys with Miles believed too, which is why they were all able to hear each other on such an extraordinary level. When Tony talked about him, Ron and Herbie getting together after shows to discuss the music, it was like mathematics. It was the thrill of playing and being able to verbalize it."

Colleen recalls the first time she met Ron, which was after the Miles tribute band finished the first part of its tour the year after Miles died. "Ron was at home and showed us all the art work in his house. Then he and Tony discussed classical music and their shared interest in classical composition," she said. On another occasion she spent time with Ron when Tony's quartet played at Birdland in New York for a week, with Mulgrew Miller and Wallace Roney. "You'd see Tony and Ron playing together and there was such a fluidity. The whole was always greater than the sum of the parts when they got together. There was nothing random in the way they played. Everything was like a ballet—the implementation of their ideas and the action of their sound."

Colleen says that when Tony was growing up, he would lie in his bed for hours listening to music and memorizing all the records—knowing all the notes so well that he could sing them. "Tony loved melodies, and when Ron plays it's deeply melodic, which Tony loved," she said. "Tony felt that they were on the same wavelength."

When Tony first came into Miles's band, they traveled to Europe. He was so young that Colleen says that he wanted to go home. But Ron proved to be a good example to Tony—passing on a sense of professionalism that got him through the tour. "Ron was like a counselor," Colleen said. "But he modeled by example. He never hesitated to say what he was thinking, and Tony felt free to disagree, which he did over the years. Sometimes he would get irritated with Ron, but he always respected him. Ron is an authoritative personality, but also extremely witty and funny."

Mulgrew says that when he played in Tony's band, the drummer would always talk about his bassist. "Tony loved Ron. He admired his tenacity and the intelligence behind his playing. Ron was like a big brother to him.

Tony would talk to the bass players in his band about how the bass playing could influence how he played his drums. He always referred to Ron."

RON ON TONY

RON SAYS THAT he and Tony were always "adamant" about the rhythm when they played. "We had rhythmic conversations every night after we performed," he said. "We didn't talk about what happened, but how we felt about what was happening." Ron, Tony and Herbie all came of age knowing the Miles book of the '50s, so they knew where Miles had been rhythmically. They, in turn, were feeling their way through the music to the next direction, not knowing precisely where they were going, but determined to find a new perspective.

"We could continue to mine in that same mine shaft, or take this ladder, climb out of the mine and go into a new direction," Ron said. "We all had the skill level, and we were all verbal, which meant we talked to each other about how we could work on discovering what we were feeling. Saying that it doesn't feel right isn't enough for me. We're dealing with different ingredients and mixing them into beakers and test tubes, turning up the heat and seeing it bubble."

Ron says that his first encounter playing with Tony wasn't so much an "ah-hah" moment as it was knowing that even though he was a teenager, he was mature and responsible enough—and even courageous enough—to try some new chemical reactions. "It developed over time," said Ron. "With Tony I knew we were going into this endless lab as skilled chemists, and we wouldn't get fired if one of us made some explosions along the way."

Recalling the first European trip, Ron said that if Tony were homesick, he didn't express that to the rest of the band, nor did he seem anxious about being in a foreign land. Still, Ron said that he probably did lead by example: "I had been to Europe before, and there's a lot to learn about the language you don't know and about what the proper etiquette is."

The first date was at a festival in Paris that featured an eclectic array of music: Sarah Vaughan and her band that included future band mate Buster Williams, a gospel group called the Harlem Beggars, Wilbert Harrison of the song "Kansas City" fame, and Miles's group. "We opened the show, which is what Miles always preferred," said Ron. "He wanted to play first and either go home or go about his business. After we left the stage, the crowd booed the next act because they wanted more of us."

Ron says that if Tony was feeling uncomfortable in the early going, he soon got relaxed and began to bask in the favorable press coverage he was getting for being a teenager working alongside Miles. He was making heads turn with his dynamic drumming. "Tony liked the attention, but I kept telling him to read the review beyond the paragraph that was about him," Ron said while laughing. "Herbie and I didn't get jealous about it. We felt, the more ink Tony gets, the more work we get."

Ron's role changed when they were in the U.S. where, because of his age, Tony wasn't allowed into a club unless an adult accompanied him. That adult was always Ron. "Tony was grown up, but he still had to stay close to me," Ron said. "Miles nominated me to be responsible for him. So, at a club, when I went in, he came with me; if I went out, he went too. If people asked about him, I'd say, 'He's with me.'"

While the rhythm team related as equals, Ron says there were times when he questioned Tony's onstage behavior. "Sometimes I'd get on Tony's case about his choices, which I felt weren't the best to be made," Ron said. "One night in London some guy in the audience yelled out to him, 'Hey, man, you got any brushes?' So Tony played brushes the rest of the set just to show this guy he could. After the set, I told him that he should have let that comment go. You want to punch this jerk out, but instead you sacrificed the rest of the band, who needed the sticks."

And if there was one distinct characteristic about Tony's playing, it wasn't his balladic style, but his volume and velocity. In Miles's band, he served as the volcanic force.

A master of telling jazz stories, producer Orrin Keepnews said that Ron told him once that he stayed in Miles's band as long as he did because of Tony. "Ron told me that when he could play the acoustic bass alongside Tony and *be heard*—that once he achieved that goal—he'd give his notice," Orrin said, and then added, "Now I don't know if that's bullshit, but Ron told me exactly that."

LISTENING SESSIONS

1. Ron on the Music of Miles's '50s Quintet

"Woody n' You," composed by Dizzy Gillespie, from the Prestige Records album, *Relaxin' With the Miles Davis Quintet*, recorded at Rudy Van Gelder's studio in 1956 (Miles Davis, trumpet; John Coltrane, tenor saxophone; Red Garland, piano; Paul Chambers, bass; Philly Joe Jones, drums)

WHEN THIS SERIES of records came out, what impressed me the most were the rhythm section arrangements. For me, it wasn't so much the library but how the band sounded. You can hear on this track how the rhythm section is such an integral part of the band, which hadn't been done in this fashion before.

Up to that point in jazz history, you had great soloists like Charlie Parker or Sonny Rollins whose rhythm sections were pulled along by their genius. This is the first clear instance of a group where the rhythm section was as important as the soloists.

You can hear on this tune how Red, after Miles's solo and before Trane's, was setting up these figures in the background. Then there's no piano at all. He's laying out. He's participating in the tune in a way that to me was a startling development for the rhythm section. No one has written about this new development—at least, not to my knowledge.

Another factor is the recording of the rhythm section itself. Today there's an unfortunate trend of "bass natural," where the player does not use a pickup. I could use this record to point out why that isn't a good idea unless you have an engineer with expertise to help you out. Without an amp you have no chance to be heard. I want my sound to be heard from the door of the club, especially when if I'm playing with someone like Tony.

But before the days of pickups and amps, Paul went to Rudy's on weekends to figure out how to get the bass sound right when recording with Miles. Otherwise, when Red played the piano, you wouldn't hear Paul's bass. So if you listen carefully here, you don't hear the bass drum prominently, but you do hear Philly Joe's cymbals, and Red is recorded more in the background, so you can hear Paul. From this point on, Rudy understood how to record the bass. He set the standard for recording bass on disc. That still holds true 50 years later.

Paul's bass is so present here, but he's not playing 1-3-5, but 9s and 11s and flat 5s. If you investigate his bass lines, you'd increase your awareness of playing harmonically. You can hear the warmth of his bass, and notice there's the snare and high hat, but no bass drum, and the piano is laying out.

This band of Miles sounded so great because of the rhythms. This made an impact. It was landmark. The rhythm section was taking charge of the music.

So, when I joined Miles, I knew that I wouldn't be playing rote. I also knew from his reputation that he liked to change styles. So, I knew it would be a learning experience. I didn't know how long it would take, but I felt like something important was going to happen.

2. Ron on the Music of Miles's '60s Quintet

"Nefertiti," composed by Wayne Shorter, from the Columbia Records album, *Nefertiti*, recorded at Columbia 30th Street Studio in 1967 (Miles Davis, trumpet; Wayne Shorter, tenor saxophone; Herbie Hancock piano; Ron Carter, bass; Tony Williams, drums)

YOU CAN HEAR Herbie being so comfortable with my bass line. You can hear my single notes that he then uses to comp. He trusts the melody and my single-note time. All I have to do is play one note to get that trust to let him know that all my notes will be OK. Rather than ignore my bass line— go over it or through it or play in spite of it—Herbie uses it. In fact, he's relying on it. When a piano player is comfortable developing an accompanying figure around the bass player's bass line, then you have a chance to play some good music.

At the beginning I'm playing a triplet figure. Tony picks up a phrase that complements it—to make my bass line work with his line rather than erase it or ignore it or wash it out by sheer volume. He can also insert my triplet pattern four choruses later. Again, if Tony does those kinds of things, you have a chance to play good music.

This song was recorded three years into the band's history, so we all were comfortable with each other and we trusted each other's judgments. Wayne is playing a moaning line on top of what the rhythm section is doing. I treated it like a chorale. That's the feeling I tried to bring to it and you can hear Herbie playing some semi-somber chords through it.

When we recorded this, we probably didn't do more than two takes. And with this song, we never developed it live, to see where it might have evolved. I would have loved the chance to play this tune night after night to see what we were missing in it. We would have been able to use the rhythm section to figure that out. I could have presented everyone in the band with some serious musical options.

That's how everyone in this band had equal footing with Miles. And we were following in his tradition of letting the rhythm section be more active.

CHAPTER EIGHT

The Miles Years, Part 3: After the Breakup

SEVEN YEARS AFTER Ron left Miles's employ, he was asked by *DownBeat* writer Arnold Jay Smith, in the magazine's March 27, 1975 issue, what were the rewards of playing with Miles? Ron curtly answered, "People often assume that everyone learns from Miles, but they never reverse the situation to ask what Miles learns from the players he hires. I feel that we both gleaned a lot of knowledge from our relationship."

At the time, Ron was in the midst of firmly establishing his own identity as a bandleader on CTI Records and focusing on shifting his priorities away from being a sideman. He added, "All of us—Tony, Herbie, Wayne—are trying not to have to answer for [Miles] any longer, now that we're not connected with him and trying to get our own personalities off the ground."

Around the same time Ron was being queried about his Quintet experience, Miles was shutting down his operation—due to ill health, being strung out on a toxic cocktail of booze and cocaine, and expressing an overall malaise with the music industry. He had suffered through the indignity of having his electric band open for Herbie's plugged-in and immensely popular Headhunters band in 1974 and '75, and finally decided to lay down his horn for an extended hiatus that lasted until 1980. Meanwhile, his former Quintet members were thriving in their own leadership roles as well as occasionally performing together.

In his autobiography, Miles remembered the end of the Quintet as he was ramping up to explore the Jimi-meets-Sly world of jazz fusion: "The group disbanded sometime in late 1968. We continued to play gigs and sometimes made some concerts together—at least Herbie, Wayne, Tony and I did—but for all intents and purposes the group broke up when Ron decided to leave for good because he didn't want to play electric bass. Herbie had already recorded 'Watermelon Man' and wanted to form a group of his own. Tony felt the same way. So they both left the group at the end of 1968. Wayne stayed with me a couple of years longer."

In early 1968, Ron began to see the writing on the wall in regard to his involvement with Miles. "Clearly, he was headed in another direction that didn't interest me," Ron said. "We'd been together for five years as a group, but going into the electronic stuff made me realize that my time was up. Also, I was becoming comfortable with my freelance operation, which meant that I had to miss some of Miles's gigs."

Ron's final hurrah with the band took place in San Francisco at the Both/And club. It was a two-week date from April 23 to May 5. "I almost didn't make that gig," Ron said. "It was after he didn't pay us right away for that show in Montreal. So I told Miles that this was the last trip to California that I was going to make with him. I told him I wanted to stay at home and be with my kids. I was going to miss Tony and Herbie and Wayne, but it was time for me to stay home. Miles said OK. He understood."

Once the band returned to New York, Ron continued to record with Miles through June, but on electric bass. Meanwhile, Dave Holland was in the wings.

During Ron's Quintet days, he always had his family in mind by sending money home from the road to pay his bills. During the famous Plugged Nickel live recording dates, he commuted from Chicago to New York for two nights because of the birth of his second son Myles. "It was important to me to have time with the new baby and give Janet some kind of rest," he said. "So, after the night's last set I took a plane from Chicago to New York, and then at seven the next night, I boarded a plane heading back to Chicago to play. I didn't worry about the lack of sleep. I wanted to show love for my family as well as keep my commitment to the band. Besides, I knew this schedule was only temporary."

On other occasions, Ron would return home from three-set gigs at three in the morning. On the way, he'd stop at Sherman's, an all-night barbeque joint on 146th Street and 7th Avenue, buy some chicken and ribs, bring it home and wake up the kids for an early breakfast. "Let's just say that Janet didn't like the idea of waking up the kids so that I could play with them," he said. "It was OK with me, but it was disrupting their sleeping schedule."

In 1968, Ron Jr. was 6 and Myles was 3, formative years when Ron wanted to be paternally present. "Back then, the school system was a mess in New York, especially for African-American kids," he said. "Janet was very active in PTA and school-district meetings, and she was doing all the work. It seemed out of balance with me being gone so much. Plus, New York was bursting with a variety of recording activities, which meant that I could work at home."

Herbie left Miles not long after Ron. He, too, was eager to return to his solo career as a leader. But his move from the working band was hastened in August when, newly married and honeymooning in Brazil, he got sick from food poisoning and had to delay his trip home. As a result, he missed a gig. When Miles heard that Herbie would be delayed, he enlisted Chick Corea, on Tony's recommendation. The once solid Quintet was in flux, adding two new players. "There was an evolutionary change going on," Herbie said. "Miles knew I was going to leave, but once he realized that

Chick could do the job, he had his agent, Jack Whittemore, inform me that it would be easier if I left right then." Even though he was angry with Miles for his punitive action, Herbie made his exit and said, "It proved to be the best thing I could have done. I left with my pride intact."

Herbie recorded a few albums after leaving Miles's working band, including a trio of exploratory funk-to-avant-to-electronic albums that have been compiled as *Mwandishi: The Complete Warner Bros. Recordings*. Then, in 1972 he founded the Headhunters, one of the best jazz fusion bands at the time.

Tony, meanwhile, stuck it out with Miles until early 1969. Being the youngest member of the Quintet, he was the most attuned to the pop and rock music that was percolating on the scene during the band's existence. "I was tuning into Jimi Hendrix and Cream and bands like that," he told me in our 1996 conversation. "Of course, I had always loved the Beatles. Hey, it was 1964 and I was 18. You can't expect an 18-year-old to not be paying attention to what all other 18-year-old kids were listening to."

Even when Tony was younger and playing in jazz bands in clubs at night, he hung out after school with his friends and listened to the pop acts of the day like Fats Domino, the Drifters, the Flamingos and the Everly Brothers. "I was always a person of my own generation," he said. "When I was with Miles, everybody else in the band was older than I was. But that didn't stop me from telling them all about the Beatles and Hendrix. At the time, they didn't particularly think much about that music or pay much attention to it."

As far back as 1965, Tony suggested to Miles that the Quintet open a Beatles tour. That never got off the ground, but it planted a seed with Miles. In 1968 he began to become very interested in the popular music of the day—partly out of necessity because jazz's star was waning in the face of the new pop tsunami, and partly because he began to envision his own music heading into the controversial direction of fusing jazz with rock.

But after leaving the Quintet, Tony beat Miles to the punch, becoming a pioneer in his own right by breaking new jazz-rock ground with his band Lifetime. The trio, comprised of guitarist John McLaughlin (soon to become a member of Miles's new band) and organist Larry Young, played a thunderous brew of intense, electric improvised music. "Toward the end of my time with Miles, around 1967 and 1968, my playing became more and more aggressive," Tony said. "There was more power to it. So, it became natural for me to go from playing straight jazz to doing the rock thing."

Wayne played one more year with Miles before teaming up with keyboardist Joe Zawinul and bassist Miroslav Vitous (both Miles alums) to form the top-drawer fusion band Weather Report. The most stable of the Quintet members, Wayne's five years with Miles had made him, as a sideman, the leader's musical catalyst. After Wayne departed, Miles blew through a series of saxophonists—five in as many years.

RON AND MILES, POST-QUINTET

MILES KNEW RON loved him, says trumpeter Wallace Roney, who was mentored by Miles in the last few years of the bandleader's life. "Miles believed that a permanent member of his band was supposed to be on call," Wallace said. "If a gig comes up, you have to leave what you're doing and come with me. He knew that Ron was a man of his word, and he liked that. But when Ron committed himself to someone else, he hated it."

Miles was not happy that Ron didn't want to continue with him on his journey, Wallace said. "He wanted Ron to play the electric bass, which is what ended their relationship. That's unfortunate because Ron did so much for him, he had his back, he was the straw boss."

During the Quintet days, Miles would invite Ron to his house, but Ron would only visit half the time. "I felt it was good to keep a distance from the bandleader," he said. "I never saw it personally, but I had heard all the stories about Miles being discourteous and trying to dominate people. I didn't want him feeling like I was dependent on his presence and existence."

After his finale with Miles, Ron would visit him from time to time, especially after 1973, when he and his family moved to West End Avenue not far from Miles's West 73rd Street brownstone. Miles loved Ron's kids, who often came with their dad. "I remember Miles as just a friend of the family," Ron Jr. said. "It wasn't like he was Uncle Miles or anything like that. But I do remember playing on his big lion skin rug. It even had a head."

Ron says they sometimes talked about music when he visited, or when Miles was sick, he got takeout at a Cuban restaurant on 77th and Broadway for him. They also watched boxing matches on TV. "Miles had a great collection of old fights on video," Ron said. "He had Joe Louis fights from 1949, '52, '53. But the screen of his television was terrible. The colors were all mixed up."

Ron asked Miles, "How can you watch that?"

Miles replied, "I'm watching the punches."

"But Miles, they're all the wrong colors."

Miles shrugged it off and continued to watch the punches.

Miles had a gym built in the basement of his house where he worked out, or sometimes he'd go to a gym downtown and box. His boxing instructor used to come to the shows. "I'm convinced that because Miles was in such decent shape he was able to delay his body from decaying because of substance abuse," Ron said. "You can't do things and not pay a price, but I believe his relative longevity had to do with his physical conditioning. Miles's body was always toned."

MILES ALUMS—RON'S GROUPS

WHILE THE QUINTET members scattered to work on their own careers, there were many instances when they came back together in a variety of combinations, all sans Miles. In the mid-'70s, during his CTI Records and Milestone Records years, Ron often hooked up with his rhythm teammates, Herbie and Tony. In 1973, he enlisted them for a band that played a series of four West Coast concerts under the banner of "An Evening With Ron Carter & Friends."

Produced by Ron's brother-in-law, Ken Huggins, the concerts were staged at large indoor and outdoor venues seating as many as 2,500 people, including the Hollywood Bowl, Santa Barbara's County Bowl and Oakland Coliseum (a show was also produced in San Diego). In addition to Ron, Herbie and Tony, the band consisted of Hubert Laws on flute and Stanley Turrentine on tenor saxophone, with Freddie Hubbard on trumpet for the Hollywood Bowl show.

At the Hollywood Bowl, Ron played a solo version of "Willow Weep for Me" while Hubert also went solo for "Amazing Grace." Tony's drums were typically punched with raucous polyrhythms while Herbie played acoustic piano throughout.

Ron, Herbie and Tony played as a trio on Ron's excellent *Third Plane* album in 1977, his third disc for Milestone, as well as on the rare *1 + 3* album, recorded live in Japan in 1978 and never released stateside.

At a live *DownBeat* Blindfold Test—a listening experience where musicians are asked to guess the performers of a certain piece of music as well as reflect on the performance—that I hosted at the North Sea Jazz Festival in 2008, I played the tune "Lawra" from *Third Plane* for the members of the jazz trio, The Bad Plus. Here are their responses to the track:

> **Drummer Dave King:** "This is *Third Plane*, with Ron Carter, Tony Williams and Herbie Hancock. The song is 'Lawra.'"
>
> **Pianist Ethan Iverson:** "It's written by Tony."
>
> **Dave** (joking): "Wayne actually went out to get some Sunny Delight. Everyone knows he loves Sunny D. He came back to the studio at the end of the tune. You can actually listen with headphones and hear him say, 'What is this shit?'"
>
> **Bassist Reid Anderson:** "I had no idea what this was at first. Ethan knew. I didn't know the music, but from the first bass note I knew it was Ron, and then there was Tony, and then Herbie came in after a few notes. This sound is something a lot of jazz musicians talk about. This certain period of jazz from the '70s has a completely different sound, especially with the bass when people started using a pickup. It's remarkable how great Ron sounds with it. It had become a taboo thing to do. Everyone hated that direct bass sound at first. But Ron really transitioned from the acoustic recording of the '60s with Miles into this. It's testimony to his musicianship and the power of his playing."

Dave: "The same holds true for Tony's drumming with those kick drums and those great floor toms. I love it. Ethan and I got totally into this Tony Williams period. We listen to him, and we're cheering him on."

Ethan: "My opinion is that whenever you have Ron and Tony together, it almost doesn't matter what the song is. It's going to be pretty good. They had a very special relationship. I don't think this is one of their best recordings. I'd be surprised if they thought that. But there's still that special vibe."

In his Bad Plus Web site blog, Ethan wrote that he much prefers Ron's *Etudes* album that he recorded in 1982 for Elektra/Musician (with Tony, but not Herbie): "This may be [Ron's] best record as a leader. His cute, singsong approach as composer benefits from not having a piano, and Ron and Tony together are flamboyantly fabulous."

In an interview with *DownBeat*'s Lee Jeske in the magazine's July 1983 issue, Ron explained why he recorded *Etudes*: "I like playing without a piano. If the pianist that's available is not Herbie Hancock or somebody of that type, it's almost necessary to play without one." Ron said that years earlier, during some time off from gigging with Miles, he, Wayne and Tony played three nights at a small club in Boston. "It's one of my fondest memories. I decided that at some point if I could get the kind of situation that would allow me to make a whole record without a piano, I'd try to do it. So [*Etudes*] seemed like a good chance."

Wayne was originally scheduled to play tenor sax on the album that also featured Art Farmer on flugelhorn, but cancelled at the last minute because of another engagement. Young saxophonist Bill Evans took his place. Ethan said, "[Bill] told me that it was all done in first takes. It took them from 11 in the morning to 12:30 in the afternoon, and then they had lunch."

Ron was an original member of Roland Hanna's New York Jazz Quartet, founded in 1972 with Hubert Laws on flute and Billy Cobham on drums. The group recorded its first albums, two volumes of *In Concert in Japan* on the Japanese Salvation label, in 1975 at Kaiken Hall in Toyko with Frank Wess on flute and Ben Riley on drums. Ron left the group (replaced by George Mraz for the rest of the band's history, which lasted until 1982) to devote time to the Great Jazz Trio, with Tony and pianist Hank Jones. It was jumpstarted by Tony and made its debut at the Village Vanguard in New York. Vanguard owner Max Gordon gave the super trio its name.

Even though Hank proved to be that trio's center of gravity during its years of fluctuating lineups, Ron and Tony were front and center for a series of live recordings in 1977 at the Vanguard: *At the Village Vanguard*, *At the Village Vanguard Vol. 2* and *At the Village Vanguard Again* (originally released on the Inner City label, now reissued by 441 Records imprint Test of Time). The two rhythm aces were also featured on such Great Jazz Trio dates as 1978's *New Wine in Old Bottles* (East Wind Records, now on Test of Time), featuring guest alto saxophonist and onetime Tony mentor, Jackie McLean, and on three dates with Japanese alto saxophonist Sadao Watanabe, 1976's *I'm Old Fashioned* (Inner City), 1977's *Bird of Passage* (Elektra) and 1983's *Carnaval* (Galaxy).

V.S.O.P.

VERY SPECIAL ONETIME-ONLY Performance. That's how Herbie's management billed a retrospective of his career in 1976 at the Newport Jazz Festival that was held in New York City. Three groups performed: his fusion-oriented Mwandishi sextet, a reunion of the plugged-in Headhunters and an acoustic group of Miles ex-pats—Ron, Tony and Wayne, accompanied by Freddie Hubbard who filled in for the indisposed leader. "People enjoyed the show, especially the Miles group," said Herbie, "It resonated with so many people that we decided to go on tour, which we called V.S.O.P."

The 1977 V.S.O.P. tour played in 16 U.S. cities, then went to Tokyo, the Montreux Jazz Festival and a corporate convention of Columbia/CBS Records in London. In an era when fusion dominated the jazz scene, V.S.O.P. proved to be a breath of fresh acoustic air.

At the time, in an interview in the tabloid newspaper *The Happenings* (in Berkeley, California), Ron said, "I wanted to go on tour as a part of V.S.O.P. for two reasons. First, of course, there's the music. That alone would be enticing enough. But from a professional standpoint, I felt that the exposure from that tour would be an asset to my own career, that new listeners would be attracted to my own quartet."

Still, Ron was encouraged by a movement afoot. The V.S.O.P. tour was "the first major indication that people today are willing and eager to investigate acoustic jazz," he said at the time. "I feel a definite responsibility to present a musically viable alternative. I listen to and enjoy all kinds of music, from the top popular stations to the symphonies. But my heart is right here with acoustic jazz."

In a preview article on V.S.O.P.'s date in Chicago for the *Chicago Daily News*, Howard Mandel wrote a profile of Herbie and his decision to buck the fusion tide by playing an all-acoustic set. (Howard identified the band with full paragraphs on Herbie, Freddie, Wayne and Tony, but neglected to go into detail about Ron.) In the article, Herbie said that even though all five members were leaders in their own right, egos were in check. "We all have a great amount of respect for each other, as people and as musicians. Nobody is going to have to take tight reins. We had no problems at Newport last year. Leadership will pass from one to the next; we'll be depending on each other more, and responding."

Reflecting on the communal nature of the music the Miles Quintet enjoyed, Herbie added, "Any one of us has enough musical sense to lead the whole band at any given time, which takes the burden of leadership off any one person. It would be wrestling with four tigers for any one of us to try to upstage the others."

Looking back at those days today, Herbie still expresses an enthusiasm for the band's existence. "It was just so great for us to be back together," he said. "It was like our time with Miles, but we had all evolved as individual players as well as human beings. We discovered when we got back together that we were almost like a sacred brotherhood—that we got to learn the secrets from the master, Miles. When we were all together, but without Miles, we interacted, we flowed, we developed the skills we had learned earlier. We weren't bound by the exact sound of Miles, but the audience enjoyed it, the musicians enjoyed it, even though the leader was only there in spirit."

The V.S.O.P. tour proved to be so successful that the group landed on the cover of *Newsweek* magazine on August 8 with the headline, "Jazz Comes Back." The story posited that jazz was making a comeback after years of being trumped by rock in popularity. V.S.O.P. was cited as one of many acts leading the charge with sold-out shows that featured revitalized versions of such tunes as Wayne's "Nefertiti" and Herbie's "Maiden Voyage."

Herbie was excited, Ron was having fun, but Wayne, in retrospect, waxed philosophical. "It was OK, but it was different than our time with Miles," he said. "When you try to go back in time, you can try to imitate yourself, but that's like an invitation to pantomime. But V.S.O.P. was a demonstration to the younger wave that 'it was something like this.'"

The V.S.O.P. ride continued for many years, with the young Wynton Marsalis even touring with the band in 1981. Many of the live albums were released exclusively in Japan. A two-LP album that garnered a five-star review in *DownBeat*, *The Quintet* was a live California date released in the U.S. in 1977 by Columbia. (While the entire group was playing at UC Berkeley's Greek Theater during the tour, Herbie, Ron and Tony gathered in a studio in San Francisco and recorded the album *Herbie Hancock Trio*.)

V.S.O.P. also recorded its 1977 tour date in Tokyo, *Tempest in the Colosseum*. After the members took a break from the group to attend to their individual projects, the quintet reunited in 1979 and returned to the Denon Colosseum to record two more nights of kinetic acoustic jazz. The shows were documented on *V.S.O.P.: Live Under the Sky*, a two-CD set that was released in the U.S. for the first time in 2006 by Columbia/Legacy. (Even though V.S.O.P. could not score a substantive tour in the U.S. at the time because of the recording industry slump, Japan welcomed the band and even broadcast the shows live on prime-time TV.)

V.S.O.P.: Live Under the Sky featured the state-of-the-art sound technology of the day. "We were recording digitally for the first time and those digital tapes captured the delicate sound of the raindrops that threatened to ruin the concert," Herbie said. "Quite the contrary, the music was so special that night that the audience felt the urge to band together as a force to defy the threat of the raindrops."

Writing in the liner notes, Herbie reflected, "I will never, ever forget the concert of the V.S.O.P. group the night we recorded ... It was a phenomenal evening ... [The audience] asked for three encores that night. Before the last encore, everyone in the band was so tired that we all said, 'No, no, we're not going out to play another one.' [But] Wayne and I had just a few more ounces of energy left, so we decided that we would play the final encore. It turned out to be an apt closing for the evening. What a night that was."

Each evening's show was launched with Herbie's explosive "Eye of the Hurricane" and continued with an array of tunes that blended elements of '40s bebop, '50s modality and '60s free jazz. The "freebop" concerts exhibited tunes by all band members except, oddly, Wayne. Herbie led the way into his grooved "Domo," Freddie contributed the highly charged and swinging "One of a Kind" (dedicated to Miles), Ron brought to the sets the lyrical "Fragile" and "Tear Drops," and Tony delivered rhythmic sophistication on two of his compositions, "Para Oriente" and "Pee Wee." On the second CD, Wayne and Herbie ended the show on a sublime note, improvising as a duo on two balladic gems, "Stella by Starlight" and "On Green Dolphin Street."

"The two concerts reflected not only the energy and inspiration of the audience, but the mutual love for one another that these musicians shared," said reissue co-producer Bob Belden. "This was a band that played together, surprising themselves with each new chorus. You could say that V.S.O.P. was a release from the tensions each musician acquired from running their own band. V.S.O.P. provided a compositional forum that the musicians exploited to the fullest."

A TRIBUTE TO MILES

WAYNE REMEMBERS THAT Miles, when he was invisible on the scene, would sometimes call him up in the middle of the night. "He'd play something on his trumpet and ask me if I liked it," Wayne said. "I knew then that the old Model T was cranking up to go out again." Miles broke his silence in 1980 and hit the road with a new band. Wayne would occasionally talk with him over the next several years. "He wanted to try something all together again after all of our experiences apart from him, to have another gathering to see what would come about."

At Montreux in 1990, Wayne's group shared a bill with Miles. Wayne went on first, and Miles was there checking out the band. Wayne said, "Miles asked me, 'Why don't we go on tour together, both our bands?' But we never got to discuss that again." It was one of Wayne's last conversations with Miles, who died in September 28, 1991 in Santa Monica, California.

The V.S.O.P. quintet arose again, this time with Wallace Roney, who was mentored by Miles, playing trumpet. He had also played with Tony's quintet, which had encouraged Miles, who told Wallace, "I know you can play since you're playing with Tony, 'cause Tony don't like any other trumpet player 'cept me." Wallace had made the trip to Montreux in the summer of 1991 for Miles's historic return-to-cool big-band outing conducted by Quincy Jones, and even got a chance to join his hero onstage.

Wallace was offered the opportunity to play with the rest of the Quintet when they decided to go on a worldwide tour for six months to pay tribute to Miles. "I got to play with the four greatest artists who ever lived," he said. "I remember Ron loosening up the groove and Herbie and Tony joining in, and all of sudden a tune would take shape."

At the tribute band's performance at Berkeley Community Theater, the tapes were rolling. Two of Miles's tunes from *Kind of Blue*, "So What" and "All Blues," were keepers for the album, *A Tribute to Miles*, recorded in 1992 and released in 1994 on Qwest/Reprise. Also featured on the CD were two of Ron's compositions, "R.J." and "Eighty-One," that had originally appeared on the Miles album *E.S.P.* in 1965. *A Tribute to Miles* won a Grammy Award for Best Instrumental Performance, Individual or Group.

Tony said that he was exhausted after all the traveling. "I took a year out of my life to do that tour," he said. "But it was an opportunity to pay tribute to Miles. It was a lot of work, but unfortunately I had to do it. I wish he hadn't died." In the CD liner notes, Tony added, "So, in our small way we offer this music, that for us recalls the essence of our love for Miles Davis. He left us much too soon."

In one interview, Ron replied to a reporter who observed that the tribute renderings of Miles's library were radically different: "Absolutely. The urgency is still present. That's really what's remarkable."

4 GENERATIONS OF MILES

WRITER CHIP STERN echoes Ron's words in the liner notes to the Chesky Records' *4 Generations of Miles* CD that was recorded and released in 2002: "Like the sons of Gabriel before him, Miles's immense body of work continues to yield fresh insights and epiphanies…. Even in divine repose, the Prince of Darkness exerts a profound influence on 21st Century music, as the trumpeter's numerous collaborators, acolytes and stunt doubles carry forth and extend upon his vision."

The concept behind the album, produced by David Chesky (and executive produced by his brother Norman Chesky), was to gather four Miles alums from various periods—and styles—in his career to play tunes from the maestro's library. The original version of the made-for-CD group comprised drummer Jimmy Cobb (from *Kind of Blue* and Miles's early '60s groups), tenor saxophonist George Coleman (from the early stage of the '60s Quintet), guitarist Mike Stern (from one of Miles's '80s electric bands) and Ron.

"I don't know whose idea it was to bring the four of us together," Ron said. "Probably the record company that wanted to make an audiophile record. We recorded live at Makor, which is a nice space [on West 69th Street between Central Park West and Columbus Avenue] with low ceilings. I tend to avoid these kinds of things, but I like playing with Jimmy. Of course, I knew George. But I had never played with Mike before. He sounded good on records, so I thought it might be interesting to see how it feels to play with him."

Stern wrote that the music (consisting primarily of Miles's '60s music) was the binding force that allowed the four players to "run the voodoo down." He added, "How else to explain the depth and ease with which these four generations of Miles Davis alumni forge such an immutable, intimate, instantaneous bond with each other?"

Ron begs to differ, labeling the gig as simply OK. What didn't he like? "First, I'm not sure if we had enough time before the recording to talk about concepts," he said. "Mike plays real different from George, and Jimmy plays real different from Mike. Everyone is a valid player, but I thought that we didn't have enough time to talk, which meant we didn't dig as deep as we could have. Paying tribute to Miles requires a lot of responsibility."

While Ron was pleased with the sound quality of the recording, he was hesitant to endorse the personnel chemistry. Intimate, instantaneous? Not quite.

After the album was released, the group played a week at the Blue Note in New York. Ron doesn't go into detail, but he and George experienced friction. "George would take his solo and then back up into my bass," Ron said. "I asked him to not do that, and he got upset."

On the first night of the week, Ron said Mike's amp was turned to "stun," which, in such a shallow audience space as the Blue Note, posed a problem. "On the stage we tried to get as close as we could to hear each other, but Mike's amp was pretty far away from him," Ron said. "He had it turned up so he could hear it. But I told him to turn it down. He was used to playing in electric bands, so I guess he felt having the volume high made him comfortable. But in a band with an upright bass and a drummer like Jimmy who's great with brushes, he was just too loud."

Ron asked Mike to lower the volume to "try to fit into the zone of the rest of the band. It wasn't a personal attack and I wasn't trying to criticize his playing. And I didn't call him out in front of his friends. I just talked to him and said, 'Hey, we've got six nights to try to play some good music.'"

Mike agreed to turn his amp down.

But Mike's attire on opening night also rankled Ron. "Let's put it this way, he was pretty casual," he said, and then added, "Jeans and sneakers. There's Jimmy in a nice sports outfit, George is dressed well and I'm wearing a custom-made suit, shirt, tie and shoes. So I told Mike the way he was dressed was not OK with me."

Ron recalls playing with Miles. One of the first things the bandleader did when he assembled the quintet was to have the entire band go to a tailor in New York to get outfitted for his gigs. The band presentation, Ron says, not only commands respect for the musicians but also signals appreciation for the audience attending a show. Plus, he said, the visual appearance of a jazz band has a tradition, stretching back to the days of Duke Ellington, Count Basie and Louis Armstrong.

So, Ron gave Mike an ultimatum: show up the next night in a dark jacket or the following night the band bassist would be staying home. "My view is that we should be dressed like we're going to work," Ron said. "Not like we're coming in from a baseball field. I told Mike I understood there were different schools of thought on this, but I let him know that he was in my school for the week and that changing his attire was going to make me feel OK with this gig."

At first Mike thought Ron was joking, but quickly realized that he meant business. The next night he showed up in a dark sports coat. Ron told him, "Mike, dressing like this doesn't make you play better, but it makes you look like you're playing better."

Needless to say, the 4 Generations band with the original lineup was short-lived. Ron says it was a good experience, but he wanted to focus on his own projects. Since then, the band continues to play its club tributes to Miles, with Jimmy and Mike in place along with different Miles alum members Sonny Fortune and Buster Williams, on saxophone and bass respectively.

MILES IN THE HOUSE

IN THE FIRST years of the new century, each Miles Quintet member was focused on individual projects that seldom found them collaborating. Rarely would they cross paths, although Ron annually called his former band mates around Christmas time to wish them well. Ron waves off reports of misunderstandings, although Wallace remembers hearing about a session of Herbie's that involved Ron on a track. "Ron came to the studio at 10 in the evening, and Herbie didn't show up until one in the morning," Wallace said. "Then Herbie immediately began writing an arrangement that took a while. Finally at two, Ron packed up his bass and left. Ron was upset that his time was being wasted, and Herbie felt spiteful. He held it against Ron for a long time."

But Wallace noted the two talked and mended their fences which led to Ron being a part of the JVC Jazz Festival New York "Herbie's World" show at Carnegie Hall on June 23, 2006. It was a four-ring affair, with Herbie performing duets with Gonzalo Rubalcaba; leading a quartet with Wayne, Dave Holland and Brian Blade; fronting a quintet with Richie Barshay, Lionel Loueke, Matt Garrison and Lili Hayden and guest bassist Marcus Miller; and helming a trio with Jack DeJohnette and Ron.

At the band rehearsals the day before at Carroll Music on midtown Manhattan's west side, Ron and Jack were already there when Herbie arrived, on time. As they ran through possible tunes to perform the next night, Ron and Herbie immediately hooked up and began to concoct new chemical experiments. Ron surprised Herbie with his note choices, which led to Herbie echoing and responding to what Ron played. They had eye contact for much of the rehearsal and exchanged smiles and laughter as if they seemed to pick up from where they had left off the last time they played together.

The trio rehearsal buoyed with another surprise: the appearance of saxophonist Michael Brecker, who was battling MDS (myelodysplastic syndrome), a rare form of cancer where the bone marrow stops producing healthy blood cells. He had experienced several ups and downs in his two-year battle fighting the cancer, but was unable to find a suitable donor for a blood stem cell and bone marrow transplant. Herbie had called Michael and asked if he would like to sit in with the trio. Michael replied that he would if he felt strong enough on one of his "good days."

Sporting a New York Yankees baseball cap, Michael arrived at the rehearsal room with his tenor saxophone. He walked in with a cane, sat down and listened to the trio practice. Several times he raised his eyebrows in amazement at the improvisation. Herbie asked him if he wanted to play, and Michael responded that this would be the first time in 15 months that he had blown his saxophone.

The foursome sped through Herbie's tune "One Finger Snap" with Michael blowing his horn fiercely. The room was on fire. Afterwards Herbie asked, "Are you sure you haven't played in 15 months?" Michael nodded and said later that he was feeling a little better. As for his display of tenor magic, he told me, "Usually when I'm playing a lot, I fall back on certain ways of playing. Today there was none of that. I had to think in the moment."

He did so at Carnegie Hall also. Unsure if he would be able to attend, there was no announcement about his joining the Herbie-Ron-Jack trio. But it was another good day, as Herbie told the audience that the next song they were going to play required a saxophonist. He jokingly asked if there were any in the house, which was Michael's cue to emerge from the wings.

Ben Ratliff, reviewing the show in *The New York Times*, wrote that Michael "looked slightly tired but otherwise gave it his all, playing long, tumultuous lines at full strength through ['One Finger Snap']."

"Michael walked out and had this smile," said Jack. "He was looking at the ceiling. The place went crazy. It was a great morale booster for him."

"It was one of those memorable days of musical history," Ron said. "Like what happened when Hank Aaron hit his 715th homerun, more people will say they were there than the hall could actually fit."

Michael went home in pain after the show, rallied in August to gather a crew of musicians (including Jack and Herbie) to record what would be his final album (*Pilgrimage*) and died on January 13, 2007.

The success of "Herbie's World" led to the JVC Festival presenting Ron the next year at Carnegie Hall with his own four-set affair (see Carnegie Hall chapter). He partnered once again with Herbie and Wayne (his first collaboration with the latter in several years), along with Billy Cobham on drums. It was an evening tribute to Ron that Wayne said was "on time but overdue." He explained, "It was not waiting until it's too late. Ron is an inspiration." As for the Miles-heavy set list they performed, Wayne said, "It's an outgrowth of those moments we had and the appreciation we have for one another." He paused and then noted, "Ron said that night that Miles was in the house. It's true. There are many times when I can feel Miles."

DEAR MILES

IN THE OCTOBER 1981 issue of a publication titled *Jazz*, pianist/educator Reginald Buckner interviewed Ron, beginning with questions about V.S.O.P. and concluding with a discussion on black student enrollment in jazz appreciation classes. In the middle of the rather tense Q&A session, Buckner asked Ron, "Would you comment on the experience of working with Miles Davis?"

Ron replied, "I never discuss that!!"

"Oh, not even what musical growth might have occurred?"

"I graciously avoid it if I can, for a whole set of reasons that would take up your whole tape if I were to answer."

End of topic. On to the next subject.

But the short and brusque exchange highlights what Ron no doubt was forever dealing with: his association with Miles that at that time, even more than a decade after the Quintet broke up, threatened to eclipse his own successful career as a leader.

It wasn't until 2006 that Ron finally decided to take the reins and give Miles his due with his album *Dear Miles*, released in 2007 by Blue Note Records (see chapter on Blue Note Records) a year after its debut in Japan and just two weeks before Ron's triumphant Carnegie Hall performance. As much an homage to Miles as it was a showcase for Ron's own quartet, the album was a long time in coming. Ron told me for my *Billboard* "Jazz Notes" column, "Until now, I wasn't ready to do an album like this for fear of getting swallowed up by the Miles aura. But since this expresses my band's personality, it's as much a tribute to them as to Miles."

COLLOQUY

Rudy Van Gelder on Ron Carter

In jazz, the RVG brand has mighty clout and speaks multiple volumes on sonic purity. It's no surprise that both the Blue Note and Prestige record labels today deliver classic RVG CD remastered series.

The man behind the abbreviation is Rudy Van Gelder, the sound engineer who revolutionized the way jazz is recorded, beginning in 1954 in his parents' living room in Hackensack, New Jersey, and continuing in his own studio in Englewood Cliffs, New Jersey, from 1959 to the present. He recorded all the jazz greats who made first-class discs for all the important in-the-day indies such as Blue Note, Prestige, Impulse!, Verve and CTI.

"Rudy defined the way several generations expect to hear jazz," said Michael Cuscuna, director of catalog for Blue Note and the impetus behind the label's RVG Series. "He's the one who got closest to the way jazz sounds live at front-row center. Most engineers in the '50s were timid and moved the microphones away from the musicians. Rudy miked up close, recorded with as much volume as possible to avoid hiss and got the power, clarity and individuality of all the players."

Freelance engineer Joe Ferla, who started recording in 1971 and has worked with a range of musicians from drummers Paul Motian and Bobby Previte to guitarists John Scofield and Charlie Hunter, sings Van Gelder's praise: "Rudy changed the way we perceive jazz recordings and the way engineers approach jazz."

Ron, who recorded many of his own albums as well as a myriad of session dates at Rudy's studio in Englewood Cliffs, said, "Rudy not only set, and maintained, the standard of jazz recordings, but he also set the standard for recording the acoustic bass."

In the Prestige remasters series, Rudy wrote in the liner notes: "I was the engineer on the recording sessions, and I also made the masters for the original LP issues of these albums. Since the advent of the CD, other people have been making the masters. Mastering is the final step in the process of creating the sound of the finished product. Now...I have been given the opportunity to remaster these albums, [and] I can present my versions of the music on CD using modern technology. I remember the sessions well, I remember how the musicians wanted to sound and I remember their reactions to the playbacks. Today, I feel strongly that I am their messenger."

In an e-mail interview regarding the dual series, Van Gelder explained that each label sends him the masters that he originally recorded. "First I examine the tapes to see if they're playable," he said. "Next step, I hook up a chain to do an analog transfer. Every tape is different, so I do a lot of listening."

When asked if he had any favorites for the Prestige sessions, at first Rudy said, "I can't have a favorite." Then he added, "But anything with Miles Davis is OK with me." Many of those sessions featured Paul Chambers on bass.

As for the Blue Note series, which included Ron on bass for many sessions, Rudy said, "They're all great music. I love them all, but Horace Silver is something special." Ron appeared on such Horace Blue Note albums as *Silver 'n Brass* (1975), *Silver 'n Wood* (1976), *Silver 'n Voices* (1977), *Silver 'n Percussion* (1978) and *Silver 'n Strings Play the Music of the Spheres* (1979).

Cuscuna said that when he first approached Rudy to revisit the Blue Note masters, he was met with hesitance. "Rudy was reticent to look to the past. But then it kicked in how much more he could do with the new equipment and what he had learned. He saw it as a challenge and opportunity. Rudy's given a new lease on life to some of these titles as he brings the music out of the tape."

In a *DownBeat* magazine interview, while reflecting on his past dates, Rudy declared, "Working with Creed Taylor was the most sonically rewarding of all of them. I started with Creed back in the Bethlehem days. Creed and I agreed pretty much as to what the sound would be, and we had great communication. He took my job beyond the five-piece bebop band to another level."

Regarding Ron, Rudy again chose to respond to e-mail questions.

Q: *Creed Taylor said that when Ron recorded for his CTI label the two of them and you got his sound right in a way that required very little conversation. How did you do this?*

RVG: Actually, Ron and I had been working on this for a long time. The way it worked was, Ron would come early before the dates, and we would experiment on getting the best possible bass sound. At the beginning of the bass pickup period, when there was an explosion of various devices to get the sound directly from the instrument, Ron had a direct line to at least one of the manufacturers. He would get their latest version, and he would bring it out to me. With a trial-and-error method, we would experiment to see which sounded the best. That process went on for a few years. So, as time progressed, the sound on one session would not be exactly the same as on another session.

Q: *How did you and Paul Chambers get his bass sound right?*

RVG: Paul Chambers required a whole different approach. Electronic pickups were not invented yet, so I proceeded on a different path. I tried to actually modify the bass itself to improve its recording characteristics. This led to my attaching various nonelectronic devices. On one album that I did for Eddie Bert, the trombone player, in the 1950s, the bass player was Clyde Lombardi. The liner notes said, "In order to get the full benefit of Clyde's rhythmic strength on these recordings, engineer Rudy Van Gelder put a mic on the bridge of the bass with a towel wrapped around it." I did variations of this with Paul Chambers.

Q: *How did you and Ron get his sound right? How was it similar to or different from the way you worked with Paul?*

RVG: The point is, they were both very cooperative and were willing to spend time with me as a friend, not an adversary. It didn't always work with other bass players, so every session was different. In those days the idea of a cable being attached to the bass was unfamiliar to the bass player. He would forget it was there, resulting in a situation where, at the end of a session, when everyone was about to go home, the bass player would pick up his instrument and start walking toward the door, trailing my cable behind him. Obviously he could only get so far. So I would dash out of the control room to catch him before the obvious occurred. One time the bass player managed to disconnect the cable but not my electronic device. I had to get his phone number and call him to remind him he had it. That only happened once.

Q: *In working with Miles Davis, what struck you about his bands and their sessions? How did you strike a balance with the rhythm team? What was Miles's response? What was he looking for and what were you looking for?*

RVG: That answer is easy. On all the Miles sessions, my ears and my eyes were focused on Miles. The groups that Miles brought in were always totally together. All I had to do was be aware of what Miles was doing and I was OK with that.

Q: *During the CTI days, what challenges did those sessions entail and how would Ron "anchor" a session?*

RVG: The [first] challenge was to make sure the toilet worked. The music in the CTI years was totally different. There was a lot going on instrumentally, but Creed was always conscious of the bass sound. For example, Deodato's *2001*. Ron always sounded great and made it easy for me.

Q: *What were some memorable sessions Ron was on and what did you see as his role?*

RVG: With regard to roles, I can only speak about mine. During those sessions, as in all sessions, my job is the audio. Memorable implies some time in the future, looking back. During the sessions, my thoughts are in the present. I have no way of knowing what will become memorable to other people while I'm recording it. I usually remember the sessions that sounded good. [I have] a list from my private files of recordings during the LP period that I made with Ron Carter playing bass. There are 105 entries. I'm really proud of that. (See discography in appendix.)

PART III
RECORDING AS A LEADER

CHAPTER NINE

The CTI Years: The Reign of Creed

IN 1960, RON had only been in New York for a year, but was already turning heads and opening ears, working with a variety of musicians, including arranger/composer/orchestra bandleader Gil Evans.

In that same year Creed Taylor was first introduced to the young bassist. A onetime trumpeter turned producer who eventually became an A&R head, Creed had started his impresario career with Bethlehem Records in 1954. Two years later he was hired as a staff producer by ABC-Paramount, the new label jointly owned by the American Broadcasting Company and Paramount Theaters. In 1960, Creed convinced the company to create a jazz imprint, Impulse!, which became home to many marquee jazz musicians, including Oliver Nelson, who recorded his classic album *The Blues and the Abstract Truth* there, and John Coltrane, who made his Impulse! debut with *Africa/Brass* and recorded there until his death in 1967.

One of the early recordings Creed supervised for the subsidiary was Gil Evans's *Out of the Cool*, a jazz-orchestra affair that grew out of Gil's multiweek gigs at New York clubs in which Ron participated. Even though the sessions, engineered by Rudy Van Gelder, were protracted—Creed told *DownBeat* they initially went for "four days without recording anything because Gil couldn't get it down on paper"—the producer experienced a revelation: Ron.

"I asked Gil why he had hired this bass player who I didn't know for the session," Creed said. "Gil said that this guy was amazing. Gil was a street person. He knew about everyone on the scene, and he told me you've got to hear this bass player. When I heard Ron, I was astounded. His sound and his awareness of how he should record were astonishing. He and I and Rudy worked together to get his sound right in a way that required very little conversation."

Creed also got an inkling of "what makes Ron tick." He said, "It's what he contributes to a record date. He hears the music in a certain way and moves with it. He would steer things in different directions. Gil loved that. He loved people taking charge at certain moments and playing a phrase in a certain way."

Thus began Ron's association with Creed, who left Impulse! to run Verve in 1961 after founder Norman Granz sold his label to MGM. It was there that, among many other accomplishments, Creed helped to usher in the bossa nova craze with the Stan Getz/João Gilberto album, *Getz/Gilberto*, which featured the classic tune "The Girl From Ipanema."

Then, in 1967, Creed officially linked up with A&M Records, owned by Herb Alpert and Jerry Moss. The following year, Creed formed his own boutique label—CTI, which stands for Creed Taylor, Inc.—under the A&M umbrella. Creed's first major hit was *A Day in the Life* by guitarist Wes Montgomery, who had followed the producer from Verve to his new label. The pop-styled recording (the title track was from the Beatles' *Sergeant Pepper's Lonely Hearts Club Band* album) earned Wes the only gold disc of his career.

In 1970, Creed launched CTI as an independent label that spun off the soul-jazz subsidiary Kudu a year later. CTI proved to be a maverick record company for its time, when acoustic jazz was waning and jazz-rock fusion was taking the music scene by storm. The music he was presenting fell somewhere in between.

With CTI, Creed was aiming for commercial respectability of jazz. He told *DownBeat* how his company was different from Alfred Lion's Blue Note Records at the time: "Alfred was interested in pure ensemble, then blowing and no nonsense. I was interested in that, plus an entertaining record that might appeal a little more to the general public."

Ron proved to be an integral part of the label's success. "I loved Ron," said Creed. "I looked forward to any date he was on. When I started CTI, he was the anchor."

Writing in the liner notes to CTI CD reissues on Epic Records years later, A&R coordinator Didier C. Deutsch—who served as CTI's press relations director from 1972–'76—took Ron's involvement with the label one step further by asserting that CTI was "ostensibly created around bassist Ron Carter, who anchored most of the albums released by the label."

While today Creed has totally disassociated himself from Didier—he said, "I don't endorse anything he writes"—he continues to praise Ron's invaluable contributions to CTI. A close friend of Oscar Pettiford, who recorded sides with him for Bethlehem, Creed saw in Ron a future jazz bass star. "Ron was a unique bassist who amazed me. He had that legato technique that couldn't be touched—the same with his glissandos and articulation. None of the notes he played, no matter where they landed on the bass, was a problem to record. Ron understood what was going on around him constantly."

Unlike a Gerry Mulligan or a Pettiford, for example, Ron was not garrulous in the studio. Rather, he was attentive and reserved, said Creed. "Gerry was real verbal, Mr. Personality, while Oscar was not quiet at all. He was like a wild man who would go off on a tangent at any time. Even though Ron had a large physical presence, he was silent except when something wasn't going smoothly on a date. He wouldn't say anything inappropriate.

He'd make a subtle suggestion or have a quiet conversation with an obstinate apple."

Didier, who calls Ron one of two jazz aristocrats on the label (the other being Paul Desmond), says that he was always first call on sessions. "People could always rely on him, and he was respected for his steadiness," he said. "If people were 10 minutes late, he'd tell them that was 10 minutes wasted. He was always ready, physically and mentally. He knew the music and would always push the others to be more creative. He lifted up all the musicians around him. He supported the other players and gave them ideas for improving the music."

THE ANCHOR

THE ANCHOR DESIGNATION cuts two ways with Ron. He was not only valued for the gravity and groove of his bass lines, but also for his session wisdom. "For many of the dates, I was maybe the most stable of the guys," Ron said. "That's not to say that the other guys were unstable. But if I saw something taking place in the studio that wasn't right, I'd say something about it. I wouldn't let it keep going. Creed trusted my maturity and sense of command of the English language so that he knew there wasn't going to be any outrageous behavior. I'd just talk to a person about doing the music in a different way."

Case in point, Freddie Hubbard's hit album *Red Clay* (produced by Creed, engineered by Rudy) in which the recording of the title track stalled. Instead of playing a regular drum kit, Lenny White had brought in steel drums that he insisted on playing. Ron traded his bass seat for diplomatic duty. "After several takes, Ron took Lenny outside," said Creed.

"I told Lenny, listen, Rudy is ready to walk up the stairs and leave and then we'd be done," said Ron. "We'd been there for two hours, and it was obvious the steel drums weren't working. The song wasn't going anywhere. Freddie was getting more and more anxious, Joe Henderson was just waiting for something to happen. The energy was dissipating, attitudes were starting to show up and the vibe was turning strange."

Outside Ron tried to talk sense to Lenny who still wanted to use the pans. "I can appreciate you wanting to get your sound," said Ron. "But playing in the studio isn't like playing in a club. Certain things don't apply. In this case, your drums don't apply. My recommendation to get some real music going here is to stash that drum in your trunk. We can't keep doing this. I won't keep doing this. We don't want to be doing take 503 with that drum."

Lenny yielded, used Rudy's drums and the tune was completed in one take.

"Creed recognized that he or Rudy couldn't say anything," said Ron. "A lot of musicians don't respect the producer or the engineer for their musical point of view. They may have valid reasons. But when another musician questions something, then there can be a level of trust. That's what I brought to those sessions, as well as sanity, levity and soberness to keep the energy going, to make the session work."

"Freddie Hubbard was and is such a mercurial person," said Creed, "and he played that way. Ron, I'm sure, made subtle suggestions to Freddie all the time to make the music better."

Freddie confirms that. "All the best stuff I've recorded, Ron is on it," he said. "He's the most intelligent guy I've ever heard. He moves the harmony around. When he first joined Miles, he didn't want to copy Paul Chambers. That's why Miles liked him so much. When Ron worked on my records, I wouldn't know what something I was playing would sound like until I heard him. He changed a lot of the music for me to make it right."

"Ron played the role of quarterback," Creed said. "He didn't mind doing that if it made sense, and then he did so in his Kissinger-like way."

Another example of Ron's leadership role during a session came early in the CTI days when Creed recorded two Wes Montgomery albums in 1967, *A Day in the Life* and *Down Here on the Ground*, both of which were released under the A&M arrangement. On the latter album, Ron overruled Creed's opinion on the tune "Georgia on My Mind." He recalls going to the studio and the band nailing the song on the first take. All the musicians agreed.

Creed liked what he heard too, but then said, "How about one more?"

Ron replied, "Creed, I'm not going to play. There's no way today that you're going to get a better take than the one we just did."

This time Creed yielded.

In remembering the session, Ron said, "This wasn't an ego trip. It was a case of knowing that when a song is right there's no point in doing more than one take. Everything will just go downhill if everyone feels the best was the first. It was simply a case of all of us feeling that what we had done was wonderful, fabulous."

Another example of Creed trusting Ron's musicality came when Ron realized that the rhythm team was getting short shrift on tunes that were later embellished by string arrangements. "I began to realize that the process was not tilted in our favor," Ron said. "The rhythm players were doing the sketches, laying out the framework essentially, that the string arranger later used. I told Creed that that was unfair, that we should be getting paid more to make things more equitable."

"Ron was right," Creed said. "He was creating music that Don Sebesky as arranger later used."

Creed asked Ron how much he wanted. "I told him," Ron said. "He agreed and then we shook hands on it."

"Only a guy like Ron could come in and make it clear that this was the right thing to do," said Creed.

"My concern was always with process," Ron said. "The guys doing all the work were getting paid the least. Creed was the first person I knew who understood that once I presented my case in adult fashion, as fact and not emotion."

Don Sebesky expresses no hard feelings on the matter. In fact, he has nothing but praise for Ron's contributions to the multiple CTI sessions he worked on. Don's history with Creed stretched back to the Verve days working with Wes on *Bumpin'*. "Ron was in most of the sessions I arranged," Don said, citing a menu of artists including Chet Baker, Jim Hall, Paul Desmond and Roland Hanna. "Ron was always the bass player. He got it all together. He made it happen. He took complex music and made it sound easy. He was the go-to guy."

Don points out that, in addition to the high caliber of musicianship Creed hired for all his sessions, he also sought sonic clarity—and purity; hence he worked exclusively with Rudy. "Ron's sound filled up all this space in the music," said Don. "His acoustic bass floated, especially with the way Rudy captured it so that it sounded like it was in a concert hall. Ron's bass was the best, like a Tiffany of jazz. And his sound is timeless, in homage to the past but also fast-forwarding to the future."

(Don, who says that Ron is the best bass player he's ever heard, enlisted him for his 1999 RCA album, *Joyful Noise: A Tribute to Duke Ellington*, where he reinterpreted classic material from Duke's songbook. "Just like Duke wrote with specific players in his band in mind, I built my arrangement for 'Satin Doll' around Ron," Don said. "I wrote it to expose his bass playing, with the focus on the bass instead of Duke's version with piano. Ron is the star of that tune.")

SIDEMAN SESSIONS

CREED TRIED TO keep the scales of artistic and commercial music balanced during his CTI years, most often succeeding despite the rumblings on the jazz scene by acoustic-music purists. Don Sebesky recalls the dismay from the shuttered Riverside Records camp, where Wes was discovered, when he recorded *A Day in the Life*. "That record was condemned as a sellout," Don recalled. "But Wes was smiling, and there were people lined up around the block when he played at clubs. He was the first in a formidable line of CTI artists who had hits."

It's also suggested that CTI spawned the soporific smooth jazz movement that arrived in the '80s. But much of CTI's brand of jazz-pop fusion had depth. Writing in the *Los Angeles Times* on January 31, 1988, critic Leonard Feather reviewed a batch of CTI records being reissued as CDs. He wrote in his review ramp-up, "There is a tendency among some artists to deal collectively with such [fusion] music and dismiss it artistically as valueless. This is at best a half-truth ... Fusion jazz can be produced and executed with good taste, in such a way that the results neither compromise the performers unreasonably nor limit the sales potential."

Feather went on to laud Creed's "unique vision, with an ear for great talent as well as for good sound quality" and single out some recordings as "illuminating testimony that fusion in many instances could achieve a healthy measure of validity." He compared that with the so-called contemporary jazz of the day, such as Spyro Gyra, Hiroshima, Fattburger and Kenny G, and questioned, "Couldn't Taylor have come up with something just as viable commercially yet more durable musically?"

The four CDs Leonard weighed in on—the compilation *Fire Into Music, Vol. II*, Kenny Burrell's sole CTI date *God Bless the Child*, the blockbuster Stanley Turrentine album *Sugar* and George Benson's last jazz recording before going pop, *Beyond the Blue Horizon*—all featured Ron as a sideman.

Even though Ron says that all his CTI dates were memorable for different reasons, for starters he singles out working with Antonio Carlos Jobim (see Brazil chapter), Hank Crawford and Wes Montgomery ("He brought so much to the table that all of us playing with him were stunned by the great music he was recording"). He also notes two dates with soul singer Esther Phillips, whose *Alone Again, Naturally* and *Black-Eyed Blues* appeared on CTI's R&B-oriented Kudu subsidiary. "I'd never played with such a bluesy singer," said Ron. "The horn section was arranged by Pee Wee Ellis, who was a student of mine from my Rochester days when I was a practice teacher. That offered me the chance to play with a wonderful singer who had great arrangements and sound to work with."

Some of Ron's favorite sessions were with tenor saxophonist Stanley Turrentine. He did five dates with Stanley, including 1970's *Sugar*. "Anytime I could play with Stanley, I was there," said Ron. "Stanley came up at the same time as Sonny Rollins, Hank Mobley, Trane and Wayne and was just as major a saxophonist as them. That's a heck of a feat. Stanley had his own sound, his own approach to playing chords. I wanted to hear how that worked, but I never figured it out. I'd say, 'Stanley, how do you do that?' And he'd say, 'I don't know Ron, I just do it.' So that stopped me asking that question again."

Ron recalls the song "Sugar," a minor blues that Stanley wrote that wasn't coming to a satisfactory resolution in the studio. Ron said to Stanley, "Can we do something other than a C-minor at the end, like an A-flat or something? When we get back to the top, I keep feeling like that C-minor is banging on my head."

Stanley paused, then blurted out with a big smile, "I've got an idea. How about if we end this on A-flat."

"You skallywag," said Ron jokingly.

Stanley laughed and said, "Ron Carter owns the last two bars of this song."

While Ron played on six George Benson CTI albums (including George's breakthrough A&M/CTI recording *The Other Side of Abbey Road* in 1969, when the guitarist was signed to the roster after Wes Montgomery's sudden death), he singles out 1971's *White Rabbit* as the record that showcased the guitarist's best performance. The jazz/classical album included renderings of such pop hits as "White Rabbit" (Jefferson Airplane) and "California Dreamin'" (The Mamas & the Papas). The recording featured an impressive sideman cast: Herbie on piano, guitarists Jay Berliner and Earl Klugh (in Klugh's first recording), Billy Cobham, percussionist Airto, and Sebesky's string arrangements.

"I don't remember having any prerecording meetings on this album," Ron said. "We were all surprised by the library as well as the arrangements, which made for an interesting date. But George came in with the intent of playing some wonderful jazz choruses. He decided that he wanted to show how well he could play guitar. Billy was a little cautious at times, but George pulled him along." As for his bass, Ron added, "It sounded good but when I listen to it now it's maybe a little too loud for the recording."

When flutist Hubert Laws, who attended the Juilliard School of Music on a scholarship in 1960, decided to explore the classical/jazz nexus with Sebesky arrangements of music by Bach, Debussy, Faure and Stravinsky, the inclusion of Ron on *The Rite of Spring* was a no-brainer. Also on the funkified 1971 date were guitarist Gene Bertoncini, vibes player Dave Friedman, drummer Jack DeJohnette, Airto on percussion and keyboardist Bob James.

Hubert knew Ron well from the commercial jingle days where musicians with classical and jazz experience were a premium, even though the two didn't discuss their common background of classical music. "Ron didn't talk too much about that," Hubert said. "I only found out later. A lot of times people will use the name and reputation of a school to elevate their celebrity. But that wasn't the case with Ron. He was all about creating the music. However, in playing with him, I did pick up on his classical music background."

"We had all done classical music for TV and radio commercials," said Ron. "But doing *The Rite of Spring* really put us to the grindstone. We were out to show how classical music could maintain its integrity. I'd like to believe that if Stravinsky were still alive, he'd have been experimenting with his composition, 'The Rite of Spring,' in a way similar to what we were doing. This is one of the most successful jazz-classical albums."

Ron said that Hubert led by example during the session, with most of the tunes being first takes. "Hubert doesn't need to tell what he wants. He just plays, and if the right guys are around him, they hear where he's going."

Hubert reflects back on Ron's solid presence on all of the records they played on together. Recently he put on a Freddie Hubbard record that he and Ron had performed on. "It was Christmas Day, and what a Christmas present it was for me to hear Ron's selection of notes, his timing, his feel," said Hubert. "I called Ron and told him how much I appreciated his gift. I told him how he played with an economy of notes, how he played at the right time with a vibrancy. It was like Miles and the way he played. I've played with virtuoso bass players, but Ron is more supportive than anyone else. He understands the right place to play in a particular setting so that he doesn't override or underplay the person he performs with. His notes are just right."

Another significant studio event in Ron's CTI career was Chet Baker's 1974 album *She Was Too Cool for Me*. It was touted as Baker's comeback recording after he'd been sidelined for five years. It featured an all-star cast including saxophonist Paul Desmond, keyboardist Bob James, drummers Steve Gadd and Jack DeJohnette, Hubert on flute, and Sebesky's string arrangements. "Chet brought a heavy rep wherever he went for whatever reasons," said Ron. "So I was hoping for this session that he wouldn't wig out. But he was in charge, he recognized that we had rehearsed and he was on time. We had one day to record. No overdubs, no fixes, so let's do it."

Ron remembers Chet being very focused on the session, even though he looked thin, unkempt and came off as meek. "It was a very nonaggressive date," Ron said. "Chet would ask us how many choruses he should take. So, since we sensed how he was doing, we turned the volume down a little, to a three from a three-point-five, to give him the boost he needed. That's a good sideman's job: to do whatever it takes to make the leader's date better."

Ron, who used Chet on his 1980 Milestone album *Patrao*, marveled at what he brought to his playing. "There were only one or two guys who understood what Miles was doing. Chet came the closest to imitating that concept. He had a good sound, good meter, and he knew how to listen to the rest of the band."

THE LEADER

EVEN THOUGH RON was the heartbeat of CTI and had signed an exclusive recording contract with the label in 1970, it didn't occur to him until 1973 to record his first date as leader there. "I was comfortable with not being a leader," he said. "Hey, getting the chance to play with Hubert, George and Milt Jackson was OK to me. I didn't feel it was necessary to record under my own name."

Still, Ron was gigging regularly with bands he led, one of which featured his new piccolo bass, the half-sized bass that allowed him to solo almost like a guitarist (see the chapter on Ron's quartets). "I told Creed about how I was developing a new concept of leader without a horn player," he said. "I was doing a date at the Village Vanguard, so I asked him to stop by. He came by one night and thought that what I was doing sounded interesting."

Creed asked him if he wanted to record an album under his own name. "Let me think about it," Ron said. "There weren't many bass players as leaders. But he told me that if I got a band together, he'd sign me to a leader contract. So I figured, let's get it going."

The result was the largely electric *Blues Farm*, a masterwork of how jazz bass not only undergirds but also soars as a frontline instrument. On the funky title opener, Ron, on acoustic, sounds like he's playing electric with his fat grooves and bluesy glissando lines as he takes the lyrical lead, then converses with Hubert on flute. In the library he created for himself as leader, Ron placed himself in a variety of musical settings where bass takes prominence, including his sublime slow song "A Soul Ballad," the churchy "A Hymn for Him" and the festive finale, the Latin-flavored "R2 M1." The only song on *Blues Farm* that is not a Ron composition is John Lewis's "Django," which was the title track of the 1956 Modern Jazz Quartet album. It was the first recording Ron bought during his second year at Eastman School of Music. It's also one of his favorite tracks on the album.

As for personnel, Ron knew pianist Richard Tee from doing commercial jingles in the studios in New York, so he asked him to come to the sessions. He was familiar with Bob James from gigs at the New York club Bradley's and from other CTI dates, and he also knew that he played with Sarah Vaughan. "That was good enough for me," Ron said. "Sarah, who was a good piano player, would not have taken on someone who couldn't respond to her needs musically."

CTI colleague Billy Cobham was also enlisted. "I was thinking that Billy was more into funk, but I liked the sound of his drums when he made jazz records," said Ron. As for Hubert and guitarist Sam Brown, they had both appeared on Ron's second date as leader, 1969's *Uptown Conversation*, on Herbie Mann's Embryo label. The rest of the band was comprised of musicians—electric guitarist Gene Bertoncini and percussionist Ralph MacDonald—who were a part of Creed's session circle.

"I wanted to surround myself with people who could respond to my needs just like I did as a sideman," Ron said. "If something's not right, let's fix it. Let's not make a big deal. It's not about embarrassing someone or showing them up. You never want to usurp a leader's identity, but it's all about having the mind-set to help make a session the best it can be."

One challenge Ron faced for the first time as a leader was dealing with overdubbed parts. "It was a new responsibility to get the sound and feeling right," he said. Overdubs on this recording were kept to a minimum, with a couple of flute parts by Hubert, a Fender Rhodes overdub by James and a few percussion parts by Ralph. Didier, writing the liner notes to the *Blues Farm* CD reissue, pointed out: "Such is Ron's no-nonsense way with things that the entire recording was done in one day, with each selection requiring only a single take. This resulted in a compact, cohesive album."

The *Blues Farm* library opened a window on Ron's compositional maturity. At the time of its release, he commented, "I take this album as a compendium of my personal experiences, and my personal musical growth, as well as my ability to pick a direction for a tune and be able to have the players understand where I want them to go."

In a review in the magazine *New Times*, Frank Conroy wrote, "Whether the tune is lyrical, funky or witty, [Ron's] writing is always clean and intelligent. This record is for the music rather than bravura instrumental performances—which is not to say everyone doesn't play very well indeed."

The title track, Ron explained, is dedicated to all the talented African Americans who weren't able to find jobs in their specific fields and thereby ended up in civil servant jobs, specifically at the post office where they were forced to wear blue uniforms. "I'd go to the post office and see these guys who would tell me that they used to play the saxophone, but for whatever reasons in or beyond their control couldn't make it and had to get a job."

The upbeat "R2 M1" was written at a time when Ron's youngest son Myles had a small dog. "Myles would take Rover on a walk, and Rover would beat him up," he said. "The dog would walk too fast or chew on his shoe. So the title of this tune is the score of the walk: Rover 2 and Myles 1." Another number Ron liked was "Two-Beat Johnson," a song he wrote in fascination with the old New Orleans two-beat style. "When we played it, it was all about how long the song would last without me playing it in 4/4 and making it swing. This is my attempt at a sound where the two-beat can go on forever."

The radio exposure was strong with "Django," "A Small Ballad" and "Blues Farm" getting the most airplay. And for the first time in his career, Ron was voted Best Acoustic Bassist in *DownBeat*'s Readers Poll in 1973.

Of special note, the cover art of *Blues Farm* was one of the most unusual and original photographs by Pete Turner for a CTI project. It's a photo of a gas-station slot machine in Nevada with a large copper-colored profile of an Indian (as in an Indian nickel), above a jackpot of Roosevelt dimes. In the coffee-table book collection of album-cover photography by Turner, *The Color of Jazz* (Rizzoli, New York), Pete commented: "How this image ties into *Blues Farm* beats the hell out of me. We had reached the point where we said, 'The heck with being constrained by titles.'"

Ron liked the artwork. "That was one thing about CTI," he said. "We never knew what the covers were until they were printed. I never quite understood what Pete's *Blues Farm* cover meant, but I thought it was unique unto itself."

Ron continued his leader's run with 1974's *All Blues*, with Joe Henderson, Roland Hanna and Billy Cobham, and highlighted by Ron's take on Miles's classic "All Blues," and in 1975 with *Spanish Blues*, a four-song outing with another Miles *Kind of Blue* song, "So What?" and three originals. The band was comprised of Laws, Hanna, MacDonald, Cobham, Berliner and electric pianist Leon Pendarvis. Writing in the original liner notes, Doug Ramsey noted how Ron integrated Spanish-music sensibilities into the mix, especially on "El Noche Sol" and "Sabado Sombrero." He wrote,

"They are compositions distilled from the Spanish style and filtered through the experience and perspective of a master jazz artist. Ron's goal was to provide frameworks within which he and his musicians could improvise with Spanish [music] feeling."

Ron told Doug that he planned to continue to focus on composition and then maintain a working band to develop those tunes on a regular basis. That took place the year that he formed his first quartet.

Ron's next album proved to be either a shock or a revelation, depending on who you talked to. Released in 1975 on Kudu, *Anything Goes* had a decidedly commercial pop influence that was spurred on in part by the rising tide of disco music across the city of New York at the time. An all-star CTI cast was assembled, including such newcomers to Ron's recordings as saxophonists Michael Brecker, David Sanborn and Phil Woods, keyboardist Don Grolnick, wah-wah guitarist Eric Gale, trumpeter Randy Brecker, and a trio of female background singers, including R&B's hot ticket Patti Austin on wordless vocals. Helping Ron with arrangements was David Matthews. Old standbys Laws, Gadd and Tee were along for the funky ride. "Dave and I met and then decided what library we could use given the intent of the album, which was CTI wanting to get into the dance zone," said Ron. "We picked songs that we felt could be manipulated into that."

The results were electrifyingly upbeat even though Ron stuck to acoustic bass, with occasional piccolo bass overdubs. It was an album to dance to. The tunes included a hip update of the Cole Porter classic "Anything Goes," an electric revisit of Dave Grusin's "Baretta's Theme (Keep Your Eye on the Sparrow)," a cover of the Stylistics' R&B hit "Can't Give You Anything But My Love," and three Ron originals: two Brazil-tinged tunes ("De Samba" and Quarto Azul") and the grand funk finale, "Big Fro," which some critics deride as Ron's concession to disco.

That song marked Ron's first meeting with Austin. "Patti came by the session one night, and I showed her the library I was working with," said Ron. "I told her, 'I'm out of my element, so I'm not sure what to tell you to do. So, you should do what you want.' So we went through the song, and Patti told me, the singers will do this here and that there. That was great. Once we determined that, I said, 'Let's get this bad boy off.'"

Many critics didn't join in the liftoff enthusiasm. They were skeptical, citing CTI's "pandering to mass tastes with slick arrangements," as Vernon Gibbs wrote in *Essence* magazine. He asked, is Ron going disco?

Ron replied, *"Anything Goes* is not a change in direction. If you listen to my other records, you'll find that each contains a full spectrum of music, including the kind of music I grew up playing—T-Bone Walker, rhythm and blues shows, strip shows, and things other than Charlie Parker, Archie Shepp and Miles Davis. Most of the jazz players I know grew up in the church, and I was also involved in all that as part of my musical exposure. I don't see that there is such a difference between playing jazz and playing music derived from the church. Technique is a relative thing; jazz can be as simple as you want it, and gospel music can be as complex as you want it."

Ron went on to say that he understands how people who narrowly define jazz were surprised by *Anything Goes*. However, he explained, "I had always hoped that this additional music would catch someone else's ear other than my own, and it seems that it happened with *Anything Goes*."

Looking back on the record today, Ron is unapologetic about its inclusion in his discography. "If people listen to the bass lines, they realize that what I'm doing is the same as what I was always doing. I didn't change lines or keys to make it sound better to a disco listener. I just wanted to make a record that stood on its own."

Anything Goes caught on in clubs, but never saw its full commercial potential. Since Creed was going for large audiences, he decided to have Motown Records distribute his Kudu imprint, a decision that proved to create glitches. "Creed took the record to disco joints where it did really well," Ron said. "Occasionally I'll run into people who still remember tunes like 'Big Fro' playing in the clubs. But something happened in the distribution paperwork. There was a lot of he said/she said, and then a lawsuit and an injunction, all of which meant that *Anything Goes* died on the vine."

That was fine by Didier who wrote in 1987 in the reissue liner notes to Ron's next and final CTI recording, *Yellow & Green*, "A year before, against his better judgment, [Ron] had recorded a pseudo disco album ... mercifully released on the subsidiary Kudu label, but nonetheless a change in artistic direction he had not totally endorsed even though it was his own album."

THE BEGINNING OF THE END

IN DIDIER'S OPINION, *Yellow & Green* was a return to form, even though the reissue included two bonus songs from the *Anything Goes* sessions, "Receipt, Please" and "Yellow & Green." However, both Carter compositions were redone on the new album with his band that included members of his newly formed quartet (pianist Kenny Barron and drummer Ben Riley) as well as such other sidemen as Cobham, Grolnick, guitarist Hugh McCracken and percussionist Dom Um Romão.

In the album's original liner notes, Ron wrote about the title: "Since my previous CTI albums have included the word blue in the titles—*Blues Farm*, *All Blues*, *Spanish Blue*—I'd like to add two more colors to these titles: *Yellow & Green*. Using acoustic, electric and piccolo bass on this album, you'll find even more colors."

Ron covered two tunes: the chestnut "Willow Weep for Me" (a solo favorite played on piccolo bass that Ron to this day performs live) and one of his favorite songs, Thelonious Monk's "Epistrophy," which he had played with the piano master. Four Ron originals are featured on the date, including "Receipt, Please" ("a very common expression that I wrote a melody for which should make it a little more fun to say") and the "colorful" title track. Ron debuted "Opus 1.5," a song he wrote for his close friend Joe Henderson ("The melody brings to mind the stillness between the last note of a song and the applause that follows") and "Tenaj," an "abbreviated waltz" he wrote for pianist Bobby Timmons, with whom he worked and recorded in the early '60s. Of the tune, Ron wrote in the liners, "Each chorus of the waltz I separated by a short cadenza that acts as a comma, allowing the soloist, in this case Kenny Barron, space to alter the shape of the piece."

In looking back at the 1976 album, Didier wrote that *Yellow & Green* was "not a huge success" for CTI, which he pointed out was facing "pressing financial difficulties that were eventually to cause its demise." Part of the problem, Didier concluded, had been that many of CTI's marquee performers "had gone to other labels, lured away by promises of greater financial rewards and greater artistic freedom."

Don Sebesky remembers the "golden days" at CTI when he would go to Creed's office and discuss the next sessions they were going to work on together. He cited the top-notch talent pool that Creed assembled for the dates and applauded the label's ability to give "artists the opportunity to have a forum. We all had that as well as we all made money during that time. It was all about the music and a wonderful group of musicians who all became friends."

However, Don pinpoints the beginning of the end at CTI with Brazilian synth keyboardist Eumir Deodato's groundbreaking 1972 album *Prelude*, on which Ron appeared. The recording included Deodato's synthed-up version of Richard Strauss's "Also Sprach Zarathustra" ("Thus Spake Zarathustra") that had been the musical theme of Stanley Kubrick's 1968 film, *2001: A Space Odyssey*. Deodato made his funky rendition a huge worldwide hit, and it reached No. 2 on the *Billboard* pop charts. "After that album, everything gradually changed," said Don. "There was less artistic clarity and a mixture of many kinds of music. Things became fragmented. There were a lot of people around who were advising Creed from a money standpoint. It became a less joyful experience."

Despite the air of uncertainty at CTI, Ron stayed at the label until 1976, even though most of his peers had already left. Didier wrote in the *Yellow & Green* reissue liners that Ron was "intensely loyal" but, in his opinion, also felt restless. He noted that Ron's last hurrah with CTI was "representative of the creative path he would follow after leaving CTI that same year to sign with the Berkeley, California-based Milestone label."

THE ALL-STARS

BEYOND THE PLETHORA of CTI recording sessions, one of the lasting legacies of the label was its innovative all-star tour that bore fruit in such recordings as the three volumes of *CTI Summer Jazz at the Hollywood Bowl Live*. "Those CTI All-Stars tours of Europe, Japan and the U.S. is one of the reasons why CTI was so successful," said Ron. "People got to see the musicians like George, Deodato, Hubert and Billy that they heard on records."

Producer/educator John Snyder, who had just come on board in 1973 to CTI fresh from law school as a music lawyer, ended up with additional duties such as serving as stage manager for a CTI All-Stars tour of Japan. During the tour, John says, Ron was the anchor just as he was in the sessions. Didier, who also ran All-Stars tours, agrees.

"Working with the logistics of touring shows like these with superstars could get hairy," Didier said. He remembers trying to find Chet Baker backstage at the Emerson Theater in Los Angeles five minutes before he was to appear onstage in a solo spot. "Chet wasn't anywhere to be found. I don't know why, but I went outside onto the terrace, and there he was smoking a joint. I told him that he had to be onstage, and he just told me, 'OK, don't worry.'"

On the flip side there was Ron. One evening Didier was looking for Ron as he was assembling all the musicians to get onstage. Instead of going outside he looked inside, specifically on the stage itself. "Ron was there already and ready to play," Didier said. "That's one of the things I admired about him. With Ron, I knew I was safe."

Drummer Harvey Mason, a youngster on the scene at the time, also toured with the CTI All-Stars. He marveled at Ron's musicianship. Plus, they found a groove together. "Ron was so natural to play with," he said. "It was like butter. There I was in heaven with all these great players, and I was experiencing the unbelievable giving in Ron's bass notes. We didn't say much, but I knew this was the beginning of a respectful friendship."

Ron loved performing on those tours. He bemoans the fact that today record labels don't recognize the marketing advantages for backing all-star revues. "As a result of those CTI tours, record sales increased," he said.

At Ron's next label stop, the same held true. "When we formed the Milestone Jazzstars, we sold a lot of records too," he said. "All of our shows sold out."

CHAPTER TEN

Milestone Records: The House of Keepnews

As CTI WAS spiraling down to a crash landing in 1976, Milestone Records, an imprint of Fantasy Records in Berkeley, California, was spreading its wings. Fantasy was still flush with money made from Creedence Clearwater Revival records. The hit pop band essentially bankrolled the label that saw a bright financial future in purchasing defunct independent labels like Prestige and Riverside. It was a catalog buy that proved to be a goldmine for reissuing recordings by the giants of jazz in the '50s and '60s.

After Orrin Keepnews's label Riverside went broke in 1964, the producer wasn't willing to sit on the sidelines for very long. In 1966, he and Dick Katz founded Milestone Records in New York, with such high-profile artists as Sonny Rollins and McCoy Tyner, and such young, but important musicians as Joe Henderson and Gary Bartz, among the label's first signees. Milestone moved from New York to Berkeley in 1972, when it also became an imprint of Fantasy Records, which, by then, was the largest independent record company in the world (in 2004, it was bought by the Concord Music Group, which now holds the honors).

Orrin also moved west with the label and became Fantasy's director of jazz A&R, signing new acts, such as Flora Purim, to Milestone as well as working with the expansive jazz catalog, including a reunion with his old Riverside master tapes.

Orrin and Ron got to know each other from the various sessions Ron appeared in for both Riverside (most notably with Wes Montgomery and Bill Evans) and Milestone (including Joe Henderson's hip 1969 record, *Power to the People*, which contained Ron's composition, "Opus One-Point-Five," and the Ron-Jim Hall debut duo album, *Alone Together*, recorded live in 1972).

So, when Ron's days at CTI came to an end, he began to shop around for another label to continue investigating his musical vision. He had Orrin's number.

Orrin recalls that it was Ron's lawyer, Alan Bergman, who did Ron's bidding. "It was offered as a production deal where Ron would deliver the albums," Orrin said. "I had never done that kind of deal. But I thought having Ron was a darn good idea so I fought with Saul Zaentz, who owned Fantasy, and Ralph Kaffel, who ran it, to get their approval. It worked, and Ron ended up recording quite a few records for Milestone as well as the live all-stars album with Sonny, McCoy and Al Foster. Ron was designated the music producer in his contract. Here was this real-life artist having the freedom to do what he wanted. That didn't come easily in those days."

During his association with Milestone, Ron formed Retrac Productions (note the name: Carter spelled backwards) and began exploring new vistas with Orrin's blessings. "I was still at CTI when I started my piccolo quartet," Ron said. "It was a low-flame band that got hot every night. I mentioned to Orrin how unique it was in terms of instrumentation and how there were four wonderful musicians playing great melodies." Orrin went to see the band and was impressed. (Ron and Co. ended up recording his new quartet live at Sweet Basil in New York. The double LP, appropriately titled *Piccolo*, was released by Milestone in 1977.)

But Ron had bigger plans for his Milestone debut, *Pastels*, which was recorded at Fantasy's state-of-the-art recording studio in Berkeley in 1976. "I always wanted to record an album with strings," Ron said. "Orrin said OK, come to Berkeley."

Ron feels that *Pastels* was his highlight moment for Milestone. "There I was, with a new label, and I knew I had a decent track record with Orrin," he said. "But to come out to California and do this kind of project showed me that Orrin must have had faith in me, that I was going to record something that had musical value. That helped to establish me with Milestone—that I was professional, that I could deliver on the production end, and that the music would be viable and commercially successful. Orrin also trusted my sense of budgetary control and music production, including every step from concept to in-store purchases."

While *Pastels* was recorded at Fantasy, most of Ron's output for Milestone was recorded in New York. "I have nothing against musicians producing their own albums, but sometimes it can be difficult dealing with the studio itself and the control room," Orrin said. "So, even though Ron produced his first couple of albums, I was credited with supervising in the liner notes. But as soon as I discovered how totally conscientious Ron was and that he was in control, I cut him loose. And Ron continued to show his ability to be in charge. He was either extremely self-confident or giving the best imitation of that I've ever seen."

"Orrin never came to the sessions after the first couple," Ron said. "He trusted me and I never let him down. He felt confident to leave me alone and not have an overseer. He knew I could give constructive criticism to the players in my sessions and that I would not abuse my role as producer."

PASTEL CANVAS

FOR HIS FIRST Milestone album, *Pastels*, Ron ambitiously assembled a wide range of musicians, including his quartet pianist Kenny Barron, and guitarist Hugh McCracken and strings arranger Don Sebesky from his CTI days.

Ron also invited another old friend from his CTI dates, drummer Harvey Mason. "I'd known Harvey for some time, but we had never made a record together," said Ron. "So I called him to see if he was available. He wasn't, but he gave me the dates when he would be. So I told him we'd work around his schedule. Harvey is such a wonderful player. He plays all styles and he brings his personality to each of those styles. He's a hard funk earthmover, but he's also great on ballads."

Even though this was Ron's first date as a leader for Milestone, Orrin quizzed him on just two basics: How long was the album going to be, and what kind of concept was he going to use? "Orrin recognized that I had a producer's mind-set and a way to talk to other musicians and people in the studio so they wouldn't take offense," said Ron. "Orrin doesn't know music in a broad sense. He doesn't know a bass clef from a treble clef. But he's keenly aware of what feels right. Orrin used to be an editor before he became a producer, so he has a sense of beginning, middle and end. Those are the kind of skills he brought to a musical date."

Ron had closely observed Orrin during the sessions where he performed as a sideman. "Some guys didn't take what Orrin said seriously," he said. "He didn't have the vocabulary, but he had enough sense of the music to convey to everyone in the studio what was missing."

As it turned out, nothing was missing from Ron's *Pastels* date, nor from any of the manifold dates he recorded for Milestone, which never returned any of his finished mixes for fixes or edits.

Playing his piccolo bass and acoustic string bass, Ron enlisted a 15-piece string section that included cellist Kermit Moore, who later became the mainstay of his four-cello nonet group, and New York Philharmonic violinist Sanford Allen, who Ron requested to be the concert master. Sanford wasn't sure he wanted to take on the assignment, based on a tiff the two had when they were working on an orchestral jingle date.

"There was a large orchestra with lots of strings, and Ron got annoyed about something," Sanford recalled. "He made it fairly clear that he was upset. I just wrote him off, and that's how it stayed between us until *Pastels*." Ron contacted Sanford through a mutual friend, and the violinist initially balked at Ron's request. Sanford held firmly to his opinion for a few months, then finally agreed to go to Berkeley to work the recording date.

"It was one long session," said Sanford. "Ron and I exchanged very few words other than about the work at hand. It was such a long day that when I returned to my hotel, the kitchen was closed. There was no place to eat, so

I bought a couple of beers and had two or three packages of peanuts from a vending machine. I was not in good humor."

When Sanford got up the next morning to check out of the hotel, he saw Ron in the hotel lobby. Still sour over the evening before, Sanford did not initiate contact. "But Ron walked up to me, put his arms around me and said thanks," Sanford recalled. "We wound up being good friends. We both decided that we needed each other."

Pastels turned heads and opened ears. Writing in the *San Francisco Chronicle*, Conrad Silvert said, "One reason *Pastels* is better than virtually anything Ron Carter made at CTI is that at Fantasy/Milestone he is producing himself." He went on to praise Ron's five originals: the humorous "Woolaphant," the big-swing "12 + 12," the "kick-ass" "One Bass String," and two romantic numbers, the title track and "Ballad." *Pastels*, Conrad asserted, made for a chamber jazz outing where melody reigns and the "blues [is] taken out of the street and put in the parlor."

Writing in the *Los Angeles Times*, Leonard Feather likewise championed the album, giving it a five-star rating and proclaiming that the LP "would win over the most stubborn opponents of the concept that bassists should lead orchestras." Earlier in his review, Feather rhetorically pondered, why bother listening to an album by a bass player? Then he replied that Ron provides the answer with *Pastels*, singling out an "azure sonata like 'Woolaphant' with its organic unity and the enveloping sound of strings" and the "exquisite symphonic encounter" on "Ballad," where, accompanied by the string section, the bassist "achieves an indescribable beauty...with his deep sound, rich in harmonics."

DownBeat was markedly less enthusiastic in its three-and-a-half-star review, as the critic complained that "the real problem is that Carter's playing doesn't fit well with the overall musical setting." The reviewer, identified only as "nolan," concluded, "It is apparent that the overall intention of *Pastels* was to explore subtle colors, but unfortunately all the shadings don't mix well on this patchwork canvas."

PICCOLO BASS AND BEYOND

BETWEEN 1976 AND 1980 when Ron ended his association with Milestone—which was incidentally the same year Orrin left the label he founded yet stayed at Fantasy as a contract producer mining the indie label's golden vaults for new reissue projects—he recorded several albums as a leader.

These dates included:

- *Piccolo* (1977)
- *Peg Leg* (his quartet augmented by woodwinds, 1978)
- *A Song for You* (the first full appearance of Ron's cello quartet concept with Jack DeJohnette in the drummer seat, 1978)

- *Parade* (a 10-member band date that included Chick Corea, 1979)
- *Pick 'em* (another quartet date augmented by the cello choir, 1980)
- *New York Slick* (a date including Art Farmer, J.J. Johnson, Hubert Laws and Billy Cobham, 1980)
- *Patrão* (a Latin-tinged affair with Chet Baker, Kenny Barron, Jack DeJohnette and Nana Vasconcelos, 1981)
- *Super Strings* (a superb adventure of the quartet, with a 27-piece string orchestra, 1981)
- *Parfait* (a new quartet group with pianist Ted Lo, bassist Leon Maleson and drummer Wilby Fletcher, recorded before *Super Strings* but released in 1983)

In each of these sessions, Ron stretched himself as a composer, a bandleader and a producer, not to mention deepening his prowess as a virtuoso bass player. And, rather than delve into electrified jazz from his CTI years, Ron, now calling his own shots, focused on playing acoustic jazz. During his Milestone tenure, Ron was consistently voted the best bassist in critics' polls in *Playboy* and *DownBeat*.

Piccolo proved to be a head's-up experience for listeners and critics because of Ron's expansive perspective on jazz at the time. Don Heckman, writing in *High Fidelity*, suggested that Ron "seems to be going through an impressive renascence as a creative jazz force," while *Playboy* praised Ron's new direction by saying that "*el numero uno* of the bass world has moved on to the piccolo bass in an obvious attempt to prove less is more."

DownBeat cheered Ron by saying that he, "not unlike Muhammad Ali or Sir Lawrence Olivier, is superior not so much because he *tries* to be, but because what he *is* demands a certain level of permanence. Study, practice and application are indispensable to anyone who would succeed, but his success flows from a deeper, richer source."

In *Rolling Stone*, Bob Blumenthal ended his review of *Piccolo* by writing that though there were some faults in the album, the final product was a laudatory outing: "Criticisms do not, however, blunt the enjoyment of hearing a magnificent player on a magnificent instrument."

And Chris Albertson, writing in *Stereo Review*, raved about Ron's originality and his band's uniqueness: "If you have heard the Ron Carter Quartet in person or on the *Piccolo* album, you already know that it can get as funky as a sanctified church on Sunday and that it can also melt your emotions with sounds that in the hands of lesser artists might be downright unctuous..."

Also in the Milestone years, Ron produced *Third Plane*, a trio date where he reunited Miles alumni Herbie Hancock and Tony Williams. It was recorded in 1977 but, despite its top-drawer quality, not released until 1982.

Under Orrin's compilation supervision, in 1988 Fantasy released *Standard Bearers*, a best-of album of Ron's material from 1972–'79.

In addition, Ron recorded several dates as a sideman on the Fantasy imprint, Galaxy Records, including

- Philly Joe Jones's *Philly Mignon* (recorded in 1977)
- Chet Baker's *Once Upon a Summertime* (a reissue of an Artist House release, 1977)
- Nat Adderley's *A Little New York Midtown Music* (1978)
- Art Pepper's *New York Album* (1979)

However, Ron's best-known association with Galaxy was with Red Garland. He accompanied the pianist on four sublime recordings: *Red Alert* (1977), *Stepping Out* (1979), *Strike Up the Band* (1979) and *So Long Blues* (1979). Ron also recorded the live album *Carnaval* as a member of the Galaxy All-Stars band that comprised Hank Jones, Tony Williams and Japanese alto saxophonist Sadao Watanabe (1978).

MILESTONE JAZZSTARS

JUST AS CTI Records earlier in the '70s had organized all-star touring shows that included Ron, so too did Milestone put its marquee roster on display in 1978 with the Milestone Jazzstars. The tour, hailed as one of the major jazz events of the late '70s, featured the *crème de la crème* of the label: Ron, tenor saxophonist Sonny Rollins and pianist McCoy Tyner with Al Foster, the only nonroster artist who had been performing with Miles, playing the drums.

While Sonny had already been on the jazz scene for several years prior to Ron's and McCoy's emergence, by the time the three got together as the Jazzstars—their first time meeting as a band—they were all considered top-tier players.

In the liner notes to the souvenir booklet that concertgoers received on the tour (it included artist bios and, of course, each artist's discography on Milestone with a focus on the latest release—in Ron's case, *A Song for You*), Orrin wrote: "You are present tonight at a most historic occasion in American music, one of a limited number of concerts bringing together three important artists, each of whom must be considered a major factor in the shaping of jazz as we know it today."

In the same program, Bob Blumenthal in his "Summit Meeting" story wrote: "All art forms have their version of the summit meeting in which acclaimed practitioners create in collaboration; and given the special nature of jazz, where (regardless of era) personal expression, collective coherence and spontaneity are always the simultaneous goals, a meeting of jazz masters may be the ultimate creative conclave."

Orrin told *Rolling Stone* writer Mikal Gilmore, "This sort of thing just doesn't happen enough," while the band rehearsed before the tour at Fantasy's recording studio in Berkeley. After listening to the band run through a tune, Gilmore commented: "Truly it is as electric a performance as acoustic musicians are capable of."

That was high praise from the rock magazine during the era where electric fusion bands (Weather Report, the Headhunters, Return to Forever) trumped acoustic groups onstage. That trend had been bucked the previous year when Herbie Hancock assembled the all-acoustic V.S.O.P. tour with Ron, Wayne and Tony, along with Freddie Hubbard on trumpet. It was a resounding success.

Orrin called the Jazzstars summit "a spiritual descendant of the V.S.O.P. tour." Ron told *DownBeat*'s Doug Clark that there were similarities between the two all-star groups, but noted, "If there is a difference, it's the level of camaraderie involved. I literally grew up with Herbie and Tony and Wayne and Freddie, having played with them since 1963, on and off. We were having an old-hometime reunion. The camaraderie of this tour is different in that we have come together as adults."

Recognizing that the underlying motivation of the Milestone Jazzstars tour was commercial in nature, Gilmore asked Ron what he thought of the buzz behind the all-star outing. He acknowledged that the tour was "grant[ing] us greater visibility" to "thereby increase our record sales."

But Ron also stated that the time was right for an all-acoustic band to be on the road. "The public has gone as far with rock and fusion as they can," he told Gilmore. "This is just another of those events mandated by the new jazz awareness. In jazz, selling 50,000 copies of an album is news, but it's nothing when you talk about rock cats selling 7 million. I hope that the people who come to see us are as impressed with this music as they are with rock ... *and* I hope they carry over their record-buying proclivities."

Ron told Leonard Feather in the *Los Angeles Times*: "There will be no synthesizers on the piano. People will see a drum kit for just one drummer rather than a whole drum-shop load of equipment. They will observe no pedals around our feet. And they will not hear Sonny Rollins's horn electrified or distorted in any way. In short, what they see will be what they hear."

The tour, which featured full quartet tunes as well as trio, duet and solo numbers, began on September 16 at the Arlington Theater in Santa Barbara and ended on October 29 at the Academy of Music in Philadelphia. The Jazzstars played 20 concerts—eight in the West, six in the Midwest and six in the East. The venues the Jazzstars performed in were top-of-the-line concert halls, symphony spaces and civic auditoriums (including the Masonic Auditorium in San Francisco, the Music Hall in Boston, Beacon Theater in New York and Kennedy Center in Washington, D.C.). The tour was pegged by *DownBeat*'s Clark as a "Major Cultural Event."

Clark reported on the band's Portland, Oregon, show, which opened with a jam-infused take on Sonny's "The Cutting Edge" and concluded with Ron's "N.O. Blues," a rousing tribute to Crescent City funeral parades. During the show (split into two sets with an intermission), Ron played a bass solo of Sonny's "Doxy" (while other nights, he went it alone on Monk's "Blue Monk" or one of his favorite solo pieces, "Willow Weep for Me").

In *Rolling Stone* (in which Milestone placed an ad announcing the tour), Gilmore commented on two shows he saw on the West Coast: "Although they patronized the rock-bred audience's predilections for volume and flash, they also displayed the sensitivity—and humor—of musical partners who've weathered seasons together."

Orrin told Gilmore, "We strove for musical integrity with this. Not that I want to demean some of the people playing fusion, but these guys belong together musically. They're part of the same jazz community. Anybody who misses this ain't ever going to see anything quite like it again."

And for those who did miss one of the Jazzstars' shows live, Milestone recorded several concerts and released, late in 1978, a double album of highlights, *Milestone Jazzstars in Concert*, that included a 10-minute solo by Ron of "Willow Weep for Me."

CODA

AFTER RON'S STINT with Milestone ended, for the next decade, he continued to record for several labels until he signed with Toshiba-EMI in 1991 (see chapter on Blue Note Records). The most noteworthy of Ron's albums recorded between his offerings for Milestone and Blue Note were:

- *Heart and Soul* (a duo with Cedar Walton on Timeless, recorded in 1981)
- *Etudes* (with Art Farmer, saxophonist Bill Evans—a last-minute substitute for Wayne Shorter—and Tony Williams, recorded in 1982 and released in 1983 on Elektra Musician)
- *Live at Village West* and *Telephone* (two duo discs with Jim Hall, 1982 and 1984, respectively, for Concord Jazz)
- *All Alone* (a solo bass exploration on EmArcy, 1988)
- *Duets* (a duo album filed under vocalist Helen Merrill's name, EmArcy, 1988)
- *Panamanhattan* (a duo album with French accordionist Richard Galliano, recorded in 1990 and released on the French imprint Capitale Jazz in 1991 and Evidence Music in 1994 in the U.S.)

CHAPTER ELEVEN

EMI:
Somethin' Else / Blue Note

WHILE FREELANCING WIDELY during the mid-to-latter half of the '80s with a range of musicians—including the two relatively new kids in town, Branford and Wynton Marsalis, on the latter's 1985 Columbia album, *Black Codes (From the Underground)*, and the former's 1986 Columbia album, *Royal Garden Blues*—Ron settled into a multirecord deal with Japan's Toshiba-EMI in 1991. A&R director Hitoshi Namekata signed Ron, inking him to a four-year contract that called for one album each year (the first being *Ron Carter Meets Bach*, released in Japan on April 22, 1992).

To this day, Ron continues to record for the Somethin' Else jazz imprint of EMI Music Japan (in 2007, Toshiba, one of the leading music companies in Japan, sold off its 45 percent share in EMI). Many—but not all—of Ron's albums have been picked up for release in the U.S. by Blue Note Records (also owned by EMI, a British company).

Historically, the Blue Note label has been the gold standard in jazz. Founded as an independent in 1939 by Alfred Lion (who soon partnered with Francis Wolff), Blue Note became an important jazz player in the '50s, helping to usher in the hard bop movement. This commitment to the high art of jazz continued in the early '60s, when Ron found himself being enlisted for many recording dates, including sessions in the decade with Miles Davis band mates Herbie Hancock, Wayne Shorter and Tony Williams. During that era Ron was also a sideman for a range of Blue Note artists, including Sam Rivers, Freddie Hubbard, Duke Pearson, Lee Morgan, McCoy Tyner and Andrew Hill.

"I never understood why Alfred didn't offer me a date as a leader," Ron said. "I did a lot of sessions for him over those years. I jumped over a lot of hurdles in those sessions. But I never talked to him about it."

Lion sold Blue Note to Liberty Records in 1966. Not long after, the label went dormant as the popularity of jazz waned in the wake of rock 'n' roll's explosive expansion. The legendary jazz label was subsequently purchased by EMI in 1980 and finally resuscitated in 1985 by record exec Bruce Lundvall (previously at CBS Records and Elektra Musician). Blue

Note regained its status as an important jazz label, both with new signings as well as the reemergence of classic albums repackaged into boxed sets by producer Michael Cuscuna for his Mosaic Records label. (Today, significant Blue Note catalog albums are being remastered by original session engineer Rudy Van Gelder for the label's RVG Series.)

It was during this new era helmed by Bruce that Lion, who had retired to live in Mexico, became reacquainted with the label, even attending shows during Blue Note concert tours in Japan until his death in 1987. "Alfred had overlooked me as a leader in the '60s, but he was impressed with me in the '80s," said Ron. "I recorded a couple of live albums at the Village Vanguard with Joe Henderson and Al Foster under Joe's leadership. The albums were called *The State of the Tenor*, but Alfred said that the title should have been *The State of the Bass*."

Meanwhile, Ron's popularity surged in Japan. He was well known for his connection with Miles as well as V.S.O.P., the Miles reunion band (with Freddie Hubbard filling in for the leader). Plus, Ron toured there often, with CTI bands especially, and came to be known as a jazz giant—partially for his music, but also for his TV commercials for a range of products, including a high-profile association with Suntory, Japan's leading producer and distributor of alcoholic and nonalcoholic beverages. (On YouTube, there's a commercial Ron made for Suntory Whiskey White, where he plays his bass in a stark studio setting, as well as his latest TV commercial for Tully Coffee.)

But it's Japan's fascination with jazz that has made it an important market for the music. In a January 10, 1988 Associated Press article written by David Thurber, Japan's love affair with jazz was investigated. He pointed out that the circulation of Japan's jazz magazine, *Swing Journal*, was 400,000—more than four times larger than *DownBeat*'s circ at the time. He also noted that most American jazz artists sell more of their records in Japan than in the U.S.

Thurber quoted Cuscuna, who said that Japan "almost single-handedly" saved the jazz recording industry in the '70s when most major and indie labels in the U.S. curtailed or even shuttered their jazz operations. Thurber asked Ron why Japanese people gravitated to jazz more than Americans. He responded, "Japanese are no different from anyone else. The difference is they've been allowed to have exposure to the music, while in the U.S. there's a lack of media availability for jazz because of its origins." Hitoshi Namekata added, "Americans are too close to jazz to love it [the way we do]."

As for his popularity in commercials, Ron expressed amazement in how Japanese companies used foreign musicians to sell their products. "On top of that," he said, "I'm a six-foot-four black American with a beard—the opposite of a typical Japanese [person]."

Given Ron's superstar status there, it made sense that, rather than being invited to join the Blue Note stable in the U.S., he got signed by its sister company in Japan. Zach Hochkeppel, who today is the general manager of Blue Note, which is part of the Blue Note Label Group, says that Ron's record sales in the U.S. pale in comparison to Japan. "Ron is a legendary figure there," Zach said. "Here in the U.S., he's not only popular in jazz circles, but he also makes a good story for a nonjazz audience. He's had stories done on him for magazines like *Vibe* and *Fader*."

Bruce Lundvall, who today serves as the CEO/president of the Blue Note Label Group (whose impact—and financial well-being—has been boosted by the series of Norah Jones pop albums), has a history with Ron. He was the head of Elektra Musician when Ron shopped him his *Etudes* album, which he had produced independently. "I love Ron, who's one of the greatest bass players," Bruce said. "I liked the concept of *Etudes*." He added, "I still have the photo of our signing agreement."

Since 1991, Ron has recorded a stylistic range of albums for EMI, including Brazilian (see chapter on Brazil), Latin, classical (see chapter on classical music) and straight-up jazz with his various bands, including the Striker Trio and his quartet (see chapters on each group). A full discography of Ron's EMI offerings beginning in 1992, including titles never released in the U.S., is in the discography appendix.

Some of Ron's best albums from the '90s include 1994's well-received *Jazz, My Romance* (a trio setting with Kenny Barron on piano and Herb Ellis on guitar), 1996's *Mr. Bow-Tie* (with Gonzalo Rubalcaba on piano, trumpeter Edwin Russell and saxophonist Javon Jackson, and drummer Lewis Nash) and 1997's *Bass & I* (a quartet date with pianist Stephen Scott, drummer Lewis Nash and percussionist Steve Kroon). The latter is the only album of the bunch that is still in print in the Blue Note catalog—the others have been deleted and are no longer available.

The following are in-depth sketches of three of Ron's albums for Blue Note in the new century: 2001's *When Skies Are Grey* (deleted), 2002's *Stardust* (in print) and 2007's *Dear Miles* (in print).

BACKSTORY—SKIES WERE GRAY

WHILE RON'S *WHEN Skies Are Grey* album—recorded in 2000 and released in the U.S. in 2001, a year after being issued in Japan—buoys with a spirited Latin vibe, it was nonetheless overshadowed literally by a gloomy, gray firmament. On April 25, 2000, only a few days before the recording session for the album, Ron's wife Janet died.

Ron dedicated the album to his band mates— pianist Stephen Scott, drummer Harvey Mason and percussionist Steve Kroon—who brought to the session stellar "awareness, sympathy and musicianship." He said, "My wife passed away during the week before we went into the studio. On Saturday we had a memorial service, on Sunday my sons, Ron Jr. and Myles, and I had a private funeral, and at nine o'clock Monday morning I was in the studio with the band. Stephen, Harvey and Steve gave me a lot of emotional support."

In the late '80s, Janet started to show signs of deteriorating health. A collector and licensed dealer of African-American art, she had a gallery on Greene Street in Manhattan, but she gave it up when her health started to fail. "Janet kept her art relationships going, but art as a business was no longer possible for her," said Ron. "We didn't understand what was going on until the early '90s. She started to lose the feeling in one foot, but she didn't tell me. She had a high tolerance for pain, which she was experiencing. I only found out later. Because of this, I didn't know how serious her condition was."

Finally, in 1995, Janet was diagnosed with diabetes, after, on her initiative and unbeknownst to Ron, she went to a clinic at Columbia University. The disease wasn't widely discussed as a condition that African Americans were genetically prone to, Ron said. "In the black community, you'd hear people say, oh, she's got sugar. Now, what the hell is that? Plus, the treatment for diabetes was not readily available to blacks then. The only thing you could do was take insulin. Now, treatment also includes diet awareness and taking tablets, but that didn't exist then."

Because of the numbness in her feet, late in 1999, Janet made a misstep in the apartment and fell hard to the floor. Ron took her to Roosevelt Hospital on 59th Street and 10th Avenue. The doctors took X-rays of her foot and hand. While there, Janet started to take a turn for the worse. "I'm watching her heart monitor going up and down, and thinking what is going on?" said Ron. "I don't watch a lot of TV, but I had seen enough to know that something was going wrong."

Ron shouted out to the doctor, "Hey, I need your help. I think my wife's having a heart attack. And she was." As he retold the story, he became emotionally irritated at the care Janet had received.

Janet was transferred via ambulance to St. Luke's Hospital at 114th Street and Amsterdam Avenue, where she underwent an operation to replace two heart valves with stents to help increase the blood circulation. The size of her heart valves had constricted because of the diabetes. Janet needed three stents, but the surgeons could only put in two. "From then on, Janet's time was short," Ron said.

He hired a nurse to watch over Janet while he continued to gig. Then one day, six months after the operation, he took Janet to her heart doctor for another routine follow-up. At the time she still had a soft cast on her foot, so Ron and the home nurse wheeled Janet's chair into her appointment. After the visit, Ron parked the car in the garage of his apartment building and had the nurse take Janet upstairs in the elevator. When he arrived on the 10th floor, the nurse said, "Mr. Carter, I think your wife had a heart attack." Janet's heart had stopped. Ron laid her on the bed and got her heart beating again while the nurse called 9-1-1.

In the ambulance, Janet's heart stopped again, at which time the ambulance workers began pounding her chest to try to get her heart beating. Ron yelled, "Hey, she's just had open-heart surgery, and she hasn't healed up yet. People with diabetes take longer to heal!"

When they arrived at the hospital, Janet's heart stopped again. They revived her again, but because her brain had been deprived of oxygen for so long, the prognosis was dire. Ron was told that if Janet continued to live she would do so with permanent brain damage. Ron consulted with the doctors and then called Ron Jr. and Myles, both living in Boston, to talk about disconnecting her lifeline.

So, after a grueling decade of declining health, Janet passed away, the day after Myles's twin sons were born. Many people, who worked with Ron over those years and who asked not to be identified, surmise that this difficult period could well have sparked some of the bassist's testy reactions to people he didn't know very well. Even though he was experiencing a lot of home-front pressure because of Janet's health, Ron kept his personal circumstances at arm's length, even to close friends.

However, Ron still had to deal with some pressing business of his own—confronting Janet's heart surgeon who, on three previous office visits, had assured him that Janet "was going to be just fine. I promise."

After Janet died, Ron drove to the hospital four times looking for the doctor and telephoned eight times without a return call. "I was livid," he said, while reliving his anger. "I'm still upset. He had continually misdiagnosed Janet's condition. He deprived me of Janet's life. I was looking for that guy. If I had found him, I was ready to do not a good thing ..."

Ron's voice trailed off, and he appeared visibly upset.

WHEN SKIES ARE GREY

GIVEN THE TRAGIC circumstances, did Ron consider postponing the recording date for *When Skies Are Grey*? "It never crossed my mind," he said. "Janet would have wanted me to do it that way. Besides, I'm sure she's enjoying it now. Of course, the first hour of recording was difficult. I wanted to be at her gravesite instead, but then I had enough music looking at me that I had no choice but to settle in. The recording was like a tribute to her. Sometimes people listen to albums without knowing the background dynamics. Well, this experience I went through gave the life to this record."

With backdrop established, Ron talked music.

When asked about the Latin tinge that imbued *When Skies Are Grey*, Ron, 63 at the time, said, "Steve had been on my case for awhile to make a record like this where the Latin element was the focus. But I kept arguing that there were plenty of other guys who had more experience. I had done a Brazilian album and that worked really well, but Latin?"

However, then Ron recalled old Latin-flavored sessions he participated in, such as Wes Montgomery's 1961 album *So Much Guitar* for Riverside with conguero Ray Barretto. He mulled over the Latin concept and then gave the project the green light. "I figured that I had played in a Latin jazz context enough times that we could pull it off by bringing a strong jazz mentality into the sessions. All of the players on this album are jazz musicians so we could bring in other harmonic choices and not wear out the Latin basics."

A key player in the recording proved to be arranger Bob Freedman, who made sure the Latin nuances of the tunes were accentuated. "Bob deserves a lot of credit," Ron said. "With his arrangements, I believe we held our own against any Latin band. We didn't just add congas to the mix; we played in the style." In addition to two numbers that came from the classic Latin songbook, Ron and company delivered four Carter originals, in addition to testing the Latin chemistry with a Brazilian tune, the Antonio Carlos Jobim beauty, "Corcovado."

When Skies Are Grey opened with a blast, as the band launched into Ron's "Loose Change," a catchy, Latin-tinged number that featured lots of changes in the musical flow. "I wrote this with an awareness of the increase in homelessness," Ron said. "So there's a little nickel here and a dime there. One of my friends Mort Goode wrote lyrics to the tune which Grady Tate recorded on one of his records as 'The Beggar's Opera.'"

The lightly swinging "Besame Mucho," the second track, is "an old Latin warhorse that we dress up as a jazz number," Ron said, adding that he hoped their version of the Consuelo Velazquez tune would "raise some eyebrows in the Latin community. Making people hear things in a new way is what music is all about."

The other Latin jazz standard was the hip, bouncy "Cubano Chant" by Ray Bryant. "This was the hardest number to pull off," Ron said. "It goes into a swing when you least expect it. But, wow, just to hear Stephen play this." At the time of the recording, Ron said, "He keeps getting better and better. He's maturing well and I'm happy to have been part of his growth."

The third track, "Caminando," was another catchy Ron original delivered with a quiet ebullience. "I was stumbling around with this until we finally got it during rehearsal," he said, and then added, "I love the way Harvey plays the cymbals here because it makes the sound of the bass shiver." This was followed by Ron's "Qué Pasa," which opens as a somber ballad then develops into a swing. "This is an early Miles-like tune with a plaintive melody," Ron said. "I like the way Steve's percussion answers my bass lines, which dictate the direction of the number."

Having played Jobim's "Corcovado" with a Brazilian band before, Ron decided to give it the Latin treatment. "The Latin vibe worked," he said, "especially with Bob's arrangement and Stephen's chord voicings."

The finale of *When Skies Are Grey* proved to be a showstopper. "Mi Tiempo," another new Ron composition, featured the bassist leading with both Harvey and Steve engaging him in a long, moving rhythmic dialogue. "It was a nice surprise that this song stood up without the piano," Ron said. "It was also a nice way to end the recording."

STARDUST

STARDUST NOT ONLY paid homage to the great jazz bassist Oscar Pettiford, but also found Ron in the company of simpatico musicians—tenor saxophonist Benny Golson, vibes player Joe Locke, pianist Sir Roland Hanna and drummer Lenny White—most of whom he had never recorded with as a leader.

"Putting this album together was a combination of the chicken coming before the egg and the egg coming before the chicken," said Ron, then 65. "I set out to pay tribute to Oscar Pettiford, but I also had in mind bringing these players together for the right project." The music on the album included three compositions by Oscar; a cover of "Stardust," one of his signature performance pieces; three Ron originals that complemented the Pettiford numbers; and a rendition of the Gershwins' "The Man I Love," which Ron felt was compatible.

The tunes were performed in various band configurations, from full quintet setting (featuring the rapt harmonies of Benny's tenor and Joe's vibes) to duo (a stunning bass-piano rendition of the Hoagy Carmichael-composed title track). The overall mood was characterized by buoyancy. Ron attributed that to both the music itself and the band's relaxed delivery, helped, in no small part, he said, by his teammates all doing their homework before the studio session.

"These tracks were all live and most were, I believe, the first and only takes," Ron said proudly. "If the musicians you enlist buy into the concept and prepare for the recording by rehearsing the music, then you avoid the false starts, the take 25s and the need for editing. All these guys sensed the music. They knew there was something there and that they only had a short time—six minutes on average—to dig it out, to get as deep and intense as possible. There was a lot of air in these tunes that the players filled in with their notes at just the right times."

Ron regrets never having met or seen Pettiford perform (the bassist died in 1960 at the age of 37 in Europe where he had relocated in 1958, a year before Ron moved from Rochester to New York). And even though Ron noted that Oscar's bass playing wasn't an influence on his own four-string prowess, he said that he was impressed by the way he wrote great bass melodies at a time when few other four-stringers were composing on the instrument. "Oscar was known as a soloist and as an excellent rhythm section player," Ron said. "But I believe he was overlooked as a composer. He wrote difficult melodies with a nonconservatory technique. Unfortunately his library is not well known in the jazz community. So this was my little attempt to bring his compositional skills to the fore."

In assembling his band for the date, one of the first people Ron thought of was Benny, with whom he had recorded and toured under the tenor saxophonist's leadership. "I've always wanted to do one of my own recording dates with Benny," he said at the time of the recording. "He's a great leader in his own right and understands what it means to take instructions because he always has to give them when he's got his own band. Plus, he's one of my favorite tenor players and a good friend who I can call if I run into problems when I'm working on one of my own compositions." Benny was featured on "The Man I Love," a tune that Ron liked but rarely had the opportunity to play.

Ron met Joe Locke for the first time three years earlier at a Thelonious Monk Institute event, and he liked what he heard. "Joe's vibes have such a bright sound," he said. "Benny has such a mellow tone and my tone is dark. So I wanted Joe to provide splashes of red throughout the record to increase the sound spectrum." Ron noted that he had heard a couple of Pettiford tunes played by Milt Jackson years ago but hadn't heard another vibes player do so since, so he asked Joe to join in.

As for bringing Lenny into the session, Ron said, "It's so nice to hear him on drums, especially when he doesn't have to slash and bash his way through a date to be successful." He singled out Lenny's cymbal work on "Blues in the Closet."

The inclusion of Sir Roland, who died in November 2002 shortly after the CD was released in the U.S., was special to Ron. At the time of the recording, Ron said, "Roland is one of my favorite piano players. He can play anything. I work with Roland anytime I can because I know I'll leave the date with a whole lot more than when I came in." While his contributions were omnipresent on the album, he was particularly brilliant accompanying Ron on their sublime take of "Stardust." Ron said, "Roland spent a long time accompanying vocalists, so I would have been a fool not to have him play with me on that number, which I usually performed solo in concert. When we finished playing, everyone in the studio was hushed."

Ron's originals included a revival of the sink-into-the-groove, blues-flavored "Nearly" that Chet Baker had recorded with Kenny Barron and Jack DeJohnette; the jaunty "Tail Feathers," which featured remarkable tenor sax-vibes harmonies; and "That's Deep," a Joe Locke showcase. Ron's tunes melded with the Pettiford pieces, which he explained were indicative of the bass elder's compositional range: the catchy, Latin-tinged tune "Tamalpais," the spirited bebop number "Bohemia After Dark" and the upbeat, blues-based "Blues in the Closet."

"These are songs that I enjoy listening to but rarely get played," Ron said. "We just settled into this session and played."

DEAR MILES

DUBBED BY MILES as the "anchor" of his classic '60s quintet, Ron had enjoyed a prolific and fertile career of his own since he left the iconic trumpeter's employ in 1968, both as a support-team member as well as a leader in his own right. But Ron finally—and fully—paid tribute to his former friend and musical revolutionary with *Dear Miles*, a quartet date that showcased the playfully unpredictable dynamic he had inculcated into his own band—comprised of pianist Stephen Scott, drummer Payton Crossley and percussionist Roger Squitero.

"I would have been offended 10 years ago if someone had asked me to do a Miles tribute album," Ron said at the time the recording was released (2007 in the U.S.; 2006 in Japan). "But as it turned out, several of the songs in my quartet's library were also from Miles's songbook." He hastened to note, however, that tribute projects can pose challenges: "Most end up with artists imitating [others] and losing themselves in the process. Even though I've been involved in projects like the 4 Generations of Miles and V.S.O.P., I wasn't ready to do an album like this before, for fear of getting swallowed up by the Miles tribute aura."

What distinguished *Dear Miles* from other homages was Ron's ability to firmly establish his quartet's personality while tapping into the essence of Miles's music. At the time the album was released, Ron had already anticipated the inevitable criticism: "People may say, 'Oh, another tribute record,' but I say, 'Check it out.' They'll hear how this band stands by itself in its sound and its library, while also paying homage."

The 10-track collection featured several tunes closely associated with Miles's repertoire spanning the '50s and '60s in addition to two Carter originals and a couple of loosely related Miles tunes. One of the high-water marks was the quartet's spirited zip through "Seven Steps to Heaven," with the band verbally expressing its appreciation of the play factor at work in the piece. "There are so many choices in that tune," Ron said. "There's so much meat on the bone that you can find ways to keep playing it over and over again."

Ron embarked on *Dear Miles* to document his quartet. "We had been working a lot and we were sounding like what I call a band—with the dynamics of a band and a library that we felt comfortable with," he said. "With this group, I feel like I can manipulate the music anyway I want to, and the guys will understand what I'm trying to do."

From Ron's experience in Miles's '60s classic quintet, he knew full well the advantages to recording with a group of simpatico collaborators willing to go to the limits in their adventurous musical interchanges. "The recording industry makes it difficult to keep a working band with the same personnel together," he said. "They figure that the more varied the personnel is from CD to CD, the larger the audience you'll pull in. That's never been my view. Look at important bands in the history of jazz: John Coltrane with Elvin, McCoy and Jimmy; Dave Brubeck with Paul, Gene and Joe; Cannonball with Nat, Sam and Louis. They all made great records because they were all working bands."

Once it was determined that Miles would serve as a guidepost to this album, Ron set his sights on re-envisioning the music in his and his band's image. The set opened with Gil Evans's "Gone," from his *Porgy & Bess* collaboration with Miles. The challenge for Ron was to reduce the big band sound to quartet, which he accomplished with Stephen's help. "So we get a bright snare drum with the piano sounding out the horn parts," Ron said, "thereby coming up with a full-band sound as a quartet."

Several Miles staples were featured, including a rapturous and swinging "My Funny Valentine" (featuring vibrant Ron-Stephen interchanges), the lyrical "Some Day My Prince Will Come" (which, to Ron, represented the "bridge between Miles's '50s quintet and ours"), the balladic gem "Stella by Starlight" (featuring Ron taking the melodic lead with deep, full-toned bass lines) and "Bye Bye Blackbird" (a favorite of Ron's that was originally recorded on the first Miles album he bought in the late '50s). Other tunes included a grooving take on Milt Jackson's "Bag's Groove" (from Miles's '50s library) and a sprightly rendition of "As Time Goes By," which, while Davis never recorded, Ron said, "honors Miles's uncanny ability to find a song no one else has tried and make it essential to the jazz songbook."

Two of Ron's originals filled out the set. The first, "Cut & Paste," was a playful jaunt with speeding bass lines and pianistic flurries. It was a genuine romp that Ron said is "something bright to add to the library to keep everyone on their toes—including me." The other track, the gently grooving "595," closed the album with a feeling that Ron likened to relaxing in front of a fireplace. "It's a nice way to end because it's like a defusing of all the emotion in the previous tracks," he said.

Dear Miles was recorded in one morning. The band rehearsed for three days before entering the studio. All 10 tracks were first takes that gave the CD a sparkling live vibe. "I'm not into recording 25 takes," Ron reiterated. "I set out to maintain a level of enthusiasm and concentration. I didn't want to have minds wander or solos meander. There was only one chance to get each song right."

Writing in the CD's liner notes, I encouraged people listening to *Dear Miles* to focus, above all, on Ron's bass virtuosity, from his in-the-moment solos, harmonically supported by his quartet, to his always-shifting, never-static bass lines throughout. I wrote, "[Ron] doesn't keep time; he creates it. He doesn't dictate; he suggests. He doesn't play it safe; he goes out on limbs."

V.S.O.P. is held up as an exemplar of new jazz on the cover of *Newsweek* magazine, August 8, 1977. The story inside posited that jazz was making a comeback after years of being trumped by rock in popularity. V.S.O.P. was cited as one of many acts leading the charge with sold-out shows that featured revitalized versions of such tunes as Wayne Shorter's "Nefertiti" and Herbie Hancock's "Maiden Voyage." (*Magazine courtesy of Willie Carter*)

Above: Debonair as always in an undated publicity photo for Milestone Records

Below Left: A late '70s press kit reprinted a *Down Beat* interview by Ed Williams entitled "Ron Carter: The Compleat Artist" (from the February 2, 1978 issue); **Below Right:** Another press kit, this one from the late 1980s

(*All images courtesy of Ron Carter*)

 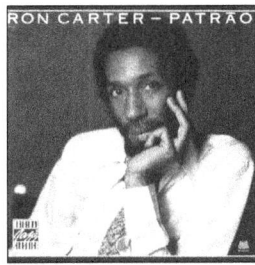 

Above and Left: A selection of album covers from Ron's Milestone and Galaxy Records years (*Courtesy of The Concord Music Group*)

Below: Some of the Milestone masters on a shelf at the former Fantasy Records vault in Berkeley, California, 2006; the Fantasy catalog has since been transferred to The Concord Music Group and the masters relocated to Southern California (*Dan Ouellette*)

Above: Ron's first quartet publicity photo for Milestone Records; (from left to right) Ron with piccolo bass; pianist Kenny Barron; bassist Buster Williams; drummer Ben Riley (*Courtesy of Ron Carter*)

Below: For *Parade*, a 1979 Milestone release, Ron assembled an all-star quartet with (from left to right) Chick Corea, Joe Henderson and Tony Williams, supplemented by an additional seven-man horn section. (*Courtesy of Ron Carter*)

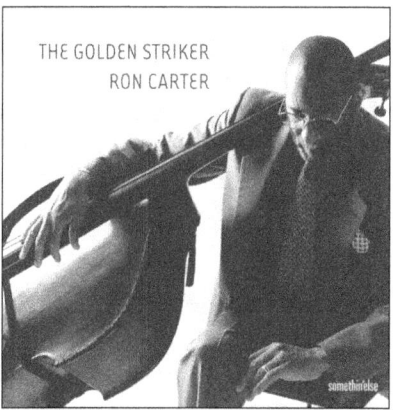

A collection of album covers from the Somethin' Else label, an imprint of EMI Japan. The top two albums were released only in Japan. All others were released on Somethin' Else in Japan and Blue Note Records in the U.S. (*Courtesy of EMI Japan*)

The Milestone Jazzstars tour featured Ron alongside McCoy Tyner (left) and Sonny Rollins (right) for 20 nights in the autumn of 1978. In the tour's souvenir program producer Orrin Keepnews wrote, "You are present tonight at a most historic occasion in American music, one of a limited number of concerts bringing together three important artists, each of whom must be considered a major factor in the shaping of jazz as we know it today." (*Reprinted from tour program; courtesy of Ron Carter*)

In Japan, where Ron has released dozens of albums that have never received distribution in the U.S., advertisements with his picture adorn subway cars and station platforms (above, 2007), and even turn up on telephone calling cards, as in a 1990s ad campaign for F-One (below). "Ron is so big in Japan," mused his friend, saxophonist Houston Person. "He's what you would call a star. We were in a department store once, and people came running up to him to get his autograph. Now that's star power." (*All images courtesy of Ron Carter*)

The Striker Trio, backstage after their Playboy Jazz Festival performance at the Hollywood Bowl, 2006; Ron, foreground; Russell Malone, left; Mulgrew Miller, right (*Dan Ouellette*)

PART IV
THE FREELANCE YEARS

CHAPTER TWELVE

Sideman: The Carter Effect— Comfort and Provocation

IT WOULD BE a herculean feat to comprehensively catalog Ron's achievements as a sideman. Read any account of his career and what stands out most, after his association with Miles, is his session work. Ron is justifiably heralded as the most recorded jazz bassist in the history of the recording industry, and he could well be the most prolific sideman overall, regardless of instrument. The estimates run from 2,000 to 3,000 recordings. Some people say sessions, others albums. Ron says that close to three thousand "sessions" is probably right, but notes that some albums require more than one session and that the tracks of live albums are usually gleaned from at least two nights of work. Then there are the dozens of albums he has recorded in Japan that have never made it stateside.

Ron's credits are spread far and wide in the industry. He has done sessions with pop singers such as Roberta Flack, Aretha Franklin, Paul Simon and Erykah Badu as well as recorded with most of the jazz titans. The short list includes Wes Montgomery, Paul Desmond, Antonio Carlos Jobim, Nat Adderley, J.J. Johnson, Jimmy Smith, Freddie Hubbard, Stanley Turrentine, Lee Morgan, Andrew Hill, Stan Getz, Coleman Hawkins, Joe Henderson and Horace Silver as well as all the alumni of Miles's '60s Quintet on their individual projects.

Not even Ron knows how many albums—including both studio and live dates—he appears on. When I recently unearthed a Bill Evans album he recorded for Riverside in 1962, released for the first time as *Loose Blues* 30 years later on Milestone, Ron remembered the session well, but never recalled hearing about the album coming out. He never received a copy, and to this day does not have one in his possession.

In May 2006, when I visited Fantasy Records in Berkeley, California, before the company was sold to the Concord Music Group, I asked an old acquaintance, Stuart Kremsky, who was the keeper of the vaults of master tapes, if I could visit the storage room again (I had done so years earlier while writing a story on Orrin Keepnews for a local paper). I took pictures in the vault (which has subsequently been stripped of its contents and relocated to Southern California) of Ron's masters for his Milestone Records years. After snapping several photos of the metal spines of his 30-year-old reels, we went into the next room where Stuart looked into his computer database of jazz recording history to see how many dates Ron had participated in. We came across close to 1,000.

But we both wondered how accurate that database was. Many micro-independent imprints and foreign labels were probably not in the system. Nor would it have identified Ron's beyond-jazz work, such as with Jefferson Airplane (1974's *Manhole*, ostensibly the group's final experimental album, where Ron overdubbed bass lines on the 15-minute title track of orchestrated rock) or A Tribe Called Quest (1991's seminal hip hop album, *The Low End Theory*).

Much of Ron's personal collection of more than 700 sideman recordings is housed in the Eastman School of Music's Sibley Music Library—a gift Ron bequeathed to his alma mater. But even that collection is incomplete. Ron says that he often gets notes from people about an album that he'd entirely forgotten about. Plus, he notes, with the Internet today, he rediscovers all kinds of albums that slipped his mind. For these reasons, the discography in the appendix is far from comprehensive.

Even now, it's a challenge to keep up with Ron. On the same day in 2006, I received two advance CDs with him prominently featured. Both albums were released a few weeks apart. One was guitarist Bill Frisell's Nonesuch album *Bill Frisell, Ron Carter, Paul Motian*, and the other was pianist Geri Allen's *Timeless Portraits and Dreams*, on Telarc.

I ran into Bill in the lobby of the Hilton Rotterdam at the North Sea Jazz Festival and told him that I had received the new CD. I asked him how this trio date came about. Painfully bashful at times, Bill beamed and said it was so special. "Ron is such an important player to me. He's one of my heroes."

Bill first came upon Ron when he was in high school and accompanying a school talent show of girls performing a dance routine to the Wes Montgomery song, "Bumpin' on Sunset," from the guitarist's 1966 *Tequila* album. "The band teacher gave me the album, and this was the first jazz solo I learned to play on the guitar," he said. "The floodgates were opened. I bought another Wes album, then one by Kenny Burrell and Miles. Soon I was listening to Eric Dolphy, Jim Hall, Sonny Rollins, Herbie, Wayne, Tony, Sam Rivers, Freddie Hubbard, McCoy. This music changed my life. I kept looking at the credits of the albums and coming across the name Ron Carter. He was on every album. Ron is the thread that runs through it all, since he played with all those guys. It's too huge a thing to even describe what he's meant to all the music. He's been the backbone of the most inspiring music."

Bill's first opportunity to meet and play with Ron came in 1997 when the drummer Joey Baron invited the bassist to participate in the sessions for his album *Down Home*, which also included alto saxophonist Arthur Blythe. They all rendezvoused again on Joey's *We'll Soon Find Out* album, released internationally in 1999 (see the Joey & Bill snapshot). In that same year, Ron invited Bill to play on his Brazilian-styled album, *Orefu*. "We'd done some gigs with Joey's band and also some club gigs at the Blue Note in New York," Bill said. "Ron's been so supportive of my music and me. I wrote a tune for him, 'Ron Carter,' on my *Blues Dream* album. The bass line has only two notes."

Regarding Geri, her first studio encounter with Ron came in 1994 when she enlisted him and Tony Williams to lock down the rhythm on her *Twenty One* trio album. Reviewing the disc in the *Los Angeles Times*, Don Heckman wrote, "Many jazz pianists deal with the disparity [of playing with tonally limited instruments] by taking a path of least resistance, using bass and drums as accompanists rather than full-fledged musical creative associates. But with this particular trio...Allen takes the classically oriented route of conceiving music that is structured around an equal and continually unfolding interaction among the players." The result, Heckman wrote, "is a surging rhythmic energy." He added that Ron "freed for once of the obligations of being a leader plays some of the finest choruses of recent memory."

In recognition of *Twenty One*, Geri became the first recipient of Soul Train's Lady of Soul Award for jazz album of the year.

A more complex and spiritual project, *Timeless Portraits and Dreams* featured Geri in a setting that included vocalists (jazz singer Carmen Lundy and George Shirley, the first African-American tenor to sing at the Metropolitan Opera), the Atlanta Jazz Chorus, horn players (trumpeter Wallace Roney and tenor saxophonist Donald Walden), and the rhythm team of Ron and Jimmy Cobb. The album opened with two Allen compositions segued together and undergirded by Ron's creative bass lines that dipped under and floated above the subtle hues of the chorus.

On the car ride from his West End Avenue home to the studio for Geri's session, Ron drove with Miles's music on the CD player. He was the picture of refinement, a dress shirt and pants, a bright scarf and long winter jacket. Halfway to the studio, Ron double-parked the car outside of a flower shop and returned to it with a huge bouquet of flowers, which he presented to Geri with a kiss on the cheek as soon as he entered the studio. She was very pleased.

"If he's not already, Ron should be in the *Guinness Book of World Records* for appearing on the most albums," said Geri. "When you bring into the studio one of the greatest musicians in the world who personifies the highest level of artistic achievement, you know the sessions will be good. When Ron walks in, he immediately commands respect. He's a consummate professional who sets the bar at the highest level and you have to rise to that. Ron makes everyone play to that higher level."

Geri calls her trio date with Ron and Tony on *Twenty One* the "highlight of my career and a breakthrough moment." She toured the album for two years, with Ron joining her along with drummer Lenny White. "I can't thank Ron enough," she said. "I learned so much from him each night. In Europe, we'd go from one country to the next, and he knew the national anthem for each that he would play in his solos."

SESSION SNIPPETS—JAZZ

WHEN ASKED WHAT advice he would give to young musicians about being a side person, Ron says that the utmost goal is to make the leader shine. "You need to do whatever you can to make that person sound good. I feel comfortable playing with people when I'm not the leader. When you're a sideman, you don't usurp a leader's identity or role. You don't embarrass. You try to fix. You treat the leader with respect. You can play with a leader who has a strong musical personality, but you have to be aware of how you can make him or her sound good."

Ron was the go-to bassist for CTI recordings and after that for Milestone. He served as the anchor for many other labels, including Fantasy Records' Galaxy imprint.

In 1975, Ron recorded as a sideman with jazz elder Benny Goodman. The Columbia Records album was *Seven Come Eleven* and included the leader playing with four different combos. Interviewed in the 2007 JVC Jazz Festival of New York program guide, Jim Hall said: "[Ron] told me a story about some kind of session he did with Benny one time. Benny played one of his short endings, and Ron hit a B-flat and it kept ringing. Benny turned around and said, 'What the hell was that?' and Ron said, 'B-flat.' I bet that note was ringing three days later."

"Benny didn't like that," Ron said in recalling the date where he supported Goodman alongside Grady Tate, Billy Taylor and Bucky Pizzarelli. "But I cut him off. I told him he couldn't talk to me like that. I remember how he had come into the studio with a terrible attitude. He didn't say a word to me until I played that note."

Ron was an essential player on Stan Getz's 1967 album *Sweet Rain*, which also featured Chick Corea on piano and Grady on drums. While Stan had been the champion of bossa nova since his *Getz/Gilberto* album in 1963 (he said that period of his musical life had put his children through college), he wanted to break from the idiom, which he did with *Sweet Rain*. He enlisted a crack team of sidemen that Steve Huey, writing in *All Music Guide*, said "were all schooled in '60s concepts of rhythm section freedom [whose] stimulating interplay helps open things up for Getz to embark on some long, soulful explorations." He continued, "The neat trick of *Sweet Rain* is that the advanced rhythm section work remains balanced with Getz's customary loveliness and lyricism."

Alto saxophone great Paul Desmond got turned on to Ron's playing through working with producer Creed Taylor at CTI. Paul's first recordings with Ron were 1968's *Summertime* and 1969's *From the Hot Afternoon* and *Bridge Over Troubled Water* (all released on A&M/CTI). On the independent

CTI, Ron served as the bass chair for Paul's 1973 *Skylark* and 1974 *Pure Desmond*. They also appeared on many albums as fellow sidemen. "His adaptability is amazing," Paul told *New Times* magazine in its December 10, 1976 feature on Ron. "Most players have a special characteristic, a certain kind of feel, and then if you want another mood, you get a different guy. But Ron covers it all. My only regret is that it took me so long to get to him. I should have been playing with him years ago."

In the early '60s, Ron appeared on several Benny Golson albums, beginning with the tenor saxophonist's 1962 quartet date, *Free*, which also included pianist Tommy Flanagan and drummer Arthur Taylor. The album features the tune "Shades of Stein." In a 2006 e-mail letter Benny wrote to Ron, he mused on that tune, noting that in writing it he kept going back to concert G over and over. "Then I decided to create chromatic motion on the bridge ... moving upward in major thirds rather than fourths as is usually done in jazz. As we usually do, I did this and moved on to other things. Then one day I heard you move upward chromatically on a blues you recorded with Milt Jackson. I almost jumped out of my socks. You, too, were onto this thought of chromatics though [using] chromatics is not considered very creative. On 'Shades of Stein,' I had created something based on this technique where nothing whatsoever existed before, but you took it a step further..."

Benny continued, "You're constantly doing these sorts of things. I do them mostly when I write, which means I have time to meticulously work out things beforehand, whereas you create them spontaneously, on the spot, at any moment. You, then, are a fearless, yet precise adventurer of the highest degree."

Benny likes to characterize Ron as a super-hero performer. He recalls working with Ron on his 1983 album *This Is for You, John*, a session where Benny paid tribute to his boyhood friend, John Coltrane, and again in 1987 on the album *Stardust*.

In 2001 Ron hired Benny to work on one of his albums for the first time, also titled *Stardust*. The session took place on April 6. In a personal letter to Ron, dated April 8, 2001, Benny expounded on his friend's abilities, both as a leader and sideman. He wrote: "It was a delight being part of your recording session. Because of your clear, creative mind, it went forward with great speed and purpose, setting things into place for posterity. As I told you yesterday, after all these years of forging ahead, I find that you're still wonderfully ascendant. I am quite delighted by this; it shows that as a dreamer, which all creative people are, you never stop dreaming and reaching into your capacious imagination where things are conceived.... As the present is overcome by the future, it's quite obvious that you are the architect of your own future. The carefully selected building blocks you use will insist that your talent and your music ... will live past your time as in the case of Diz, Bird, Tatum and Duke."

When reminded of his missive, Benny said, "That's true. Ronnie is a no-nonsense guy. I try to be the same myself. He's not frivolous in anything he does. Once he plays something, it's there for all of posterity. He buys into that spirit."

While veterans praise Ron's prowess as a sideman, the bassist has also proved to be a valuable addition to sessions led by young jazz artists. Prime example: Kenny Garrett's breakthrough album, *African Exchange Student*, recorded in 1990 when the alto saxophonist was playing in Miles Davis's final band. Kenny has gone on to top-tier jazz status. More recently Ron has mentored another young saxophonist, his former student Ignaz Dinné, who featured him on his second CD, *The Next Level* (with Ron's name on the cover as being the featured artist), released in 2008.

Cuban-born pianist Gonzalo Rubalcaba, who moved to Santo Domingo in the Dominican Republic in 1992 and eventually to the U.S. in 1996, was signed to a record deal through EMI/Toshiba in Japan, which issued his albums in the U.S. on Blue Note Records. While mentored by bassist Charlie Haden, who met the young piano phenom in 1986, Gonzalo also entered into an inspiring, on-the-road trio tutelage with Ron in 1993 along with drummer Julio Barreto.

"I was very young, and Ron was our teacher in every aspect," Gonzalo said. "We spent weeks touring Europe, and Ron never imposed on us an attitude of follow me. He's a smart musician who's very sensitive. At each concert, he was always trying to get us to do something different, like changing tempos, harmonies, rhythms."

Ron performed anchor duty on Gonzalo's trio date, *Diz*, which was released in 1995. "People think that Ron is closed, but he's a musician who's a lot more open than you'd think," said Gonzalo. "He was always open to experimenting."

Michael Cuscuna, who produced pianist Benny Green's 1997 Blue Note Records album *Kaleidoscope*, recalls Ron's settling presence at that recording date. "Benny was young and could be very indecisive about what to play because he was somewhat of a perfectionist," said Michael. "In some ways he was driving people around him mad. That's the first time I saw another side of Ron. He got into a teaching attitude. He took Benny aside and helped him think through what he wanted to do. That's when I saw Ron as a gifted teacher and guidance counselor."

In an article that appeared in the *Detroit Free Press* in 1997, journalist Mark Stryker raved about Ron's "impeccable taste, rock-ribbed groove, harmonic imagination, rhythmic freedom, seductive tone, lightning reflexes, imperturbable profile and uncanny ability to bring out the best in others" and how all these attributes have led to him being an invaluable sideman whose phone continues to ring. Stryker quoted Herbie Hancock as saying, "Playing with Ron feels like being cradled in your mother's arms, it's so comfortable. But at the same time, it's so provocative that it inspires you to create new ideas."

Stryker then gives an example of what he calls the "Carter Effect" by citing tenor saxophonist Eric Alexander's 2003 album *Nightlife in Tokyo*. He characterized the young leader as "a rousing but mechanical player who often relies on pet tricks." He then singled out Ron's glissando lines in the minor blues tune "Nemesis" just before Eric's solo and quoted the saxophonist from his press material as saying, "[That] really influenced the way I played. I found myself playing something entirely different than what I was preparing myself to play. It was a magical moment."

Drummer Joe Farnsworth, who appeared on Eric's date along with pianist Harold Mabern, enlisted Ron for his 2004 album recorded for 441 Records. *It's Prime Time* also featured Golson, Alexander and Curtis Fuller. Joe told a writer, "Playing with Ron Carter and Benny Golson was very nerve-wracking for me, especially on 'Five Spot After Dark,' which Benny wrote. Ron helped me out a lot. [At first] I was really intimidated playing with Ron, but he was extremely supportive during the session." Also on the album is Joe's take on Ron's composition "Third Plane." He said that when they recorded the tune, he and his young band mates "were trying to be like Ron, and we were in the same room with him playing together...It was great seeing the older guys integrating with younger guys ... The cross-generational mix we had was quite an experience."

Ron also influenced Joe's original, "It's Prime Time," a piece he wrote to have an easy melody and a boogaloo beat. Pianist David Hazeltine wrote the chords, Joe developed the melody and, he said, "Ron added the bass part like only he can."

SESSION SNIPPETS—POP

APART FROM JAZZ, throughout his career, Ron has performed with pop artists, most prominently on Aretha Franklin's *Soul '69*, a jazz-gospel-blues-infused recording produced by Jerry Wexler and engineer Tom Dowd for Atlantic Records. The sessions, arranged and conducted by Arif Mardin, included an all-star cast of jazz musicians with, among many others, guitarist Kenny Burrell and baritone saxophonist Pepper Adams. Featured tunes included Smokey Robinson's "Tracks of My Tears" and a gorgeous balladic cover of the tune Billie Holiday put on the map, "Crazy He Calls Me." Recorded in 1968 and released the following year, *Soul '69* is probably the most underappreciated album the Queen of Soul has recorded. Ron sings her praise: "Aretha has a great voice, a great sense of music, and she doesn't mind stepping in a different arena to see how things works. Today pop musicians like Rod Stewart and Queen Latifah are playing the standards like they're jazz singers, but Aretha was the first. She gets the r-e-s-p-e-c-t."

In 1970, Ron was enlisted to perform on singer Roberta Flack's debut album, *First Take*, which yielded her soulful and romantic rendition of folky Ewan MacColl's 1957 song, "The First Time Ever I Saw Your Face."

While the Joel Dorn-produced album didn't make big waves at first, the song leaped to the top of the charts in late 1971 and early '72 when it appeared in Clint Eastwood's film, *Play Misty for Me*. It won the Grammy for Song of the Year. Ron was also on board for Roberta's 1971 album, *Quiet Fire*, and 1973's *Killing Me Softly*, which featured another hit, "Killing Me Softly with His Song."

In addition, Ron recorded with Paul Simon on his eponymous debut as a solo artist in 1972, laying the bass line on the tune "Run That Body Down." Ron recalls the rhymin' Simon session as taking place the same day that he was going to see a prize fight at Madison Square Garden. He said that he'd do the studio date as long as he was finished in time to get to the fight. With pop record sessions having an infamous reputation for being long, drawn-out affairs, Ron had reason to doubt. But he laid his bass lines down and made it to the fight without a problem.

Drummer Harvey Mason recalls working with Ron and three-fifths of the Miles quintet on Carlos Santana's 1980 album, *The Swing of Delight*, recorded when the pop guitarist had adopted the name Devadip from a poem written by his guru Sri Chinmoy and decided to explore his instrumental fusion leanings. The album sessions took place over the course of five days at The Automatt in San Francisco. While Harvey had become friends with Ron during a CTI All-Stars tour and had gigged with Herbie in his Headhunters band, he was anxious about this particular session because of the Miles legacy of Tony.

"When I was young, I hitchhiked once to see that band in Philadelphia from my home in New Jersey," Harvey said. "It was amazing. But when I was asked to be a part of Carlos's session, it blew my mind. As soon as I saw Wayne, who I didn't know, and Herbie and Ron in the studio, I got nervous."

What initially perplexed Harvey was the absence of Tony who had played the day before. "Why isn't Tony here?" he thought. "Tony lives out here, so he should be here. I guess he must be busy."

As a result, Harvey was thrown for a loop. He says that he didn't feel at ease playing and admits that he wasn't thinking clearly. "I was trying to think like Tony, play like Tony," he said. "We were all feeling each other out, but then all of a sudden we took a break because it wasn't working. Ron put his bass down, pulled me aside and said, 'Hey Mason, if they wanted Tony Williams, they would have called Tony Williams. Play your shit.'"

The rest of the session for Harvey was a dream.

In an interview with Jazz.com, when asked what some of his favorite recordings were as a sideman besides his dates with Miles, off the top of his head, Ron answered, R&B guitarist Eric Gale's 1987 *In a Jazz Tradition* and Herbie Hancock's 1968 *Speak Like a Child*.

Were there any artists whose sessions he missed out on because of his schedule but wished he'd been a part of? "Phoebe Snow," Ron said. "I played on only one of her songs [on her self-titled album in 1974] not long before she retired and decided to raise a family. I'd like to have a chance to play with her again now that I've gotten a few years older and she's settled into a nice place raising her family. She's a great singer, and I think I could have some fun playing with her."

While he did record with Lena Horne (1975's *Lena & Michel*, a co-leader date of the songstress with French pianist/composer Michel Legrand that also included Grady on drums and Joe Beck on guitar), Ron was busy when asked to work with her again. "I got called a couple of times, but I was out of town," Ron said. "I wish I could have spent more time with her just to find out how she does what she does."

When Jazz.com asked Ron what he learned from being a sideman to musical elders like Coleman Hawkins and Eddie "Lockjaw" Davis, he said, "Anytime you play with people of that [age], and certainly they were 30 years older than me at the time, it's like going to school with them. You learn how they pick the tunes, how they pick the speeds, the personnel, how they go into the studio prepared or not prepared. Those kinds of things affect me more as a complete musician than as a bass player in and of itself."

SESSION SNAPHOT NO. 1: HOUSTON PERSON

"WHEN PEOPLE HEAR this record, they're going to think that jazz is such a 'light' art," said Ron when talking about the fourth duo album he made with veteran tenor saxophonist Houston Person, *Just Between Friends*, recorded in 2005 and released in 2008 on HighNote Records. (The duo dates are Person recordings identified as Houston Person With Ron Carter.)

Ron then scoffed at such an assessment with a growl: "Ruff."

He continued, "Someone listening to this for the first time may assume it's just two people deciding to get together to play. But it's a lot more complicated than that. This kind of date doesn't just happen. It's not like we go into a date blindfolded and hope that lightning strikes the studio. We discuss the libraries, we figure out where to solo, we have rehearsals. Houston is the perfect person to play duos with because he brings so much to the table. You know that what he plays, he's playing it right. I bring the rhythmic stability to the tunes with interesting bass lines."

Houston returned the compliment and added, "I like the freeing up we do with just the saxophone and the bass. When there's just the two of us, we can take the music wherever we want it to go. We don't have to worry about any constraints from a piano or drums. Ron and I like this concept, this setting. He's the rhythm; he plays the melody and harmonies. He's such a virtuoso that he's the whole band." As for what it takes to make it work, Houston shook his head, laughed and slyly said, "We can't give away our trade secrets."

Houston and Ron have been friends for many years, sharing session dates with Prestige Records in the early '70s and in 1987 getting reacquainted when Ron produced Eric Gale's soul-jazz-meets-bop album, *In a*

Jazz Tradition on EmArcy Records, also featuring Grady and organist Lonnie Smith. The pair recorded their first duo album, *Something in Common*, in 1989 on Muse Records, followed the next year by another Muse duet disc, *Now's the Time*. The two were reissued as a two-fer called *The Complete Muse Sessions* in 1997 by the now-defunct 32 Jazz label co-owned by Joel Dorn.

Dorn sent a copy of the reissue to Dr. Billy Taylor, who liked what he heard. "Those sessions Houston and Ron did knocked me out. The way they played together was so melodic. I point to this album when I explain to people the kind of music I really like."

After *Now's the Time*, Ron and Houston again went on their separate paths, not collaborating on record until Ron's 1999 *Orfeu* disc. But they did spend time on the road together, which Houston remembers fondly. "Ron is so big in Japan," he said. "He's what you would call a star. We were in a department store once, and people came running up to him to get his autograph. Now that's star power."

Houston also recalls their favorite tour pastime: Scrabble. "I won't tell you who was better," he said with a laugh. "Ron's an intellectual, but I can keep up with him. He's a great gift giver too. After a tour of Japan once, he gave me a Scrabble tie that received a lot of compliments."

Ron and Houston revisited the intimate duo format in 2002 with the appropriately titled album *Dialogues* on HighNote. Like the earlier recordings and the most recent CD, *Just Between Friends*, the focus of the songbook was mostly on lyrical standards, such as "Polka Dots & Moonbeams," "How Deep Is the Ocean?" and "Darn That Dream."

"Ron knows the lyrics to all the standards," said Houston. "He can even sing some of them."

Ron doesn't wholly agree with Houston's view. "I know the melody and the verses, but not necessarily the lyrics. Houston must know 20,000 songs, and I know at least six." He laughed and said, "I trust Houston's judgment because he's played with singers like Etta Jones for such a long time. He knows moods and the right keys for a song."

On *Just Between Friends*, the pair stepped outside the Great American Songbook zone by bouncing into a take on "Blueberry Hill." While written in 1940 and performed by such artists of that era as Sammy Kaye, Gene Krupa and Glenn Miller, the song is most associated with Fats Domino who made it an international R&B/rock 'n' roll hit in 1956. "That was Houston's suggestion," Ron said. "Jazz players traditionally tend to shy away from those tunes for whatever reason. I hadn't heard that song in a long time, and though I thought it was interesting, it's nothing I would ever have considered playing. I have a different view of what I'd like to record, but this was Houston's date."

But not for a moment does Ron question Houston's integrity, noting that the saxophonist has been performing long enough to judge an audience's response. "If he chooses this song for the duo, then my job is to make sure I can make it come true," said Ron, who added, "I'd like to have Fats hear this to see what the jazz boys can do with his song."

While Ron has performed with hundreds of artists during his session career, he said playing with Houston is special. "When I make my list of friends, Houston is very high on the list. I'd stop in a heartbeat for him."

SESSION SNAPSHOT NO. 2: DONALD HARRISON TRIO

WHILE RON IS to the studio what a gym rat is to an indoor basketball court, he's also been a session man in the live-in-a-club recording setting. In late April 2005, he joined alto saxophonist Donald Harrison and drummer Billy Cobham for a week's stint at the Blue Note in New York that resulted in Donald's scintillating album, *New York Cool: Live at the Blue Note* (recorded and released in October 2005 by the club's home label, Half Note). It was a reunion of sorts from when Donald assembled Ron and Billy to record *Heroes*, released by German label Nagel-Heyer in 2002 and in the U.S. in 2004. (The threesome also recorded together on Billy's 2006 quartet album, *Art of Four* on In and Out Records, with pianist James Williams—one of his last studio dates before his death.)

In the upstairs dressing room before the show, I asked Ron how he was doing. "I'm working," he said with a smile and then walked downstairs and onto the stage where he demonstrated how much play can infuse his work.

All three players, dressed to a tee in suits, dress shirts and ties, started in a flurry as Ron, reading the charts in front of him, began walking while Donald blew an exhilarating avant-garde-like solo. Ron followed with a solo of his own: low-toned, bluesy, lyrical. With eyes closed, he quietly hummed along with the melody he created while Billy calmly comped before opening fire with a barrage of drum detonations.

During the set, Billy's bright red mallets blazed while Ron's dark brown bass provided the earth tones to allow Donald to soar and weave and romp—inside and outside the lines. They played "The Harrisburg Address," a whimsical tune where Ron gleefully contributed a walking bass line and Billy accelerated the beat midway through. That pushed Ron to speed his notes and Donald to blow with a frenzy that settled into a New Orleans-styled swing—a gentle rain after a wind-swept thunder shower.

More velocity came on the standard "I Remember April," where again Billy and Ron spurred each other on. The drummer shot flames while the bassist sped up and tossed his lines into space. Donald smiled and leaped into the free-for-all.

The most serene moment of the set came with the ballad "Easy Living" that featured Ron's solo, which elicited "ahhhhhs" from the audience. He graced his spotlight moment with hammer-ons and harmonics, strong-fingered single notes and lushly strummed chords.

After the set, Donald praised his *Heroes* trio: "First of all, Ron and Billy have a lot of musical knowledge. I'm in a situation where I'm learning every night. We're sharing, going to the outer limits to find new ways to find the right notes."

Like most sessions Ron engages in, this one, Donald says, teemed with surprises. "We've been around each other over the years enough to know how to move with the music," he said. "We move according to what we're feeling in the music. For example, on 'I Remember April,' the song is different every night. This band takes it and shapes it into something new. We're all listening to each other."

SESSION SNAPSHOT NO. 3: STEVE KUHN TRIO

IN JULY 2006, on the second night of a four-night stint at Birdland in New York, pianist Steve Kuhn set up shop with his trio comprising Ron on bass and Al Foster on drums. The next night Blue Note Records would be recording the date for a live album.

Arriving at Birdland, I spied Ron in a suit with a gold vertical-striped tie and gold pocket square in his suit's breast pocket. "How did it go on opening night?" I asked him.

"A little rough around the edges, but interesting," he said.

"Tentative?"

"No, not tentative," he said as he took the stage.

The set started with a rousing version of "If I Were a Bell," where Ron laid down a deep-grooved walking bass line, spiced with his trademark blues-inflected, sliding glissandi. He launched into a lyrical, almost guitar-like solo, then returned to the walk that opened the door for Al to charge in.

Steve introduced the next tune, Fats Waller's "The Jitterbug Waltz," by citing the jazz great as "one of my heroes." There was an overarching sense of humor in the piece, with Steve's graceful, eloquent lead. Ron's tone was thick, buttery, deeply resonant. He took a bluesy riff into the middle section of the number, after which the tempo accelerated.

Steve then reflected on how 20 years earlier this same trio played a four-night stint at the Village Vanguard (March 27–30, 1986) that was recorded live. The fruit of the sessions yielded two albums: *The Vanguard Date* (Owl Records) and *Life's Magic* (Blackhawk Records).

In a *New York Times* review of a Kuhn trio show at the Vanguard in 1984, writer John S. Wilson remarked about how distinct the pianist's new group was in comparison to his other bands: "One difference is the caliber of his colleagues ... Ron Carter, a musician of unusual versatility, imagination and skill, and ... Al Foster, taking a brief leave from Miles Davis's group." Wilson concluded his review by writing, "Mr. Kuhn is a positive, two-handed pianist who can be effectively spare and sketchy but who also builds rolling, sometimes oddly accented lines that eventually sweep relentlessly along, driven by the rhythmic juggernaut supplied by Mr. Carter and Mr. Foster."

At the Birdland 20th anniversary reunion, Steve and company performed several classics, including "Stella by Starlight," of which Steve explained later, "My mother's first name was Stella, so playing this is always an emotional experience for me. I always like doing a ballad in each of my sets and this is one of the most beautiful. We do it here in three different keys."

The group also weighed in on Kenny Dorham's "Lotus Blossom" (which featured a piano intro from Debussy's "La plus que lente"), Billy Strayhorn's "Passion Flower," Charlie Parker's "Confirmation" and one of Steve's originals that didn't make the final album cut, "Poem for No. 15," a piece written in homage to the late New York Yankees catcher Thurman Munson. Throughout the set, Ron played evocative bass lines, unpredictably morphing from comps to lead runs. He composed as he played and veered from keeping a straight pulse, opting instead to fully engage the bass in the ongoing onstage jazzspeak.

At the end of the set, Steve took a moment to acknowledge his band, calling Ron and Al "none better on this planet."

After the set, I asked Ron, how did it go, in his estimation, tonight?

"It's getting better. It was better than last night. That was more like a rehearsal. Tonight the music is taking shape."

When I point out how unpredictable his bass lines are, Ron said, "I'm having to figure out how to resolve playing with Steve and Al. I'm beginning to make choices. Maybe not the best choices. But tomorrow I'll be making better choices."

I told him that he'd better because that's when the tapes will begin to roll.

"Well, it's not just about that. It's about making better choices, about finding the right notes to play. Tonight was OK. But it could have been better. Tomorrow *will* be better."

How did Steve feel? He was elated. "[This trio is] one of the best in the universe," he said. "Inarguably, absolutely."

What does Ron bring to the session? "Ron is so knowledgeable. He knows everything about the history of the music. He's creative, has great time, great bass intonation. I love his ability to play time, his harmonic knowledge and especially his risk taking, which is what I love about his playing."

Risk taking in what way?

"In his rhythms and harmonies. He fucks with me. I fuck with him. And Al fucks with us. It's a communal fuck."

Does Ron help steer the music?

"Absolutely. It's a democratic trio. At any given point, you think that maybe either Ron or Al is going one way, then they go another. It's unpredictable. It's like a conversation."

After the two-night warm-up, the next two nights' sets were recorded, which gave birth to *Steve Kuhn Trio Live at Birdland*. On the CD, the trio rendered two of the leader's compositions, "Two by Two" and "Clotilde," and Ron's "Little Waltz," all three originally recorded on *The Vanguard Date*. On *Live at Birdland*, each song took on a new life. For example, Steve said he wrote "Two by Two" "back when the trio first started playing together, and I'm still trying to figure out how to play it. This take feels fresh to me."

The trio also interpreted a tune that's not performed often: "Slow Hot Wind," a Norman Gimbel/Henry N. Mancini song that Sergio Mendes recorded on *Brasil '66*. "I've never recorded that and to my knowledge no one's ever recorded it as an instrumental," Steve said. "It's usually done with a Latin feel, but knowing how great Ron walks on the bass, I decided to do it straight ahead."

Shortly before *Live at Birdland* was released, Steve said he was pleased with the disc, especially in how well the trio jelled. "The three of us playing together is a unique thing. It's something special. It didn't take long for us to get back into the music. We didn't rehearse prior to the Birdland shows. We just played. There was no angst. There was the greatest amount of mutual respect. That's what makes this album so exciting to me."

He added, "The three of us are of an age. Ron, Al and I grew up listening to the same music and have the same point of reference. And we care for each other."

Additionally, Kuhn noted, the Ron-Al team makes a leader's life easier and the music richer. "Years ago [critic] Stanley Crouch told me that my role as a leader meant that I had two jobs: leading and pulling the extra weight. But with Ron and Al, there's no extra weight. There's a commonality, and we all share responsibility for the music, harmonically and rhythmically. For me, it's like being a kid in a candy store. There are a lot of surprises. I enjoy the challenge of not knowing what's going to happen from chorus to chorus or from bar to bar."

SESSION SNAPSHOT NO. 4: McCOY TYNER

"Where do you want me to sign?" asked Ron, when Derek Trucks handed him his red guitar at the conclusion of McCoy Tyner's recording session for his album, *Guitars*, at Clinton Studios in Hell's Kitchen (officially the New York neighborhood of Clinton) in the fall of 2006. Also in the studio were producer John Snyder and drummer Jack DeJohnette. The aim of the album—released two years later in September 2008 on his own McCoy Tyner Music, a subsidiary of Half Note—was to put the pianist in foreign territory to buoy his creativity. The concept was to have McCoy set up with an all-star rhythm section and perform with such special guest guitarists as Derek, Bill Frisell, John Scofield and Marc Ribot, and for a special twist, Béla Fleck on banjo.

Derek had already got McCoy's autograph on his guitar. With Ron, Derek said, "You can sign here," pointing to the bottom of the front.

Dressed down today in jeans and a visored baseball cap, Ron quipped, "OK, but I think I'll sign right here over McCoy's name."

McCoy and Derek laughed as Ron signed, not over the pianist's signature but to its side.

The exchange provides another window on Ron's personality. He likes to joke and laugh, though many people who don't know him think of him as a stoic character: serious, impatient, prone to perfectionism, quick to reprimand. That no-nonsense quality is certainly one of Ron's traits, as witnessed earlier when he opened the sliding glass door of his isolation booth and chided the engineers for toying with Derek's sound levels during a take on "Greensleeves" that the guitarist had arranged for the session.

"Once you set the level, keep the level," Ron said sternly in a severe tone of voice that exuded authority. "Anytime you change the volume, you never get back to the right sound. We're struggling to hear [through the headphones]."

As it turned out, it was Derek—and not the engineers in the booth—who was tweaking the amp and the dials on his guitar to remove a crackling sound from the mix. The engineers changed cables to fix the problem and then promised not to mess with the mix from the control room. The band completed take two of "Greensleeves." It was a keeper, all parties agreed.

For the last song of the day's recording, Derek chose "Plastic Blues," a McCoy tune from early in his career. McCoy hadn't played it in so long, he wanted to hear the recording that Derek had brought to the session on his iPod. The engineer struggled to feed the iPod through the studio speakers. First, he cued up a gospel-singing track, which cracked the band up. Ron joked, "We doing this, McCoy? You didn't tell me this is what we're doing."

Finally "Plastic Blues" came over the speakers so McCoy could relearn the tune. Meanwhile, Jack had joined Ron in his isolation booth where they talked about sports. At one point, Jack pointed to the headlines in *The New York Times*: "Bush Acknowledges CIA Prisoners Exist." They both sarcastically laughed.

After several minutes' delay, John asked if everyone was ready to play the first take. Sensing his rhythm team's unrest, he apologized first: "Thank you for your patience," he said.

Ron replied, "That's OK...well, that's not true." He laughed. John laughed too and said, "I didn't think so."

John then tried to rally the troops. "We're in the home stretch now. One more. It's the seventh inning."

The song took three takes. The first was the longest but was marred by no one taking charge about how to end it. The second was a mini version that McCoy ended quickly, thinking that they were doing one more take on the end part only. That brought more laughter. John said, "McCoy, that's the shortest take you've ever recorded."

Jack chimed in, "That'll get you radio play," to which McCoy laughed and said, "That's what I've been waiting for."

Finally the third take sped off with Derek playing bottleneck lines and Ron taking a walking bass solo and comping during McCoy's sprightly solo, knowing that his longtime piano friend would be listening to him and responding in kind with left-hand thunder. The ending was nothing like the version everyone had just agreed to and practiced, but it pleased all parties nonetheless—at least that's what they all said, given that this was the last song to record after a long day in the studio.

With the session over, a half hour early, Ron sighed and packed up. It had proved to be a good day. He comes to the studio to do business, but he also comes to play with friends—and laugh.

Ron has been in McCoy's corner for many albums throughout his career, including *The Real McCoy*. Recorded in 1967, it was McCoy's first date with Blue Note Records and his first album since he had left John Coltrane's employ two years earlier as the pianist in the saxophonist's classic '60s quartet. Also on the session was Trane alum, drummer Elvin Jones, and tenor saxophonist Joe Henderson. The next year McCoy asked Ron to play cello on his *Expansions* LP. Other McCoy albums with Ron in the bass chair included 1970's *Extensions* (with Elvin again as well as Wayne Shorter on saxophone and Alice Coltrane playing harp).

During McCoy's Milestone Records years, Ron recorded with him on 1973's *Trident*, a trio date with Elvin; 1976's *Fly With the Wind*; two 1977 recordings, *Supertrios*, with Tony Williams on drums, and *Inner Voices*; and the live *Passion Dance*, with Tony again. Ron reconnected with McCoy in the studio when the pianist returned to Blue Note in 1985 with *It's About Time*, co-starring alto saxophonist Jackie McLean.

"Ron is an amazing bassist," said McCoy. "You can see and hear the love he has for the music and his instrument. He's a valuable guy for a session. He has a sensitivity, and he knows what he's doing. He's very musical. That's why Miles loved him so much."

With regard to *Guitars*, McCoy says that Ron's flexibility in playing with several different guitarists was an asset. "Ron is on the spot and creative. He's able to deal with changing situations, and he helped me to figure out the direction I wanted this project to go."

Snyder agrees. "Ron is so confident in a relaxed way," he said. "There's no arrogance. When he did Trane's 'Mr. P.C.' with Sco, it was unbelievable. He played his ass off. He was wailing. Ron Carter kicks ass. He's relentless but also perfect. If he hears something he doesn't like in the music, he'll let you know, either in his music or in words. In that sense, Ron is terrifying."

John goes a long way back with Ron to the days when Creed Taylor hired him as the lawyer to run CTI's publishing company. But one of his first assignments was to listen to a test pressing of Ron's album *Blues Farm* with him for his approval. "Ron had sunglasses on and didn't say a thing," John recalled. "It was intimidating. He listened and I didn't say much except to tell him how much I liked the song 'Da-jango.' I didn't know any better how to pronounce the name. Ron could have cut me into pieces, but he corrected me by telling me the 'd' is silent in 'Django.'"

"Yes, I could have wrung him out," said Ron, with a laugh.

Ron remembers his first dealings with John, a North Carolina native with a distinct Southern accent. "John was shy, but I was wary of someone who spoke like that," Ron said. "My age category has gone through those days where it was never good to travel too far south of New York. I wasn't prejudiced against John, just wary of that twang in his voice." However, Ron soon discovered that he had a lot to learn from John's expertise in the music business. They became friends when John served as the road manager for two CTI All-Stars tours in Japan.

John recalls that the *Guitars* sessions were not without their tense moments, especially when Marc Ribot came to the date with a casualness that Ron didn't appreciate. He brought music, but McCoy couldn't hook into it. Marc said that that was OK, they could overdub later, which Ron protested. "Marc's not a straight jazz player," said John. "He's used to fixing things in a studio setting. Ron's philosophy is to be prepared and do a tune in one take."

John asked Ron, "Why did you get on Ribot's case?"

Ron replied, "I have a certain reputation to maintain."

John smiled and said, "Well, your pain-in-the-ass rep is intact," then laughed.

"Ron is demanding, but he's also giving," said John. "He's the most giving player I've ever seen in the studio. He'll support you and give you things that no one else could, but then he'll pick your pocket if you're not careful. He's patient, but he also takes no prisoners."

As it turned out, McCoy and Ribot played free on three duos.

John appreciates Ron's professionalism in the studio because it makes his job as a producer easier. "Let's describe Ron as 'demanding strict,'" he said. "He has his standards and you have to toe the line with him. You have to hold up your end, otherwise you'll suffer. In between takes, you'll see him just reading the newspaper as if he's not engaged. But when the session is ready to go, he's there. Bam! Zero to 60 in three seconds. No wasted energy. He's more like an athlete, like a basketball player ready to play, or a lion. A lion in winter."

Ron concedes that John had challenges to face on the *Guitars* sessions, especially with the variety of personalities. "Sometimes musicians take advantage of a producer, by coming in late or not being prepared, which I think is rude and is also draining on the rest of the band. But John, like Orrin Keepnews always did, found a way to keep this date going."

One of the highlights of the *Guitars* CD is Bill Frisell's contributions, especially his teaching McCoy the sublimely rhythmic tune "Baba Dramé" by Malian guitarist/composer Boubacar Traoré. (Bill had recorded the song on his 2004 album *The Intercontinentals*.)

"Bill is so sympathetic, so humble," John said. "He's so kind and has a light that makes him glow with expectation. He's great to be around."

Ron agrees. "Bill has such a wonderful guitar sound and he's always so aware of being in tune." He likes to tell about enlisting Bill for *Orfeu*, the first time he used him as a sideman for one of his own projects. With Bill's early-'90s reputation in the progressive Downtown New York scene and his being a one-time member of John Zorn's avant Cobra band, people questioned Ron, "What is Bill Frisell doing on one of your albums?"

Ron replied, "Man, just listen to the music. That tells you why."

SNAPSHOT

The Joey & Bill Show

Photograph by Stuart Brinin

Bill Frisell is the champ of contemporary jazz guitar, hands down, with his reflective, quiet but subtly quirky lines that flow from the lyrical to the angular. He can also sling arrows into the mix, but in the company of two of jazz's greatest rhythm players—as well as two of his musical heroes—on 2007's *Bill Frisell, Ron Carter, Paul Motian*, he steered away from sudden blasts and settled into the fluidity of cliché-free improvisation.

What's remarkable about the 10-song date is how untethered the trio sounded. Ron steered with his unpredictable bass runs, countermelodies and motifs as Paul flicked the cymbals in dance-like support while Bill mused soulfully and whimsically through pop stand-bys like Hank Williams's "I'm So Lonesome I Could Cry" and the folksy Americana oldie "You Are My Sunshine," which ironically was sketched in a melancholic mood. It was also significant that the trio delectably covered two Monk tunes, "Raise Four" and "Misterioso," given that Bill is the Thelonious of jazz guitar.

In celebration of the release, the trio played the Blue Note in New York in December 2007, largely covering the tunes from the album, albeit with the kind of spontaneous recreations befitting jazz. Miles's critics used to be vociferous in their complaints about the trumpeter's proclivity for playing with his back to the audience. They cited arrogance as the reason. No one could accuse Bill of that, though he too did not face the crowd. Some people in the club could only see his back, others his side. Where was Bill looking? Right at his two band mates, attentively watching them throw changeups into the music, sometimes using one note or a cymbal tap to shape a new framework or shift perspective.

"Bill was physically in tune with the band," said Ron, who noted that he liked the fact that all the trio members were right in front of the bandstand.

The live set, just like Ron's quartet dates, used segues throughout. "It's the only way to get to those rings of Saturn," Ron said. "You allow the song to take you there, then let it dissipate during the interlude where you're going into a new song. It's a musical thread."

Those interstitial improvisations often developed into free playing—stretching out without the gravity of a song form to ground it. "I really like playing that way, especially with musicians who don't feel the need to depend on that form to be musically successful," said Ron. "I haven't played much of this free type of music since the early '60s, when I was backing Jaki Byard and Don Ellis."

As for his appreciation of Bill's musicality, Ron said, "What I find so interesting about Bill is how he's able to go into so many different environments in his music. What's he have, four or five different groups? And he makes records with lots of different people, yet the music is always so viable just from his presence."

This comfort zone for Ron began when he first played with Bill on drummer Joey Baron's 1997 Intuition Records *Down Home* album, also with alto saxophonist Arthur Blythe. A longtime associate of Bill's who played on his albums throughout the '80s, Joey is a self-professed "bass freak" who has always appreciated a strong bass foundation in a rhythm section. He grew up and started gigging in Richmond, Virginia, where, he says, good bass players were hard to come by. However, he did hook up with one good bassist, Mike Ross, "who took me under his wing. I savored every minute playing with him."

Joey picked up on Ron in the early '70s on Roberta Flack's *First Take* album. "Roberta is pure soul, and Ron's grooves were so soulful," Joey said. "The way Ron played upright was as greasy as I've heard anybody play with integrity. That album was a major influence on me about how to articulate time, how Ron worked with the drummer where they weren't playing a pattern, but were loose." He laughed and added, "They weren't shuckin' and jivin.'"

Another Ron recording that struck Joey was his performance on Miles's "My Funny Valentine." That, he says, should go down in history as one of the world's greatest pieces of art. "The whole group was incredible in the way that they all gave up the ego. But listening to Ron's notes—the growl, the timing—was a dream. It's every drummer's fantasy to feel that underneath the time pulse."

Over the years Joey paid close attention to Ron, from his work with Stan Getz (*Sweet Rain*) to Antonio Carlos Jobim (*Wave*) to Jim Hall (*Alone Together*). He loved his funkiness as well as his harmonic advances, though he could never quite figure out exactly what he was doing. "But I thought, wow, this cat has some serious ears to be able to play with so many different kinds of musicians on that level," he said. "Ron to me defined the line between knowing about music and knowing about soul. That's what a drummer likes. He's got the perfect balance. Some guys know one, but not the other. Ron's got it all."

One particular vinyl disc that Joey wore the grooves out on was Kenny Burrell's all-star big-band album *Blues: The Common Ground* (recorded in late 1967, released in 1968 on Verve). Ron, Herbie Hancock and Grady Tate were a part of the orchestra that played Don Sebesky arrangements. In the beginning couple of bars of "See See Rider," featuring versatile funk-to-swing drummer Donald McDonald, Ron played a bass line that Joey said "just killed me. I listened to it over and over again. It's so funky the way Ron keeps the integrity of the line while still keeping it loose. Ron never lets the bottom fall out."

When Joey was in his late teens in the early '80s, he moved to New York where one of his first gigs was with vocalist Carmen McRae. "Carmen was one of the greatest leaders I've ever played with," he said. "There I was this drummer from Richmond with no money, no class, no PR, no connections, and I got to play with one of the heaviest musicians to ever walk the planet. I auditioned with her in her living room. I played three bars, she stopped and said, 'You got the gig, motherfucker.' It ended up being such a great relationship. Eventually, working with Ron had the same effect."

As a teenager, Bill often traipsed into the city from his suburban home in New Jersey, where he grew up. Just as Bill had been hearing Ron play bass on almost every new record he bought, so too did he keep catching Ron in live shows. He went to the Village Vanguard to see the Thad Jones/Mel Lewis Orchestra that usually featured Richard Davis in the bass chair. Ron was subbing for him. Then he went to see Thelonious Monk's saxophonist Charlie Rouse play a show, and there was Ron again. He wanted to see Hank Jones play one evening and who was playing in the rhythm section but Ron and Tony Williams. When Bill attended Berklee College of Music in Boston, he saw Ron's piccolo bass quartet several times. But Bill never approached Ron to meet him, not even years later when he was playing in Paul Motian's band and it shared a festival date with the Miles Davis tribute band.

Bill's first meeting with Ron came in the studio with Joey for *Down Home*. Both Bill and Joey were petrified. Joey had met Ron briefly once at a concert he performed at the Museum of Modern Art in New York. Joey's neighbor, Horace Arnold, knew Ron and introduced him. "Ron shook my hand and told me he had heard my name but not heard my work," Joey said. "By that time I knew I wanted to ask Ron to record my next album, but I was nervous. I had heard nothing but scary stories from second- and third-hand sources that Ron could be temperamental."

The request was made by Joey's producer, Lee Townsend. Ron signed on to the project, but made some stipulations. The session needed to be done professionally. Joey says he didn't sleep much for weeks before the recording dates, and when he did sleep, he suffered nightmares. "This was a lifetime dream for me to be in the same room with my hero and just be normal. I couldn't play like Tony Williams, but who cares? Ron's already heard that anyway. I just wanted Ron to like the music and then to like me."

Bill says that Joey did his homework, working up a library that was modeled around the kind of playing Ron did that they both loved. Joey wrote out the charts, even suggesting bass lines, and made copies for each band member. They made sure they were punctual.

"Joey's like my brother," said Bill. "We were so excited to be playing with Ron. But we were like Beavis and Butt-Head, and Ron is such a classy guy. Joey and I had been in some strange and unreal situations before, and then even performing with the L.A. Philharmonic. But in thinking about playing with Ron, it was kind of dreamlike."

For the session rehearsal, Joey remembers Ron entering the room and going straight to the corner, unpacking his bass and not saying a word. "I was as nervous as a whore in church," said Joey. "Ron is dressed in sharp clothes. He looks around the room and sees Bill first, who's not exactly a fashion plate. Then he sees Arthur, who's dressed soulful and down-home. I never dress to kill. In fact, I went out and bought a new pair of pants that was uncomfortable for me. Ron looks at us all, and the first thing he says is, 'I think I'll have to dress down a bit for this gig.' He looked at me and winked. Then we all busted up. From that moment on, Ron was the absolute easiest person to deal with. He was exactly the opposite of all the stories we had heard. He totally shattered all that misinformation we had gotten."

When asked why he thinks Ron gets that rap, Joey figured that the stories come from people who don't understand why Ron commands so much respect. "Ron is one of the smartest people I have ever met," he said. "He's a genius. From moment to moment, he's so sensitive to the music. He's hyperaware. And he doesn't wear that on his sleeves. That's just who he is. If he feels a lack of respect or a sense of laziness or unpreparedness by people in a session, he has a lot of integrity and speaks up about it.

Just based on my limited history with Ron, he can be very intense and very rewarding."

Bill agrees. "I didn't know if Ron would like my playing because I don't play in that traditional guitar way," he said. "But he seemed to like it."

Joey remembered the sessions being a dream date as the quartet developed "that certain interaction thing that you can't write. It's telepathic."

"Ron doesn't come in and dominate the session," said Bill. "He comes in and pushes the music around. He finds his way into the center of the music, the deepest center, and then works his way out. He responds to everything around him in the moment."

Ron liked the session so much that afterwards he asked if the quartet was going to play any gigs. He pulled out his date book and then asked Joey if he could use his tune "The Crock Pot" for his classes at City College, which thrilled the drummer.

Three years later, the quartet reassembled to record Joey's 2000 album, *We'll Soon Find Out* (Intuition). They also performed gigs together, but these were limited in number because of the busyness of all their individual schedules. They played a week at the Blue Note in New York as well as a couple of shows at the Knitting Factory in New York's Tribeca district. The latter was the kind of funky, unkempt venue that Ron would rarely perform in. But because it was Joey's date in support of *We'll Soon Find Out*, he agreed to play.

Joey went to check out the performance space earlier in the day. "There I was going to play with one of my biggest musical heroes and the place looked like a shit hole," he said. "I talked to the owner, and he didn't do anything about it. So I went down to a store on Canal Street and bought Spic and Span and scrub brushes."

"Joey spent the whole afternoon on his hands and knees, cleaning the dressing room and scrubbing the bathroom," Bill said. "That's the respect Joey has for Ron. He wanted to make the space comfortable for him."

"I was scared, embarrassed and by the time the show started I was completely exhausted," Joey said.

The story doesn't end there. Bill recalls that Ron, as usual, arrived at the Knit wearing a suit. Before they went onstage, a patron who appeared to have had too many beers accidentally spilled his latest on Ron's leg. "Ron was totally cool," Bill reported. "He wasn't thrilled, but I guess he's had worse things happen than that."

CHAPTER THIRTEEN

Jingles:
A Different Kind of Session

Ron may be renowned as the right-stuff session man for recording dates, but he has also served as the underpinning for hundreds, maybe thousands, of radio and television commercial jingles. On the albums, he is credited. On the jingles, he's anonymous, which makes chronicling and quantifying this different kind of session work virtually impossible.

During the jingle heydays of the '60s, '70s and '80s, Ron was in a New York City studio for jingle duty as much as, if not more than, for artistic sessions. He remembers that world as encompassing "a small circle of friends who were always busy." Off the top of his head, he mentions a few of his fellow jingle pals: Hugh McCracken, Richard Tee, Eric Gale, Hubert Laws. He could have easily identified more musicians such as Jay Berliner, David Sanborn, Steve Gadd, Grady Tate, Patti Austin, and Michael and Randy Brecker, all of whom Ron came to trust enough as musicians and friends to enlist for his own recordings.

In the feature article, "Music's Most Valuable Players," that ran in the *Boston Globe Sunday Magazine* on September 7, 1980, writer Stephen Davis explored the commercial session world of turn-of-the-decade New York where he found the "pride of studio lions [to be] composed of the elite master craftsmen of the American recording industry." Davis followed Jay Berliner on a typical day in his life, traveling from studio to studio in a hectic pace to keep up with all his jingle gigs. After profiling the guitarist, he focused on Ron. "If Berliner is one of the workhorses of the industry," he wrote, "Ron Carter is one of its aristocrats."

RON BREAKS IN

Ron got his start doing jingles thanks to his association with Miles. "The producers were from the age group that knew all about Miles," he said. "That helped me slide into gigs." Even so, in his early days, there was a pecking order, with Ron third or fourth on a list of bassists to ring up for a session. "I usually had to wait for a producer to see if George Duvivier or Richard Davis were available. If they weren't, I was usually next on the list."

Ron quickly rose through the ranks thanks to a combination of several important factors: He was always punctual to a session (even those early in the morning, when most jingle sessions took place); he was a quick study who could handle the time constraints (often having to deliver a 30-second jingle in three minutes); he worked well in a team setting (especially with serious musicians, who were always the kind of session people who got called back); he could play a wide variety of musical genres (from classical to jazz to funk); and he could sight-read in a flash. In the December 1981 issue of *Black Enterprise* magazine, Ron told writer Hershel Johnson, "You need to be able to read right away, to play the ink the first time down. That's critical. Jingle producers don't have time to have someone play by ear or hope to get the part right by the third or fourth take. It's too expensive."

In the *Boston Globe* piece, Davis wrote that New York's clearinghouse for session musicians, the Radio and Television Registry, listed a membership of nearly 700 working musicians in 1980. He figured some 200 were in demand daily and that there were some 25 superstar session aces. Competition for the top jingles was stiff. He wrote that the rigors of being a go-to session player "usually means years of study and practice, a natural flexibility, an iron body and will, and then more years of forming a personal and professional rapport with producers, arrangers and other players." Davis put Ron into that upper echelon of jingle titans.

Unlike Ron's album dates, where freedom of personal expression was an asset, the producers of commercial jingles frowned upon their session musicians taking creative liberties. They sought performances that stuck accurately to the written notes and looked for a finished product that had an emotional thrust so that the jingle would pop, though unobtrusively enough so as not to interfere with the sales pitch.

In that same feature, Davis interviewed Richard Tee and asked him if jingle session work drained a musician of his most cherished creative moves. Richard replied that it didn't and added, "You never know what your best stuff is." He explained how tightly structured jingle sessions are and how you follow the producer's lead. It's why he formed his own group, Stuff, to be able "to stretch out" and record albums "that are just an extension of what we do in the studio, sort of like putting our own signatures on *our* music for a change."

JINGLE MAESTRO

RON'S JOB AS a jingle specialist was to bring a depth to the music at hand. Even so, sometimes he would be asked to come up with a bass line. In one case he balked. "I was doing a commercial for an auto company," he said. "The music that had been written wasn't working, and the ad agency wasn't happy. So one of the guys asked me to come up with something. I asked, 'Is this going to be in the commercial?' The guy said, 'Yes.' And I told him that I'd have to talk with the agency's lawyer to see how this was going to work out and if I would be collecting a writer's royalty. Well, they didn't like that. I was never called back."

That, Ron says with a laugh, is one way in which he talked himself out of the industry.

Though he was a high-profile session man, Ron also faced prejudice during the jingle prime-time period because of his stature in the recording business. "I like doing jingles, but I don't get that many because they don't think I'll take 'em," Ron told the *Boston Globe*'s Davis. "I've spent a lifetime gaining a reputation, trying to build an aura of esteem around my music, and so the industry guys, some of them, tell me they feel their jingle music is beneath me. It's a shame because I find jingles to be a challenge." He described one he had done recently for Manufacturers Hanover Trust that called for a series of half notes and whole notes. "I tried to get them perfectly pitched so the engineer wouldn't have to equalize it on the mixing board. When I'm doing this kind of work, it means I have to practice less at home, so I wish I had more of it."

Ron also ran into discrimination of another sort, which he talked about in the *Black Enterprise* story. One of the premises of the article was that white producers in the early '80s favored white musicians in standard commercials while pegging blacks into soul or funk spots. Ron said, "I've done big orchestra dates with 45 players, and I've been the only black person there." He figured that contractors had their own set guys and that they'd rather hire "a stranger who is white than one who is black." He bristled at the closed-mindedness of some producers who "are still dealing in stereotypes about how black players can't be punctual or can't read music."

As far as compensation for these sessions, the price was right for Ron. "The hours are short, the money is really good, and you get to work on trying to make a piece of music be successful for a 30-second spot," he said. "For me, that's like going to school." Keeping in mind the inflation rate between then and now, in 1981 when talking to *Black Enterprise*, Ron said, "It may take me six hours in the studio to make $2,000 on an album date, while the time would be much shorter on commercials." Johnson wrote that busy jingle players could earn $100,000 a year just working that trade.

In the *Boston Globe* piece, Ron talked about "the old days" when he would play a cigarette commercial and receive, as a bonus, cartons of cigarettes after the session. Given that Ron does not smoke cigarettes (he's a pipe man), that was hardly a gift. But he told Davis, "I thought about that when I did a commercial for Porsche last month. I wanted to know where I could pick up my car." Given that Ron is a car buff (read: fast cars), this would have been quite the perquisite. Of course, when Ron said that to Davis, he was smoking his pipe and laughing.

The history of using jingles to sell products began in the mid-1920s when radio had become a popular medium. Many of the jingles were singing commercials (the first and most popular of early radio was the General Mills pitch: "Have you tried Wheaties?"). The jingle movement continued with TV, selling all kinds of products, using songs or instrumental music as a catchy backdrop. But for top-tier musicians, the business began to wane in the '80s.

MACHINES TRUMP MUSICIANS

RON ATTRIBUTES THE end of the jingle golden days to computers and synthesized instruments that could take the place of players who were paid according to union scale. However, he admits that he also found himself at odds with some commercial producers as his association with the jingle industry was fading out. He recalls one session in the '70s when the show *All in the Family* with the bigoted character Archie Bunker was all the rage. Some musicians and studio people were talking about the sitcom when Ron—who concedes he might have been in a "grumpy" mood at the 9 a.m. session after a late night playing in a club—said, "It seems a pity that with all the homelessness we have today that a show would be mocking that situation and those people who are homeless. I don't see the humor in that."

Ron recalls that his remark put an end to the conversation. "And they didn't call me back," he added.

In another jingle situation, he was called to do music for an oil company TV commercial. The clip he was playing to was about an eclipse of the sun that would be seen across the United States. "They showed this person looking at the eclipse with his naked eyes without protection," he said. "I told everyone, hey, you can't show that. If a person really looked at the eclipse like that he could go blind. They all looked at me as if I had three heads."

Ron said, "That comment shut me out too." He added, "That's what could happen in the jingle world. I have plenty of interesting stories about the ramifications of what would happen if you spoke out against something."

Today Ron's appearances on jingles sessions are few and far between. Ron says that he misses that world and the camaraderie of the session players. "I miss seeing the guys on a regular basis," he said. "And I miss those jingles where I could get some new schooling."

CHAPTER FOURTEEN

Film: Celluloid Jazz

WITHIN A LITTLE more than a decade, Ron was involved in three of the most classic jazz films of all time: 1986's *'Round Midnight*, 1988's *Bird* and 1996's *Kansas City*, all of which boasted music at their cores and included the bassist in onscreen performances.

Even though he appeared in those "co-starring" roles as a member of an onscreen band (to the best of his recollection he has never spoken one word of script), Ron also served as the behind-the-scenes score composer and performer on numerous projects, including director Frank D. Gilroy's *Desperate Characters* (1971, starring Shirley MacLaine and Kenneth Mars), Bertrand Tavernier's French film *La Passion Béatrice* (1987, starring Julie Delphy and Bernard-Pierre Donnadieu, released theatrically with English subtitles in the U.S. as *Beatrice*), Volker Schlondorff's *A Gathering of Old Men* (1987, with Louis Gossett Jr., Holly Hunter and Richard Widmark), Ernest R. Dickerson's *Blind Faith* (1998, starring Courtney B. Vance, Charles S. Dutton and Kadeem Harrison) and Tom Vaughan's *What Happens in Vegas* (2008, starring Cameron Diaz and Ashton Kutcher).

While Ron applies his patented lean-and-rapid modus operandi to recording his own albums as a leader—thorough rehearsing, then first-take, never-look-back sessions in the studio—working on film is an entirely different animal. "You take and then you take again," Ron said. "And if you're playing to track, you're not really playing but mimicking. Then, you work on the same scene, and it needs to be shot from four or eight different angles. That's so different from the way I work in the studio where it's 'Gentlemen, we have one chance. Let's not fool around.' Everyone agrees, and then we see what happens."

When Ron first started working on film, it took him a minute to understand the process. He recognized that he had to go with the flow, that the image was the dominant factor, and that shooting from different positions was essential. Case in point: *What Happens in Vegas*, where Ron was called upon to appear as part of a jazz trio playing in a gazebo at an outdoor party. His music was prerecorded. The shoot was in Long Island, a bus ride away from Ron's New York home. "I left home at five in the morning, and I was there all day," he said, then added with a wry smile, "All that for 15 to 25 seconds on the screen."

Ron says the long days require a lot of sitting and waiting while the tech guys perfect the sound and lights for the shoot. While he's used to being in the mind-set of "OK, here's the job, let's just get going," he finds himself on the sidelines in a waiting mode. "It's strange and a bit lonely," he said. "I bring along a book to read and just kill time. When they're ready, here I am, the bass player, who's an integral part of the scene. But I also know I could just as easily end up on the cutting room floor during the edit."

Still, Ron marvels at the editing process of putting a film together, tipping his hat to the unsung heroes who do the grunt work of choosing among the multiple filmed takes to put together a scene that appears fluid on the screen. He believes the editors are the ones who should get the top Oscars. "It's amazing how they go back and forth with the reels and make it all work out physically," he said. "They can do that for hours just to get a 10-minute scene cut right."

However, there's a downside to the experience for Ron. "After being on a set and knowing all that it entails, it's hard to see the movie onscreen," he said. "After I had done a couple of films, it made me not want to go to the movies anymore. Knowing how they get the scenes cut took the mystery out of the film for me. It took me out of the ballpark. I lost my zone."

BIRD

AN UNUSUAL FILM opportunity came in 1988 when Ron was enlisted to participate in the music soundtrack to *Bird*, produced and directed by Clint Eastwood who sought to retell the tragic story of Charlie Parker. While the drama of the jazz titan was ably told with Forest Whitaker (then only 26) taking the lead role, music was integral to the telling of the story. Veteran Los Angeles alto saxophonist Lennie Niehaus (best known for his stint with the Stan Kenton band) was entrusted with the musical director role.

Niehaus and sound recording engineer Bobby Fernandez took original Parker music and eliminated the poorly recorded rhythm section behind his playing by cutting the highs (drums and cymbals) and lows (bass). Niehaus then brought in several modern-day marquee jazz players to "accompany" Bird on his solo flights. (One tune, "Moose the Mooche," features a sound-alike alto sax performance by Charles McPherson in lieu of Bird.)

Ron was among three bassists used for the sessions (the other two being Ray Brown and Charles Berghofer). He "performed" with Bird on "Now's the Time," "Lover Man," "Cool Blues" and "Ko Ko." Additional musical support on those tunes came from trumpeters Jon Faddis and Red Rodney, pianist Walter Davis Jr., and drummer John Guerin.

While proud of his work, Niehaus exaggerated the end product by saying, "I went to the filming of all the musical scenes, and I also helped with all the editing. Unlike past films on jazz, this one [is] 100 percent authentic." Likewise, in reviewing the album, *Bird: Motion Picture Soundtrack*, critic Jim Santella wrote that the film is "the stuff dreams are made of," and the soundtrack "is arguably the best recording Charlie Parker has ever issued ... This is Bird at his best."

"I appreciated the opportunity to play with Charlie Parker," said Ron. "Not many guys in my age group can say they played with Bird. Still, I didn't understand musically and sonically why we were doing what we did. No one ever said to play in the style of the original bass player or if it was all right to play my own style. Nevertheless, it was fun to do, and I'm happy that Clint Eastwood made the film, even though I would have liked for it to feature more of Bird's musical contributions."

While Ron broke into the soundtrack scene with *Desperate Characters* (he provided original music along with Jim Hall and Lee Konitz), it took him another 16 years to be involved in a significant way with film scores, with two movies that were released in 1987, *A Gathering of Old Men* and *La Passion Béatrice*.

A few years earlier, in 1982, Ron decided to sharpen his orchestral writing skills by taking a class with Don Sebesky that was held during a summer session at Carnegie Hall. "I knew how to write for the cellos in my band and I was interested in recording string orchestras," he said. "But I didn't know how to notate. Writing for the cellos was writing on instinct. And that was not good enough, so I knew I had to go to school. Don's class proved to be very profitable for me in learning how to do string writing for film."

A GATHERING OF OLD MEN

A GATHERING OF Old Men was basically a consolation prize for Ron who had met Volker Schlondorff, the director of the 1979 film *A Tin Drum* that had won the Academy Award for Best Foreign Language Film. Volker asked Ron to do the music for a 1985 televised version of Arthur Miller's play *Death of a Salesman*, starring Dustin Hoffman, Charles Durning and John Malkovich.

Ron agreed, composed the music and recorded it for use in the film. Volker arrived in California with the tapes for final editing only to be told that he was off the project. It seemed that Miller had stipulated that, should any music ever be associated with the play, noted American film composer Alex North (of *A Streetcar Named Desire* and *Spartacus* fame) would be in charge. "It never occurred to anyone that my doing the music wasn't possible," Ron said. "After months of writing and recording, I was crushed. As a footnote, they ended up using some of my music but rewrote it, without me receiving credit. I was bent out of shape."

Embarrassed by the foul-up, Schlondorff told Ron that he had another made-for-TV project he was just beginning to work on. Having already proven his ability to write music for screen, Ron says that the director was convinced he'd make the right note choices. "Volker knew enough about music and trusted me so he didn't ask that I provide samples of the music for the scenes," Ron said. "He was good to work with. I've been on dates where directors have humiliated composers, where they talk down to them and the level of communication is not good. My feeling is, if you don't like the musical cue, let's talk about it so we can both agree on how to get it right. Otherwise, it's as if the people in charge are on the third floor and I'm just trying to get out of the subway."

Ron met with the musical coordinators for *A Gathering of Old Men* in Los Angeles, and they worked together on where to insert the music. They may not have always agreed, but Ron submitted to being overruled. "This was the big time, this was the real deal," he said. "It's not like doing something for prom night. I had to learn to trust someone else's judgment, which is what I don't normally do in situations involving music. I know what I hear, but the people who do the musical editing have been at it for way longer than I have. So I put my musical tastes at their mercy."

A Gathering of Old Men centers on a murder mystery in the sugar cane fields of Louisiana where a well-respected black sharecropper is accused of gunning down a racist Cajun tenant farmer. Based on the novel of the same name by Ernest J. Gaines, the story unfolds with the black community rallying to the defense of the alleged killer, who in years past would have been lynched without arrest and a trial. Ron's music is generously spread throughout the film, with ominous cello parts, string lyricism and slow, bluesy bass slides. While Ron doesn't show up onscreen, fiddler Papa John Creach does, as an actor and a musician.

While composing the score, the music coordinator asked Ron what he was thinking of doing. He replied that he wanted to work with his nonet: four cellos and a rhythm section. "I was in New York and the guy in Hollywood told me, 'Write it and we'll see if it works,'" said Ron. "So that's what I did, and I also called in Jerry Dodgion who is a great reeds player. He played flute and helped a bit with the arrangements. But overall, I was determined to make the bass be the focal point of the music without dominating it."

Writing in *The Hollywood Reporter*, Miles Beller called *A Gathering of Old Men* "a moral vision of conscience at work in an imperfect world, presenting with indisputable force the price of responsible action." He also commented on the score: "Musically, Ron Carter's soundtrack... is a revelation—a spare, soaring aural offering that must win an Emmy."

Unfortunately, neither the film nor the soundtrack got nominated.

LA PASSION BÉATRICE

MEANWHILE, RON WAS working on a completely different soundtrack, one that forced him to do some self-schooling in the musical styles of medieval Europe. The film was *La Passion Béatrice*, a horrific view of French soldiers who suffered humiliating defeats in battles against the British in the Hundred Years' War (in French, Guerre de Cent Ans), which lasted from 1337 to 1453. After four years' absence, the lord of a French castle returns home in a state of posttraumatic stress and wreaks havoc on the entire family and serfs, singling out his daughter, played by Julie Delpy, as the focal point of his vindictive anger. It's a dark tale of the depravity of the human spirit that ends with existential uncertainty.

On bass and piccolo bass, Ron contributed music that plays to the action and seamlessly acts as scene transitions, with eerie arco lines, twisting classical music lyricism, glissando solos, bass lines with drops of percussion and overall a Renaissance orchestral feel. In one scene where Béatrice rides her white horse over the hills in a state of despair, Ron contributes the sobering music that accompanies her, as if he is in her mind as she rides. Joining him in performing the score is the ensemble Concert Dans l'Oeuf, a second bassist Yves Chabert and percussionist Cheikh Tidiane Fall.

"When Bertrand first contacted me, I told him I definitely did not want to write a bebop score that wouldn't fit with the time period of the film," said Ron. "So I went to the New York Public Library and researched the music of the king's court and the instruments of the time." Ron discovered the sackbut, a medieval/Renaissance-era trombone, and viol, a six-string bowed instrument with a fretted fingerboard and low-arched bridge.

His next challenge was to find a group that could play his score using period instruments. As it turned out, there was a group, Concert Dans l'Oeuf in France, which specialized in medieval European music. Ron wrote the score in New York and decided to augment it with percussion parts. He enlisted a local percussionist and practiced the music before the trip to Paris to record it.

However, the percussionist was a no-show at the airport. Ron called him and asked, "Where are you?"

His reply was, "I can't go."

"Why not?"

"I just can't."

Ron was exasperated and embarrassed. "Hey, if the guy had said, I broke my leg or my wife is sick or my kid got arrested, I'd say, OK, that's a good excuse," he said. "But he didn't tell me anything. So I telephoned Bertrand and asked him to find a French percussionist that I could work with."

When he arrived in Paris, Ron was introduced to Cheikh, an African percussionist who at first did not fathom Ron's concept for his rhythmic contribution. "Luckily, he could speak English, so we talked," Ron said. "I told him I liked his playing, but that it wasn't fitting with this type of European music, where there wasn't percussion like congas, bongos, thumb pianos, talking drums. We were going to have to make do with triangles, bells and maybe tom toms. So, that's how we got it done with Cheikh's percussion, my basses, and the ensemble's viol, sackbut and hurdy-gurdy."

BLIND FAITH

RON CONTRIBUTED TO many other projects during his career, ranging from writing the score for Nigerian director Ola Balugun's *Haraka* in 1980 (four cellos and Dodgion on flute), to supporting jazz vocalist Jimmy Scott during an early '90s episode of David Lynch's classic TV series, *Twin Peaks*, to composing original music for the 1999 PBS-TV documentary, *The Black Press: Soldiers Without Swords*, a history of black newspapers in America, written and directed by Stanley Nelson.

Ron's strongest high-profile film project in recent years was writing the score for the compelling courtroom drama *Blind Faith*. It debuted on the Showtime premium cable network in 1998 and then had a theatrical release in 1999. In *The New York Times*, critic Janet Maslin praised the film as a story that "describes a hate crime and the miscarriage of justice that it engenders ... and manages to explore more kinds of prejudices than might be expected."

Ron can't remember how he got the call, but he threw himself into the murder mystery set in Van Cortlandt Park in the Bronx in 1957. The story centers on the case of a young black man—the son of an aspiring, hard-nosed cop (played by Charles S. Dutton)—being accused of killing a young white man. Ron colored the story line with subtle background music, used strings to express tension, delivered bass glissandos, employed jagged piano lines to express the thick racial tension of the story and, on occasion, set in motion swinging jazz bop of the time. Ron's support team included Stephen Scott on piano, Lewis Nash on drums, Steve Kroon on percussion and Bill Easley on saxophone.

In a pivotal scene near the end of the film, the attorney (played by Courtney B. Vance) working the case of his nephew, who is hiding the secret of his homosexuality, visits his estranged brother (a jazz saxophonist portrayed by Kadeem Hardison) during one of his gigs in a Greenwich Village jazz club. Hearing a song sung by Bobby Soul, and especially a powerful saxophone solo (played by Easley), the attorney breaks down in tears, overcome by the raw emotion of the music, which expresses the tragic story of discrimination that is unfolding.

'ROUND MIDNIGHT

ONE OF THE best-known jazz films is Bertrand Tavernier's *'Round Midnight*, which features saxophonist Dexter Gordon in his one and only starring film appearance. The story line is roughly patterned after the friendship between pianist Bud Powell and French jazzman Francis Paudras in Paris in the '50s. Gordon, whom Tavernier tracked down living in relative obscurity in New York, plays the alcoholic, down-and-out saxophonist Dale Turner, who is befriended by a French jazz buff named Francis, played by François Cluzet. The year is 1959. As Francis goes to see Dale play in the Blue Note Club in Paris every night, he gradually gains enough of the saxophonist's trust to persuade him to move into the apartment he shares with his daughter. Francis's mission is to support the addled musician until he can get back on his artistic feet. Writing in *The Daily Breeze/News-Pilot*, A Southern California newspaper, critic Jerry Roberts called the film "a heartfelt submersion into the world of jazz and a heartbreaking story about friendship."

While Dale eventually returns to New York, the music scenes in the French club buoy the story. Herbie Hancock, who won an Academy Award for his original score, appears in the film, as does a full cast of jazz stars, including Ron (in a tux, no less), Tony Williams, Billy Higgins, Freddie Hubbard, Bobby Hutcherson, Chet Baker, John McLaughlin and Cedar Walton, among others. Interestingly, also co-starring later in the story is Martin Scorsese as Dale's fast-talking New York agent. Tunes include compositions by Thelonious Monk, Cole Porter, Bessie Smith, Johnny Green, Dexter, Herbie and Ron, who won a Grammy for his instrumental "Call Sheet Blues" from the film's soundtrack.

The abundance of music is live and spirited, including a scene where Wayne and Dexter engage in a classic bebop cutting scene. Roberts wrote, "The musical scenes...are lovingly created by Tavernier, who seems to have an absolutely thorough understanding of and love for the time and place and mood of the film."

"I wish I could speak more French because there was a lot going on during the filming where I kind of felt left out because of the language barrier," said Ron. "But it was OK, because they were going for authenticity. It was pleasing to be part of a project where they had such a high regard for the music, which came first to them. They also highly regarded us as musicians and made sure they got the right sound."

Ron also notes that the club takes were all played live. "I'm not sure if the audience realized how effective that was," he said. "It made a big difference versus recording a tune in the studio and then trying to make a song come alive by playing to a track. In this film, you can feel our energy and enthusiasm. We were not faking notes."

KANSAS CITY

THAT WAS THE same strategy Robert Altman employed on his feature film *Kansas City*, which was set in 1934 during the Great Depression and shortly after Prohibition ended and the jazz clubs of the Missouri city were hopping with all-night jam sessions. The story line uses the club scene (The Hey Hey Club) as its anchor, so music is featured throughout. Musical director Hal Willner assembled a large intergenerational cast of jazz musicians, including young upstarts like Joshua Redman, Craig Handy, James Carter, Cyrus Chestnut, Kevin Mahogany, Christian McBride, Nicholas Payton, Mark Whitfield and Russell Malone; seasoned players such as Geri Allen, David Murray, Olu Dara, Victor Lewis and Don Byron; and vets such as David "Fathead" Newman and Ron. The music easily trumps the story that features actors Jennifer Jason Leigh, Miranda Richardson and Harry Belafonte, who plays the Hey Hey's gangster owner named Seldom Seen.

Altman told *Los Angeles Times* music writer Don Heckman that he was faced with a challenge while putting the film together. "The problem," he explained, "is that most jazz is very hard to use as background music in film because it has such an insistent voice. I'm a jazz fan, obviously, myself. It was the first music I ever heard. But I didn't want to do a film where the characters are jazz players, which makes it very hard. How do you do it?"

Altman pulled it off by having the jam sessions of that time take a starring role. He knew the music from his experience of having grown up in the city. He told Heckman that he remembered the jazz jams he witnessed as a young man, including the young Charlie Parker starting out in Jay McShann's band. "I didn't know who [Bird] was at the time," Altman told Heckman. "I was just a kid, but I knew he was good."

The nonstop sessions are at times scintillating, especially given that they were performed live by a crew of musicians who appeared to have enjoyed the opportunity to play for themselves as much as for the camera. Verve Records released the soundtrack under the title *K.C. After Dark* by the all-star ensemble named the Kansas City Band. In addition, Altman made good use of the raw footage of performances that were only shown in truncated version in the film by putting together a 55-minute film titled *Robert Altman's Jazz '34: Remembrances of Kansas City Swing*. Belafonte narrated and the various bands played. It was shown on TV and is available today on DVD.

Ron recalls working on the set, which he joined for the last two days of shooting because of previous commitments. "We were just told to play," Ron said. "It would have been good to know what the story was, which I didn't find out until I went to the screening. But I enjoyed getting to know Robert Altman through Harry Belafonte, who was my neighbor at the time. Mr. Altman respected me as a person first, which means if that's in place, then we can talk about questions he may have with the music. I thought the music was done well, even though I always feel that the sound guys can never get enough bass in the mix. I had a great time playing with all those guys. And most of the music was live, first takes."

Geri Allen remembers how rowdy—bordering on cocky—the young musicians were on the set. "They were having fun, clowning around and being silly," she said. "It was a new thing for all these young guys with the cameras and the encouragement to just play." She recalled that the whooping-it-up atmosphere sometimes went over the top. But all that stopped when Ron showed up on the set. "We watched this man walk in with that dignity and elegance, and the attitudes immediately shifted. Everyone knew that when Ron arrived, he meant business. He was there to be responsible for the music. He settled everyone down."

The end performance on *Robert Altman's Jazz '34* features Ron playing an after-hours bass duet with McBride, which runs while the credits roll (the duo performance also closes the feature). "That was Robert Altman's suggestion," Ron said. "I generally don't like to do random two-bass performances. It takes both guys being willing to step back, to not jam things up by interfering with the other person developing a good idea. You have to deal with issues like timbre, tone, range and even bass concept. Sometimes you get put into the role of second fiddle, which you have to be open to. I don't mind being second fiddle because it's all about the big letter M—music, not me."

The lack of respect for big M, Ron feels, also may figure into why more score work may not be coming his way these days. "Everything is done by computers now with translating the score and sending it digitally," he said. "I'm not sure I want to write that way. Besides, most of the film work is done in Los Angeles. You really have to be out there and that's out of the question for me. So today, writing scores may be difficult to come by, but that's OK. I'm working. I've got gigs, so I'm doing fine."

As for that *Kansas City* duet with Christian, Ron feels the one-take on-camera tune worked out well. "Christian is a sensitive young man who was learning the ways of the bass at the time," Ron said. "I think that what we did together was musically successful."

SNAPSHOT

The Tales of Christian McBride

Photograph by Stuart Brinin

The *Kansas City* duet as it turned out proved to be one of the more compelling moments of the live performance shoot. Christian recalls that he and Ron played two songs, sans rehearsal: "Solitude" and "Body and Soul." He also remembers that they didn't say much to each other during the taping on the stage at the makeshift club the crew had built. Plus, he's got a vivid memory of Robert Altman's enthusiastic approval ("That's a wrap!") and the standing ovation he and Ron received from all the other musicians who had assembled to see this rare summit of cross-generational bassists performing a duo.

"They were screaming and hollering," Christian said. "Everybody was standing." But he also added that what happened next took him completely by surprise because he was upset by a very uncomfortable event that had happened earlier in the week. "I was prepared to shake hands with Ron and then get out of there. So, I put my bass down and went over to Ron to shake his hand, and he gave me the longest, deepest hug I've ever had in my entire life. He was hugging me and I kept thinking, huh? Wow, he hasn't let me go."

Christian smiled and added, "That's when all the tension lifted."

At the time, Christian was a 23-year-old bass phenom who was the talk of New York and already one of the go-to players of his generation. A bassist since the age of 11, he singles Ron out as one of the most important influences of his early life. While trying to master the instrument, his mentoring uncle—bassist Howard Cooper who's still active on the Philadelphia music scene—dropped off a stack of records and said, "You're starting out on the bass, so now it's time to turn you on to the cats." Ron's work with Miles and as a leader was prominent in that pile of LPs.

With the elder statesman of the bass elevated to hero status (as a teenager, Christian even had a photo of Ron from a fashion shoot in *Ebony Man* that he tore from the magazine and tacked to his bedroom wall), the neophyte set off on a journey of learning about the instrument, the history of the jazz idiom and the players with whom he would later share a stage. Ron became an integral part of Christian's odyssey, but initially at least, it was not the dream relationship the young and slightly naïve man had hoped for. In fact, after a few early positive experiences both in his hometown of Philadelphia and later in his new home of New York, Christian learned, as many people had warned him, that Ron could on occasion be "prickly and testy."

Through Christian's lens, between 1990 and 1995 when the *Kansas City* filming took place, his relationship with Ron was "highly intense." Before that it had approximated extreme idol worship.

MEETING RON

"A lot of people assume that I got to Ron through Miles, but that wasn't true," said Christian, who was born on May 21, 1972. One of the albums his uncle gave him to listen to first was *Parade*, with Chick Corea and Tony Williams. Then it was Ron's sideman gigs on the Galaxy Records label including trio dates with Red Garland and Philly Joe Jones. Later came *Piccolo*, with Ron's quartet of Buster Williams, Ben Riley and Kenny Barron. "So I got to know Ron's music from the late '70s through his Milestone LPs. Then I was influenced by Ron on Miles albums like *Four and More* and *Seven Steps to Heaven*."

Christian says that both Ron and Miles's former bassist Paul Chambers served as early role models primarily because of their ability to play with fluidity. "For an 11-year-old bass player, you can imagine how cumbersome it was to play good notes with a clean sound and a good tone," Christian said. "Ron could get around his instrument. I could hear clearly what he was playing versus other records where you could, at best, only take an educated guess as to what the bass player was doing. What both Ron and Paul did turned me on."

Paul was Christian's first influence, specifically how he played Miles's "So What" on the live album *At Carnegie Hall 1961*. Then, he said, it took him "a lot of listening to hear how Ron's style evolved out of Paul's. In Miles's classic quintet of the '60s, Ron expanded the harmonic and rhythmic possibilities in the music. The band went to the outer limits. Ron really was the most pivotal figure on bass in the '60s. I was attracted to his sound, which is the characteristic I've come to most admire in a bassist."

Throughout his teenage years listening to records, studying and going to jazz clubs in Philadelphia, McBride said that his "admiration for Ron grew by leaps and bounds. I got every album he was on, all the Miles and V.S.O.P., the Milestone records and CTI and Blue Note. I had nothing but deep admiration for Ron."

In 1987, Christian finally got to meet Ron at Philadelphia's Mellon Jazz Festival where he and Milt Hilton were giving young musician workshops. Hundreds of students jammed the overall sessions, but when they were separated by instrument, the class sizes were considerably smaller, with only five bassists working with the two pros. "The other four guys were rock 'n' rollers," said Christian. "They were all appreciative of who they were going to work with, but I was the only one there who knew Ron's and Milt's genius from their records."

The first thing Ron asked Christian to do was play a scale. Then he asked him to do it again, this time two octaves higher, making sure every note was crystal clear and with full value on the bow. "It was like, wow, I'm at a real lesson with Ron," said Christian. "He was not unlike my teacher Neil Courtney of the Philadelphia Orchestra. Intense, straight-ahead, no nonsense but not mean." Likewise, Milt was very helpful, and Christian left the session feeling elated. "Wow, an hour with those two—it doesn't get any better than this," he said.

The following day Christian played in an all-star student band after which both Ron and Milt exchanged addresses and telephone numbers with the youngster should he ever come to New York. Ron, in fact, gave Christian a big hug and told him, "Kid, you're going to be all right."

Christian was thrilled.

Ron also cautioned him to stay in school, to finish before he moved north. "New York will always be there," he said.

PHILLY TO NEW YORK

Fast-forward two years to February 1989 when Christian went to New York with his grandfather to audition for Juilliard. They drove from Philly and to Christian's surprise stayed in a hotel on West End Avenue directly across the street from Ron's apartment. "I was totally freaking out," he said. "My grandfather said, 'Why not go over there to say hello.' But I was too nervous about the audition to go."

However, after the audition, Christian mustered up the courage to stroll across the street from his hotel, only to discover from the doorman that

Ron was on the road. But again, the youngster was euphoric. "Wow, I've been to his building," said Christian. "Total dreamland."

He got accepted to Juilliard and began in August. Early on in his studies, he was doing a gig at Indigo Blues, a club underneath the Edison Hotel, with fellow Philly friends B-3 bomber Joey DeFrancesco and drummer Byron Landham. Christian proudly announced that he had Ron's address, so he convinced Byron one afternoon to come with him just to pop in on him. "I can't believe I did this," Christian recalled. "Not only was I intruding on Ron Carter's privacy, but I was also taking someone with me."

When the pair arrived at Ron's building, there were four string players waiting to enter the elevator. The doorman informed everyone to go upstairs to see Ron. Christian and Byron joined. The elevator door opened into Ron's apartment. He welcomed the quartet, which was there for a rehearsal, then said to Christian and Byron, "Can I help you?"

"Mr. Carter, I met you in Philly, remember?" said Christian. "This is my friend Byron, who's a great drummer."

Ron held the door open and cordially told the pair that he was busy, then added, "I'm playing at Sweet Basil tonight with Cedar Walton and Billy Higgins. Come down and we can talk."

Christian left with another victory under his belt. "That's all I needed," he recalled. "I was a teenager and I was jumping up and down. I had seen Ron again and he hadn't thrown me out or cursed me."

As it turned out, Christian's gig at Indigo Blues was taking place at the same time as Ron's shows at Sweet Basil, so he couldn't follow through on the invitation. The next time he ran into Ron was a year and a half later when he was playing fourth-string bassist at Bradley's. He was getting so many working gigs in New York—playing in Freddie Hubbard's band, working with Betty Carter—that he quit school and became a full-timer on the scene.

In late 1990, early 1991, Christian met Ray Brown and the two became friends. At the time, Christian was playing in Benny Green's trio, which was patterned after Oscar Peterson's trio with Ray in the bass seat. "That's when Ray took over as my primary influence," said Christian, "even though anytime Ron played New York I was there."

It was around this time that Christian began to hear stories about Ron from people who were making observations about him from a distance. Some warned that eventually it was "guaranteed that Ron will not be nice to you," said Christian, who replied, "Why, what did I do?"

"You're a bass player and you're not studying with him," they told him.

"That's silly," he responded.

SWEET BASIL CHILL

Not long after, Christian met with what he viewed was a chilly response from Ron as a result of being an innocent bystander—attending one of his shows with a heckling Betty Carter. A member of her band at the time, Christian attended one of Betty's Jazz Ahead events at the Brooklyn Academy of Music. Afterwards, she inquired of him, "Who's playing in town tonight?"

"Ron's at Sweet Basil with Stephen Scott, Lewis Nash and Boots."

"Let's go mess with Ron," she said.

"What do you mean?"

"Why is he always so mean to you young cats? He should be open to teaching you all. I'm trying to teach, so is Art Blakey, so is Ray Brown. Why not Ron?" (Ron had actually been teaching fulltime at The City College since 1983.)

Betty also failed to note that both Stephen and Lewis were former members of her band who were being schooled by Ron within the workaday context of his group. (Stephen notes that Betty was upset when he left her employ and eventually joined Ron's band. "She never forgave me for leaving," he said, "especially after I started working with her No. 1 enemy.")

Christian also wasn't aware of when and how Betty's animosity toward Ron had begun. In the early '70s, she went on tour to Japan with a band that comprised Kenny Burrell, Roland Hanna, Ben Riley and Ron, who recalls that the tour was rocky throughout. "Kenny was kind of out of the picture and Roland and Betty didn't get along at all," he said. "So I was left to bring the band together each night so that Betty could sing."

While they were in Japan, a record producer approached Betty to record an album with the band and have Ron share the billing. But he was under contract with CTI and there was no time to work out permission rights. "So, the record date never took place," said Ron. "And Betty never forgave me."

In the cab ride to Sweet Basil, Christian recalled that Betty "was getting hotter" about Ron's treatment of young jazz musicians. But he said to her,

"I don't want you doing anything because that man is my hero. I don't want you making a scene and me being there with you."

But Christian noted, "If you knew Betty Carter, she was very good about kicking up dust."

And that's just what she did that evening. As fate would have it, she and Christian were seated in the front row, at the dead-center table. During the set, Betty kept nudging Christian in the side in an obvious manner, telling him that he could play better than what Ron was doing. Meanwhile, Stephen and Lewis were watching it all and became distracted, while Ron was stoic but aware of Betty's behavior. Christian kept pleading with her to stop, but she persisted. After the set, he told her, "You're awful," then told her he was going to say hello to Ron. She replied, "Don't waste your time. He probably won't even say anything to you."

Nevertheless, Christian went up to Ron: "Mr. Carter. Christian McBride. It's great to hear you again. You're still the greatest in my book."

But Christian figured he was caught in a guilt-by-association situation because, he recalled, as Ron was zipping up his bass bag for the night, he didn't look up or shake his hand. "I was so crushed. I went back to Betty who told me, 'See, I told you. He should have been nice to you. You're one of the few young bass players who give him his props.'"

Christian left the club wondering what happened: "There I was watching my hero Ron, and Betty, who didn't like my hero, was blatantly dissing him. I almost felt like I was being forced to take sides."

Six months later, Christian went to another one of Ron's shows at Sweet Basil, where this time he was playing with Cedar Walton and Billy Higgins. Even though he was anxious about seeing Ron, Christian approached him after the set to shake his hand. From the young bassist's perspective, Ron's handshake was cold.

COVER STORY

That was around the same time that *Bass Player* magazine ran a December 1994 cover story on electric bassist Anthony Jackson in conversation with Ron. At one point, Anthony asked him, "Are the young upright players like Christian McBride, Charnett Moffett and Robert Hurst receptive when you talk to them?"

Ron replied, "I can't speak for what's inside their heads, but they're respectful and try to come hear me play. That's not the same as taking lessons, though. I get the vibe from some of the young bassists that they're not into hearing what I have to say.... A lot of them have expressed interest in getting together with me, but they're all busy working. Good for them, man—somebody's got to play bass in the band. But I'd recommend to each of them that they take three or four months off to study the instrument with someone. Their curiosity about their own playing is underdeveloped..."

Christian read this and said, "OK, I'll fix this right now." The next day he called Ron and left a message requesting a lesson. For the next two months they traded messages. But the hookup never took place because of conflicting tour schedules. "I wanted to keep on it," Christian said. "Ron had to know how much I loved him and wanted to learn from him."

But then life for Christian went into a whirlwind. He signed with manager Mary Ann Topper, he was playing in Ray Brown's SuperBass trio with John Clayton, and he got signed to Verve Records for his debut recording. With his star rising, *JazzTimes* magazine decided to put him on the cover, with Ron. With Bret Primack as moderator, the feature story spotlighted Christian interviewing Ron. The session took place in December 1994 for the April 1995 issue.

Because of his two previous encounters with Ron, Christian felt tense about doing the interview. "I felt like I was going to be walking on eggshells."

For the photo shoot, Christian appeared in a suit, with a red pinstriped shirt and tie, while Ron was the more casual of the pair, with a forest green cardigan sweater and button-down blue dress shirt.

In the intro to the piece, Primack previewed the "cross-generational colloquy between two bad bassists: Ron Carter, the tribal elder of world renown, and Christian McBride, the young lion certain to inherit an abundance of accolades." In print, the interview seemed to go smoothly, with Christian asking Ron for his wisdom on such matters as how to get depth from a basic blues composition and what the difference was in playing with drummers Tony Williams and Elvin Jones.

After the interview, Ron put on his jacket and left without any fanfare. Again, Christian felt hurt, but he still gave Ron the benefit of the doubt. "I can't believe the interview ended that way," he said. "But hey, this is Ron Carter. Ron's the king."

IN KANSAS CITY

When the *Jazz Times* story appeared on the newsstands, Christian was pleased and hoped that it would thaw his relationship with Ron. Soon after, in May 1995, the two were enlisted by musical director Hal Willner to be in Altman's *Kansas City* film. Again, Christian got excited: "I'm going to be in a movie with my hero!"

He was on the first shift of the shooting, working a few days, then flying to New York to do a gig and coming back the next day. Because of previous engagements, Ron was coming in on the second shift, arriving from New York on the same day as Christian, but on a flight one hour later.

"I love telling this story," said Christian. "It was intense. The guy who met me at the airport told me to put my bass in the equipment van and he'd deliver it to me later because he had other instruments to pick up. He told me he'd give me a ring once he got to the hotel. Sure enough, sometime later the concierge told me that my bass was safely in storage at the hotel. That night all the musicians—Geri Allen, Cyrus Chestnut, Victor Lewis—and Harry Belafonte who starred in the film went to see the daily screenings. I got there and Ron was talking to a few people. I went over to pay my respect and bam! He laid into me."

Christian was not only embarrassed that he had been singled out by Ron, but also angry because other people witnessed the exchange.

The way Christian remembers it, the following conversation took place:

"What's your problem leaving me with your bass?"

"Mr. Carter, excuse me?"

"You left your bass at the airport with the equipment person."

"That's what he told me to do."

"No, you don't leave your instrument with anybody. You take full responsibility for your instrument."

"But Mr. Carter, I've been trusting him all week long. It's in a hard case. What's going to happen to it?"

"That's blatantly irresponsible to leave your bass with a nonmusician. Not only that, but when we got to the hotel, I'm the one who had to take it out of the van and put it in storage for you."

"Mr. Carter, no one said to do that. And if there's a problem with how I handle my instrument, not everyone here has to know that."

Christian left the screening, upset and embarrassed. He called Mary Ann Topper and told her how angry he was. "I will always love that man's bass playing, he's legend," Christian said. "But as a man, to hell with him. I don't ever want to speak with him again. I don't want to study with him. Nothing. Just keep him away from me."

Ron recalled the event through a different filter. "It was my concern that a young bassist should learn to take care of his own instrument and not let someone handle it who's unaware of how delicate his instrument is," he said. "I tell that to any bass player who thinks he can just leave his bass, for example, onstage after a gig and let one of the stage crew guys take care of it. I've seen instruments get damaged that way. So, I told Christian that he needs to be more responsible. I think he took what I said personally."

Soon after the event, Harry called Christian in his hotel room. "Christian, it's Mr. B.," he said. "Let's have dinner tonight." At dinner, Harry said to him, "Now, what's going on between you and Ron?"

"Mr. B., I know he's your friend, but he totally hurt my feelings, and he's done it more than once. And frankly I'm sick of it."

"What do you think the problem is?"

"I don't know."

"I've known Ron for several years. I used to live in that same building he lives in. I watched his family grow. He's a good man and wants the best for you."

"No, he doesn't."

"I know he can be harsh sometimes but give him a chance. I'll talk with Ron and see if we can straighten this out. You guys should get along."

"I don't want you to feel obligated to do that."

"No obligation. Ron's my friend. We'll talk."

However, Ron doesn't recall his friend Harry interceding on Christian's behalf.

For the rest of the week, the rising-star bassist avoided the elder, he said, "like the plague" until Robert Altman informed him that he wanted to end the filming with a bass duet. Christian recoiled in fear. "My first reaction, was, oh no. I knew everybody would be on the set, and I could just imagine that it would be like Ali versus Fraser. Who will they place their money on? Who's going to pop their cork first? McBride or Carter?"

Christian talked to Mary Ann who smoothly told him, "Just do your job and it'll be all right."

And, as it turned out, the music healed.

In fact, Ron, unaware that Christian was upset, went into the session unfazed. He adopted the professional stance he takes for any session: We've got a job to do and let's make it work. It's all about the music. "Christian played great," Ron said. "I'm sure he felt some pressure. But that could well have been the first time he played with someone clearly his equal who didn't act superior toward him, but gave him all the room he needed on his bass to succeed."

CLEAR SAILING?

From idol worship to estrangement and disappointment, Christian recognized that his relationship with Ron righted itself from that moment and then remained on an even keel.

Christian says that, with the ice melted for him, he contacted Ron about trying to work out their schedules so that he could study with him. But the attempt met with another round of phone tag.

In 1998, Christian taught a clinic at the New England Conservatory of Music in Boston and talked with some students who had studied with Ron at the Thelonious Monk Institute of Jazz Performance, where he had started the program and served as artistic director beginning in 1995.

"One kid told me that Ron had spoken to a class and he was asked who he liked as a young bassist," said Christian. "He said he'd been listening to me and that Ron talked about me a lot. Well, after hearing that, I went home floating on a cloud."

For his 30th birthday party, Christian sent an e-mail blast to about 300 people. Ron replied, "Dear Christian, I can't make it to your party. I'll be out of town. Love, Ron."

They met up again later that year when they were both on the bill of the Newport Jazz Festival. Ron was playing with his trio of Mulgrew Miller and Russell Malone, and he was dressed in his refined suit and tie. On the other hand, Christian had a gas attendant outfit on backstage with a long platinum chain and was smoking a cigar. "Ron came out of his trailer, and seeing him made me want to go back to my trailer and change," he said. "But he was the sweetest I ever saw him. We hugged and talked. I felt that day solidified our relationship."

Their paths crossed again in December 2006 at the Waterside Jazz Legends Gala tribute to Frank Foster in Norfolk, Virginia. The two bassists were invited in addition to Frank Wess, Donald Byrd, Branford Marsalis, Billy Taylor and Nicholas Payton, among others. Christian approached Ron and said, "Mr. Carter, it's so great to see you."

Ron pulled him aside and said, "It's good to see you respecting the music so much." He then added, "And it's good to see you in a suit and a tie for a change."

Christian called his friend Lewis Nash, who was part of Ron's quartet for many years, and asked him, "Was that a loaded comment?"

Lewis replied, "Of course it was loaded."

"OK, I guess it was," Christian said. "But I still love him."

He accentuated that comment when he made reference to Ron while talking to me a few years ago about the influence electric bassist Jaco Pastorius had on him. He had tried to emulate Jaco's style when he was young and listened avidly to his music in Weather Report. Jaco died while Christian was still in high school, but he felt like he got to know him a little through his later associations with Joe Zawinul, Wayne Shorter, Alphonso Johnson and Victor Bailey.

Christian then recounted what he called one of Jaco's "famous ego tirades" where he said there were only three great bass players: himself, Ray Brown and Ron Carter. Christian agreed, but thought that Paul Chambers also had to be added to the list. "If I had a bass Mount Rushmore," Christian said, "I'd actually have four bass presidents: Ron, Ray, Paul and Jaco."

As for Ron, when he heard a tune played by Christian at the live *DownBeat* Blindfold Test at the International Association for Jazz Educators conference in January 2007 (see Colloquy in Part V), he concluded his critique by saying fondly, "Christian has been a friend for a very long time. I would hope he'd go back and listen to this track to find out what I'm talking about."

In the audience at the time, Christian said he loved Ron's response and totally agreed with his criticism.

Perhaps if they can both free their busy schedules, that long-overdue one-on-one lesson will finally take place.

CHAPTER FIFTEEN

Brazil: Bass Undulation

THE DEPTH OF Ron's relationship with Brazilian music stretches back to 1967 when producer Creed Taylor, then at A&M Records, recorded the seminal Antonio Carlos Jobim album, *Wave*, for his CTI imprint at the label. Ron was called upon to play bass on that session. Having been aware of the bossa nova craze that had spread around the globe earlier in the decade, Ron knew who Jobim was, but he admits that he was not very conversant with his style or with Brazilian music in general. He didn't have guitarist Charlie Byrd's Brazilian-influenced album, 1962's breakout bossa hit *Jazz Samba*, or the Stan Getz/João Gilberto classic, 1963's *Getz/Gilberto*, that featured the lush tune "The Girl From Ipanema," sung by Astrud Gilberto—both of which were produced by Creed for Verve Records.

So, Ron says that he went into the *Wave* session blind. "I just played what I thought would fit," he said, then added simply, "Mr. Jobim was quite pleased."

Actually, like many others—musicians and listeners alike—Ron first became aware of Brazilian music in 1959, when he heard the score to *Black Orpheus*, composed by Jobim and Luiz Bonfa (the film won the Academy Award for Best Foreign Film). "Not only did that give an impressive visual image of Brazil," said Ron, "but it also highlighted my ignorance about the music."

Historically, Brazilian music derived from African roots. When Europeans introduced enslaved Africans to their New World colonies in South America, the indigenous people (prominently such Caribbean Amerindian tribes as the Caribs and Arawaks) were largely eliminated. The two newly established cultures blended together, with elements of European classical music merging with the drum rhythms of Africa.

African rhythms took hold on the mainland of South America most significantly in Brazil. Growing out of the late 19th-century choro tradition based on such European dance music as the waltz and the polka, samba (named after the Congo-Angolan dance *semba*) was born in Little Africa in Rio de Janeiro. It was there that ex-slaves generated a percussive style of music with a massive drum soundscape and syncopated dance beats to buoy the Carnaval celebrations that had previously been European-music affairs. In 1928, composer Ismael Silva formed the first samba school, Deixa Falar, and the style soon became Brazil's official music.

Its new-wave, cooled-down offspring came three decades later. Cofounded by Jobim, who was the music's leading composer, bossa nova officially celebrated its 50th birthday in 2008, honoring the anniversary of Gilberto's 1958 recording of the Jobim tune "Desafinado (Out of Tune)," followed the next year by his "Chega de Saudade (No More Blues)."

Brazil-born, New York-based pianist/vocalist Eliane Elias notes that the early bossa nova movement got its start when Jobim began to collaborate with poet Vinicius de Moraes in 1956. But it wasn't until Gilberto arrived on the scene that bossa fully bloomed. "In 1958, a young singer and guitarist came out of nowhere and gave these [early] songs a new vocal interpretation and a new beat," Eliane said. "That singer/guitarist was João Gilberto, whose seductive vocals caressed the ear as well as the soul, while his guitar played an infectious swinging rhythm." She added that he "recognized the possibilities inherent in the beat—how it simplified the rhythm of samba and allowed for a lot of room for the modern harmonies Tom [Jobim] was creating."

Gilberto's version of "Chega de Saudade" wasn't the first take on the tune. Brazilian singer Elizeth Cardoso recorded it originally, with João on guitar, on the limited edition record, *Canção do Amor Demais*. Then the vocal group Os Cariocas delivered its own rendition, also with João, after the ensemble's guitarist Badeco couldn't duplicate the syncopated beat Gilberto bestowed upon the tune.

"While Elizeth was learning Tom's songs, João tried to show her how to delay and advance a chord's rhythm the way he thought the song should be sung," said Eliane. "But Elizeth would have none of it and let him know she could do it without his advice. She sang the song the conventional way. Only João's guitar hinted at what was to come."

With Jobim's encouragement, Gilberto finally recorded the song in 1958, as one side of a 78-rpm single for Odeon Records. Initially the label was reluctant because, according to Eliane, artistic director Aloysio de Oliveira "saw no commercial potential for an artist who sang quietly and used no vibrato," but relented thanks to Jobim's intercession. Recorded on July 10, 1958 with the tune "Bim-Bom" on the B-side, the single was dispatched to Rio record stores where, said Eliane, "it remained in total obscurity for several months."

Even though *Black Orpheus* had exposed bossa nova to a wide audience, the biggest surge of the music came in 1963 with *Getz/Gilberto* (which included Jobim as a piano player).

JOBIM

WHILE JOBIM WAS famous for his compositions, his recording career first bloomed when Creed took him under his wing, beginning with *Wave*. Since he had previously worked with Ron on various recordings, including Gil Evans's 1960 masterpiece for Verve, *Out of the Cool*, Creed called the bassist to see if he were available for *Wave*. Even though Ron was still playing with Miles at the time, he had a hole on his schedule that enabled him to join the session, which also included trombonist Urbie Green, orchestrator Claus Ogerman, who arranged the string section, and several Brazilian musicians.

"I went to the studio and was introduced to Jobim and the rest of the Brazilians," Ron recalled. "They all spoke English, but I didn't speak one word of Portuguese. Not one word. Nothing."

Ron said that at first he spoke with the session leader by addressing him as Mr. Jobim. But he replied, "Please, no, call me Tom."

Jobim asked Ron, "Have you ever played Brazilian music before?"

"No, but I am a little familiar with it."

"I think you'll find it fun to play. Let's see how far we get."

Jobim gave Ron a lead sheet and told him to play the way he likes to play and have a good time. And that he did. Three years later he was enlisted again by Tom and Creed for the second A&M/CTI date, *Tide*, which also featured Jerry Dodgion on alto sax/flute, and an all-star cast of Brazilian musicians, including Hermeto Pascoal on flute, Eumir Deodato on piano/acoustic guitar and Airto Moreira on percussion. Recorded around the same time for CTI was Jobim's *Stone Flower*.

In an interview with *DownBeat*'s Ed Williams in 1977, Ron replied to the journalist's comment that Jobim "seems to be very fond of calling you," by saying, "Yes, Brazilians in general call me." He added, "When Brazilians come to New York, whether from Rio or wherever, when they want to hire a bass player, they hire me. When I ask why, they say, 'Because you play Brazilian music better than the Brazilian bass players.'"

At the time, Ron had not gone to Brazil nor experienced what he called "pure Brazilian music" nor had he listened to a Brazilian record, other than the ones he had played on. Williams noted that the way Portuguese is spoken in Brazil reminded him of the sonority of Ron's bass tone. He said, "There's something about your note length and the way that you use it, especially with Brazilian music, that captures the undulating movement of the people."

"It's strange because that music is not indigenous to my background at all," Ron said.

It was a horizon for him. Even while he was perfecting the rhythmic communication as the anchor in Miles's band, Ron was plunging into an entirely new ocean without a lifejacket. "With Miles, we were playing our music," he said. "With the Brazilians, I had to figure out what was happening, how the different rhythms worked, how the triangle figured into the music like the clave in Latin rhythms. In Brazilian music you listen to the triangle, which allows you to figure out where the percussionist thinks the beat is. My job became finding the notes to be compatible with that rhythm that's played by that tiny instrument as well as the drummer who's playing rimshots that are different than what Americans play."

Ron also discovered that with Brazilian music he played with more freedom because the bottom of the tunes wasn't dominated by a bass drum. "I had the freedom to do different kinds of things without worrying about the bass drum drowning out what I was playing," he said. "They have a bass drum but it's played in a different pattern, almost like a snare drum. That allowed me to find different notes that could change the sound of a chord being played. I was able to play bass notes not expected in bossa nova. The chords of the music aren't complicated, so I was able to trust my sense of working with the drummer."

In the end, Ron says, his challenge was "to play music in the bossa nova style that was different than what they played in Brazil." He calls it a trial-by-error endeavor that he developed over the years, working with such Brazilian percussionists as Airto and Naná Vasconcelos. "I wasn't looking to throw curve balls, but I was into using their rhythms as a new palette where I could add in a splash of red," he said. "I was always looking to find the right notes to make their percussion sound good. I would think, what note makes him not play this figure, what note throws him out of one groove and into another?"

BRAZIL IN PERSON

WHILE RON CONTINUED to be fascinated with the new world of Brazilian music that he encountered in New York, he knew that he'd have to visit the country to get a firsthand look. He told Williams in *DownBeat*, "I would just like to go down there to do some musicological and ethnological research." Citing his passion for working with Airto and his wife Flora Purim as well as multi-instrumentalist Pascoal and vocalist Milton Nascimento (whom he called "a folk hero"), Ron said that a trip to Brazil was essential for a deeper understanding of the music: "There's that whole Brazilian music cult that I've become involved in, and they play [the music] with such native purity that they feel they must have me on [their dates]. I have to find out at some point, go see and hear how those guys do it down there and see where we're coming from."

In fact, Ron says that as more Brazilians continued to come to New York to work with him, they began to tease him about not going to their country. "They told me that everyone there was playing bass like me," he said. "So, I kept threatening to go, just as a tourist, and have someone take me to different areas of the country. I wanted to see for myself how it was that it was not only possible for me to play their music, but also be able to change the way they play their music from the bottom up because of me."

Ron finally made it to Brazil in 1988 on a gig. In September, he performed at the Free Jazz Festival (sponsored by the Free cigarette company) in Rio with a trio comprising Tony Williams on drums and Mulgrew Miller on piano. Mary Ann Topper, who was managing Tony at the time and traveled with the group there, recalls that the young drummer was in a hyped-up mood, telling everyone that the band was "not going to take any prisoners in Brazil." In contrast, she said that Ron was low-key: "He was reading a book, probably a mystery novel, as we took a cab from the airport to a press conference. Tony got upset about something and walked out, but Ron and Mulgrew stayed on. The next day there was a picture of Ron on the front page of the newspaper."

In the 20 years since that first trip, Ron figures that he and his bands have gone back to Brazil at least 15 times, either playing at festivals or in clubs, such as Mistura Fina in Rio and Bourbon Street in São Paulo. He also recalls playing an all-star tribute to Jobim at the Free Jazz Festival in São Paulo on September 27, 1993, a little more than a year before the composer died (December 8, 1994) in New York. For the show, concert producer Oscar Castro-Neves, a longtime Jobim associate, enlisted several American musicians, Ron among them, to come to Brazil to pay homage. Additional guests included Alex Acuña, Gal Costa, Joe Henderson, Jon Hendricks, Shirley Horn, Harvey Mason and Gonzalo Rubalcaba, as well as musical director Herbie Hancock. Jobim also joined in the festivities, as did his son Paulo Jobim. The live recording, *Antonio Jobim & Friends*, was released by Verve in 1996.

Once Ron got to Brazil, one of the first things he heard on Brazilian radio was his own bass lines. "They'd play Jobim records with me on them," he said. "That was a thrill." He says that while in Brazil he and his band mates would go to Brazilian music concerts "to see how the musicians present the music. I may have some of a band's record, but seeing them live, up close and personal, is different."

As for his performances in Brazil, Ron says that audiences are intrigued by the fact that he knows the Brazilian "library," but also brings his own voice to the music. "We're a jazz band," he said, "And I like that word jazz. We're not a Brazilian band or a bossa nova band, but we figured out a way to play Brazilian music more like Brazilians would play versus how Americans typically play Brazilian music. At the same time, we modified the melodies and brought in new chords, but still had the Brazilian intent. People would say, 'How do you do this?'"

As a result, people there began to call Ron "the bass player of Brazil."

ORFEU

A MILESTONE RECORDING where Ron fully integrated Brazilian music into his sensibility, 1999's *Orfeu* featured him in a sextet setting with his quartet at the time (pianist Stephen Scott, drummer Payton Crossley—in his first recording with the leader—and percussionist Steve Kroon) and tenor saxophonist Houston Person, all of whom had traveled to Brazil as a quintet. The other voice in the mix was guitarist Bill Frisell. Two tunes were written by Luiz Bonfa, the rest by Ron, including his variation of a Dvorak melody lifted from his symphony *From the New World*. The quintet had just come back from Brazil (playing in Rio and São Paulo) where they had road-tested the tunes for the studio date. Bill, meanwhile, studied a demo Ron had given him and met up with the band in New York.

While in Brazil, Ron, Stephen, Payton and Steve frequented a local samba school where they sought to learn the real Brazilian thing from local musicians, talking to drummers and percussionists about what rhythms are most appropriate and authentic in Brazilian music. It was through this absorption of the music on an intimate level that the rhythm section was schooled for the recording.

In the liner notes to *Orfeu*, Ron said, "In my arrangements, I've tried to interweave what we develop in terms of rhythm with what the lead instrument is playing. This distinguishes our music from the usual American version of bossa nova. For instance, there might be as many as three different rhythms simultaneously progressing behind the soloist, or four different beats played by piano, guitar, drums and bass, all intertwining. The soloist can then join the rhythm established by the guitar, or play against the rhythm created by the drums, or even match what is happening in the percussion. The bass creates the groove at the bottom of all this." He then cited Bonfa's tune "Manhã de Carnaval" and his own song "Por do Sol" as prime examples of the band interplay.

ROSA

OVER THE YEARS, Ron has been the go-to guy for sessions by top-tier Brazilian artists, including vocalists Flora Purim, Astrud Gilberto and Ithamara Koorax, keyboardist Deodato, drummer Dom Um Romão, percussionist Airto, and composers Pascoal and Bonfa. One of his most significant recent Brazil recordings, *Entre Amigos*, a co-billed date with Brazilian singer/guitarist Rosa Passos, was released by Chesky Records in 2003. Ron likes the album so much that he singled it out when DJ Alisa Clancy on radio station KCSM-FM in San Mateo, California, asked him to talk about his "desert island" discs.

JazzTimes magazine also marveled at the recording, remarking first how Passos, singing in Portuguese, is able to "convey emotional nuance [that] transcends linguistic barriers." The review continued by acknowledging the "profound, embedded presence of Ron Carter. Right at the center of this graceful, melodic music is the big beat of his bass, and it changes everything. Carter is in tune with Passos's particular cultural concept of time, but he also pulls her his way, toward a more aggressive drive. The synergies create a groove that throbs like life."

Ron recalls the session, produced by Cliff Korman and recorded in St. Peter's Church in New York, as an opportunity for him to have his ears opened to a new talent. "Originally I wasn't interested in doing the project, but I agreed to it to learn more about Brazilian music from Brazilian musicians," he said. "I wasn't interested initially because as a co-leader I thought I'd have to be responsible for the library and the arrangements. I felt like I'd be walking into a lion's den without a whip or a chair. I don't speak Portuguese so I thought it could be a problem, but then I figured, OK, let's see if I can have some fun playing this kind of music."

Heralded as Brazil's best bossa nova singer to come on the scene since João Gilberto and arguably the country's most esteemed female vocalist today, Rosa's bossa/samba performance ranges from the intimate to the ebullient with dreamy, gently bouncing numbers as well as jaunty rhythmic rides.

It wasn't until 1996 that she made her American premiere, at the invitation of Oscar Castro-Neves, to a Brazilian music event at the Hollywood Bowl. After that, she collaborated with Sadao Watanabe, Paquito D'Rivera and then with Ron on *Entre Amigos*.

Rosa said, "It was marvelous, an honor for me to record with him. I consider Ron Carter a living jazz legend."

"I met Rosa at a rehearsal for the session and she was a little, bitty lady," Ron said. "She had heard my music with Jobim, Hermeto and Gal Costa and always wanted to work with me. Once we rehearsed I was flabbergasted at how well she sang and how well she played the guitar. Her voice is pure and her pitch good."

Still, Ron felt a little shy about what he would be able to bring to the sessions. "Everyone expects magic from me," he said. "I don't mind having that responsibility, but what people expect isn't always what they hear on the playback. So, that tired me out a little, but I went into it hoping to learn some new music and learn new things about Brazilian music that I didn't know before."

Rosa enlisted two Brazilian musicians to be a part of the session: guitarist Lula Galvão and percussionist Paulo Braga (Billy Drewes also contributed on tenor saxophone and clarinet). The group played several Brazilian tunes. Seven of the 11 were composed by Jobim, including "Desafinado," "The Girl From Ipanema (Garota de Ipanema)" and "Insensatez," arranged to be performed as music of the moment.

Once again, before the session, Ron felt embarrassed that he didn't know Portuguese when the rest of the band huddled to discuss a tune. "I felt a little inept, like I couldn't help out with making things right," he said.

But as it turned out, Ron's intuition with Brazilian music did the trick. *Entre Amigos* liner-note writer Chip Stern said that the band "recreated

Brazilian music in their own image. Given the splendid recording quality of the recital, we have a front row seat to bask in the sepia glow of Ron Carter's warm, woody acoustic bass violin, as he uses his singing sound, big percussive beat and canny harmonic sensibility to rudder this ship of song with the firm yet gentle understatement of a true Brazilian.... [His] playing evinces great depth, dignity, simplicity ... and authenticity—a decidedly definitive recital." Stern marveled at the high level of communication of the collaboration given the language barriers, saying, "It's remarkable how well Carter and company have captured both the letter and spirit of these traditions."

In looking back, Ron is pleased with the *Entre Amigos* sessions. "It was a successful recording session musically," he said. "The bass sounded good, and the drumming wasn't too thick for the bass. I'm glad I did it. I learned some new music and made some wonderful new friends."

JAZZ MEETS BOSSA

AT THE BEHEST of his record label, Somethin' Else, the imprint of EMI Japan, Ron joined in the international commemoration of the 50-year anniversary of bossa nova by returning to the Brazilian music well he had drawn from so many times in his career. On *Jazz & Bossa* (released in Japan in 2008 and not scheduled to be released stateside), Ron continued his exploration of the connections between jazz and bossa nova, bringing the two styles intimately together—essentially approaching bossa nova tunes with the jazz vocabulary and infusing the bossa sensibility into the jazz realm.

Arranged by Robert Freedman, *Jazz & Bossa*'s nine songs include three written by Brazilian musicians (including Jobim's "Chega de Saudade"); the Benny Golson standard, "Whisper Not;" and five tunes written by the leader that reflect his relationship with Brazilian music over the last 30-plus years. Music from Ron's songbook includes "Ah, Rio," "De Samba," "Por-Do-Sol," "Obrigado" and "Saudade," the solo guitar endsong that for the first time in his recording career the composer sat out.

"Even though I've recorded some of these tunes before, I'm playing them in a different way and in a different musical environment," said Ron. "These aren't updates, but they represent how I'm hearing the music differently today than I did 20 to 30 years ago. It's like what artists such as Miles did, revisiting their library more than once and bringing it into a new light."

For *Jazz & Bossa*, Ron was joined by two of his current quartet members, Stephen on piano and percussionist Rolando Morales-Matos, as well as longtime tenor saxophone friend, Javon Jackson. The CD also featured two Brazilian musicians, guitarist Guilherme Monteiro and drummer Portinho.

"No matter how well American musicians can play the bossa nova beat, Brazilians play it differently," Ron said. "I knew that to make this CD come out the way I envisioned it, I'd need to include Brazilians. I've played with Portinho on and off for several years, and I met Guilherme several years ago. I knew they would do a great job. My biggest challenge was nailing them down because they're constantly on the road, going back and forth to Rio."

As for Rolando, who hails from Puerto Rico, Ron enlisted him to play whistles, tambourine, triangle and small hand drums to augment the rhythms after the two talked about how comfortable he was playing in the Brazilian style. Ron said that he's pleased with what his percussionist brought to the mix—likewise with Stephen. "Stephen and I have been to Brazil several times together, and we've sought out music there to see how the players write and comp for each other," Ron said. "Because Guilherme kept the rhythm going, Stephen was freed to solo in an unrestricted way. He didn't have to concern himself with stepping out of the rhythm section. That's the way it works in most Brazilian bands where there's usually two guitarists or a guitarist and pianist to keep the rhythm flowing."

An unusual overarching concept for *Jazz & Bossa* was the diminishing size of the ensemble as the CD spins, beginning with the full sextet and ending with a solo piece. Ron explained this in the Japanese CD liner notes: "The concept was to go from a large group—and large sound—to smaller and smaller groups, ending with a single player. It's like a novel with a complex plot that reaches a conclusion and resolution at the end."

Ron said that closing the CD was solely in Guilherme's hands, playing "Saudade," a song that Ron wrote for *Orfeu*. They discussed the tune at rehearsal—the chords, the melody line, the intent. "Guilherme played a little, then I told him not to play anymore," Ron recalled. "I wanted to let the song marinate until the studio session. I told him, OK, it's your job to end the story. It makes for the perfect conclusion. It's kind of like it took eight tunes to figure out that the butler did it."

Jazz & Bossa opened with the full sextet swinging into an upbeat take on "Salt Song" (*Canção do Sal*), composed by Milton Nascimento. It featured charged guitar/tenor sax lines, a sparkling piano break that turns a corner into a percussion fiesta, and a rhythm jam at the end. That's followed by a Brazilian-tinged version of "Whisper Not." "That song is so great, but it has a bass line that's almost dictated because of the melody," Ron said. "My job was to turn it somewhere else, to give it a Brazilian feel, to make it feel like a Jobim song." Featured on this track once again was a catchy piano/tenor sax unison line and percussion interludes after each solo.

The two other Brazilian songs included "Chega de Saudade," which marked the first time Ron recorded the festive tune. He heard it in the '60s when Dizzy Gillespie would play it with his band and make it sound like a bop number. "Dizzy played it like he invented it," said Ron. "I wanted to keep that bop idea but still make us sound like a Brazilian band playing it."

It featured one of Ron's best solo spots on the album—deep grooved bass lines with his characteristic glissando slides. The other song was another Jobim number, "Wave," which Ron had recorded with the songwriter. The breezy guitar-bass duo was arranged differently than the original. "It was difficult because I kept hearing Tom's sound in my ear," Ron said. "I sent the original to Bob and told him not to arrange it like that, otherwise I probably wouldn't have been able to play it."

Besides "Saudade," two other Ron tunes from *Orfeu* were revisited on *Jazz & Bossa*: the dance-filled "Obrigado," given a new Freedman arrangement, and "Por-Do-Sol," a sprightly bossa-steeped number that Ron said was "one of the brighter songs on the album in terms of key sound." A real samba cooker with the bass percolating beneath the melody line, "De Samba" originally appeared on Ron's 1975 *Anything Goes* album for the CTI imprint Kudu. "Again, I sent Bob a copy of the song and told him, that was recorded more than 30 years ago," he said. "Let's not do this again, but let's take it into a completely different zone."

One of the strongest tracks on *Jazz & Bossa* was the sweetly melodic "Ah, Rio" that harked back to Ron's introduction to bossa nova: *Black Orpheus*. "Ah, Rio" was originally recorded on Ron's 1980 album *Patrão* on Milestone Records. His frequent travels to Brazil since that time influenced this new version that's transfixed and transported by Rio de Janeiro's splendor. "It's stunning just flying into Rio," Ron said. "You see the sun coming up and the giant statue of Jesus [Christ the Redeemer on Corcovado Mountain], and then when you land, you immediately get the feel of the culture. You're awestruck."

Ron said that the entire CD reflects that sentiment, from the beauty of the dramatic landscape to the rhythm of the bossa-grooved soundscapes. And there's still so much more to explore, he said. "Every time I go to Brazil, I'm listening. I listen to hear what new direction the Brazilians are taking their music. I'm always learning."

CHAPTER SIXTEEN

Classical Meets Jazz

IN 2006, WRITER Dave Helland asked Ron if studying classical cello as a youngster was a factor in his prowess as a jazz bassist. In his typically taciturn manner that reveals his wry sense of humor, Ron replied, "Probably not. I'm a pretty disciplined person with a focus on what it takes to make things better. If I had started out as a lamp maker, I would have been just as good a bass player."

All kidding aside, Ron's classical music training—whether on cello or on bass—has undergirded his oeuvre as a leader and session man. He was classically trained, beginning years before jazz registered on his radar screen, and it was on this cornerstone that he pursued his never-satiated quest for finding the right notes. So, it comes as no surprise that, beginning in the mid-1980s and continuing through the present, Ron has more fully embraced an amalgam of jazz and classical in his recordings.

Ron recorded a classical/jazz album in 1985, originally slated for Columbia Records, but later issued by Phillips in Japan as *Ron Carter Plays Bach*. In 1991 he recorded *Ron Carter Meets Bach* for EMI/Toshiba (his first session for the label), which released the album in 1992. (Both albums have never been released in the U.S.) In 1993 Ron recorded *Friends* and in 1997 *Brandenburg Concerto*. (Both were recorded for EMI/Toshiba and released stateside on Blue Note.)

BACH TO MONK

RON RECALLS HIS first jazz/classical outing that was recorded in 1985, originally for Columbia, between his association with Milestone Records and EMI/Toshiba, when he said he was a "free agent" as far as record contracts went. "I called myself the Catfish Hunter of bass players," he said, in reference to the star baseball pitcher who, as the first free agent in the major leagues, left the Oakland A's to become a New York Yankee in 1975.

At the time, Columbia was enjoying success with jazz musicians recording classical music, most prominent among them young trumpeter Wynton Marsalis. In 1983 and 1984, he recorded *Concertos* (with material by Haydn and Mozart), *Haydn: Three Favorite Concertos* and *Baroque Music for Trumpet*. "Dr. George Butler at Columbia Records called me up and asked me to do a classical and jazz album," Ron said. "So I talked to the person in charge and told him I wanted to do Bach's suites for solo cello on the bass. He said, great idea, so for the next six months I practiced my brains out."

When Ron was ready, he went to Rudy Van Gelder's studio in New Jersey and recorded the solo bass album (the cello suites as well as two lute suites with overdubs). When Columbia received the final product, they wanted to hire a baroque musician in Boston to add in percussion parts. While at first Ron hesitantly agreed, he wasn't happy. Then he nixed the idea. "They really busted my chops," he said. "Eventually, they told me they couldn't do anything with the album. Since Columbia hadn't paid Rudy yet, he owned the master tapes. So I borrowed some money and bought them from him."

Not long after, Ron passed the tapes on to Japanese producer/radio DJ Kiyoshi Koyama, who liked what he heard. He shopped the album to various record companies in Japan. He settled on Phillips, which issued the album as *Ron Carter Plays Bach*. It sold more than 80,000 copies in Japan.

At the same time, in 1985, Ron joined the avant-garde classical group Kronos Quartet as the marquee artist on its adventurous classical-meets-jazz album, *Kronos Quartet Plays Music of Thelonious Monk*, on Landmark Records. Produced by Orrin Keepnews—who not only oversaw Monk's piano brilliance on the Riverside label in the '50s but also enlisted Ron for several sideman sessions as well as signed him to his Milestone imprint in the '70s—the disc features Ron on Kronos's expansive "Monk Suite." The piece, arranged by Tom Darter, highlights Ron improvising on bass while the quartet plays the classical-oriented notation on several Monk works, including "Off Minor" and "Epistrophy."

Comprising violinists David Harrington and John Sherba, viola player Hank Dutt, and cellist Joan Jeanrenaud, Kronos performed "Monk Suite" as one part of its performance at the Brooklyn Academy of Music in November 1986. Ron appeared as a guest. Writing in *The New York Times*, critic Bernard Holland asserted that the entire concert highlighted the quartet's innovative resolve to break down musical barriers, demonstrating "that music and performing style are of a piece, that the fissures between past and present really do not exist."

Holland singled out the "Monk Suite" performance by writing, "The addition of Ron Carter's bass gives an apt percussive element to the bowed instruments—which by themselves seem to puree jazz's sharp, cutting edges." While criticizing Ron's amplified sound that "overly dominated balances" and his "cadenza-like improvisations [that] had an interruptive quality," Holland championed Ron as "a brilliant player [who] added a sense of authenticity to a basically unjazzlike configuration of instruments."

BACK TO BACH

RECORDED IN 1991, *Ron Carter Meets Bach* featured him taking the full plunge into classical repertoire: an entire album of Bach compositions that he interpreted with new arrangements. On the disc he performed all the parts, overdubbing his double bass and piccolo bass to create a one-man multitrack ensemble. The Bach library he chose included works originally written for flute, violin, clavichord and organ as well as chorales and chorale preludes.

In the album liner notes, Kermit Moore, the esteemed classical cellist who is a member of Ron's Nonet, wrote that Ron "has a lifelong love for the music of Johann Sebastian Bach..." and that he studiously chose "works from the various periods and disciplines of Bach's productive life." Kermit went on to say that Bach would have approved of Ron's "thoughtful adaptations" as well as his use of the piccolo bass—the small bass Ron employs in his Nonet—given that the baroque composer wrote solo works for the double bass (violone and its diminutive, the violoncello), the viola di pomposa, the viola da gamba and lute.

On the album, Ron played with embellishment and improvisation on such works by Bach as "Air" from the Orchestral Suite No. 3 in D Minor (playing the violin lines from what is often called "Air for the G String"), the chorale "Christ lag in Todesbanden" (based on a Lutheran hymn), "Jesu, Joy of Man's Desiring" (with Ron playing the four chorale parts on the piccolo bass and walking the bass line on the double bass) and "Prelude, Interlude and Fugue" (a Bach prelude and fugue with Ron inserting his own bass interlude in between). While Ron took many liberties with Bach's music, he also stayed close to home on some pieces, such as the lyrical "Arioso," where Kermit wrote that Ron played with a simple, respectful and strict adherence "to Bach's architectonic structure."

Ron was a student of Bach, especially his chorales. "There's something like 375 chorales that I studied on my own over and over again to see how the bass lines make the music work," he said. "I never patterned my jazz bass lines on Bach, but by studying his music I came to understand how his lines could alter chord changes and make a solo different. He showed me how the bass line affects everyone else in an ensemble. Anyone who analyzes music, who is a scientist of music, has to acknowledge that Bach's bass lines for chorales are the most perfect."

While *Ron Carter Meets Bach* was a popular album, it met with some rough resistance from the classical music crowd as well as jazz aficionados who bristled at Ron's approach. In one online chat room Ron was called a Bach "beginner" who was playing "nonsense," a "fabulous jazz bassist... who has no business recording Bach and trying to tell us it is something of quality" and "a deluded old jazz legend [afforded] the chance to make an ass of himself."

However, two critics from prominent publications, Don Heckman, writing in the *Los Angeles Times*, and Greg Sandow, from the *Wall Street Journal*, disagreed. Don wrote that the album "revealed both his affection for and his understanding of baroque music." Meanwhile, Greg called Ron's album "a deeply serious tribute in which he multiplied his solo bass with multitracked clones, allowing him to form an ensemble of bassists all by himself." He added that Ron's recording, scored for bass, was "the deepest low-pitched Bach we'll ever hear. The effect is distinctive, maybe even unique, strikingly nocturnal and intimate."

However, Greg criticized Ron for "slipping" out of tune, though he wondered, "or is he simply playing in the language of jazz, where 'blue' notes are allowed and harmony is more ambiguous? Whatever the reason, people with ears attuned to classical music might balk, though I got used to the sound, especially when I played the disc at night."

MORE BACK TO BACH

STILL CONFIDENT IN his ability and passion to explore the classical-jazz zone, Ron continued to record albums that featured classical works—arranging them to open them up for jazz commentary. Released in 1993, *Friends* featured Ron assembling his then-nascent four-violoncello Nonet along with such classically trained guests as flutist Hubert Laws and pianist/harpsichordist Alison Deane. They re-envisioned such classical compositions as "Minor Mood" by Sergei Rachmaninoff, "Freefall (Gymnopedie)" by Eric Satie, "The Beginning (Prelude No. 4 in E Minor)" by Frederic Chopin and "Vagabond Vision (Après un rêve)" by Fauré. Ron's principal solo instrument was the piccolo bass.

Kermit, who appeared on the album as well as penned the liners, wrote that the big group outing of Ron's Quartet, augmented by the four cellos and guests on various instruments, afforded Ron lots of opportunity to explore: "This unique grouping gives Ron the resources with which to mold infinitely variegated scores. The rhythmic and harmonically coloristic variety are the fortuitous results of this formulation."

On the album, Ron also delivered two originals (the title track, written for his father, and a piece he wrote in 1969 for Joe Henderson, "Opus One Point Five") and a cover of John Lewis's "Django."

On his next classically oriented album, *Brandenburg Concerto* (1997), Ron assembled an 18-piece string ensemble to re-envision Bach's "Brandenberg Concerto No. 3" as well as pieces by Ravel, Bartók, Grieg and Handel. Heckman weighed in on the concerto by writing in the *Los Angeles Times* that Ron "deals with the work by moving freely through its textures, a kind of dark, shadowy musical wraith slipping in and out of sync with the music." Don felt the Bartók and Ravel pieces are "more appropriate choices for Carter's jazz transformations" and heralded Ron's original, "Vientos del Desierto," as the most intriguing tune of the album. Don said that the disc was "an eminently listenable collection" with Ron's "good taste never [allowing] him to do anything that either distorts the original works or his own spontaneous ideas."

The *Wall Street Journal*'s Sandow lauded Ron's version of Bach's concerto, writing, "Bach is an exuberant yet organized composer, always precise about the way his music moves. Mr. Carter stays with Bach's conception, never getting off the road, though always putting up signposts of his own along the way."

Greg's *WSJ* piece (March 11, 1997) looked at the bigger picture of the classical/jazz nexus and how the classical purists have problems with what they consider to be trespassers and even heretics when it comes to the tradition. He quoted Ron as saying, "It's not necessary to build walls between jazz and classical music. It's just been the view of the keepers of the classical world." Ron added that the classical world is changing, with classical venue producers adjusting their opinions so quickly on the matter that they're "leaving skid marks behind their ideas. If they play their cards right, they'll get more people in their subscription series."

Greg, recognizing that Ron was angling to perform in classical venues, wrote, "Mr. Carter deserves to be booked. All his classical adventures work."

To Ron's disappointment, *Brandenburg Concerto* was not picked up by many classical radio stations for airplay.

Ron's friend, violinist Sanford Allen, the first African-American musician to be a fulltime member of the New York Philharmonic, was privy to the criticism of Ron's interpretations of Bach's music. "Ron was aware of the reaction because we discussed it," said Sanford, who got to know Ron when the two of them worked in jingle sessions. "I personally feel Ron's Bach records weren't entirely successful, but the reasons for this are extremely complicated and involve people that I'd rather not talk about. I'm not interested in trashing people."

One of Sanford's critiques was Ron's insistence on recording first takes. "I view that as a mistake unless you make people aware in the liner notes," he said. "First takes are not what [classical music listeners] expect. It's OK if a recording is live in concert. Then people are more forgiving."

CLASSICAL KIND OF BLUE

RON GOT INVOLVED in another project of taking jazz liberties with classical music in 2001 when he began working with arranger/producer Bob Belden. Belden wanted to work up classical works for a quartet and enlisted Ron to put a group together. He first contacted pianist Kenny Barron and then brought on board vibraphonist Stefon Harris and drummer Lewis Nash to form the Classical Jazz Quartet.

"Bob wanted to arrange for the talent of the band like Duke Ellington did," said Ron. The first project was Tchaikovsky's *The Nutcracker*, which had been recorded for the Vertical Jazz label. Then in 2002, the quartet recorded an album of Bach tunes. Both albums were reissued in 2006 as *The Classical Jazz Quartet Play Tchaikovsky* and *The Classical Jazz Quartet Play Bach* on the Italian label, Kind of Blue Records. The quartet also released another pair of Kind of Blue albums in 2006: *The Classical Jazz*

Quartet Play Rachmaninov and a disc of Tchaikovsky and Bach holiday tunes called *Christmas*.

"The library is entertaining," said Ron. "Bob's treatment of the music is meant to maintain the classical integrity and melody while allowing us to have the latitude to use our judgment in how far we can take it."

The group created some misconceptions within the jazz community. "Unfortunately people want to equate us with what the Modern Jazz Quartet did," Ron said. "My concern is that they don't know who MJQ was. We are moving in such a different direction and with such a different mindset. I don't understand why a group can't stand on its own without being compared to others. It's like when people compare my Striker Trio to Nat Cole's trio."

To the best of his knowledge, Ron says there weren't any classical-music reviews of the quartet's albums. He also regrets not being able to tour the group. "We're all so busy and we each have our own projects," he said. "There's just not enough time to do a series of shows with this band. We played a concert in Portland once and played at the Detroit Jazz Festival. I was so busy that I even had to miss a couple of gigs."

While the Classical Jazz Quartet still performs on an irregular basis, Ron has bigger aspirations for a classical-jazz project: to work up arrangements of his own compositions for symphony orchestra. But that, he said, will have to wait for another day.

CHAPTER SEVENTEEN

Pedagogical Ron: A Retired Schoolteacher, Working on Weekends

IN THE FORWORD to *The Ron Carter Collection*, lead sheets and solo transcriptions for 19 of Ron's compositions published by Hal Leonard, Ron said, "Education has always served to increase my awareness. Teaching helps me better understand what it is that I do. The students walk away with the history of string bass; they become more cognizant of jazz history. Also, their questions—about music publishing, copyright laws and recording contracts—are answered firsthand."

One of the unheralded chapters of Ron's life is his pedagogy. In the midst of becoming a master bassist, he also donned the robe of master teacher.

Ron received his bachelor of music degree from the Eastman School of Music in 1959 (where he earned credits as a student teacher and in 2002 was awarded the prestigious Hutchison Medal, the highest honor bestowed by Eastman's parent school, the University of Rochester). He then received his master's degree in double bass from the Manhattan School of Music in 1961 (he later taught there), and merited honorary doctorates from the New England Conservatory of Music, the Manhattan School of Music, Berklee College of Music, and the University of Rochester.

When the Thelonious Monk Institute of Jazz Studies was located in Boston, Ron was its artistic director. (It relocated to Los Angeles and is now based in New Orleans.) But Ron's greatest contribution as a teacher came during his nearly 20-year tenure as a music professor at The City College of New York, where he was awarded a Distinguished Professorship in 1993 (The City University of New York's highest professional title).

Ron is the author of five books on the craft and art of bass playing: *Building Jazz Bass Lines* (a series of books on playing jazz); *Ron Carter, Bass Lines*; *Comprehensive Bass Method* (for classical bass studies); *The Music of Ron Carter* (with 130 of his published and recorded compositions); and *The Ron Carter Collection*. Ron also self-published the 1966 book, *Building a Jazz Bass Line*, with Oliver Nelson writing in the forward how the young musician was "considered to be by many of his associates one of the finest new bass players on the American music scene today." (In the book, in addition to blues progressions, Ron included two original compositions, "Little Waltz" and "R. J.," complete with melody, chord progressions and sample bass lines.)

Even while Ron served as an exemplary classroom educator throughout his career, he also opened his apartment to give private lessons to aspiring neophytes as well as seasoned veterans. Since retiring from City College in 2002 until his appointment to the Juilliard faculty in 2008 as the jazz program's bass instructor, Ron's main outlet for passing on the instrument's tradition besides clinics has been in his own home.

ACOUSTIC VICTOR

IN PUTTING TOGETHER an overview of Ron's pedagogical career, I felt it necessary to view him up close and in person as he bestowed his bass wisdom. Years earlier, when I had arrived at his apartment to do an interview, he excused himself to finish up a private master class he was teaching. Five minutes later he emerged from his office with Larry Grenadier, the young and highly esteemed jazz bassist who was playing in pianist Brad Mehldau's popular trio while co-leading the trio Fly.

Even though I talked with Larry about what he was learning, I still wanted to see Ron in action. I asked him if I could be a fly on the wall for a session. Ron agreed.

I asked him when? He replied that Wednesday was his lessons day. He said he had a session the next week at 11 a.m. that I could come to, but I needed to clear it with his student. I asked for the student contact. Via e-mail Ron sent me the name—Victor Bailey—and his e-mail address. Then, he added, "Yes, THAT Victor Bailey."

I wondered, why is Victor Bailey—one of the most important electric bassists in popular music who made his name in the seminal fusion band Weather Report in the early '80s, fusion band Steps Ahead in the late '80s and early '90s, as a member of Madonna's touring band in the mid-'90s and then with the Zawinul Syndicate later that decade—coming to Ron for acoustic bass lessons?

When seeking Victor's permission to observe, I asked him why. "When I decided I wanted to get my upright bass playing together, who else is there?" he said. "Everyone thinks I'm all electric and all about fusion, but when I was at Berklee I was always into real jazz, like knowing how to play 'Giant Steps' when I was 16. I knew in the back of my mind that I was always going to get back to acoustic bass. Since I was young, two people kept telling me that I had to play the upright: Stanley Clarke and Ron. Ron would always see me and say, 'I've got a spot for you,' which meant a lot to me because everyone knows how selective he is about taking on students."

At the appointed hour for his lesson, Ron was finishing up with another student. Since Victor had yet to appear, Ron sat down at his dining room table and noted how odd it was that he hadn't shown yet because in the past he'd always been early. Finally, at 11:20 or so, the doorbell from the lobby rang and a few minutes later Victor arrived on the 10th floor via the elevator that opens right into Ron's apartment.

"I'm sorry I'm late, but I didn't have your phone number on my new phone, and I forgot whether you lived on West End in the 70s or 90s, so I've been driving around trying to find your building," said Victor, dressed in a white shirt, jeans and shiny black dress shoes. He was thin, and wearing a belt to keep his jeans up, although he'd missed a loop so his jeans were cinched up awkwardly at his waist. He was also walking with a silver and black cane, necessary because he's in the early stages of MS, which also afflicted his father.

Usually a stickler for punctuality, Ron, casually dressed in a green T-shirt and dark blue jeans with black and gray athletic shoes, amiably gave Victor a pass and said, "OK, but let's get going."

Victor apologized again, noting that he too was committed to punctuality. "I never was until I became a bandleader," he said, with a laugh. "Then I realized how important it was to be on time."

After Ron pulled an acoustic bass from the closet in his office, the lesson began with the teacher asking the student to slowly play a chart—four bars of F, played as a blues—set up on a music stand. Facing the floor-to-ceiling wall mirror in the practice room, Victor began with Ron noting problematic habits in his student's playing.

At one point after giving Victor instructions on how to correct his playing, Ron summed up what he needed to remember: "First, don't press down on the strings so hard. Second, make sure the fingers on your left hand are spread out at all times; if they're squeezed together, you're not going to be able to get from F to F-sharp very easily. And third, don't look at your left hand. All you'll see is your fingers attached to your wrist. Trust your feelings. Trust that you'll find the right notes. Make yourself feel like you're in the right neighborhood, even if you haven't found the right apartment yet."

Ron was a patient teacher who joked and instructed gently. He pointed out to Victor several times that he doesn't have to press the strings harder on the fingerboard than is necessary, even though Victor said that he wanted to make sure the strings don't buzz. "The harder you press," said Ron, "the more tired you'll get. Let your hand relax while still doing the work. You don't have to press so hard that the strings will push through the fingerboard." Ron also warned Victor to "keep the spacing between your fingers instead of having your fingers scrunched up."

Ron snapped his fingers to a 4/4 beat as Victor played a melody based on a chart. He repeated to Victor not to look at his fingers while finding the notes. "Feel the difference," he said. "Trust your feelings."

Then Ron noted where Victor was placing his left thumb on the backside of the neck—pointing straight up at 12 o'clock instead of nine o'clock. "You won't be able to get from a B-flat to a B-natural that way," he said, "because of the positioning of your thumb." To help Victor get out of the habit of his incorrect thumb placement, Ron put his fingers above Victor's in the 12 o'clock position. He held his hand there while Victor played the chart.

Ron pointed out that the whole time the exercise was being played on the upper end of the neck. "They are a lot of great notes there," he said. "A lot of great choices. The key word is horizontal when playing the fingerboard, and not vertical. Of course, you can add the vertical in." He took the bass and demonstrated by playing high on the neck, then added in vertical slides to another position lower on the neck before returning to the upper end. "I can stay here all week and still find the great notes."

After an hour passed and the session concluded, Victor was pleased. "That's a good lesson," he told Ron. That evening he sent Ron an e-mail thanking him.

The next day I called Victor and asked him about his experience. "I feel more like I'm hanging with a friend than I am being with a teacher," he said. "I went to Berklee and took lessons when I was a kid. I had the formal lessons. I'm not looking for a teacher offering technique or theory. I've had all that. I don't need a music lesson. I need someone to say to me, don't bunch your fingers."

The lesson was Victor's third with Ron. Because both are in and out of town due to the demand for their services, the lessons take place sporadically. But that's fine with Victor. "We're both busy and on the go," he said. "And I don't need a lesson once a week. I just need refreshers on the basics of the instrument."

Victor said that Ron is teaching him what he teaches his electric bass students. "Ron shows me exactly what I lecture," he said. "You get guys who know every note that I played or that Jaco [Pastorius] or Marcus Miller played, and they know how to play fast. But are they positioning their fingers on the neck in the right way? And are they moving their right hand around a lot?"

Victor said that lately he's been playing more acoustic bass gigs where he applies Ron's advice. "I play every day, so I remind myself what Ron has told me," he said. "So often we have a tendency to pick up our instruments and just play. So I have to remember what Ron has told me, stuff like keeping my hands in the right positions so that I can get my intonation correct."

In Ron's office/lesson room, there are a couple of full-length mirrors that he says he often uses to critique his own playing and positioning. Victor did the same at home, moving a few mirrors from other parts of his house in Brooklyn to his practice room. "On acoustic bass, just like Ron instructs, you don't want to be looking at the instrument so that you can get the feel for where the notes are. So, by using the mirror, you can see the position of your fingers, to make sure they're not squeezed together. It's so easy to fall into bad habits, especially when you're playing onstage, in an emotional place, feeling good."

Victor said that Ron's instructions are always helpful. "Ron just knows how to play. He plays the way I want to play on the upright. It's not so much about chops all the time, but the swing, the feel. A lot of guys from my generation like bass players such as Jaco, which is fine because he was so special. But I prefer guys like Ron, and Ray Brown, and Paul Chambers—great musicians in addition to being great bass players."

And what's so special about Ron as a teacher? It's all about how natural his style is, Victor said. "It's like being with a friend who's giving you advice. I know some guys who went for a lesson with Ron one time and didn't go back. They were looking for technique or theory. But Ron's lessons are basic. Ron gives a life approach to the bass versus a formal or university-type lesson. Ron's approach is natural, and he doesn't try to come off sounding intellectual about the bass."

THE CITY COLLEGE OF NEW YORK

AT THE APOLLO Theater in 2006 at the Jazz Foundation of America annual fundraiser, in between acts emcee Bill Cosby engaged in an impromptu onstage conversation while the equipment for the next band was being set up. He queried one performer, pianist Seth Farber who had just accompanied folk icon Odetta, about where he went to school to get his music education. He replied, The City College of New York.

Cos then asked Seth, "Who was the professor that was the most challenging, but was also the teacher you're most proud to say you studied with?"

Seth replied, "Oh, that's easy. Ron Carter."

Cos made one of his classic comic facial expressions, which prompted audience laughter. In reflecting on that exchange, he said later, "I didn't hear him saying that Ron instilled fear, but looking at him I saw it. When you think about it, here's this guy who at the beginning of a semester gets this teacher that he may not want because of his reputation for being tough. But he gets him and figures, OK, I'm going to have to work for this guy and I can't cut any corners, I can't cut any slack, I can't ask for a break. But then he learns how to play and do things correctly. And when he graduates, there's no teacher on the face of the earth that he'll be indebted to more."

An educator himself, Cos speaks from experience. "The reason why you think that is because you know the teacher saw more in you than you saw in yourself," he said. "You end up getting more from yourself than you ever expected."

Cos's anecdote exemplifies Ron's career at City College. When Jazz.com's Andy Karp asked Ron in 2007 what he counted as the most important accomplishment in his career, he said that it was his tenure at City College.

He cited his commitment to the students and the principles of teaching, noting that he would rarely take a job during the course of the school year that would require him to miss a class. "I would travel only on weekends, so I could get back to New York on a Sunday night or Monday morning," he said. "I would often go from the airport right to class, and I would only travel on extended tours during the summer."

Ron stressed the importance of class continuity. "They came to school to study with me, not a substitute, and so I had a game plan for them. I had a 16-week syllabus that consisted of arranging and composition. In order to teach a class, I couldn't be gone for three or four weeks at a stretch. I didn't mind that sacrifice because it was for the students. I never felt that I was shortchanging my career or missing a chance to do something."

Ron started teaching at CCNY in 1983, first as a substitute for John Lewis, who was planning to go back on the road with the re-formed Modern Jazz Quartet after a hiatus. Ron taught four courses: Jazz History After World War II, a small-ensemble class that he wrote arrangements for, Advanced Improvisation and a rhythm-section class. In the history class, he taught sessions on Charlie Parker, Miles Davis (several classes, since he had influenced jazz in so many ways during his career), Ornette Coleman and John Coltrane. Of the latter, Ron bought records to analyze what made Trane tick and then passed on his analysis to the students.

In reflecting on his students in those early years, Ron says that many were unaware of the jazz titans he was discussing. They came to his classes and listened to records from his collection. Then Ron assigned them not only to go to the school library to dig deeper, but also to get out into the city's clubs and write live reviews.

Ron's friend Ed Summerlin had founded the jazz program at CCNY in 1974. It was an uphill climb given that the music department had always been classical and was reluctant to accept jazz as a course of study. But Ed, who graduated from North Texas State, which had a large jazz program, insisted that jazz should not be treated in academia as a stepsister. With the help of Professor Barbara Hanning, who was chair of the music department's curriculum committee at the time, Ed convinced the school to institute a jazz program, saying that it was high time for a large school like City College to recognize the music's impact and history. Barbara points out that Ed had the support of philanthropist Leonard Davis, who shared his views. (Over the course of his life, Davis gave more than $10 million to his alma mater and was responsible for the creation of City College's performing arts space, Aaron Davis Hall, and funding the Leonard Davis Center for the Performing Arts, which housed the "preprofessional training" curricula of several departments.)

"The jazz program was Ed's fiefdom," said Barbara. "He designed the classes—which included private instruction, improvisation, ensembles and arranging—and he advised students in his office, telling them which classes to take. From the beginning, it was separate from the music department, though it was under the department's jurisdiction."

But Ed alienated some of the rest of the faculty who felt that he was overstepping his boundaries and not heeding the department's right to oversee the curriculum or have any input. "There was a sense at the school that the jazz program was autonomous," Barbara said. "The students felt they were not members of the music department, but were there only for Ed and the other jazz faculty."

An early-music historian, Barbara says that Ron came on board while she was on a sabbatical. One day, when she happened to be visiting campus, Ed called her into his office, introduced her to Ron and asked if she could help him do research for a film score he was writing. (Later she learned Ron was scoring Bertrand Tavernier's *La Passion Béatrice*, set in medieval Europe.) "Ed sweet-talked me into helping Ron research early instrumentation for the film," she said. "But I didn't know Ron. He was this tall, lanky guy who was almost too shy to speak for himself. I was skeptical, but I stuck a book in Ron's mailbox. A couple of weeks or months later, he returned it to mine without a word."

Ron remembers coming to CCNY and seeing many problems with the classical program as well as feeling the jazz/classical schism. The classical music population was dwindling and because of budget cuts throughout the city's music-education programs, the once-proud school marching band and full orchestra were history. "The student body was changing," he said. "Ed pushed for jazz and saw the necessity of getting students prepared for performing."

When Barbara assumed the music department's chair in the mid-'80s, she made it her mission to heal the rift between the classical and jazz factions in the faculty and student body. By that time she and Ron had become friends. "Ron played a big role in making this happen," she said. "When Ed retired, I asked Ron to supervise the program." As jazz surged in popularity, Barbara, who had taken on the role of advising jazz students, worked closely with Ron to develop the program further. "Ed had been possessive of the program and defensive about its curriculum, and didn't have the time or inclination to consult," she said. "Ron was more involved. I consulted with him about the hiring of instrument teachers and adjuncts, and about what students should be in which ensembles. He came to auditions for the undergrad BFA program as well as for the Masters program, sat on juries, attended committee meetings, and participated in comprehensive oral exams. He was an excellent colleague. I relied on him a lot."

Another factor that Barbara appreciated was Ron's championing of classical music. "He urged students to play in the orchestra and formed a bass ensemble to play classical pieces. He was far better studied in classical music than I was in jazz. I remember telling him about a Schubert string piece I was teaching, and he stunned me by whistling the melody of the second theme."

Eventually, Barbara says, Ron's teaching duties were tailored to his greatest strengths, including ensemble work and private lessons. Ron focused on the importance of students knowing jazz library in his classes, bringing in music by Duke Ellington, Benny Golson, Randy Weston and Miles Davis. "Compositions by those musicians were fading out because guys were so determined to write their own tunes," he said. "But I wanted to show them music that has stood up to the wear and tear of years. Believe me, standards have been performed terribly, but there's enough in those songs that make it hard for them not to exist anymore."

Ron assigned his students seven tunes for the semester to discuss and understand. The exam required the students to take one of those tunes, write a lead sheet from memory, with changes that a sight-reader could play. Ron also taught classes where the final exam consisted of an essay, written in class, on such subjects as what did you learn in this class, what didn't you learn, what did you want to hear more of?

"I wanted my students to be able to put their thoughts into writing," he said. "Some of my students had poor writing skills—literary as well as music manuscript. I told them that not everyone would be playing music in the future, but all of them needed to learn how to write. Writing to these kinds of topics also gave me insight on what to change in the next semester."

As department chair, Barbara was required to observe instructors' classes in order to document their qualifications for tenure and promotion. In Ron's case, she chose a rhythm-section class. "I remember clearly that Ron was standing with his back to the sax player and only addressing his remarks to the rhythm section. I felt that was out of line, and that the sax player should be getting something out of it too." Barbara soon learned Ron's rationale and understood the classroom dynamics better.

"I had already told the saxophone player that I wanted him to play lines that would raise the eyebrows of the guys in the rhythm section," Ron said. "I wanted to see how they were responding to this musical idea that the saxophone player hadn't played last week. Theoretically, the saxophone player gets better each week as the rhythm section becomes more aware of their choices, how far they can take him out or how much they can change the tempo. A good band is aware of that. They're having a conversation, and you can see the physical response."

During Ron's tenure at City College, in addition to history, composition and ensemble classes, he put together an undergrad elite ensemble and installed a four-to-five-member bass choir. "Ron wrote the arrangements for the elite group," Barbara said. "His first ensemble entered a competition, was invited to San Sebastián, Spain, and brought back first prize in 1987."

As for the bass group, Ron said that he taught the bassists to play Bach chorales. "I felt it was important to play in a section of bass players, so they could differentiate tones, note lengths, sounds, pitch. I was finding that many of the bass students I had were only thinking of themselves in terms of what they were bringing to the bandstand. They were not attuned to the subtleties of pitch or weren't playing octaves or unison lines."

Barbara notes that while Ron didn't come off as an academic type of jazz historian, he was indeed a scholar of the music. "I'm sure a lot of what Ron knows is from first-hand experience and not from books," she said. "Once when I asked him to look at a general music appreciation book, he pointed out how the author was not telling the right story about jazz. Ron marked up that section of my book with corrections."

"I always told the students to compare the histories they were reading in different textbooks," Ron said. "I told them not to stop when the class was over, but go the library if they were curious. I felt it was important to instill in them not to take one source as the ultimate fact. For example, one jazz textbook author wrote that jazz players couldn't make a living just playing jazz. My reply to that was, 'What do you think I've been doing for the past 25 years?'"

Barbara also recalls the days of the "turf war" in the '80s. Ron proved to be loyal to the music department when the Black Studies department wanted to take control of the jazz program. That department was chaired by Leonard Jeffries, who was controversial for his alleged black supremacist and anti-Semitic views. "Professor Jeffries argued that because jazz was an outgrowth of black culture, it should properly be taught from a black studies point of view," Barbara said. "Ron stood up for the music department whose faculty was largely white."

Ron explained that the seeds for the attempted takeover were sown during the black student uprising and campus unrest at City College in the late '60s and early '70s. He recalls Jeffries saying that white people came from a cold country and black people from a warm country. "Len wanted to take jazz and put it in Black Studies, but those guys didn't have a high regard for the music as a broad category. The best I could tell was they only knew about John Coltrane and that was it. But jazz is a lot more complicated that that."

Ron wondered, what if a student didn't like Coltrane? Or what if their approach didn't recognize the achievements of Benny Goodman who was the first white jazz artist to play Carnegie Hall with an integrated band? "I can appreciate the direction, but it was the wrong one for me," Ron said. "They were not able to come up with a good intellectual answer for me. They were dealing with a lot of emotional shit." The clincher for Ron's decision was that all of these people who wanted jazz to be in the Black Studies Department had never come to the clubs or concerts. "They were not on the scene, so how could they be connected to understanding jazz history? If their knowledge started and stopped with John Coltrane, how could the jazz program survive?"

Barbara and her colleagues felt that Ron's achievements and commitment to the college merited a Distinguished Professorship and she asked for his help in preparing the case. The process involved submitting a *curriculum vitae* for Ron that listed all his recordings and compositions, concerts, club dates, tours, master classes, and clinics, plus a report that included letters from dozens of people in the jazz world. Once all the information was compiled, it had to be screened by various committees at the college and finally sent to the Board of Trustees, which awarded Ron the title (the first in CUNY history for a jazz musician).

"Ron was thrilled," Barbara said. "He felt affirmed. He's a man who was always trying to prove and improve. He was always looking for new challenges."

That also included getting a doctorate, which was a subject that came up at City College. The doctoral program at CUNY had decided to offer a DMA (Doctor of Musical Arts) degree that was intended to complement the PhD program in music at the City University Graduate Center. Barbara was privy to the plans for the degree, and, as chair of the music department, she was asked to assign Ron to the doctoral program as part of his CCNY workload.

"Ron, however, not being on the PhD faculty, had only the vaguest notion of how the doctoral consortium operated," she said. "When he heard that this DMA degree was being planned, he naturally wanted to know how to get one. He was surprised and delighted when I told him he didn't need one because the planners were already anxious to have him on the faculty."

When he asked Barbara about getting his own DMA, he wasn't prepared for her answer. He said, "At the time, the University of Massachusetts in Amherst was giving doctorates to jazz players, so I figured I'd get my own and work out a time frame to do it."

Was Ron surprised by his role in the program? "No, I felt qualified."

Today he points to the honorary doctorates bestowed upon him. "I've heard that even with a honorary degree I could be called Dr. Carter if I wanted," he said. "Tony [Williams] used to call me Doctor all the time when we were in Miles's band, because he said I knew how to 'operate' on all the changes."

When Ron retired from City College in 2002, he received a grand farewell reception in his honor in CCNY's Great Hall. Attendees included school president Gregory H. Williams, Benny Golson, Mona Hinton (the widow of Ron's friend and fellow bassist, Milt Hinton) and more than 100 of Ron's current and former students from the school. Today a Brazilian-music scholar, teacher and pianist, Clifford Korman, who attended graduate school at CCNY under Ron's tutelage and subsequently entered the DMA program at Manhattan School of Music, presented an homage to his former teacher. He began by reading from one of his end-of-the-semester exams titled, "What I Learned in the Carter Ensembles," and continued with a short history of his CCNY experience. Evidently, one of the things that most impressed Cliff was Ron's way of beginning his student critiques with the words: "You might consider..."

In his speech, Cliff recalled going to see Ron play at the Village Vanguard while he was a student, noting how he was "taken by the elegance and clarity" in Ron's performance. After the set, he shyly told Ron how much he appreciated the music. He recalled Ron's response: "I'm just looking for some good notes."

Cliff: "I think... that's it? Ron Carter is looking for some good notes? No big deal? I shall now go home and look for some notes that might have fallen off my instrument, since I haven't found them on the keyboard as yet."

As he began to wrap up his speech, Cliff addressed Ron: "Professor Carter, you have passed on a state of mind, a state of being and doing. From that perspective, we, your students, can continue to look for *our* good notes, to sound them with good time, in a good place, clearly, with commitment to the details and vision of the whole. And just as importantly, we can pass that skill and that state on to *our* students."

How good a teacher is Ron, whether at City College or as a private tutor? The following testimonies from his students open windows on that question.

STUDENT TESTMONY NO. 1: DAVID WONG

AT THE NORTH Sea Jazz Festival in 2008, Ron performed with his quartet, while on the same night on another stage bassist David Wong played with vocalist Sachal Vasandani. The two friends met up with each other in the musicians' dining room. After David left, Ron said, "This is one of the best young jazz players today."

At the time, the 26-year-old had been taking private classes with Ron consistently for more than three and a half years. David reflected on the experience:

> I went to Juilliard for four years to study classical music. I never studied jazz. The summer after I graduated I broke my wrist playing basketball in Italy while I was on tour with the Juilliard Orchestra. That totally burned me out. To make me feel better my friend [bassist] Ben Wolfe told me that when I got better I should hook up with Ron Carter for lessons.
>
> I had always been aware of him, but I had never met him. I did see him on occasions because I grew up above the [New York City club] Knickerbocker where he used to play duo shows with Sir Roland Hanna. I also listened to Miles's records. Someone told me once, "Check out Paul Chambers and Ray Brown. But if you want to get to the next level of bass playing, listen to Ron Carter."
>
> When my wrist was recovered, Ben asked me if I had called Ron yet. He told me he had told Ron about me and that he was waiting for my call. But Ben warned me that Ron would be teaching very basic things at the beginning.

I called Ron and my first experience was playing the F-major scale, which is something that you learn on a bass when you're 12 years old. At first I was confused. Why did I have to work at this? But Ron had a lot to say about how I was playing it. He had very specific ideas about my left hand, and he gave me good reasons for every critique. He taught me how to play the scale feeling natural about it, but also controlled—not letting any one note stick out but each having equal tone, length, release.

After awhile Ron had me playing an F blues, which was a great exercise for me. I had never studied with a jazz teacher before. It was so loose, so unregulated. And here I was with the greatest living jazz bassist telling me exactly how I needed to practice—not telling me how to play. Ron had me practice etudes that were relevant to walking bass lines and taught me how to play the bass horizontally.

The first time Ron heard me perform was at Dizzy's Club in New York in Roy Haynes's band. We played Wayne Shorter's "Fee-Fi-Fo-Fum" that Ron had recorded with him. Every note that I would be playing he had played. So I thought, should I play his notes or come up with something else? I did a little of both. Afterwards, Ron gave me a hug and a kiss. He was very sweet, very kind.

The second time he saw me was much later with the Heath Brothers at the Village Vanguard. After the show, he said, "Mr. Wong, we have a lot to talk about." One of the first things he talked about was how lazy I had become with my left hand. I realize how high a standard Ron sets, but it's an honor to be held to that and inspiring to achieve those standards.

Before I met Ron I had heard that he might not be so friendly. That was his rep. I know a lot of bass players have been rubbed the wrong way, that he wasn't warm. But I think it's all about whether you pay him the kind of respect he deserves. He's played jazz for his entire life, so it's important to be treated in a respectful way. And I think Ron is so sensitive that he can be offended easily. From the first moment we met, Ron has only been generous to me in his teaching. And he's also given me two ties along the way.

STUDENT TESTIMONY NO. 2: LEON "LEE" DORSEY

Bassist Leon "Lee" Dorsey did his undergrad work at Oberlin Conservatory of Music (class of 1981), and then got two masters, from the University of Wisconsin, Madison (1983, under the tutelage of jazz bassist Richard Davis) and one from the Manhattan School of Music (1986). Today he's the head of the University of Pittsburgh's jazz department. Leon was Ron's first bass student in CUNY's DMA (doctoral) program. He mused on the impact of Ron in his career and life:

When I moved from Madison to New York in 1984, Richard Davis told me that I needed to look up Ron. So, that was a priority. At the time City College didn't have a doctoral program, so I took lessons with Ron while I was at Manhattan. That was my only way to study with him. We started in the spring of 1985.

I first met Ron in Pittsburgh when I was visiting my parents during a break at Oberlin. Ron was conducting a jazz seminar at the university, and I was a student volunteer, driving musicians to and from the airport and to the seminars and rehearsals. Ron was one of my heroes, so it was a great honor to drive him around.

After that I got to see Ron perform on a number of occasions, with the Milestone All-Stars at Oberlin and then at the Kool Jazz Festival when I visited New York. Shortly before I moved to New York I saw Ron perform with the Great Jazz Quartet at Hartt College of Music at the University of Hartford in Connecticut.

When I first started taking lessons with Ron, I was 24 and had already taken a lot of bass-playing classes and sessions. But he could see the gaps in my training. He was like a personal trainer. It was like, do 200 jumping jacks, 50 sit-ups and 20 push-ups once a day for six days a week and you'll be in shape. Ron would point out specifics, and he was so thorough. You keep practicing what he tells you and your playing gets in shape. I started with Ron by playing walking bass lines, constructing them and coming to fully understand them. He uses the blues as a device for understanding chord structure.

What I was also impressed by was how Ron could talk about any dimension of music. He was renowned as a jazz bassist, but you should hear him talk about Bach.

I also took classes with him at City College where we went through the jazz library. There were maybe four or five people in the class. I was dumbfounded that he didn't have 500 students there. So, over the years, I recommended a variety of people to go there and learn from Ron.

Ron was 100 percent giving if you wanted to learn. He'd play a date at the Village Vanguard that got out at two a.m. and he'd be at his class or lesson at nine a.m. I was blown away by Ron's dedication. I think that commitment to teaching is a part of Ron's career that's not recognized. He's honored for the totality of his work as a musician and recording artist, but he should be just as much celebrated for his teaching.

STUDENT TESTIMONY NO. 3: SAADI ZAIN

BASSIST SAADI ZAIN spent a lot of time learning from Ron, figuring that during some semesters he met five hours a week with him: one hour in a private lesson in his studio and then two hours in one ensemble and two in another. He first became aware of Ron while an undergraduate at Hartt School of Music where he was a student in the Jazz department, headed by saxophonist Jackie McLean. As a freshman, he hadn't been exposed to many jazz recordings, and was unfamiliar with many of the jazz greats. Later that year (1985), his bass teacher, Nat Reeves, had gone to New York to hear Ron play live, and came back raving. The rest, for Saadi, is history:

> After Nat told me about Ron, I went out and got some of his records. I became a huge fan. That's when he became my mentor and idol. After a while, I had to stop listening to him because I worried I would sound too much like him. In 1986, Ron did a master class at Hartt.
>
> I moved to New York in the summer of 1994, after getting my masters at Penn State. I had no intention of going back to school, but Nat told me that I should try to take some classes with Ron. In January 1996, I was temping five days a week at a bank and getting one gig a month if I was lucky. I spent a lot of time at home practicing, but it was pretty desolate.
>
> I went up to City College to see if I could sit in on one of Ron's classes. I took a half-day off from my temp job and went to the music department office, pretty much expecting that I'd run into red tape. I was sitting in the office when Ron casually walked in. My heart started beating ten times faster. I walked out into the hallway to compose myself. I went back in and he asked me a question about an amp. I answered seriously, and he said, "Ok, just checking." He took me to his studio and asked me to play a B-flat major scale. I said, "one octave or two?" He said, "one." I played. It was extremely basic. He gave me feedback, which I came to find out was typical of his teaching style, and he said, "OK, I'll take you on." He walked me down to the chair of the department. I thought about starting in the fall (the following semester), but a friend said not to hesitate, so I left my temp job. I entered City College as a post-baccalaureate student, then started my masters and graduated in the spring of 2002, when Ron retired.
>
> The first class Ron suggested that I take was a study of baroque music history, taught by Professor Hanning. He said I should take it to study how the basso continuo bass lines work. I started to work with him, not just studying bass lines in bebop, but other music as well. Ron taught music in a more complete way. I decided to do whatever Ron asked me to work on, out of respect and esteem. I'd seen people go in and argue with Ron about what he expected them to do. He got frustrated by that, feeling they were wasting his time. If Ron had

asked me to go to the George Washington Bridge, jump in and swim three times a day, I would have done it.

Ron taught in such a logical and systematic way, just like he plays.

I remember telling Ron about the bad experiences I had while playing gigs. He told me, "as long as you have the bass in your hands, you can always be learning something. It could be working on your time, your intonation, your endurance; or what to do to make that ensemble sound better, to be aware of what the bass can do." That was important because it made every little gig different for me. That was revolutionary to me.

Ron could be hard on me in a lesson. But then the next time he saw me he'd give me a sweater. There's an old proverb about a fisherman with a large catch of fish being approached by a beggar. The fisherman told him, "I won't give you any fish today, because you'll be hungry again tomorrow. But come back here tomorrow, and I'll show you how to fish so you won't go hungry again." Ron taught me how to be a better bass player, and I began to get more and better gigs.

Since Ron has retired, he's been traveling and touring more, and I've become busier myself, but I still try to take a lesson at his house once in a while.

I still call him Professor Carter.

STUDENT TESTIMONY NO. 4: SIMEON CHAPIN

TODAY THE DIRECTOR of marketing and promotion at Cumbancha in Charlotte, Vermont, drummer Simeon Chapin has fond memories of Ron at City College:

One time in his rhythm-section seminar, Ron was on one of his monologues in response to a poorly played version of "Oleo" by Sonny Rollins when he began to make marks on the chalkboard (something he rarely did). Arcs were split by triangles as he attempted to impart musicality to young players working to overcome the technical aspects of their instruments. After a few moments of reflection, Ron said something to the effect of, "Man, people walking by this classroom... they're gonna look at this chalkboard and say, 'That's the secret to Nefertiti!'"

I remember Ron as a teacher who was concerned with preparing us for life on the bandstand—getting cut, getting over, getting paid. He wasn't always the nicest teacher, but he was always honest and told it like it was.

On a particularly special day, he criticized my ride cymbal (not my playing, but the cymbal itself). At a break he took me to his office and asked me to get a 24-inch sizzle out of his cymbal bag and bring it back to the classroom. As it turns out, that cymbal was once owned by Billy Higgins, and Ron had got it from him because he loved Billy's cymbal sound. Later that year Billy passed away. The cymbal felt so good under my sticks—I don't know if it was the cymbal, the knowledge that it was Billy's or the magic pushed into the metal by millions of strokes by a master artist. I'd say that a good deal of those cymbal strokes were right in time with Ron's low lines.

PLAYING TIP NO. 1: TIPS FOR PLAYERS

RON, IN HIS own words, from *Bass Player* magazine:

1. Find a teacher. Period.

2. Don't watch the piano player's left hand. Piano players often tell bassists, "Watch my left hand. The note I play with my left little finger is often the root of the chord." But that's not always the case; good piano players don't always play the root. They may play the third, or they may play no chord at all. To get a sound like Horace Silver or McCoy Tyner, the chord's sound and rhythm are what's important. If you rely on being visual to figure out what the chord is, you miss the point of hearing the music. You have to be able to hear the chords; you can't rely on the piano player's left hand to bail you out.

3. Learn some keyboard. Bass players should know what the chords look like on piano. That gives you an idea of how your bass note affects the quality of the sound—whether you play a C or a B-flat under a C7 chord, for example. If you have some keyboard skill, you can hear what that stuff sounds like. It also helps when you're learning a new tune; if you can get to a piano and figure out what the chords are, you can stumble through the melody.

4. Play as often as you can. The more you play, the more you can make mistakes and learn how to fix them. Don't limit yourself to one band and one concept of rhythm-section playing. The more experiences you have, the more you can bring it all under one umbrella.

5. Always know what your bass really sounds like. Go into a corner and play some scales, without trying to knock down the walls—you'll hear what kind of quality you actually have in that small space. Is the sound dark or light? Are the notes short, or are they long? Is the sound warm? Is it flat? Is there any resonance? I still do that because I want to know what happened last week—maybe the bass wasn't standing up straight enough, maybe the angle was too great or maybe my hands were too high. I just like to get an idea of what's going on with my bass and its sound.

Source: *Bass Player* magazine, September 2003, as told to feature writer Brigid Bergen. Used by permission of Brigid Bergen and *Bass Player*.

PLAYING TIP NO. 2: TACKLING IMPROVISATION

RON, IN HIS own words, from *Strings* magazine:

The first thing any improviser must know is what chords are attached to each note. Classical players tend to saw away at notes or scrape the bow or pluck at random. They don't think about chords. They don't think to analyze. That's not the job of a second violinist in an orchestra. Knowing what the chords are is not their concern.

Our concern as jazz improvisers is much more complicated than just playing a note. You need to know what chords are attached to this note and what other chords can be used to give harmonic validity.

So, the first thing I'd suggest is learn harmony and theory to understand what chords do to certain melodies. Second, stay away from trying to play a lot of notes. Half notes are fabulous. Half notes and rests are two of the greatest things invented.

Improvising doesn't mean you have to have a different technique or skill. Jazz requires the same skill level as classical music, but it's more complicated because you play notes that you don't know are coming in advance. It's hard to prepare your left and right hands so as to make those notes easily attainable.

I'd recommend listening to as many jazz musicians as possible who play an instrument different from your own. A violin player could listen to Charlie Parker on saxophone or Miles Davis on trumpet. A cellist could listen to bassist Oscar Pettiford or me. By listening to others, you can get some ideas about how you could sound on your own instrument. For example, if you're a violinist and you listen to Jean-Luc Ponty, you may not learn what your own violin playing could be. That's what Ponty has done. Why not listen to a saxophone player to hear what other choices are available?

Last, don't worry about trying. You can't learn to improvise in three weeks. You can just keep working at it, and it'll come.

Source: *Strings* magazine cover-story, "Ron Carter: Dean of Jazz Bass," May 2004, issue number 119, as told to Dan Ouellette. © 2004 by String Letter Publishing. All rights reserved. Used by permission.

2005 COMMENCEMENT SPEECH

In 2005, Berklee College of Music in Boston not only honored Ron with a doctorate of music, but the school also asked him to give the commencement speech to the graduates. The following is Ron's presentation, which includes a healthy dose of his pedagogical philosophy:

> Mr. President, honored trustees, faculty, parents, assembled guests, and ladies and gentlemen of the graduating class of 2005: Good morning.
>
> I was quite surprised to have been asked to give the commencement address this year. After all, who notices the bass player? He, or she, is usually buried behind something—either three or four horn players, or a very tall and wide music stand, or sometimes an anemic palm tree or two.
>
> Only when he, or she, stops playing, do people miss something—the pulse or heartbeat of the music. Then, and only then, will he, or she, hear, "Well, what do you have to say for yourself?"
>
> And for the first time—and he, or she, hopes not the last time—others hear a thunderous voice ring out with the following comments, attempting to explain what might lie in store for you.
>
> OK, now that you have reached this point in your career, receiving a diploma, accompanied by a sigh of relief from your parents, a sigh of hope from bill collectors waiting to get paid and a sigh from the world at large awaiting your next move, what will you bring to the table?
>
> Here are some suggestions, some words that have accompanied me that I've tried to live by—arranged in an order that forms an acrostic with my name—to help you remember them after you leave here and when you think back on this day five or 10 years from now, or more.
>
> What will you bring to the table?
>
> First, I hope, R for responsibility. You can be responsible not only for the count off—1, 2, 1-2-3-4—but also for being there on time and doing your best in every situation. Letting people know they can count on you is what makes other musicians want to play with you.
>
> Then O for objectivity. By that I mean not letting your emotions get in the way of the music. I'll tell you a secret: People who think that music requires great passion are wrong. Of course, music can communicate passion and can move us to extreme emotions; but to be a good player, you better be calm, cool and collected. As soon as you get emotional, man, it's over. Then the music controls you instead of you controlling the music.

Let's see, where were we? R-O-N. Yes, we're up to N. I'll bet you'd never guess what word I'm going to spring on you here. Ready? N is for north, as in north star. The North Star is a beacon for others, a lone light in the sky—sometimes the only one visible—that people can look to for direction, to point the way. So, shine like the North Star, and I don't just mean in your combo, but also in your future roles as teachers, parents, and partners or spouses. Remember, too, that the light from the North Star, or any star, is soundless—and realize that sometimes the most eloquent music is silence. That may come in handy, especially with a spouse.

Well, that takes care of my first name; now let's get started on my last. (You thought I might have quit here? Nope. I have a few more words of wisdom for you!)

My last name begins with a C; and C makes me think of compassion. You can bring compassion through your music. By that I don't mean a concern about whether this is the right or best song for the occasion, but a concern for your fellow human beings. Show them that you care for each and every one of them, that you share in their good times and hard times, that you welcome the challenge of trying to improve a situation. This is the kind of compassion and sensitivity you can show, not only through your music, but also through your words and actions.

Next, A for awareness—not of the best key for this song or that song, but of the problems or challenges others may be facing, and how you can deal with them so as to make them less painfully aware of their difficulties or shortcomings.

R for resilience. If you've already come this far, you must have some resilience, but in order to make it in this business, you're going to need a lot more. When you flunk an audition or get a bad review, you've got to go right back out there and try again. When you are the butt of someone's thoughtlessness or the target of another person's racial prejudice or hostility, let it sharpen your resolve to be better, to be the best.

Then comes T, for time. You can have great time, not only by playing and swinging in the tempo at hand, but also by knowing when to push and when to slow down in life; when to work overtime and when to rest. All of us have an inner clock that we have to learn to listen to. Unless you can do that, you can't be in time or in step with others, whether family and friends or other players.

And E. Well, E is for energy. You should play your instrument with great energy and enthusiasm, but you also have to learn to conserve energy, to pace yourself, to step back and assess your development and figure out what you have to do to get to the next level of achievement as a performer. Don't make the mistake of thinking that enthusiasm and energy can substitute for discipline and practice.

Finally, R is for resources. You can use all of the resources you learned at the Berklee College of Music to the music's best advantage, and even be willing to share them with others; but you still have to be ready and able to take risks, to go out on a limb for an idea, to search for new ways to make it work. You still have to find ways to keep learning and improving.

So, if you keep these words in mind and act by them throughout your career, when your final chorus is played, and the applause we all hope for has died away, I suspect you'll be able to feel that you played well—that you did a good job, not only on the bandstand, but also in life.

I've tried to live by all of these words in my more than 50-year career as a parent, teacher and performer. And I'm comfortable enough with my past efforts and with who I am right now that when I'm asked by the security person at the airport, "What do you do?" I can say, "I'm a retired schoolteacher, working on weekends."

Congratulations, graduates, and I'll expect to see you at the Village Vanguard!

Used with permission of the Berklee College of Music.

SNAPSHOT

Sergio Larios on "Pops"

Photograph courtesy of Sergio Larios

Being a student under Ron's tutelage changed Sergio Larios's life.

He's been deferentially calling him Pops for the last 10 years, and on most evenings when Ron plays in New York, he's right there in the dressing room before the show, whether it's just hanging with Ron, snapping photos on his digital camera or rushing off to attend to an onstage sound concern.

A bass player who began taking classes with Ron at The City College of New York, Sergio is now not only a respected music teacher at Eleanor Roosevelt Intermediate School in New York's Washington Heights neighborhood, but he also serves as the arts coordinator for Community School District 6, where he founded the impressive student jazz ensemble Claveazul. At a recent awards dinner presentation that featured Claveazul as the musical entertainment, Sergio told the gathered crowd, "There were times when I had it rough growing up. But because there were people like Ron Carter who helped me in college, now I'm an educator."

Born in Honduras and raised in the South Bronx, Sergio was interested in both music and the visual arts. He began studying the latter at Parsons The New School for Design. He pursued this for three years before enlisting in the service, where he spent 12 years in the Marines and National Guard. He then decided to take up music, first at Bronx Community College where his teacher was pianist Valerie Capers and then at The City College, where Ron gradually took him under his wing.

While Sergio hadn't been playing bass for very long, he still passed his audition. "I didn't have any chops or skills, but that didn't matter," Sergio said. "Ron saw something in me. He took a chance. I didn't know who he was when he walked down the hallway before the audition, but after a friend told me that he was the biggest bass player going, I went to the library and record stores and tried to find all his records." By the time the first classes started in September, Sergio knew all about Ron Carter.

In his first semester, Sergio took a jazz history class that Ron taught and also took a class that was a private lesson. He learned early the importance of being prompt. On a Monday morning, during a driving rainstorm, Sergio arrived at his nine a.m. lesson soaked and running several minutes late. Ron was waiting. He looked at him and asked, "Do you know where I was this weekend?"

"No, Mr. Carter."

"I was in Europe doing a record date. I flew all the way from France to be here on time for your lesson."

"I'm sorry."

"You need to be on time, always. Now get dried off and let's get started."

The next semester Sergio took Ron's small ensemble class in which five students learned how to perform together under his guidance. They delved into five or six songs each semester. "We got to hear history," said Sergio. "We learned who played the tunes, what the chord changes were, how to play over the changes, and then how to move the melody around. It was almost like an arranging class."

Sergio continued taking private lessons, writing walking bass lines. During one lesson, he played a wrong note in the bass line that he had written out. Ron told him to stop.

"Do you know what note you played in measure four, beat three?"

"Mr. Carter, I don't know."

"Did you realize that the one wrong note you played there changed the sound of the whole chorus?"

Sergio thought, this man is not only a genius as a player, but he has huge ears.

"You made that wrong note sound like a mistake," Ron said. "When you play the second chorus, play the same note because you could use it as an extension of the chord or as a passing tone. Once you play that note, try to understand what it could mean."

The lesson stayed with Sergio—that even if you make a mistake by playing the wrong note, you can try to make it be a part of what's happening in the tune. "Ron showed me that it could lead to something else," he said. "You can make that note work for you. That one note can make a big difference. It can take you almost anywhere."

A key event happened during the next couple of semesters. Sergio had a 1962 Fender electric bass because he couldn't afford an acoustic bass. One day, a thief broke into his Bronx apartment and stole the bass as well as all the money Sergio had in his home to pay the bills. He couldn't get to school because he didn't have any money and his electricity was shut off for failure to pay the bill. After missing school for four weeks, Sergio made an appointment with Ron to explain his absence.

After telling him what happened, Ron asked, "Why didn't you call me sooner?" He pulled out his checkbook and said, "Here, pay your rent and your light bill." Then he gave Sergio the address of Manny's Music instrument shop on West 48th Street in midtown Manhattan. "Go there and they'll be waiting for you."

"Mr. Carter, I don't know how to repay you for this."

"Don't worry. You'll pay me back."

"How?"

"By doing three things."

First, Ron got him a college work-study job in the music department. Second, since he recognized Sergio had good music copying skills, he enlisted him to do his copyist work, which continues today—but with pay. Third, Ron told him, "Pass the library down."

"I didn't question him, but I thought what the hell is the library?" said Sergio. "What does he mean?"

The copying work strengthened Sergio's relationship with Ron. He came to a deeper understanding of harmony in the way Ron wrote the voicings for his cello group. But the learning was also reciprocal. Ron called Sergio one night late, woke him up and told him he needed to see him right away. Slightly alarmed, Sergio rushed from his Bronx home near Fordham University all the way to the Upper West Side, went upstairs to Ron's home and found him in his office at the piano. "Sergio, listen to this," Ron said, playing him a chord progression and showing him the score. "What do you think?"

"It was a big lesson for me," said Sergio. "I was honest with him." He questioned a chord or two and helped Ron work on the arrangement.

As the years went by, Ron entrusted Sergio with more work. At one point, he offered to give Sergio money for doing the copying. "As hard up as I was, I refused to take it," said Sergio. "That made me feel good, like I wasn't taking advantage of him." Finally Ron prevailed.

Over the years Sergio was afforded the opportunity to get to know Ron not just as a musician on stage, but also as a friend. He remembers once going to one of Ron's shows with some friends who were mesmerized by his playing. They told Sergio, "The only problem is that you can't get near Ron Carter. He's like a myth. How do you talk with him? He must be hard to get along with."

Sergio was surprised. "I'd been able to meet Ron Carter the person. He's a wonderful man who really cares about people. If a musician friend is in the hospital, he sends flowers. He knows I like T-shirts, so he often brings one back for me when he's on the road. I don't like to take time away from him, but he invites me over. Those are special moments for me, just talking about the little things or taking me out to lunch or dinner."

As their relationship grew, Sergio approached Ron one day about calling him Mr. Carter. "Ron had been more than a mentor to me. He was like a father to me. He treated me like a son. So I asked him if I could call him Pops. He said yes."

It wasn't until Sergio began to teach that he finally glimpsed what Ron meant by passing the library down. Inspired by Ron's commitment to students like himself, Sergio began to teach, first in elementary school, where he exposed the kids to the elements of jazz, including harmony, melody and scales. He taught them the blues as well as Latin music and soon had his students in ensembles that were playing in the neighborhood outside of school.

While Sergio plays in his own band, sometimes he feels slightly uncomfortable in some of Ron's circles, especially when jazz stars gather. Case in point: a lawn party in Central Park for Ron's 70th birthday that his friends and colleagues attended. Sergio pulled Ron aside. "Pops, I don't belong here."

"You have to be here," said Ron. "Don't you know that you're very special? You inspire me."

"Me?"

"Yes, you're one of the people who has made a real impact on my life."

The incident reminded Sergio of years earlier when Ron returned to Eastman School of Music to perform with his nonet. Sergio was invited to come along. "It was an emotional time for Ron to be invited back there," he said. "I saw that emotion. He allowed me into that circle of his space. Ron comes in layers. The more you earn his trust, the more he allows you to enter those deeper layers."

Funeral service for Tony Williams, St. Ignatius Church, San Francisco, February 28, 1997

Top: Ron performs with Wayne Shorter, Herbie Hancock and Wallace Roney.

Bottom: Max Roach recalled how fellow musicians were so impressed with Tony's footwork that they used to call him "a four-legged monster."

(*Both photographs by Stuart Brinin*)

Top Left: Ron signs Derek Trucks's guitar at the recording session for McCoy Tyner's *Guitars* album, 2006; **Top Right:** Ron backstage with vibraphonist Joe Locke

Middle: Ron, Michael Brecker (left) and Herbie Hancock (center) prepare for the "Herbie's World" show at Carnegie Hall, June 2006. The show, a multiple-band affair presented by the JVC Jazz Festival New York, was Brecker's final public appearance before his untimely death.

Bottom Left: Ron and Herbie review a chart; **Bottom Right:** Ron with Dave Holland, who played bass with Herbie in a quartet at the "Herbie's World" show. Ron performed in a trio with Herbie and Jack DeJohnette.

(*All photographs by Dan Ouellete*)

Above: Ron performs at Yoshi's in Oakland, California. (*Stuart Brinin*)

Below Left: Ron at soundcheck at Yoshi's; **Below Right:** Ron at soundcheck/rehearsal for Nonet performance at Merkin Hall, New York (*Dan Ouellette*)

Above: Ron at home with his prized Tetra Speakers (*Stephen Fenn; courtesy of Adrian Butts, Tetra Speakers*)

Facing Page: A busy schedule creates a cluttered desk; modern art and tasteful furnishings define Ron's living space; Ron at work on his Apple laptop; time to go (*All photographs by Dan Ouellette*)

Above Left: Ron autographs a program for a fan at the Blue Note in New York; **Above Right:** In the studio at jazz radio station KCSM-FM, San Mateo, California (*Dan Ouellette*)

Below Left: A pensive moment before signing an autograph after the IAJE *DownBeat* Blindfold Test, January 2007 (*Evantheia Schibsted*); **Below Right:** Victor Bailey, already a world-class electric bassist, comes to Ron's place for a lesson on the upright. (*Dan Ouellette*)

An assortment of magazine covers from around the world: *Swing Journal* (Japan's leading jazz magazine), June 1997; *Jazz Hot* (France), April 2007; *Strings*, May 2004; *Bass Player*, September 2003

Ron leads his trio at Carnegie's Zankel Hall, December 14, 2005. (*Jack Vartoogian/ FrontRowPhotos*); a ticket from the event

PART V
CONTEMPORARY RON

CHAPTER EIGHTEEN

The Art of Jazz Criticism

Raise Ron's ire and be prepared for his rancor. Early on during the course of our conversations, he made a request: Could I track down an old issue of *JazzTimes* where critics exercised their voices in attack mode on jazz artists whom they considered to be overrated? The article was from several years ago, he told me, but he wanted to express his opinion, a rebuttal of sorts.

As it turned out, said story was nearly a decade old. But Ron remembered it well and still considered that what was written about him and his colleagues was insulting—musically and personally—as well as grossly ill-informed. He was not amused. He harbored a smoldering grudge, and, although he didn't articulate it, I sensed that he was hurt. He wanted to set the record straight and also set forth his opinion about what criticism of the arts should entail.

Some people might conclude that Ron has a two-by-four on his shoulder about negative reviews. Those *JazzTimes* pages, by now most likely rotted in a landfill or mildewing in stacks of magazines in a cellar, are ancient history, so why fret? Isn't it a testament to how tall he stands in the jazz world that he should have to endure pot shots taken at him? And besides, who really believes what critics say anyway? Yet, the underlying question remains: Don't all artists who take their art seriously and express it with integrity desire to be critiqued with equal candor?

Pianist D.D. Jackson, who pens the "Living Jazz" column in *DownBeat*, tackled the topic of "Jazz and Criticism" in the magazine's November 2002 issue. He wrote: "But the reality is that musicians are an insecure lot, and in a profession where one's soul is seemingly on the line at every performance, hypersensitivity is more often the norm. I'm probably not the only one who has written letters to writers [about] what I considered 'unfair' reviews of my work."

Jackson noted that it's open season as soon as an artist's star rises: "To artists in the public eye, reviews are an inevitable—and regular—part of existence, and we all have our own often highly evolved systems for dealing with them."

Ron may agree with some of what D.D. said, but he won't advance any notion of insecurity.

FIGHTING WORDS

I CALLED LEE Mergner, publisher and editor of *JazzTimes*, and asked him to dig through old volumes to find the article Ron requested. Obligingly, he sent me the issue, September 1997, with the thumbs-up, thumbs-down cover story: "Who's Overrated Who's Underrated: The Critics Sound Off!" Two writers, New York-based Bill Milkowski and Chicago-based Neil Tesser, both veteran jazz journalists, snarkily singled out Ron as one of their five jazz artists who were valued too highly.

In the introduction to the piece, which was comprised of 13 critics weighing in on the subject, then-editor Mike Joyce called the art of criticism "the sport of contrarians" and expressed surprise at "the high number of unguarded responses" and "mind-boggling choices." He concluded: "We don't expect you to agree with the critics ... but after reading the following pages, we know you'll be better informed about where our critics stand."

Opening the critics' coverage, Milkowski acknowledged that while Ron had contributed to such classic Miles Davis albums as *Sorcerer*, *E.S.P.* and *Nefertiti*, his "own post-Miles work has been lackluster at best." He called Ron's two classical music experiments, *Meets Bach* and *Brandenburg Concerto*, respectively, a travesty and a "sad interpretation." He then tagged Ron a "sacred cow," and wondered why no record producer would ever challenge him by saying, "Hey Ron, you wanna check your intonation?"

Also on Milkowski's overrated list were Keith Jarrett, Ginger Baker, Eddie Daniels and Benny Carter, whom he dissed as "classy, elegant, refined, graceful, full of urbane panache and all that ... yet ultimately too gentile, a tad too 'Republican' for my taste." High fives went to Brian Lynch, Rodney Jones, Jeff Clayton, Randy Brecker and Walt Weiskopf.

A few pages deeper into the survey, Tesser opined that while Ron was "obviously accomplished" as a bass player, he was "mystified by the totemic stature [Carter] has achieved." He complained about Ron's "meandering solos that almost always last a chorus or two too long" and the "cloying fulsomeness of his tone." Like Milkowski, Tesser nixed *Brandenburg Concerto*, citing it as "a definition of artistic hubris."

Others on Tesser's hit list: Chet Baker (whose "near-divinity stature" he questioned by slamming the plethora of the trumpeter/vocalist's subpar recordings), Abbey Lincoln (whose songwriting earned his thumbs down), Oliver Nelson (overrated for his "mildly pedestrian to wildly off-base" large ensemble arrangements) and Joshua Redman (dismissed for his "formulaic solos and crowd-pleasing shenanigans"). Plusses went to Buddy DeFranco, Eddie Harris, Sir Roland Hanna, Russell Malone and Phil Woods.

When reminded of the exact words, phrases and sentiments of these critiques, Ron paused for a few seconds, and then responded. He began by saying that his first impression, in general, had to do with the audacity of such an approach to critical journalism, whether it was about music, the visual arts, film or dance. Specifically, as it pertained to him, Ron said, "It's obvious these guys have a better bass player in mind than me. They have their favorites—bass players they feel are better and who should have gotten the calls for the jobs over the years that I got."

That was fair, Ron conceded, then continued, "But for these guys—and I don't know who they are and have never seen them to know who they are—to have the unmitigated gall to say I'm overrated, what does that mean? That means to me that they feel that my career up to this point has been based on bullshit gigs—gigs that required nothing from the bass player, that required no standard for him to be involved with, gigs in which the leaders were just taking him for a ride, whatever that ride may have been. That, to me, seems to be their premise."

Ron said that he was offended musically. "I've been playing the bass probably for as long as they are old," he said. "Not one of these guys has ever been in the studio for my recordings or at all the gigs I've done or rehearsals I've led. They know nothing about other musicians asking me for advice. And my records, whether with Cannonball, Miles, Herbie or Red Garland, speak for themselves. Not one of these critics stood next to me when guys I worked with told me how happy they were that I could make their projects—and these are leaders who had 20 other bassists to choose from in New York or worldwide but called on me. These critics weren't standing next to me when decisions were made that relied on my input. So for them to single me out as someone who hasn't carried his weight through these years and hasn't earned a high level of respect, well, this is an insult to my musical tenacity."

After pausing to let that initial musical slap in the face momentarily lose its sting, Ron got fired up thinking about the personal attacks both the critics made. Granted each writer had a word-length requirement that limited their assessments (50 words or less), but the choice of words—sacred cow, cloying fulsomeness—cut deeply. "Hey, everyone's got a favorite person for a job, whether it's an electrician, florist or cleaner," he said. "I went to a cleaner someone recommended who did an awful job on my clothes so I went out and found someone better. I didn't stand on the corner and tell everyone who went by how overrated this cleaner was. So, for these guys to assault me and question my musical integrity—that got personal. For them to suggest that I hadn't earned the right to be on certain projects was really a low blow."

Actually, in Ron's estimation, these were fighting words. It's a good thing he didn't run into these critics after they shot their barbed arrows. "I thought at one time, that if I ever saw one of these guys that I'd call them out in public," he said. "And after that, I'd strangle them. And I meant it."

His anger was also aroused because the article was aimed for the jazz audience. "It's not for the readership of *The New York Times* or *The Daily News* or the *New York Post*, but for the jazz community, which isn't that big," Ron said. "A critic's job is to swing people's opinions, and here are these two guys telling readers who may like what I play that they're wrong, take our word for it. They're not saying, we've been listening to all of Carter's records in detail for the past 10 years as well as his sideman gigs, and we can assure you that he's highly overrated. They're not going into any of this kind of background. Their examples are minuscule compared to the big picture."

He took direct aim at *JazzTimes*, accusing it of sensationalizing the issue to gain readership and acknowledging that maybe some people would subscribe because of its "nasty, hostile" intent to hurt. "People like that," he said. "You see it in the magazines that they sell in the checkout lines at grocery stores. But I question why a magazine like that would devote an issue to putting down so-called sacred cows. Why not try to increase circulation by having more substantial reviews and hiring a better set of writers?"

Saying that he has "no regrets whatsoever" for publishing the article, Mergner countered Ron's appraisal. He explained that *JazzTimes* wanted to shake things up a bit by showing how "subjective and varied music criticism can be," thereby giving readers the opportunity "to hear the voices of our contributors in the most candid way." Mergner said that the motivation for the survey came from what he suggests was a lack of integrity on the part of his critics: "We felt that often writers would write one thing about an artist or a release, but then, when speaking confidentially with us about that same artist or record, would have a totally different take. We wanted readers to hear the confidential take."

Mergner hastened to note that critics weren't asked to assess who the most important or least important musicians were, but who they felt received too much or too little attention from the jazz press based on their true merits. "This section was very much about critics evaluating themselves and their peers," Mergner said. "In the end, readers got a real handle on the true biases of our writers."

HOUSTON WEIGHS IN

RON DIDN'T KNOW the extent to which what was written in *JazzTimes* affected his career. He said he'll never know. "But even if one producer read this and thought, well, maybe these guys know something, so I'll hire someone else, then that matters," he said. "The fact that these guys have been allotted that kind of persuasive power over me really offended me."

In response to both critics' slam on his *Brandenburg Concerto* CD, Ron replied, "I think it's a fantastic record. If either of those critics had been at the session, they would have seen that there were no overdubs. These are all first takes, no rehearsals. If they don't like the *Brandenburg* album, that's fine. But I'd challenge them to sit with me and listen to it and tell me exactly what about it bothers them. They're giving a blanket criticism." He paused again, lit his pipe, and continued, still fuming. "I'd ask these questions as I was being led off in handcuffs after being charged with a felony for attempt to do serious harm to an individual."

He also questioned whether Milkowski and Tesser had sufficient authority to level their critiques. "Are these guys Bach experts? Do they know that he was one of the great improvisers of all time? To imply that I didn't do a good job suggests to me that they understand how Bach would have done it. Is that true?"

As for the intonation criticism, Ron said, "Can you find me a bass player who's made records where the bass has been totally in tune all the time, where the pitch is perfect? We're talking about an instrument that has no frets, no markings on the fingerboard, is susceptible to the environment it's in, and that is constantly being played by changing locations to find the right notes. I'm satisfied that my intonation is great."

Ron took umbrage at Tesser using the words hubris and cloying. He joked, "What is the cloying sound? Is it purple; is it maroon? Is it bright or dark? Is it too long or too short? Writers have a way of hiding their ignorance by using words that no one will question the meaning of."

Ron's response to the *JazzTimes* story at the time was to cancel his subscription. Other artist friends did the same. "I don't want to support this critical mind-set that allows them to do a story whose partial purpose is to put people down without justification," he said. "As tough as it is to get work, this kind of thing makes it even tougher. I'm personally not worried about getting work, nor was I worried about that when this article came out. I see this as a pretty underhanded way of trying to increase magazine sales at the expense of the artist."

I read Ron a transcription of a conversation I had done with another artist who remembered that issue of *JazzTimes* well. (Before I read it, Ron said he didn't want to know who that person was. Why not? That wasn't the point of our conversation, he said, to have people lined up in his support. After I read the quote, Ron told me again to not reveal the source to him.)

The person? Saxophonist Houston Person, whose musical path has crossed Ron's many times in their careers. He spoke of the high standard Ron exercised in his musical projects. "Ron's star power has everything to do with having respect for the music and its history as well as respect for self," he said. "Ron never sacrificed any principles—or any person for that matter—for the betterment of his music. He gets things done, no matter what it takes. Of course, a lot of people misunderstand this." The example he cited was the *JazzTimes* article.

"It hurt me," said Houston. "I never mentioned it to Ron, but it really, really hurt me. I live by the same standards he does. One of those same critics also singled out Benny Carter. How can you pick two of the most stellar jazz artists with impeccable credentials as performers, composers and bandleaders? How can you do that?"

Houston was both befuddled and furious. "I don't think an article like that was necessary," he said. "As hard a time as jazz musicians have, to be knocking them, taking potshots...Sometimes these kinds of critics don't understand dignity, especially the dignity of black musicians. Ron and I have talked about the business of music and the jazz world, but I've never said a thing to Ron about the article. But that one hurt me, for him especially after this body of work he's created. It was painful. He doesn't have to explain himself. It's concrete what he's done. You can't wipe that away. This is respect for a musician and performer—for a man. That article hurt every musician. We're the ones in the trenches. We're out there. Ron has done so much to educate. Benny Carter too. You can't pick two better role models."

After hearing me read the transcript, Ron picked up on the selection of Benny as underrated and rallied for him: "Benny, whom I had the pleasure of working with, was a trailblazer for 75 years. I can't imagine why any critic with a sense of jazz history would scrounge around to find something negative to say about him just to make his own day."

When he read anew Milkowski's assessment of Benny, Ron saw red. "That's a concern I've always had about the critics," he said irritatedly. "If a person doesn't fit some stereotypic view of a jazz musician, they have a problem." He ran off a list of qualities belonging to such a stereotype from the '50s: an unkempt figure with dark glasses alongside a brown paper bag and blowing a saxophone with a reed that resembles a popsicle stick, playing it "down on the floor on one knee" with mismatched socks and shoes, wearing an oversized sweater that looks like it belongs to someone else and perspiring like they're in a shower. He added, "People like to think of jazz musicians as dressing inelegantly; having rough, crude language skills; playing high, loud and hard all night even if they have limited technique; and telling sob stories from the bandstand about how they just got thrown out of their apartment by the landlord. Some writers think that if you don't fit that image, you can't really be a jazz musician."

Ron suggested that the reason some critics have a problem with him is because he doesn't fit their stereotype: "I never borrowed someone else's bass because I was without one. I never slept in someone else's apartment because I didn't have one. I've never gone to work without taking a shower. I've always made it a point to dress up and look good when I perform. Because I—or Benny Carter—have this image, I think some critics feel they can complain."

As for the party-politics snipe (Benny looking like a Republican), Ron said that he challenged any critic to be able to "define the political leaning of a saxophonist from hearing his B-flat. If he could determine that there's a Republican B-flat and a Democratic B-flat, I'd kiss his ass in Times Square."

DELVING DEEP

MERGNER SAID THAT the response to the *JazzTimes* piece was overwhelming, with the majority of letters to the editor being emotional rejoinders characterized by anger and agitation. "People seem galvanized by any negative criticism," he said. "And, apparently there is an assumption out there that critics cannot speak negatively about certain artists."

He said that the magazine printed most of the letters, pro and con, and believed that the article served a purpose in generating a critical forum, which "we felt was a good thing. The love of jazz is not a cult demanding uniformity of opinion," he said, adding that the magazine did not "counterattack people who attacked us.... We felt that if we could dish it out, then we could take it too. A few artists and labels pulled advertising, but we're always threatened with that action by labels and artists who are unhappy with our coverage."

All of which brings up the question: In the relatively small, close-knit jazz community, what is jazz criticism and is there a place for it? Mergner said that the most common complaint *JazzTimes* receives from its readers is that if every album is "great and worthwhile," which ones should they go out and buy? "I know that musicians often feel that critics have no right to say anything negative and that the magazine is too negative, but fans and readers feel differently," he said. "We don't need less candor. We need more. Jazz criticism should be informed, passionate, thoughtful and well-written."

On Mergner's final point on jazz criticism, Ron agrees, but only if you replace the word "should" with "needs to be." He said, "Arts critics have a place in our society so they can help the public form some opinion on their own," he said. "There needs to be someone whose job it is to help interpret Shakespeare, or to help read between the lines of a play by [Pulitzer Prize-winning playwright] August Wilson, or to explain to an audience how Langston Hughes's poetry works."

Yet, Ron said, jazz is a different arts animal primarily because of its improvisational character. "When you play the notes, they're gone, they're out of here," he said. "To analyze a solo that's like a whiff of smoke is incredibly difficult—it's all in the feeling and in the moment. Once that puff is gone, you can't define it. A critic trying to analyze an Oscar Peterson solo or a Herbie Hancock solo based on that smoke coming out of this atomizer is impossible, especially from someone who has never worked a jazz gig with an upper-echelon player. Otherwise, a critic can't put himself in a position to factually tell a reader why he believes this bass player is awful because his B-flat was a little too flat when maybe what happened was the piano was flat or the trumpet player played a note that was flat. That may all sound very technical, but that's what critics should have the awareness of and the ability to comprehend."

Ron said that if critics take on the role of weighing in on a performance, they have to delve deeper than "this band didn't swing," "they were too loud," "I didn't like their last record," "it didn't move me." "Too often critics put themselves into a position of making judgments without the background knowledge or experience to make any judgment," Ron said. "They need to have some understanding, limited though it may be, of what it takes to make this thing called jazz work. That would give their opinions a little more weight."

Jazz players are OK with criticism, Ron said, but not if the critique comes from an unfounded opinion and especially when such an amateurish approach has the power to make or break someone's career. Jazz musicians aren't afraid of opinions on their playing, he said, because they hear that every night on the bandstand. "Musicians tell each other all the time, 'Hey, you're playing too loud' or 'You're playing too sharp,'" said Ron. "There's nothing new about someone giving you negative feedback on your playing because it's all about your life's work. But it's different when a critic in the audience is griping about the music while camouflaging his ignorance and remaining invisible. That's when artists don't respect them."

Ron recounted an experience he had where a former student asked him to attend a show he and his band were performing at Smoke, the jazz club on the Upper West Side. Ron called the group competent, even if it wasn't "making any new statements or startling me with their approach." But he said that he enjoyed hearing these young musicians trying to find a way into the music. Much like a teacher, he said he'd feel free to critique the band with a goal of helping them get better, suggesting basic things like placing an amp in a different place to improve the sound and to make adjustments to the bass line. And, he added, "I can assure you that if I were to review this band, I would not do so as to discourage people from going to the show. I'd give my opinions and write in a way to encourage the band to keep playing and to encourage the audience to go hear them. I wouldn't use my 'power' to shut them down."

AHEAD TO THE FUTURE

SOME CRITICS ARE frustrated musicians who sharpen their spears to take aim at those who, unlike them, overcame the odds and through talent and perseverance found an audience and a fount of creativity. Then there are critics who are fans. They like having a friendly association with an artist—not to drag a musician down but self-servingly to buoy themselves up in the presence of heightened inspiration. A fan-critic will never express anything but cheery optimism and acceptance.

In the middle somewhere are the critics who have honed their own understanding of the music—its tradition, its cultural significance, its beauty, its complex weave of structure and improvisation. They celebrate the very act of an artist's commitment to their art, and sometimes stand in awe or at least acknowledge the high order of imaginative impulse at work, whether it's Bach-inspired, fusion-oriented or straight down the middle. They congratulate the true artist who moves the art form forward.

In this critical scenario, the true overrateds are those who are on cruise control, going through the motions of some past glory. And the true underrateds are those who go out on the edge, seeking new adventures in their 50s, 60s, 70s, even 80s with the giddy but earnest excitement of trying to create something new.

CHAPTER NINETEEN

The Ron Carter–Jim Hall Duo: Hugging Buddies

ONE OF RON'S most potent contemporary bands is his duo partnership with guitarist Jim Hall. It's a meeting of masters that's based on a longstanding history of performing together, stretching back to the early '60s. While their personal relationship has had its share of tension, their professional hookup makes for intimate discovery and sublimity charged by adventure.

Where and when exactly they met and began their onstage association is partially obscured by the passage of time. Jim, who traces its genesis to circa 1963, enjoys telling the now legendary tale of how Miles Davis tried to wrench Ron from Art Farmer's group in 1963. Jim was an eyewitness to the historically significant jazz moment. The guitarist, who had moved from Los Angeles to New York in 1960, was playing in Art's quartet (some sources, including the NEA Jazz Masters bio on Jim, contend that he was a co-leader with the trumpet/flugelhorn player), which included drummer Walter Perkins, during a stint at the Half Note in New York.

"Miles was skulking around the club one night," Hall recalled. "He wanted Ron for his band so he approached him after a set. But Ron told Miles that he'd have to go talk with Art because he was working for him. That's when I knew that Ron was a classy guy. He didn't have a contract, but he had a commitment."

Of course, Art freed Ron to leave and enlisted Steve Swallow as his replacement. Jim said he believed Ron had just come to New York at the time (actually, Ron had beat Jim to the city by a year) and that that was their first interface. But it turns out their working relationship started a year earlier in the studio, as sidemen for a Bill Evans project that didn't see the light of day for 30 years.

The date was *Loose Blues*, recorded by producer Orrin Keepnews in August 1962 for Riverside Records (Jim had also recorded a duet album with Evans, *Undercurrent*, that year for United Artists Records, which is now owned by Blue Note Records). But the session's eventual release as a complete album—on another Keepnews label, Milestone—didn't take place until after the pianist's death. Jim and Ron were both in the studio band along with marquee tenor saxophonist Zoot Sims (his only recording with Evans) and veteran drummer Philly Joe Jones.

Some critics assumed that Evans refused to release the record—the lone album in his immense catalog that featured all of his own compositions—because his sidemen for the date couldn't negotiate the harmonic and rhythmic twists of such hip, yet obscure tunes as "Funkallero," "Fudgesickle Built for Four" and "Fun Ride."

"Clearly the music was original, but I don't remember the tunes being that difficult," said Ron, who admits that he lost track of the album when it wasn't initially released. "I think the critics writing about this album might be guessing after the fact. I can't imagine how musicians like Jim, Zoot, Philly Joe and me couldn't negotiate them. What could Bill have written that was that far out that guys of our experience couldn't figure them out. I think the critics were blowing smoke."

Ron laughed at this, then added, "Jim Hall is one of the greatest guitarists of our century. I can't imagine that Bill wrote something that he couldn't decipher."

Orrin agrees. He recalls the *Loose Blues* date, which took place a month after Evans' *Interplay* album sessions and "was part of a big flurry of recording activity primarily caused by Bill's extreme need for cash," he said. "Ron was on this session only because Percy Heath, Bill's first choice at the time and the bassist on *Interplay*, was out of town with the MJQ." Similarly, Zoot replaced Freddie Hubbard (also on *Interplay*) because Evans wanted a tenor saxophone as opposed to a trumpet for this new material.

"These tunes might well have been newly written so Bill could get publishing advances," said Orrin. "But Bill was always honest about music-related matters, and so these were good pieces—and not easy to play."

The album took two days to record but Orrin figured that to get the album in shape would take a lot of editing. They worked on the title track, but then, Orrin recalled, the album "never had Bill's primary attention. Indeed, we were coming to a position [at Riverside] where we couldn't continue to support Bill's [drug] habit. And Creed Taylor was leaning on him real hard, waving Verve's checkbook. Anyway, Bill kind of drifted away from working on the editing project, then we turned him loose to go to Verve, and the next thing you know it was mid-1964 and Riverside was out of business."

When Keepnews was working at Fantasy Records, which had acquired the Riverside catalog, he rediscovered the *Loose Blues* sessions, and with Ed Michel worked on the final editing. The tunes were included in an Evans box set of all his Riverside recordings. Later the full album was released as a CD.

THE JIM HALL SOUND

WHILE RON CAN'T pinpoint his first meeting with Jim, the guitarist had been on his radar screen for some time. Jim had played in Ron's future bandleader Chico Hamilton's quintet in 1955 in Los Angeles, but it wasn't until the guitarist met up with adventurous saxophonist Jimmy Giuffre that Ron became aware of him. It was the Jimmy Giuffre 3's 1957 mini-hit "The Train and the River" that opened his ears. "I thought, hey, this guy has a nice guitar sound," Ron recalled. "I'd like to play with him some day."

At the time, Giuffre's trio included bassist Ralph Pena, who was soon replaced by Jim Atlas. Valve trombonist Bob Brookmeyer, in turn, supplanted him. The new iteration of the Jimmy Giuffre 3 recorded the landmark *Travelin' Light* album in 1958 that Ron tuned into. "What interested me about that record was that there was no bass player," he said. "Now, as a bass player, I was critical of any kind of record that didn't have a bass, but Jim's chord choices and sounds, where he voiced the bottom notes, made the bass player's absence acceptable." He laughed, then added, "But only for a 37-minute record."

Jim's guitar sound was appealing. "Everyone has their own distinct guitar sound, whether it's Wes Montgomery, George Benson, Grant Green or Russell Malone. But Jim's sound was so round," Ron said. "I didn't understand how he got that by just using a pick. I couldn't figure it out. Even when I got the chance to watch him, I kept wondering, how does he do that? I still wonder. But I stopped worrying about that. I figured, just give me those notes and we'll make it work."

Work they did several years later. And when they finally got their chance to dance together, the collaboration was pure play and unfettered exploration into the secret recesses of songs.

Jim, of course, followed Ron's career post-Farmer, by listening to the Davis Quintet's "marvelous recordings." He said, "I always had a lot of admiration for Miles. He could play silence better than most guys could play notes." Meanwhile, in 1965, Jim got married and decided to retire from the grind of the road. He secured a job in the Merv Griffin television talk-show band. "I hated it," he said. "I took the subway uptown to work every day, from the Village to 48th Street near Sardi's Restaurant." He said the gig wore thin which prompted him to start gathering dates as a leader.

When Ron left Miles's employ in 1968, he settled into New York to enjoy his two sons while doing local gigs in a variety of settings. "At the time there was a lot of recording in New York, whether it was for albums or commercials," he said. "Plus there were two or three live studio bands. There was always a call for an upright bass player. It was either Richard Davis or me. I was busy."

Evening dates were plentiful also. The clubs—including the Village Vanguard, Hickory House, The Embers, Half Note, The Five Spot, Count Basie's, Wells Chicken and Waffles, among others—were hopping, and bands were booked for as many as eight weeks at a time. "There was a circuit," Ron said. "In between circuits, Jim called me and asked me to play."

One of their first hookups was in 1969 in a trio setting with pianist Tommy Flanagan at The Five Spot in the East Village. The stand lasted eight weeks. Jim remembered it as a nightspot on 4th Street between 1st and 2nd Avenues while Ron recollected that it was on 3rd Avenue and 8th Street. Whatever and wherever this mystery club was, Ron said that it had yet to secure its liquor license. Oddly, the venue at the time nixed drums, perhaps because some of the windows had plastic sheeting rather than glass panes. "It was really cold in there, and it was a physical chore to get through the night without freezing," he said.

Nonetheless, Ron welcomed the date. "Jim and Tommy both knew a lot of songs that I had heard but had never played," he said. "Working with those guys not only broadened my musical horizon, but it expanded my song library."

Ron recalled Tommy's "harmonious and velvet touch" as well as Jim's uncanny knack for developing a solo. "I wanted the chance to see how Jim did what he did on the guitar, where he'd play his chords as he comped for me, how he got that texture to his sound and what range I would have to play in to make my notes heard. My job playing with Jim wasn't so much finding the right set of notes, but finding the right range to play in so that our separate sounds could be heard. Every night playing with Jim was a lesson about all those possibilities."

THE DUO BEGINS

THAT TRIO DATE led to Ron and Jim playing duos beginning in 1969 at a small midtown West Side club on 10th Avenue called The Guitar, which was partially owned by guitarist Kenny Burrell. "It was a fascinating place," Jim said. "A lot of Brazilian groups had come to New York and people like Airto Moreira would come to play. I remember Airto playing the forks and knives and this other Brazilian playing the flute. That's also when I met Pat Metheny for the first time. He was 15 and Attila Zoller, who was running a summer guitar camp that Pat was attending, brought him in."

Ron recalled that the club was so small that it fit only a guitar/bass duo. The club attracted a lot of people who would drop by after attending Broadway shows a few long blocks away. (The Guitar ended up being evicted from its space because the building was scheduled to be demolished. It relocated to the East Side. But, Ron said, it didn't last long because its clientele didn't follow the move. As it turned out, the West Side building was spared from the wrecking ball, and the club space went through several incarnations over the next 20 years, including a bookstore and daycare center, before it was brought down.)

"It seemed like the logical choice for Ron and me to play together there," said Jim, who had hooked up musically with him in the trio with Tommy. "I knew Ron had the ability to listen really well and also lead with just the bass lines he played. He was always coming up with unique ways to harmonize tunes. I'd listen to him while I was playing and then play something odd to see what he'd do. Then he'd say, OK, I'll play this in response. In that way he'd lead you to new places. We quickly learned to listen and to react. We had great rapport."

Jim summed up his successful duo partnership with Ron by saying that it's "like a personal relationship, where no matter how much you may talk about things, you either have it or not." In the as-told-to "Sharp Dressed Man" article that he was asked to contribute to the 2007 New York JVC Jazz Festival guide in *JazzTimes* magazine, Jim said, "Ron has this way of playing through chord changes, so I'd listen carefully to where he was going and I'd stay out of his way on the guitar and likewise."

Humor also plays a big part in their musical relationship. "It's something subtle in the music and it always cracks me up," Jim told Evan Haga in the JVC festival guide. "Somehow I think humor is part of music, certainly improvised music. It has to do with surprise. I see Ron's sense of humor when something musically happens—like when we step on each other's feet in our interplay."

Ron and Jim are on the same page when it comes to solo breaks. "I learned early on that Ron hated the quiet bass solo," Jim said. "He liked to have me comping, but that can be dicey because you don't want to play so loud that you drown out the bass sound. So I play a lightly amplified rhythm."

"I love how Jim never stops playing," Ron said. "It wasn't like me playing by myself at my house. I don't like that feeling. In a duo setting, if the person stops when I solo, it's like the bottom falls out of everything. It bores me to tears. Jim is a great accompanist."

After The Guitar, Jim and Ron played at the Playboy Club on 5th Avenue and 56th Street, which was a hotbed of music in the early '70s. In August 1972 at Playboy, they recorded the chamber jazz album *Alone Together* for Milestone, the first of three live duo discs. In the most intimate of performance settings, with no safety nets, Ron and Jim musically conversed, cracked jokes, surprised each other, reacted with emotional sensitivity and improvisational pliancy. The tunes included the title track, several standards such as "Autumn Leaves" and "Prelude to a Kiss," a jaunty ride through Sonny Rollins's "St. Thomas" and a swing through Ron's original "Receipt, Please," all of which are part of the duo's songbook.

While *Rolling Stone* magazine today makes scant mention of jazz, back in its open-eared heyday in 1973 when *Alone Together* was released, it raved that it was a "jewel of a little album" with "improvisations [by] two of the finest instrumentalists in America" engaging in "an exercise in comparative musical temperament."

That album opened the door to more collaborations, including the classic recording under Jim's name, *Concierto*, recorded in 1975 for CTI with an ensemble cast that included saxophonist Paul Desmond, trumpeter Chet Baker, pianist Sir Roland Hanna and drummer Steve Gadd. It was recorded by Rudy Van Gelder and arranged by Don Sebesky. Side two of the LP featured Sebesky's 19-minute adaptation of Joaquin Rodrigo's guitar concerto, *Concierto de Aranjuez*, which became somewhat of a hit.

THE DUO RETURNS TO ACTION

BECAUSE BOTH JIM and Ron were on a roll in their individual careers as leaders, they didn't reconvene as a duo until 1982, when they received a request from the club Blues Alley in Washington, D.C., to give the collaboration another spin. That led to more shows, both in the U.S. and overseas, in Europe and Japan. They also set up shop at the Greenwich Village restaurant/club Village West, where they recorded their second album, *Live at Village West*, in 1982. Originally taped and broadcast by the National Public Radio series *Jazz Alive*, the recording rights reverted back to Jim and Ron. They shopped it to Carl Jefferson, the owner of Concord Jazz, and he liked what he heard. The album was released in 1984.

Tunes included another upbeat take on "St. Thomas," a Ron original, "New Waltz," whose arrangement he said developed spontaneously, a bluesy "Blue Monk" by Thelonious and a gemlike rendition of Oscar Pettiford's "Laverne Walk," along with a six-pack of standards.

In the liner notes to *Live at Village West*, Jim Ferguson passed on what Jim had told *The New York Times* when asked why he likes playing with Ron so much: "All I have to do is just start, and he finds something that complements. Ron has a compositional approach that I like. If I had to boil it down to one word, it would be listening."

Jefferson was so pleased with the recording that he invited Jim and Ron to perform in 1984 at the annual Concord Jazz Festival in Concord Pavilion in Concord, California, east of San Francisco. The tapes rolled, and their intricate and creative interplay was captured for the duo's third album, *Telephone*, which was released the following year. Liners writer John S. Wilson quoted Ron as saying, "The sound of each instrument is distinctively different. In addition, Jim's personal sound is different from mine. When you have someone as sensitive to music, with a capital M, as Jim is, you can try anything you want. You're not limited to a certain frame of reference."

The tunes included "Alone Together" again, two standards, two Jim originals ("Chorale and Dance," originally written for a duo treatment with Bob Brookmeyer, and "Two's Blues" from the *Concierto* album) and two penned by Ron (the quiet ballad "Candle Light" and the title track that he wrote while playing with Cedar Walton, of which he said, "It shows people how a bass and guitar can play almost unison lines and sound like a trio rather than a duo").

In the 2007 JVC festival guide, Jim commented on Ron's bass identity and singular sound: "I love the sound he gets out of his bass. His solos are very pronounced, and he outlines the harmony very clearly."

Ron returns the compliment. "Jim has a way of playing any melody and making it sound like his own," he said. "'Alone Together' is our signature tune, and even though it's a standard, it sounds like a Jim Hall original. Not many musicians can do that."

THE FIGHT

IN THE '80s, they continued to tour as a duo, but there were problems. Jim admits that "Ron put up with a lot of crap from me" over the years. He attributed that partly to "my heavy-drinking days. I'd been playing my guitar in saloons since I was 15 growing up in Cleveland, and alcoholism runs in my mother's side of the family," Jim said. He had given up drinking during his Merv Griffin show years and figured later that he could handle it again. "But I couldn't," he said.

At one date in Spain on their European tour, Ron returned to his hotel room, but Jim went to a flamenco concert and ended up getting mugged. "These guys kicked me and I ended up in the hospital," Jim recalled. "My shoulder was dislocated. Ron was great. He said not to worry about the rest of the tour, let's just go home."

As for Jim's "problem," Ron is politic. "It's true that Jim and I had some difficult times because of it," he said. "I came to an understanding about him. My role shifted from being just a musician to being a musician and a friend. I believe there were times when Jim couldn't have found a better friend. We both understood that."

Even though the two kept in touch regularly, there was another pause in their playing together until 1996 when Jim enlisted Ron to be a part of his newly formed Grand Slam quartet, which included tenor saxophonist Joe Lovano and drummer Lewis Nash. The group's first gig was a week at the end of January and early February at the Blue Note in New York, with Christian McBride substituting on bass because of Ron's previous work commitments. After that stint, the band was off to Japan, with Ron in the bass chair as Jim had originally envisioned the group.

The first stop was at the Blue Note franchise club in Osaka, where Grand Slam played Thursday through Saturday, February 8–10. "It was a bit rough," said Mary Ann Topper, who was Jim's exclusive booking agent at the time and had booked many of Jim and Ron's duo dates in earlier years. While it wasn't fully apparent to her at the time, trouble was brewing.

From Osaka they went to Tokyo for a week at that city's Blue Note club. After the second night, February 13, Jim disappeared after the show and made his own way back to the hotel. The rest of the group took the Blue Note bus, Mary Ann remembers. "Everyone was real quiet," she said. "I was the first person out of the bus when we got to the hotel, and there was Jim standing outside with his Indiana Jones-like fedora pushed up over his scalp and his hands on his hips. He looked upset, but I didn't say anything.

Joe, Lewis and I walked into the lobby while Ron got his bass out of the back of the bus."

Then the sparks flew. Jim remembered the incident: "It was something about Ron complaining that he didn't get enough solo time. It was just the way he said it that really bugged me."

Mary Ann witnessed the confrontation that started with Jim angrily saying to Ron, "What's the matter with you?" She remembers Jim throwing his hat to the ground. It was a strange sight, she said. "Here are these two soft-spoken guys angry with each other. You've never seen the gentle soul of a tall man get so mad."

She remarked how Ron could turn quickly if he felt he was wronged. According to her recollection, at that evening's show Ron cut Joe's solo off prematurely which irked Jim. "That pissed him off," she said. "He felt like this was his band and Ron had no right to interrupt a solo because he felt like it was going on too long. It was a territorial thing as opposed to their duo where all things were done equally."

Joe and Lewis witnessed the incident but were too far away to hear. Joe recalled, "It was right around Valentine's Day. And I remember what a thrill it was to play 'My Funny Valentine' with Ron because of the Miles connection." He recalled that the way the tune developed, Ron didn't have the opportunity to play a solo or follow through with a solo that he started. "I can't remember exactly what happened, but I think Jim cued me in when Ron was soloing," said Joe, who recalled "tense, strange moments" with Ron in the past, including his first recording date with him in 1974 on Dr. Lonnie Smith's 1975 *Afrodesia* album when Ron played an electric bass. "Knowing Ron, if it was something that I did, he would have talked to me about it after the set."

But Ron's need to vent had more to do with Jim than Joe, as it turned out. After that second evening in Tokyo, Ron unleashed his feelings about what he felt was a certain amount of injustice happening on the bandstand.

Ron recalled the incident as if it had happened yesterday. "I was so upset," he said. "We didn't have time to rehearse in New York and Jim couldn't find the time to rehearse in Japan. I understand that, and I'm usually OK with those reasons. But it seemed that Jim was not hearing me about the need to do something when I had been called in to play a book that only Christian had played before. I was expecting some kind of chance to play with the other guys in the band, but without rehearsing I knew I couldn't play to my expectations. I felt like the low man on the totem pole. Everyone had the music, which was complicated, in the bag before I came on. A rehearsal or two would have taken care of that."

The solo spotlight is what rankled Ron. "Yeah, I was pissed off," he said angrily in recollection. "Everyone was open to take a solo except the bass player. What's that shit all about? If the solos are spread around, everyone's equal and I'm OK with that. I had as much experience as anybody else on the bandstand, but to have them come in while I was playing—when *they* thought I was through—was an insult to my integrity."

Ron bore the brunt of the situation for the first part of the tour. He noted, "The first nights, if you haven't rehearsed new material, are like the set-up nights to get the sound right and the library in place." But by the time the group reached Tokyo, the second night proved to be the breaking point. Impatiently, Ron began to take the initiative with moving the set along, which pushed Jim's buttons.

After Jim's verbal foray at the hotel, Ron countered: "I told him, 'Jim, what the hell's wrong with you? I've been doing this for as long as you.' Jim was mumbling about it, as if he didn't realize how upset I was, not just about the soloing, but the imposition on my integrity. Why am I to take one chorus each night when Jim and Joe get to play as long as they liked? We had four more nights to go, so I objected, "Where's the equality?"'

Ron recalled the incident as seemingly ugly, with onlookers gawking about the two men "getting into a fight." While Joe and Lewis didn't know exactly what was going on, it appeared to Joe that it was a quick blow-up that soon passed. "The next night, everything went great," he said. But Mary Ann noted, "I don't think Joe fully realized that he was at the center of this drama."

HUGGING BUDDIES

IN RETROSPECT, RON said that all turned out well. A flash of anger, a flame-throwing expression of that inequality, and let's move on and get back to the business of playing the music.

"At the time, Jim and I were both old enough to realize that we had to get on to the next tune," he said. "Hey, Jim and I are hugging buddies now."

Jim said, "I think we both got fed up with each other for awhile. I remember hearing stories about guys in big bands who would get so upset with each other that they never talked to each other again. At least we made it back together."

Even so, Jim and Ron didn't work again for several years. Four years after the Tokyo incident, on January 20, 2000, Jim got his first opportunity to document the quartet with the album *Grand Slam: Live at the Regattabar* (Telarc) in Cambridge, Mass. George Mraz played bass in the band.

That same year, when Ron's wife Janet died, Jim wrote a letter to him, which began to mend the hurt feelings. "Ron came to the Vanguard one night when I was playing, and he gave me a big hug and kiss," he said. "So that helped to straighten things out."

While Ron presented Jim with the NEA Jazz Masters Award in 2004, it took another two years for them to share a stage together. In the interim, Ron said the Tokyo incident was ancient history: "I had just gotten my groups working, with the nonet and the quartet finally settled, and Jim had his different projects, with various sized groups. We were just doing our own things."

Jim and Ron reunited onstage in 2006, playing an Oscar Pettiford blues at a private benefit concert at the Apollo Theater (as a quartet—though not billed Grand Slam—with Lovano and, Ron recalled, either Lewis on drums or Ben Riley). Their first reunion as a duo took place in a Tuesday-through-Sunday stint at the Blue Note in New York during the first week of April 2007. In the first set of their second night, they opened the show by easing into "Alone Together," with Ron's deep-pulsed bass lines interacting with Jim's expressively warm, cool-toned, fluid yet spare guitar action. The piece revealed a quiet introspection as well as harmonic sophistication that on careful listening opened a window on each player's sense of humor.

Jim played electric, but sounded acoustic. A couple of years earlier, he had told me that that approach "was partly my personality. I'm stuck with it. Frankly, I don't understand the volume guys are playing at now. For one thing, it's dangerous to their hearing, and eventually it's also a turn-off. It's like they're pushing people away." He held his arms out stiffly and leaned back in the chair in his home office in the West Village. "It's overkill. It hurts. I've gone to see guys who I really like, and I have to wear earplugs. It'd be better if at least there were some contrast. I don't believe in all-soft or all-loud."

The set continued with a bluesy tune that had pockets of dissonance and a tinge of funk, the standard "All the Things You Are" rendered as balladic waltz (introduced by Jim as his wife Jane's favorite song) and a Brazilian beauty with Ron in low-toned lyrical lead. After that song, Jim beamed and introduced Ron, joking with him by saying, "He's tall and handsome, and he still has all his hair." He paused, and in reference to his own baldness, quipped, "No one likes a showoff."

The audience laughed. But that wasn't the only onstage contrast. A propos for any Ron gig, he was dressed to a T, wearing a blue suit and a tie. Jim wore a blue shirt with a skinny rainbow-colored tie and a frumpy brown vest. Commenting on their disparity of appearance in the JVC festival guide, Jim said, "[Ron] dresses beautifully... Each night at the Blue Note, he wore a different suit!"

Talking prior to the weeklong date, Ron said that he and Jim approach the shows differently. Rehearsing once or twice and agreeing on the library is all the prep he needs. "I prefer not to put a lot of time into getting ready," he said. "But Jim puts a lot more time into what we're going to play. He works on making what he plays on his guitar sound great and gets the feel of an orchestra on his instrument. He sets up the arrangements. After each show, I'll go home and then show up the next night knowing that I'll be working with an arrangement that Jim spent more time on. Then it's up to me to play catch up, to see how quickly I can figure out what Jim has done to make it sound like we both came up with the new ideas together. I trust what Jim does with the arrangement, but by the second night it'll be our arrangement."

For Jim, the rehearsals "refresh our memories" and provide for an infrastructure for song choice. "Ron and I agree that a set must have shape," he said. "I went to the Village Vanguard one night to see an up-and-coming guitarist who played four or five blues tunes in a row. I thought that he really needed to plan his set out better. I was bored. With Ron, we mix it up with a standard, one of my tunes, one of Ron's and make sure we end with something zippy."

Back at the Blue Note, Jim and Ron gained strength in the second half of the set, seemingly more in sync with each other. After all, Ron said later, that was to be expected given that this was only the second night they had performed together in several years. They launched into Ron's "Receipt, Please" with a playful buoyancy, then followed with a beautiful treatment of the Hoagy Carmichael classic "Skylark," which Jim told the crowd had lyrics by Johnny Mercer "that I promise I won't sing." Ron smiled in appreciation. Jim opened with a prelude, and Ron joined with a walking bass line. It proved to be the standout slow song of the set.

Rather than tinker with the arrangement, the duo played it straight, without changeups and harmonic surprises. Jim had told me years earlier, "Playing 'Skylark' is like revisiting an old friend. It has some zany lyrics, but I just love playing it. I don't arrange it differently. I feel that I'm paying respect to a song I heard when I was growing up." He paused and added with a laugh, "It feels great. It's like aftershave lotion."

The set ended with roaring applause after Ron and Jim cooked up "zippy" Caribbean energy with "St. Thomas." Jim introduced it by saying that Sonny Rollins was ahead of the curve when he wrote this song and talked about global warming. He then praised the recent initiative to deal with climate change by former Vice President Al Gore.

Later, Jim wrote in the JVC fest piece, "With regard to my talking politics onstage during our recent stand at the Blue Note... Ron and I hadn't talked politics specifically beforehand, because I hadn't seen him in so long. But I remember saying something one night on the microphone, and I realized that maybe I should have run it by him first. I said, 'Ron, I'm sorry I said that,' and he gave me a kiss! So we're on the same page. You pretty much have to be."

After their triumphant week at the Blue Note, more dates were set up, including a short set at Ron's 70th birthday celebration at Carnegie Hall and a stretch in Japan. They both expressed pleasure at working alone together again. Instead of nostalgia, it was all about seeking new vistas—both players committed to not playing it safe.

"For me, it's a challenge every day," Jim said. "It's never over. It's like a carrot on a stick. I don't concern myself with anything other than allowing myself the opportunity to grow. More and more I use the guitar as a tool. I have the instrument in my hands and try to use it to produce music."

He added that the duo has "become more prone to exploration and we take more chances." He said that Ron's voice on bass is palpable. "I can recognize Ron's playing from one note—his sound, his attack—and my ability to do that has grown over the years. I also wasn't really using effects pedals when Ron and I first played together, but he seems to be OK with it. I think of effects as orchestration, and he feels the same way."

Given their history, does Ron's playing still surprise him? "Oh, yes," Jim replied. "It's like a conversation. If a person you're with is bright and aware, he'll say surprising things and you'll react to them."

A NEW DUO

JIM AND RON were ramping up to play another week at the Blue Note in the second week of April 2008. However, Jim was waylaid with a back injury that led to a lengthy hospital stay and back surgery. Rather than cancel the dates, Ron enlisted a new guitar duo partner to fill in: Russell Malone, from his Striker Trio with Mulgrew Miller. As it turned out, the set was also all about conservation, this time with a different flavor.

Backstage before the opening-night set, Ron was giving Russell an impromptu lesson of how to get from G to A. Then they talked about the recent Lent season with Ron telling a story about how his friend asked him if he was going to give anything up for Lent. Ron laughed and said that he told her, "What? Lint?" He actually did give up red meat. A month later, he announced, he had yet to eat red, to which Russell asked, "What's your favorite red meat?" Ron replied: "T-bone steak."

Russell talked about a great Chinese restaurant he had gone to in the neighborhood before he arrived and then the chat shifted to the cost of parking and the price of gas. They were still talking as they headed down the stairs (Ron saying, "Hey, I'm not going to play like last night. I already played that and tonight's going to be different"), through the aisle between the crammed-in tables and onto the stage, where the conversation continued with their instruments.

The set was distinctively different from a Jim-Ron performance. Ron ran through his bass lines and Russell responded with, at turns, discordant chords, meat-on-the-bone blues licks, heartfelt lyricism. At the close of the first song, Pettiford's "Laverne Walk," Russell resolved the piece with a chord, but Ron threw out another cluster of notes. Russell tried to resolve again, but Ron, with a smile, kept going. It took several false endings before the piece ended. Both laughed and the crowd roared.

Ron laughed when reminded of the practical joke the next day. He said that the jazz community feels like it's lost its sense of humor. "Humor is always available and is not always taken advantage of. It's not a minstrel show or an entertainment event. It's just that there is a lot of humor that happens on the bandstand if you allow yourself to be more open to get the inside joke. Russell quoted 'Three Blind Mice' in his first chorus. The audience may be stunned to hear such a simple song in a jazz piece. I may be startled at first, but if I play the same three-note phrase back to him, we could go on and on with that theme for the next set and a half."

As for the fluidity of their set, Ron said that it comes from their work in the Golden Striker Trio. "In the trio we already have our alphabet in place. We just have to come up with the right combination of letters. We talk about the music all the time, in between sets, after the night's show, about how to either try or avoid something the next time out."

With Jim, the alphabet is different as well as the approach. Ron said that both guitarists are offshoots of Charlie Christian but they've gone in different directions. "Russell is more aggressive on the attack so his sound is more insistent," he said. "Jim's attack is rounder. I hate to use the term mellow because it's not. It's just a more laid-back volume versus Russell's smash-mouth volume. Both work for me."

However, Ron is forced to take more of a leadership role when Jim is sidelined. He and Russell chose the tunes together, weighed in on what their favorites were, then decided the keys and tempos. "We share the program of music and the determination of the library," Ron said. "But it's more on me to make Russell play good every night, to make him set a standard of presentation. That's not necessary with Jim. He's already at that stage. My job is showing Russell how we can develop a song night in and night out so that by Saturday night an arrangement we stumbled onto Tuesday night could evolve enough to sound fabulous."

As for further comparing the two guitarists in the duo format, Ron explained, "It's like the difference between a 35-year-old cask of wine and a 25-year-old cask of wine. They're both good, but one is aged 10 years longer. It's not that one is better, but they're clearly different."

CHAPTER TWENTY

The Golden Striker Trio: Panning for Gold

IT'S A SCORCHING mid-June day in Southern California at the Hollywood Bowl when Ron and his trio of guitarist Russell Malone and pianist Mulgrew Miller take the stage at the 28th edition of the Playboy Jazz Festival in 2006. The sun beats down on the bowl-shaped outdoor venue, with temperatures in the mid-90s, far away from the California shoreline with its cool breeze. Yet the crowd of 18,000 people is elated—not so much with Ron taking the stage, but with a pervasive air of festivity as befitting a beach holiday. The designer coolers are packed full of ice, the champagne is pouring freely into plastic glasses. Picnic baskets brim with grapes and cheeses and fancy paper plates. The only thing missing is a volleyball game on a sand court.

The crowd basks in the rays with UV-blocking suntan oil applied liberally. A variety of fancy and floppy sunhats, the latest-fashioned Ray-Ban glasses and visor-front baseball caps advertising different brands (radio stations, record labels, hip boutiques) fill the picture—all craving an association with jazz (preferably smooth). Indeed, it's a party, with old friends gathering together in their special box seats close to the stage and the general-admission audience higher up the hill sitting on bleacher benches. With few exceptions, the crowd continues its gregarious—and at times boisterous—affair as Ron's Striker Trio gets spun into view on the revolving stage that insures sound checks will not slow the proceedings. Dressed in dark suits, white shirts and green-striped matching ties (picked out and supplied by Ron), they are in stark contrast to the crowd's casual attire. As Ron and Co. break into a couple of ebullient, striding tunes, surprisingly many in the Bowl stop their socializing and watch the show, nodding in appreciation. The groove momentarily conquers.

Then Ron calls "My Funny Valentine," one of his favorite songs and one of the group's highlight tunes. Even though the trio is outside in an expansive amphitheater—foreign territory, given its regular bookings into classy theaters and intimate clubs—Ron does not compromise. This is his show and, one guesses, his attempt to win over the crowd with sublime beauty. But from the perspective of the audience, it's a wrong turn. A ballad means it's time to return to chatter, laughter and the hollow clinks of plastic crystal.

Ron's bass lines evoke the heart of the tune, with its quiet, sobering, bittersweet romance. His single notes and his chordal strums are blue-tinged, while Mulgrew sprinkles mellifluous notes and Russell punctuates with soft-toned chords in support. But the lyrical sentiment of the song is lost in the din of the Bowl, where the music now only provides the soundtrack to the revelry. Ron follows the ballad with a bright, bouncy swing tune where all the trio members dance out the rhythms. It's a gallant endeavor to recapture the crowd's attention, but the party buzzes on. Surprisingly, the most attentive listeners are at the lip of the bowl, patiently listening to the amplified sound coming out of the mighty hillside speakers. They're here to catch Ron, not to bask in the glow of the event.

Backstage after the set, Ron doesn't seem to be affected by the inattentive audience. He's been there before in so many different venues throughout his career. He admits his patience wore thin while having to speak loudly to the crowd to be heard, but he shrugs.

Russell, who is sweating after being in the brutal full-sun exposure during the set, smiles and says, "Man, was it hot out there today." What was it like having to wear a suit and tie on a day like this? He replies, "Ron Carter is the only man in the world who I would wear a dark suit on a hot stage for."

TRIOS OF OLD

RON HAD PREVIOUSLY recorded in the same instrumental configuration as the Golden Striker Trio: the 1994 Blue Note CD *Jazz, My Romance* with Kenny Barron and guitarist Herb Ellis.

Ron also set up shop in a trio format with pianist Cedar Walton and drummer Billy Higgins in the '80s (they never documented their group on record under Ron's name). That trio developed out of a duo Ron and Cedar had formed. "We played without rehearsing," Cedar said. "We were just developing treatments of various pieces. Rather than stay at home and watch TV, we'd go out to play and work through the tunes."

Cedar remembered one of the venues they frequented: the Knickerbocker in Greenwich Village. "That was the test of all time," he joked. "It was always really noisy there. I remember that the management would tell the staff to not bother people who were loud. Therefore it was hard to listen to the music."

Soon after, in 1981, Ron and Cedar relocated their duo to the Star and Garter not too far away. In a *New York Times* "Going Out Guide" article dated Jan. 28, 1981, reporter C. Gerald Fraser wrote: "These days, Ron Carter is recognized as an outstanding bass player, and tonight he will perform at the Star and Garter, in Greenwich Village, with Cedar Walton, a fine and thoroughly seasoned pianist, whether functioning as a soloist or an accompanist. Star and Garter specializes musically in soloists, duos and trios—keeping the noise down—at 105 West 13th Street. Basically a restaurant with music, Star and Garter entrees are from $4.50—the ubiquitous hamburger—to $11.95. There is a $5 minimum. Music begins at 9:30 p.m."

"That's when we started to develop repertoire," Cedar said. "When Billy started to play with us, he fit right in with what we were doing." The trio played at Sweet Basil in the West Village every few months, Cedar figured, before each went their separate ways.

STRIKING GOLD

THE STRIKER TRIO takes its name from Ron's self-produced 2003 Blue Note album *The Golden Striker*, which featured him leading his new trio of Russell and Mulgrew (the CD was released earlier that year in Japan by Somethin' Else Records, a division of Toshiba-EMI). Like nearly all of his group associations as leader, the trio proved to be a draw on the touring circuit (the exception being his nonet, which because of its size, rarely leaves New York City). While Ron had worked with both musicians before in various contexts, prior to their July 20, 2002 recording at Avatar Studios in New York, he had never worked with them under his leadership. But in planning the creation of his latest trio and its subsequent recording debut, Ron had big plans, with a hope that the grouping would be a sustainable entity rather than a one-off outing.

"I knew the session I had in mind would be a challenge," said Ron. "The music on *The Golden Striker* was complicated, and the setting is difficult because you don't have drums and a conductor. That's a tall order, made even taller by our busy schedules, which meant we didn't have a lot of time for rehearsals and recording."

But Ron was confident Russell and Mulgrew could handle the demands of the date. "They were the guys I wanted to play with on this album, but first I wanted to make sure they were up for what I had in mind."

The requirements for making this trio work were very explicit. Reading music—not just a sheet of changes—was essential so that the twists of the arrangements could be properly negotiated. "It's not just three guys going out and blowing off steam," Ron said. "The music has specific parts, specific effects, specific times, so that, for example, we're all playing bar 27 right. And, there must be the time spent on the material because it's demanding. If they didn't take care and concern for the music, they wouldn't have been able to camouflage their deficiencies. This session wasn't one where someone could just walk in off the street."

Ron proved to be a hard taskmaster, making a couple of rigid requirements before the project was underway: Each member must commit to two lengthy rehearsal sessions, then be willing to approximate a live set in the studio with first takes the goal. The results? "Under the challenging recording circumstances because of the time constraints and with difficult music, Russell and Mulgrew both sounded great. And we were all focused. On this album, these are all first takes except for two tracks."

Ron's studio goal was to mirror a club setting and play the songs (four of his own compositions, one each by Russell and Mulgrew and three covers, including the CD leadoff track, "The Golden Striker," written by Modern Jazz Quartet pianist John Lewis) on a continuum, taking few breaks and avoiding distractions.

"This music required a high level of concentration," Ron said, noting that because of the prep the date was fully completed in six hours. "We didn't have people in the studio hanging out, and we didn't take an hour off for lunch. We didn't take a two-hour break between tunes so that everyone could check on their solos. I wanted to maintain the flow of the music. It was the opposite of call waiting where you're interrupted in the middle of a sentence or a thought. We all maintained focus. We sounded fresh for each tune. This wasn't about getting every note perfectly clean and completing every phrase. It was about achieving a trio sound. So, the album sounds complete, not like nine takes strung together."

So impressed with the session, which featured inspiring interplay among the three virtuosos, Ron set into motion plans for live trio dates "to bring new life to the arrangements." He expressed his pride in his newfound band: "I'm looking forward to meeting up with Russell and Mulgrew again so we can continue to explore what we've started here."

Ron added, "They're both first-class musicians and people."

THE SWEET GEORGIA PICKER

WHILE RUSSELL, A Georgia native, had been listening to Ron's work for years ("Everyone born after 1960 listened to him, snapping our fingers to his bass lines"), he first caught Ron live in a duo performance with Jim Hall in Atlanta in the early '80s. When he moved to New York, Russell sought out Ron in various clubs, including the Knickerbocker where he was playing in a duo setting with pianist James Williams as well as in a quartet led by pianist Rachel Z with saxophonist George Garzone and drummer Lenny White at the Iridium.

"I remember how elegant Ron looked onstage in any situation," said Russell. "And it was as if everything musically gravitated to him. There was such a poise and confidence that he possessed."

Russell's first interchange with Ron came in 1996 on the set of director Robert Altman's film *Kansas City*, in which several jazz musicians provided the backdrop to the '30s-era story line. "Ron is quiet, which a lot of people misconstrue," said Russell. "I just think he's shy. I was looking at him from afar, and then even though I was nervous, I walked up to him and introduced myself. I told him my name and what I played, and how much I appreciated his playing. I told him, 'Mr. Carter, you're on my list of someone I'd like to play with some day.' He replied, 'Well, you're going to have to call me to get me off that list.'"

Russell and Ron shared dinner together there and agreed to meet up back in New York. That didn't take long, as pianist Benny Green asked both players to record his Blue Note album *Kaleidoscope* (which was released in January 1997). Also on the session were alto saxophonist Antonio Hart, drummer Lewis Nash and, as a special guest, tenor saxophonist Stanley Turrentine. But it was Benny's decision to play the tune "My Girl Bill" in a piano-guitar-bass setting that provided a partial glimpse of what would a few years later morph into Ron's own trio with the same instrumentation. (Benny's mentor and friend Oscar Peterson had two such trio groups, with guitarist Herb Ellis and bassist Ray Brown in the '50s and guitarist Joe Pass and bassist Niels-Henning Ørsted Pedersen in the '70s.)

To support the release, Benny enlisted the band to play the Village Vanguard in New York and the Regatta Bar in Boston. After that, Ron called Russell to play a few gigs, and he in turn called Ron to play on his third album as a leader, *Sweet Georgia Peach*, released in 1998 on GRP/Impulse. During this time (from 1995–'99), Russell was best known as the foil in singer/pianist Diana Krall's trio.

In 2002, Russell appeared on two CDs on Telarc International, helmed by bassist Ray Brown: the first as one of the six-stringers on *Some of My Best Friends Are Guitarists* and the second in a bass-piano-guitar trio format, titled *Ray Brown/Monte Alexander/Russell Malone*, which proved to be the bassist's final recording session before passing away on July 2, 2002.

Meanwhile, Ron had already contacted Russell about his trio vision. "I knew immediately how interesting that would be," Russell recalled. "I thought of Nat Cole's and Oscar Peterson's trios, but I knew that the arrangements Ron would come up with would be far trickier. Playing with Ray Brown in that trio format was pretty much straight down the middle. Ron can be straight down the middle too, but he's also very flexible about where the music goes. I knew that I'd have to really listen to what Ron was playing on the bass, being in that constant experience of not knowing where we would be headed next. Ron was big on interaction. He talked about Miles and how that band had five musicians who trusted each other. So, I knew that the element of trust would be essential, and that I'd have to be ready to take the music anywhere."

EXPLORING NEW TERRITORY

MULGREW MET RON when he first moved to New York in the early '80s. He took in a Ron show with Kenny Barron on piano at Bradley's one night. He introduced himself to Ron and told him that he'd like to play with him some day. "Ron looked at me and said, 'Well, OK, man, I want to play with everybody's who's good,'" said Mulgrew. "But he didn't even know me." He added, "Of course, for everybody in my generation, Ron was an idol on bass. I listened to him a lot on the Miles albums and all the stuff he did with CTI."

While Mulgrew continued to run into Ron, his first performance meeting with him came in 1983 when both played on Branford Marsalis's debut album, *Scenes in the City*, that was released on Columbia in 1984. Mulgrew was one of two pianists on the date; Ron was one of four bassists. "I was very much influenced by McCoy Tyner at the time," Mulgrew said. "I was playing that style where you pound out the bass notes with your left hand, then play the chords. That got Ron upset. He told me that when I pounded that way it handcuffed him on the bass. It locked him in and didn't allow him to suggest things on bass that are different than what's already been stated."

Two years later in 1985 Mulgrew recorded his first album as leader, *Keys to the City*, on Orrin Keepnews's new label, Landmark, while at the same time he played with drummer Tony Williams on his 1985 Blue Note album, *Foreign Intrigue*. That started Mulgrew's association with Tony that lasted until 1994 and included his fourth Landmark date as a leader, *The Countdown*, with Tony, Ron and Joe Henderson.

"I'm unique," said Mulgrew. "I'm one of a few people who had a long-term relationship with two members of one of the most important rhythm sections in jazz. As a young fan listening to Miles's '60s albums, I would have never dreamed such a thing. If someone told me in 1973 when I was listening so much to Miles's *Four and More* that I'd be in Tony's band for more than six years, then be in Ron's band for just as long, I'd have told them they were insane."

As for the Striker Trio formation, Mulgrew said that Ron called him one day. He had a record date set up and had the music and arrangements all ready to go. "Ron told both Russell and me that he wanted to play with us and that we deserved more recognition than we were getting," Mulgrew said. "What better compliment is that?"

Ron's vision for the drummerless trio was quite different than what Mulgrew was expecting. He thought of the Nat Cole group, while Ron had a more chamber-jazz concept. "Ron is a huge Modern Jazz Quartet fan, so he was thinking along that classical-like idea with contrapuntal lines and countermelodies," said Mulgrew. "He wasn't interested in swinging like Nat Cole, but you know when you're playing with Ron that the music will swing anyway, in its own way."

Mulgrew knew that Ron was trying to break into new territory with the trio, which proved to be a challenge. "Ron's arrangements were more notey than what I usually did," he said. "I was asked to play a lot of written-out lines. I was more dictated to than I was used to. But Ron prepared us."

Russell added, "We had the charts and arrangements, but they weren't confining. We didn't even think much about it. We respect Ron, we love him, we knew what to do and we did it. No big deal."

Both Russell and Mulgrew agree that the two rehearsals prior to the recording date were key. "Ron isn't the kind of person to go over and over the music in the studio," said Mulgrew. "He's a one-take guy. He's Mr. No-Nonsense. The session was probably the shortest record date I ever did. We were in at nine in the morning and walking out the door at noon."

Russell likewise remembered the brevity of the session. He arrived a half hour early and liked the fact that they had a wrap by noon. "Ron doesn't waste time," he said. "He doesn't like to listen to playbacks. The songs were done in one take or two. We finished, and Ron stayed to do the mastering and mix to send to Japan. I was thinking, doggone, he's efficient and fast, but he never does anything halfway."

CITY SLICKERS

THE GOLDEN STRIKER opened with the spirited title track, a jaunty rendition of Lewis's tune that served as the perfect introduction to the buoyant set that followed. "John is one of my favorite writers," Ron said. "I wanted to find something right for this trio. When I found this, I thought, this sounds like a Percy Heath tune, so let's do it. It's a medium tempo, the changes aren't hard, the arrangement is not fingermashing. This gave us a chance to get loose and have some fun. It set the tone for the rest of the record."

Other covers included "Autumn Leaves," delivered with a sprightly feel, and Joaquin Rodrigo's "Concierto de Aranjuez (Adagio Theme)." In regard to the former, Carter applauded arranger Robert Freedman for providing "a new view of an old chestnut." He added, "Mulgrew, Russell and I all knew the piece, so the solos took care of themselves. We've all played this in our travels, so we didn't face any difficulties making this our own."

Not so with the latter tune, the most difficult piece of the CD that had been recorded by, among others, the Modern Jazz Quartet, Miles Davis and classical guitarist John Williams. Freedman's chore was to make this be unique to Ron's trio. "Bob had to arrange in ways that we don't normally play. This tune required us to do our homework," said Ron, who, while being immensely pleased with the results, conceded that this was one of the pieces that required a second take to nail.

Ron contributed four of his tunes to the date. The playful "NY Slick" was originally written for his 1980 Milestone album *New York Slick*, featuring Hubert Laws, Kenny Barron, Billy Cobham, Art Farmer and J.J. Johnson, who came up with the title for the speedy number. The lighthearted "A Quick Sketch" was originally recorded for Herbie Hancock's 1982 *Quartet* album (on Columbia) that also included Tony Williams and Wynton Marsalis. "We were short of material for the session," Ron recalled, "so I got out a pad and pencil and literally made a quick sketch. It's a long form, so on the trio album Russell, Mulgrew and I got to stretch out. There's not a lot of confinement here, so playing this number in the session relieved some of the physical tension."

Two other Ron originals were from his 1979 Milestone album *Parade*, with a support team that included, among others, Joe Henderson, Chick Corea and Tony Williams. The Striker Trio delivered the carnival-vibed title track and the lyrical ballad "A Theme in 3/4 Time," originally written as a showcase for Joe. On *The Golden Striker* Ron's bass sang, Mulgrew developed classical-like piano voicings and Russell offered feathery runs.

True to his vision of giving his new teammates more visibility, Ron opened the door for each to bring in a song. Mulgrew contributed "On and On," a reflective number with a gorgeous melody. "It's harmonically different than anything else on the CD," Ron said. "I can't write melodies like this, so I like having my band mates bring different kinds of writing to my sessions. This song is a great showcase for Mulgrew, who is not only a wonderful player but also a skilled composer."

Russell offered "Cedar Tree," a tune that pays homage to Cedar Walton. "Again, this is not my writing style," Ron said. "While I play bass figures like the one Russell came up with here, I don't usually write them. This song is in a strange key for bass and is a little brighter than what I usually write, but it sounds wonderful and reflects our shared responsibility in making this session work."

As Ron had hoped, the invites for the band after the CD was released became widespread, not only in the U.S. but also in Europe and Japan. "My agent in Europe tells me that even though people just want to see me, they really love it when I come with Russell and Mulgrew," Ron said. "Sometimes it's a matter of musical personalities working the right way." However, getting to the point of truly syncing up required "more time together," he said, "where we can play the band library for 14 one-nighters in 18 days versus one night every four months. When that happens, we're basically playing the music for the first time, even though Russell and Mulgrew are as determined as I am to make this work."

Ron referred to his days with Miles Davis. "The more this trio plays together, the more we can allow the music to take us somewhere else," Ron said. "I have a lot of ideas in my head about where this can go. It's like with Miles. After playing that library so often for five years, we knew what possibilities would no longer work and what possibilities were worth developing." Knowing the library and keeping that songbook small enough is crucial. "It's easier each night," he said. "You can actually be more creative. That's the band's job: to make more possibilities within any given tune. It's like you're fighting songs every night of your life to discover something new." He paused, laughed and, with the voice of a sage, said, "You're fighting for your life every night."

A key factor in the trio's success is the rapport the trio has established, recognizing Ron as leader and as facilitator. Ron recalls working with Russell one night at the Village Vanguard with a group. Of course, Ron was at the back of the stage, while Russell was in front of the drummer. "The bass drum and ride cymbal was right there, so Russell put his amp in front of him so that he could hear," Ron recalled. "On the first set, he had his amp up so loud, so that he could hear himself, but it was way too loud. So I asked him after the set, 'Can you turn that down because you've got it at stun right now.' He said, 'Mr. Carter, why?' I told him no one else on the bandstand could hear. I told him to make adjustments—either turn the amp so he could hear it more directly, or get in front of the amp and project it out to the audience. Russell made the right changes, and the rest of that evening everything was sonically right—I can't remember if it was musically right, though."

In the trio, Ron voices his concern about wrong notes, sound, sensibility. For example, he may ask Russell to play a guitar note in a different place on the fretboard because it interferes with his bass note or may request that Mulgrew soften his playing. "The trio is such a fragile environment," Ron said.

While he serves as the benevolent dictator in his bands, Ron said that a critique of an evening's performance is open to all members. "One of the things that I pride myself on is that whenever someone asks for something musically, it gets done. No arguments. Let's get it done right, without sacrificing my musicality, my adulthood, my manhood."

Of course, the buck stops at the leader: "If someone has something to suggest, I say, let me hear it, but I have the final vote. Russell and Mulgrew want to know who they are musically, but they also know that the trio is my view. I dictate the shape of the band and the shape of the solos—how long, how loud, what notes to play. After a passage is done and I ask to change something, hopefully that person can walk away feeling that not only did he respond to what I was asking for, but he also did it fabulously well—and he's still a nice guy. That's the level of comfort Russell and Mulgrew give me."

PIVOTING ON THE BASS

WHAT IMPRESSES MULGREW so much is how Ron insists that the bass be the pivot for the band's performance. "Quietly, Ron became one of the greatest contributors to jazz bass," he said. "He's not a guy who just walks a bass line. He has the audacity to assert in any situation that his choice of notes, his sense of design will move the music. You can't sleepwalk through a performance with Ron. You never know what note he's going to put on you. You have to be keen and attentive. He keeps you on your toes."

Especially for the piano, where the player can demonstrate immense amounts of harmonic knowledge, flexibility is key. "Ron looks for me to react, to respond to what he's doing," said Mulgrew. "He's always seeking to challenge you, from night to night, from chorus to chorus."

Russell echoes Mulgrew's sentiments. "Ron never allows you to play it safe," he said. "You can't rely on patterns or licks. He throws curves so that you can never become self-indulgent. It's all about listening and interplay. It's amazing how he can play the same tune so many times and still find something fresh in it. He's always listening, always searching for the best notes."

Russell said that even though Ron has a reputation for being prickly (read: unafraid to voice his opinions), he doesn't blame him for not acquiescing to low expectations. "Ron doesn't have to sit around and take crap," he said. "He's very particular and very observant. He watches everything. He pays attention. Some people may be put off by him being outspoken, but he has every right to voice his concerns about things that aren't going right. If people see that as prickly, that's their problem."

As for prepping for a gig with Ron, Russell said that he not only "commands respect," but he also "makes you want to come correct. That even goes for how we're dressed for each show. I like that. I like to get dressed up. It shows the audience respect. I remember a show in Europe where our luggage didn't arrive, so we had to play the show in our traveling clothes. Man, even when Ron dresses casually, he's slick."

Russell observes how happy Ron is with the trio. "Ron smiles a lot on the bandstand," Russell said. "He's having a good time. I haven't seen a black musician have so much fun since Elvis died."

Elvis was nowhere in the house at the Blue Note in New York in 2007 when the Striker Trio once again took the stage at their home base. Ron was all smiles, as he looked to his two band mates as they lifted off for a set in front of a full house. He was front and center, flanked by, what he likes to say, two of his closest eight friends on the planet.

ABOUT TIME

THAT SAME YEAR, Ron, Russell and Mulgrew returned to the studio to record their second album, *It's the Time*, that was initially released in Japan on Somethin' Else (it has yet to be issued in the U.S.). It has four Ron originals (three of which appeared on earlier albums) and five standards, including the trio's live-set standby, Oscar Pettiford's "Laverne Walk," and Kurt Weill's "Mack the Knife" (co-written by Bertolt Brecht, whose lyrics were later translated into English by Mark Blitzstein).

How different was the experience of recording the album after having been tight with his trio mates? Ron refers back to their shared experiences. "Over the past three or four years, Russell and Mulgrew have understood how low my tolerance is for carelessness," he said. "I don't mind if a guy misses a passage if he's trying to go for it. You miss it, then there's one more set to try to get it. But carelessness, not caring for the music, well..." His voice trailed off without finishing his thought. "But they've gotten used to my impatience. I write out a set list for a gig, so that when I call a number, I expect to not hear the crumpling of paper looking for it."

Ron also notes that because they've been playing more frequently, they are more simpatico to each other's needs. "We've all realized how easy it is to play when we're all listening to each other and contributing to the music. When one of us solos, we trust that both will accompany—or maybe just one—and that that source of information could be helpful in reforming our solos or coming up with another chorus based on this other information."

For the new album, some of the material had already been introduced to the trio's songbook while others were fresh. Ron called rehearsals not only to discuss the arrangements but also discuss the sound and intensity he was looking for. "Actually, there was more to talk about with Russell and Mulgrew this time: I wanted the [record's] concept to be clear, so there wouldn't be any element of uncertainty," he said. "When we recorded, we had all first takes again, except for maybe one false start. When you spend an hour on a tune and it requires 25 takes to get it right, everyone loses their enthusiasm for the song, and therefore the quality of the music takes an unpleasant dip down."

The solo choruses were short on each tune, with Ron for the most part playing his bass into the rhythmic marrow of each song. Mulgrew's piano sparkled throughout and Russell played into the heart of the melodies. The album opened with the title track, which was a brand-new Ron number that he wrote for a Tully's Coffee commercial that aired on TV in Japan. (Ron also appeared in out-of-door advertising throughout the marketing campaign, including blown-up photos of him placed on the sides of subway trains.)

On the Japanese version of *It's the Time*, the bonus track at the end featured Ron tracking the tune in Japan with an all-Japanese quartet, comprising pianist Mitsuaki Kishi, drummer Makoto Rikitake and percussionist Motoya Hamaguchi. The trio version opened the album with a hip swing as Ron slid into a quick solo, and then scooted right out. "That song sets the pace for the whole album," Ron said. "It's a fun piece that we'll have in the tour book."

That was followed by "Eddie's Tune," a joyous mid-tempo number that Ron originally wrote for the movie *Blind Faith*, a story about racial prejudice in the African-American community in the Bronx in the '50s. The seed of the tune appeared in a scene where actor Courtney B. Vance's character leaves his house to get into his car to meet Charles Dutton's character. Saxophonist Bill Easley was on the original. The director, Ernest Dickerson, requested a "theme for the transition from the stairs of the house to the car," Ron said. "I always thought, let's see if I can work it up for three minutes. As it turns out, it's one of the trio's favorite tunes."

The two other Ron tunes were the slow-tempo "Candlelight" that he originally wrote when he and Jim Hall toured and decided they needed a strong ballad for their live set, and the driving-with-glee "Super Strings," from the album of the same name. "I thought it would be nice to use the melody as the interlude between solos," he said. "It's just another song form for me to fool around with."

Why the fade out at the end of the song when it sounds like the frolic is still going strong? "That's a call by EMI which is always concerned about the length of the CD," said Ron, who agrees with the less-is-more line of thinking on recordings. Fifty minutes is max, not the 79 minutes a CD can hold. "By the time listeners get to 60 or 70 minutes, no one's probably paying attention," he said. "Hey, Miles's *Kind of Blue* was, what, 37 minutes long? It's concise and doesn't give your mind the chance to wander."

The Pettiford tune, "Laverne Walk," opened with deep-toned bass riffs and closed with false endings. "I don't know of another bassist who wrote more tunes that were a perfect fit for a bass player," Ron said. As for the anticipation at the end, he said, "In a live performance, the audience likes that kind of suspense. It's a nice way to open the night. It's a way of saying, 'Here we are, ladies and gentlemen.'"

In addition to "Mack the Knife," the trio covered another Weill tune, "My Ship" (written in 1940 with lyrics by Ira Gershwin). Ron knew well the former song's history (including versions by Oscar Peterson with his trio, Louis Armstrong and Ella Fitzgerald, and Sonny Rollins, of which he said, "Sonny just tore that sucker up"). "I wanted to give the song a different harmonic sense," he said.

Ron knew "My Ship" from playing it with Gil Evans in 1960 when he was a member of his orchestra that played at the old Jazz Gallery on 8th Street and 2nd Avenue in New York. "I had heard Grady Tate do a version of this too, but I was not aware of a trio playing it," Ron said. "So, it was interesting enough to me to work it up."

Ron recalled seeing Charles Mingus play the emotive "I Can't Get Started" (another tune graced by Ira Gershwin's lyrics, over music by Vernon Duke) at the old Five Spot in New York in the '60s. "I remember him playing the melody different than someone like Oscar Pettiford or Slam Stewart, who are two of my favorite bass players," said Ron. "I decided to make this song the bass feature on the CD. Even though my goal is always to show how the bass is such an integral part of a band's sound, I do solo pieces just because people expect that from a leader who is a bass player. I hope I don't overdo that, though."

Russell and Mulgrew don't believe that. In fact, they feel like they're riding high in the Striker Trio. "Ron's the best," Russell said. "And you know what they say, a band is only as good as its bass player."

CHAPTER TWENTY-ONE

The Quantum Quartets: Yesterday and Today

IN TALKING ABOUT his trio, Ron says that his job is to insure that the audience "doesn't miss the drums." As for the Ron Carter Quartet, he says his job entails making sure listeners "don't miss the horns."

And since 1975, he's been true to his word in the foursome setting, which gradually evolved from a two-bass affair (with Ron on piccolo bass plus another bassist, pianist and drummer) to one that features Ron solely at the bass helm with the additional rhythmic support of a percussionist. The current lineup comprises pianist Stephen Scott (the band's vet who came aboard in 1988), drummer Payton Crossley (who joined the band in the mid-'90s) and relative newcomer, percussionist Rolando Morales-Matos (whom Ron enlisted in 2006).

At Yoshi's jazz club in Oakland, California, in April 2007, Ron set up shop with his Quartet for a five-night stint that was the epitome of jazz elegance, refinement and, though not obvious to the untrained ear, unabashed adventure. Front and center, Ron led the group as it sprinted and danced through the segued tunes that the group wove together into a multi-hued tapestry. Unlike most jazz performances where there's a round-the-horn solo sensibility (each band member offering an expression of self in a pocket reserved for individual glory), Ron set up that rare state of full-band interplay with a wellspring of unpredictability inherent in each tune. He set into motion a journey of new notes, harmonies, vistas. Levity played a significant role in the interchange, with frequent inside jokes and comic surprises expressed through the music.

For the first two nights, Ron led off with his composition "595," which alludes to Miles Davis's "So What." While anchoring the Latin-tinged beat, Ron walked, played harmonics and glissandos, and cued a bossa feel that opened into a Brazilian percussion break for Rolando's spice. Then to the audience's surprise, the number took off into a rousing canter tempo before the suite moved into a coda where Ron's repeated two-note bass motif signaled the end.

Ron served not only as beat keeper, but also as the instigator of transformation, agent of modification, and lyrical lightning rod. In a slow piece, Ron played a quiet bass riff that he repeated until it morphed into a swing that enticed audience members to clap and the rest of the band to fly. Then Stephen changed directions again into a down-and-dirty blues where Ron soloed with a fluttering strum and rapid lead line as if he were playing a guitar. On both nights, the Quartet concluded the set with "My Funny Valentine," where Stephen again starred with his impressionistic prelude before Ron took over, closing his eyes and playing with rapturous meditation.

A year earlier at Yoshi's a young man encountering Ron for the first time wrote about his experience taking in the Quartet's transcendence in his blog "Darin's Drivel." He first described how he ended up at Yoshi's—on a whim going with friends to a jazz show to catch someone he knew nothing about. After what he called a "pricey" sushi dinner, they found themselves immersed in a "wonderful jazz master class surprise" that was "undeniably spectacular." He wrote: "From the first note that came out of the speakers toward us, we knew that we had stumbled onto something special, and boy is that an understatement."

Darin concluded, "It's difficult to describe what the music sounded like because it was many things all at once: experimental jazz, Afro-Cuban rhythms, a moist tropical rainforest and a music studio master lesson with traditional jazz drums combined with otherworldly noisemakers. [There were] off-beat chord changes, sections where it seemed almost cacophonous—everyone playing their own disparate pieces of music—and then in a moment, a crash cymbal and a snare drum would bring them all back together as if they had been playing a piece that was written to confuse but also return you to the central theme in an instant. Unbelievable. We could hear people in the back [of the house] saying 'Wow! And 'Yeah!'"

Even novice jazz listeners fathom the Quartet's sublimity, though they might be hard pressed to articulate what they've just seen and heard.

THE FIRST QUARTET

AFTER HIS SESSION work and leader dates at CTI, Ron decided to form his own quartet, circa 1975. By 1976, he had enlisted band mates who could free him up to play his piccolo bass as the lead melody instrument. The unprecedented two-bass setting featured pianist Kenny Barron, bassist Buster Williams and drummer Ben Riley. That band made its mark both in New York and on the road for the next four years. (Within one week in 1979, Ron's Quartet opened a new venue, Fat Tuesday's, on 17th Street and 3rd Avenue in Manhattan, and closed a venerated club, playing the farewell show at Rosy's Jazz Hall in New Orleans.)

The band was built around the piccolo bass. Contrary to popular belief, Ron did not invent the instrument, but he certainly made it popular, introducing it in 1973 while experimenting with a larger group of musicians that would eventually become his nonet.

"I wanted to be a leader," Ron told *Frets Magazine* in 1979, "and in a piano/bass/drums trio, unless there is a specific physical instrument arrangement, a person walking into a club and looking at the band would not usually assume that the bass player is the leader. The piccolo bass puts me physically in that position, and because it's tuned up a fourth higher than a standard bass (A-D-G-C), it puts me in the musical spotlight too."

The bass, which Ron called piccolo because of its ability to play in an upper register, is a half-size bass and has a brighter sound and a lighter tone quality, which allows it to blend in well with the standard upright. Historically, the piccolo bass had been used in small chamber music ensembles, but was gradually supplanted by the standard bass as classical composers wrote music for larger orchestras that required more volume.

Ron contacted an instrument-maker friend in New Jersey, Fred Lyman, who built him a piccolo bass that was retired in 1990 when Ron found one in a bass shop in Cincinnati. It's a French Tyrolean that was built in 1890. Originally it was a three-string instrument that was modified to a four-string bass some time before Ron bought it. He retuned it to C (top string), G (second string from the top), D (third string from the top), A (the lowest open string). It's the same tuning as a cello, but upside down. That enabled Ron to get the quality that made him feel like a bassist, while also attaining a cello-like sound. "This instrument is older and has a more mature sound because of its age," Ron said. "Because of the higher tuning, it didn't settle for two years, but now it has a nice warm tone."

Ron told writer Kalamu ya Salaam of *The Black Collegian* (March/April 1978) that his intent for the band was "to play music that will leave the audience with a melody that they can take home with them. My goal is to have this Quartet be successful enough that it will allow me more time to write and play with the band, and take on fewer outside projects."

Ron's Quartet members came to the group with impeccable musical backgrounds. Ben Riley played with Thelonious Monk and Roland Hanna. Buster had played with Miles and Art Blakey. And Ron had gigged some with Kenny, whom he knew best from his stint with Yusef Lateef. While the four musicians had never played together, Ron said that he knew enough about their musicianship ahead of time that, were he to form a band, these would be the people he'd want.

Ron knew that Buster had filled in for him in Miles's group while it was playing dates in 1967 on the West Coast. The first time Buster hooked up with Ron personally came with Herbie Hancock's new sextet at the Village Vanguard, and then later they swapped the bass chair with Herbie Mann. It didn't take long for the two bassists to establish a good friendship.

Kenny remembers running into Ron in San Francisco when he was playing with Yusef. Kenny recalled, "Ron came up to me and said, 'I have something to talk to you about when you get back to New York.' I assumed it had something to do with music, so I just let it go. Apparently, even though I had run into Ron previously, Ben had told him to check me out."

Meanwhile Buster, who after performing with Hancock from 1969 to 1973 and gigging with McCoy Tyner and Sonny Rollins, got a call from Ron. "At that time we weren't on any kind of talking-daily basis," he said. "Ron called me out of the blue. He just asked me to come to his apartment for rehearsal. I thought that was strange. He didn't mention anything about the concept. He said Kenny Barron and Ben Riley would be there. I thought that maybe he was going to produce a trio project. When I arrived, Ron brought out his piccolo bass and only then did I realize that we were rehearsing his new band and that it was going to be a quartet."

Was that daunting? "It was. I had mixed emotions," Buster said. "Here I am playing in a band with someone I truly admire, but I'm playing the same instrument. He's going to hear me every night. I'll be under the microscope. I wasn't sure about that. But then I thought, yes, but I'll be hearing *him* every night. Wow, how exciting is that?"

Buster says that their basses meshed. "The timbre of Ron's piccolo bass with mine was wonderful," he said. "We went to work right away." The Quartet opened at Sweet Basil, and then played at a club in New Jersey, in West Paterson, called Gulliver's that was owned by a former boxer, Amos Kaune. "Ron had all these hookups to keep working, so the band went on for five years."

In 1977, Ron gathered the Quartet at Sweet Basil to record a live album over the course of two nights (March 25 and 26), which became the double-LP *Piccolo* for Milestone Records. On it he soared above the rhythm section that supported his extended solos. But some listeners were confused. Was Ron playing a cello or a guitar?

The program included the 1930 Tin Pan Alley hit, "Three Little Words," Monk's "Blue Monk," Oscar Pettiford's "Laverne Walk," and two Latin-tinged originals by Ron, "Saguaro" and "Tambien Conocido Como." One reviewer commented, "The sophisticated swing and high-caliber musicianship by the late, lamented Modern Jazz Quartet [then on hiatus] are to be found in the Ron Carter group, and a commensurate popularity will surely follow."

Later that year, Ron recorded with the Quartet again at Rudy Van Gelder's studio in New Jersey. However, *Peg Leg* (released in 1978) featured an expanded version of the group as Ron began to explore more complex arrangements. He brought in guitarist Jay Berliner and four wind instrument players: Jerry Dodgion (piccolo, flute, alto flute), George Marge (piccolo, flute, oboe), Walter Kane (flute, clarinet, bassoon) and Charles Russo (clarinet, bass clarinet).

During this time Buster got his share of schooling from Ron. One of the biggest challenges was keeping his bass lines distinct from Ron's. "It took a lot of discipline to make it work," he said. "But it was exciting, rewarding. I learned a lot, especially in how to solve problems in the midst of improvisations. I learned how not to be afraid to set myself up, taking the lead from Ron in the way he handled himself onstage, leading the band without saying much. His composure and confidence were remarkable."

Working with Ron in the context of the Quartet proved to be an ah-hah experience for Buster, who said, "Ron turned on the light for ideas. He helped me to solve problems in my playing. I allowed myself to become a sponge, to absorb as much as I could from him."

Likewise, Kenny grew from his experience in the Quartet. "Ron always wrote interesting runs," he said. "As a bandleader, he knew exactly what he wanted. I learned how to play soft with Ron, to play the nuances but also be intense." Kenny said the band had a lot of fun, especially making those "mad rushes" to catch transportation in Europe with not just one bass, but two.

Ron and Buster developed a deeper relationship during those years. They talked a lot about the bass itself—the different ways of playing it and practicing. They also talked about their experiences with Miles and his clothes, cars, and days with Bird.

Did Ron ever ask Buster for advice on the bass? "No, but I know he was listening to me," said Buster. "He hired me because he liked the way I played. He made no bones about that. We'd talk about what he was hearing night after night, and how that affected the things he was playing. It was rewarding because I realized I wasn't the only one stealing. I was definitely stealing from him. There was no way to not influence each other. We'd trade fours and trade eights, and we enjoyed playing together."

Buster also remembered how Ron would show his appreciation in ways that "warmed the cockles of my heart." Once while they were touring in California, Buster recalled that Ron had a recording date with McCoy Tyner. "Of course, Ron only had his piccolo bass on the road, so he asked me if he could use my bass. I said, of course. That night when I got to work at our gig, Ron had a gift for me. Inside this box that was wrapped with classy paper was a beautiful silk scarf. That was Ron's way of saying thanks. I never expected a gift. I was just doing him a favor."

As late as 1979, Ron was telling reporters that the Quartet was solid. At a show at the Earth Tavern in Portland, Oregon, in January, he told *Pacific Front* writer Randy Davis between sets when asked about the band's future, "I have a great love for the musicians in this band, and I sense that we are on a direction that pleases me. I can't see any alterations to this group in the near future. I may record with different ensembles, but as of 9:39 p.m. on January 8, 1979, this is it."

However, over the next year, a confluence of factors—including all the band members being involved in different projects and the increasing complexity of the compositions and arrangements Ron was writing—led the leader to think about disbanding the group.

The Quartet officially ended in 1980 after a weeklong stint at Sweet Basil. After the final set, Ron informed Kenny, Buster and Ben that the ensemble's run was over.

"Sure, it surprised me," said Kenny. "Well, it did and it didn't. Ron seemed unhappy. I'm not sure why, but I could feel something. I thought, well, that was a good run."

Did he ever ask Ron why? "Not really," said Kenny. "Ron is a private man and I respect that. We've worked many times together since then."

"I have my own thoughts as to why," Buster said, who recalls that Ron came into the club's kitchen to announce the band's end. "I don't remember him saying anything else. We'd been together for a while, so it was a bit of a shock. No, not so much a shock, as much as it was abrupt. But it didn't really bother me. I was ready to move on anyway. I figured that the band had run its course. But there wasn't any explanation, and I don't remember any of us asking why."

Ron said that his original intention was to continue working with Kenny as often as he could. But as it turned out, Kenny, Ben and Buster, who had gigged as a trio during their time with Ron, formed the Monk tribute group Sphere that included saxophonist Charlie Rouse. Between 1982 and 1988, the band (named after Thelonious's middle name) recorded eight albums.

"I didn't talk a lot to the guys about what I was thinking," Ron said. "I just let them know it was time for another point of view. That's how it went down, and I was comfortable with how that ended."

Ron told writer Lee Jeske in *DownBeat* (July 1983) that he had been musing on the break for a year, while still feeling emotionally tied to the band members and responsible for the bulk of their gigging work. "But there's no way to pleasantly break up a band—you either do it or you don't. You can't mail 'em flowers or give 'em candy or a gold watch. You just blurt it out."

THE NEXT QUARTET

THE QUARTET FORMAT with piccolo bass still promised a steady flow of creative juice for Ron. He set out to reform it. He told Jeske, "I was looking essentially for the same qualities that the band I no longer had could do. I had to have a bass player who could read and play in tune. I had to have a piano player who knew songs other than Chick Corea tunes. I had to have a drummer who could manage brushes."

Ron said that the bass player in his new band had to be a perfect fit, someone who not only could play the right notes and be centered on a concept but also be willing to take directions from him. "Here's a chance for a bass player to get free lessons and get paid for taking these lessons," Ron said. "Because what I tell him is not only going to make my band sound better, but it's also going to make *him* sound better, if he follows my instructions.... All I'm trying to do is be a bandleader with three young guys who want to play some music."

Ron's first hire was 23-year-old bassist Boots Maleson, who had just moved to New York from Boston and who today continues to perform with

Ron in his nonet. Boots had heard rumors that Ron was looking for a new bassist to replace Buster. He got up the nerve to call Ron, who told him to come to his place at 10 the next morning. "How do you prepare?" Boots said. "I was as nervous as any bass player might be. But, show-no-fear is the motto."

Ron got down to business quickly, asked Boots to play a D-flat scale, then walk a blues bass line and sight-read a melody. "It was a brief musical audition as well as a personal audition," said Boots. "We talked for a few minutes, and he thanked me for coming."

Ron auditioned four or five bass players. "Some guys came late and brought their coffee and napkins," he said. "Some couldn't read the parts, some suggested that a piece I wrote should be played in a different way. Only Boots came completely prepared for the audition. He was on time—early, in fact. He played the parts that I wrote, not interpreting them. He played in tune, had a great arco sound, could sight-read really well and played a classical bass that had five strings. That low C string wasn't a prerequisite for the gig, but it was nice to be able to have the opportunity to write notes that are readily available on a guy's bass."

A few days after the audition, Boots got the call from Ron—"the greatest phone message I ever got in my life"—who asked him to pick up the book of tunes for the Quartet.

Boots felt comfortable in the setting. He too had played cello before becoming a bassist and listened to cello-bass records by Oscar Pettiford and an old double-bass recording (on a 78) by Charles Mingus. He loved the sound of Buster and Ron playing together, but he knew he'd be facing a steep learning curve in coming to understand what Ron was looking for.

"It's hard to get that kind of thing across," said Boots. "But each time we played together, he'd talk to me later, about how to play certain notes. He didn't try to get me to play everything all at once, but was patient that I was making gradual improvements." Later he took lessons with Ron, learning how to shape his bass lines and understand more deeply what was at work in the music.

"Boots was experienced enough and sensitive enough that if we did have a problem, we could talk about it and he'd make the adjustment," said Ron. "But above all, I liked that he wasn't intimidated by me as the bandleader, that he was comfortable enough to make suggestions for a part or what I was playing."

With Boots on board, Ron formed a new quartet that included Ted Lo on piano and Wilby Fletcher on drums. The group lasted less than two years. Boots recalls a few "sparse" Quartet years with a revolving cast of different performers—on piano, Kenny Barron, Mike Longo, Kenny Werner and Roland Hanna; and on drums, Kenny Washington, Marvin "Smitty" Smith and Lewis Nash.

Lewis came aboard as a sub for Smitty at Sweet Basil in 1984, then after intermittent gigs became permanent in 1985, working with Boots and

Roland. Lewis remembers the close friendship and intimate musical bond Ron and Roland enjoyed. "They were very different in many ways," he said. "Ron tall, Roland short. When they were together, they looked like Mutt and Jeff. But onstage I loved watching how they interacted. There were times when Ron would be visibly moved and tear up when Roland played."

Ron proved to be a mentor for Lewis, who came to grasp the important professional values that were paramount to the bandleader, including promptness, readiness and focus. "When we recorded, it was important for Ron to do one take," Lewis said. "You learn what you need to before, you practice so you will be at your best musical level and then live with what you document in the studio." He added, "I was in my mid-20s, so Ron served as a brother, father, teacher, friend. As a young professional, it was so important to be around him, someone of his stature, to see how he conducted himself with people after gigs and with promoters on the road."

Lewis calls Ron the Beacon. "I look at him that way," he said. "It's his physical stature—you can see him far away, for example, in a Japanese airport—as well as his consummate musical sensibility. He's soft-spoken and shy, which some people mistake as him being standoffish, and he's understated in so many ways."

Ron so appreciated Lewis's ability to react quickly to musical experiences that he also introduced the drummer to the waning, but still lucrative, commercial jingle studio scene. "Ron did it all through his career," said Lewis. "In the '60s and '70s, the jingles world was big, and there was Ron, even though he was also doing lots of club gigs and recording dates with others. In the '80s, he brought me in because, first, he knew I could sight-read and second, because he knew I'd show up and be on time."

Plus, Lewis points out, Ron inspired by example as a pro still curious about how to find the right notes. Once in Japan, as the band was in a van going from the airport to the hotel, Ron had headphones on. Lewis asked him what he was listening to. He said, "Paul Chambers and Israel Crosby. I'm still doing my homework." Lewis said, "That let me know a lot about him."

Another experience in Japan told him about Ron's camaraderie for the band. There was a huge dressing room reserved for Ron at a venue and only a closet-sized room for the rest of the band. "Ron went to the management," said Lewis, "and had all of us move into his room. He was uncomfortable that his friends weren't being treated fairly."

RETIRING THE PICCOLO BASS

LEWIS WAS IN the drum chair when in 1987 Ron decided to change the Quartet's format, retiring his piccolo bass to nonet service only, bidding farewell to Boots who continues to play in the nonet, and bringing aboard a percussionist. "After a while I was feeling the bass sound of the sound spectrum was getting crowded, and I wanted a little lighter texture," said Ron. "That meant that I would have to replace Boots with a percussion sound, and that I would have to return to the big bass."

Ron tried out several percussionists, but Steve Kroon got the gig. Lewis was pleased with the changeover. "What drummer wouldn't be happy?" he said. "When Ron played the piccolo bass, he played the melody a lot and strummed rhythms like a Freddie Green type of playing. But with Ron playing the bass, I'd be able to learn a lot more from him about playing together. It opened a lot of doors and created possibilities."

Indeed, Ron schooled Lewis to be a better drummer. They talked often about how to work together, for example, about how he could tune his drums to not interfere with the sound of the bass. "The relationship of the drummer and bassist is the key to everything in jazz," Lewis said. "I became more conscious of how my bass drum and tom toms could wipe out bass notes. I figured out adjustments to allow Ron's notes to flow freely."

Lewis also learned how to stay aware during a tune. "Ron's the type of bass player who's not trying to force a view," he said. "He allows it to take shape and then he steers it. He's very patient and suggests subtleties."

Lewis marvels at Ron's ears. "He listens intently," he said. "I'd play a rhythmic figure, and he'd repeat it with a different twist during the course of his walking bass line. He's always in the moment, which is the essence of creativity. He playfully manipulates the pulse, while also doing something different harmonically, like playing a note on the bottom of chord. Ron likes to challenge others as well as himself. We'd talk about young players who would only play a certain set of changes and how boring that was. Ron can play a song dozens of times, still searching for the best notes and finding something fresh."

With the Quartet's new drum-based rhythm section, Lewis and Steve had to work together to figure out their roles. "We talked a lot about not getting in each other's way and being careful not to wipe out Ron's bass," Lewis said. "In the beginning we decided to err on playing less, but as time went on, the percussion Steve played got more dense, and Ron began to write things that had more space for the percussion and drums."

THE NEW QUARTET

MEANWHILE, THE QUARTET was ready for another change, this time with the piano chair. In 1988, Roland wanted to curb his traveling and focus more on teaching. That opened the door to Stephen Scott, who shortly after his 19th birthday was invited by Ron to rehearse for a gig as Roland's sub.

Stephen came up in the New York jazz scene a year earlier as the youngest piano player that vocalist Betty Carter ever hired. He replaced Benny Green who left to become a member of Art Blakey's Jazz Messengers. Stephen was just shy of 18. He recalls learning an early lesson when accompanying Betty. She was singing a ballad and in the middle of the tune he was called upon to solo. "I started to play and figured that the first eight bars I'd do my Kenny Kirkland, the second my Mulgrew Miller, do Wynton Kelly for the chorus and then close out with Monk," he said. "I was getting into my solo when Betty got the mic and told me, 'No, kid, be honest!'" While Stephen began to develop his own voice, Betty praised him, proudly proclaiming her new protégé a "genius."

A year later Stephen met up with Ron for the first time when he was producing the debut record of the hard-bop revival group, the Harper Brothers. Led by trumpeter Philip Harper and drummer Winard Harper, *Harper Brothers* featured the nucleus of Betty's trio. "My first experience with Ron was that he was very cool and very thorough," Stephen said. "And also very generous."

Around that same time, Cedar Walton called Stephen to sub for him one night in his trio with Ron and Billy Higgins at Sweet Basil.

Recognizing that Roland was ready to part ways from his employ, Ron called Stephen and asked him to check out the music for his quartet and nonet groups. Soon after, he got the call. "At the first rehearsal I was overwhelmed," he said. "I'm just barely 19 and here I am subbing for Roland Hanna who came after Kenny Barron. I felt like I had to fill big shoes that didn't fit. I knew Ron had played with Tommy Flanagan and Hank Jones, so I started playing these wide-open chords and then two-fisted chords."

All of a sudden Ron stopped and asked Stephen, "What kind of piano is that?"

Nervously, Stephen replied, "A Steinway, a Steinway & Sons."

"Well, if you play below the S in Steinway, you're in my register."

It was not only Stephen's first lesson from Ron, but as he looks back, it also offered a glimpse at his humor. Stephen passed the audition that ostensibly greenlighted him into the piano chair. "I thought I was going to be Roland's sub, but I realized soon that I was pretty much the guy," he said. "It was my gig to keep or lose."

Early on, Stephen faced "my all-time worst experience," when he accompanied Ron and Lewis on a Japanese tour as a trio. He admits that he was overwhelmed and intimidated. "I was the new guy and I was a fish out of water," he said. "Ron and I were hearing things differently, and there was a lot of clashing. He was very articulate about what he wanted and wasn't afraid to tell me, but I never quite met the mark. I hadn't developed his trust, which takes time. I knew he respected me and that he trusted I would find where he's going. But I dropped the ball on that tour and Ron made sure that I knew it."

With Steve Kroon in the picture, Stephen says that a lot of rhythmic weight was taken off his shoulders. "Things began to change," he said. "I had to develop my sound, my vocabulary and my confidence. I grew up before Ron's eyes. It's come full circle to a place where today he fully trusts me."

One of the key developments of the Quartet was Ron's decision to segue tunes together at shows. "It's like saying no to call waiting," Stephen explained. "Stopping a tune and announcing it is like saying, hey, we're having this great conversation and the flow stops by taking another call that's coming in. We develop segues, one big collage of ideas. Instead of call waiting, we're in a conference call. No interruptions, just a stream of consciousness. We can be in the middle of a tune and I may throw another tune right on top. That could end up in a train wreck or there could be a merging into a new emotional space."

Writing in the *Los Angeles Times* about a show in 2004 by the Quartet at Catalina Bar & Grill, Don Heckman remarked about how wonderfully the set was delivered without a break: "Songs surfaced, then receded into the distance: 'It Might As Well Be Spring,' Wayne Shorter's 'Footprints,' 'I Thought About You.'"

As Lewis began to take on new projects, including a leader role, he slowly phased out of the Quartet, with Ron's blessing. One of the regular subs was Payton Crossley, a former drummer in Ahmad Jamal's band who can't exactly remember when he officially became a part of the Quartet. "When Ron started sending me the complete itinerary of upcoming shows, it spoke for itself," Payton said. "It naturally evolved." He also became a member of the nonet.

Understanding that Ron has many projects in the works, Payton says he doesn't mind when he's left out of a recording session, such as 2001's *When Skies Are Grey* album with Harvey Mason, and the new album *Jazz & Bossa*, where a Brazilian drummer was enlisted. "Ron handpicks people he wants on certain records," Payton said. "And that's fine with me. Ron is an institution and is all over the place. No one gets 100 percent of him. I get my piece and I'm happy with that."

Having been a sub for Lewis, Payton found his place in the Quartet without much anxiety, though he hastens to note that Ron doesn't shy away from commentary about his playing. "You can't have thin skin playing with Ron," Payton said. "You may feel you're playing with fire, and he might say, don't do that anymore, it's not working. He takes you off your guard, and he makes you think about what will work. He hired me because he trusted that I would take direction from him and not take what he says personally."

Trust is a word that comes up frequently with Ron's band members. "That's what happens among the four of us," said Stephen. "Once that trust is developed, that's when the fun and magic happen. If respect and trust is not there, it's hard to make magic, it's hard to do great things together. It's when we mix everything together as a band that we experience our highest moments. It's not just a solo, but it's where I solo along with the percussionist, and then Ron reharmonizes, and a tune goes in a new direction. I know he used to play with Bobby Timmons, so I might play a few notes like him to set Ron up, then Payton responds and Rolando responds, and we're all smiling."

Payton is continually fascinated by Ron's quest for finding the right notes night in and night out. "I watch Ron play, and I see the authority of an old master, but also the curiosity of a 10-year-old," he said. "He's always trying to find some other way to play a tune. He's incredibly creative. Most people his age have figured that they've already made their statements and they'll just ride into the sunset."

THE NEW PERCUSSIONIST

THE PERCUSSION CHAIR in the Quartet in recent years has been in flux. Kroon, Ron's first permanent percussionist who appeared on six of his recordings, left, the leader surmised, because he began to take critiques personally. He was replaced by Roger Squitero, who was around long enough to appear on the Quartet's *Dear Miles* album, recorded in 2006 and released stateside in 2007. Then Roger was hired for the Broadway show, *Tarzan*, which required a six-month commitment with no subbing allowed, and was replaced in 2006 by Rolando Morales-Matos.

Like the others in the band, Rolando, the percussionist/assistant conductor of the orchestra of the Broadway musical, *The Lion King*, began as a sub, on Roger's recommendation. "I met Ron at my first rehearsal and it was very challenging," he said. "Even today, it's still challenging." But Rolando's background—he was trained classically with symphony orchestra experience and familiar with Latin music from playing in bands in his native Puerto Rico—made his transition to working with Ron easier, even though he was not conversant with the breadth of the bandleader's career.

Rolando's willingness to work with Ron on what sounds he was hearing in the music made him a valuable collaborator. "I understand that you need something to drink, but you don't like water? Then, I'll give you the liquids you need for your body," Rolando said. If Ron called for a cowbell at one point, Rolando said that it "has to make sense to me musically, that it relates to the tune and the key. Ron may give me a B-flat note that I then will convert into the colors that match the sound."

The discussion is ongoing, says Rolando. "That's why I like working with Mr. Carter," he said. "We talk about the music, the chord progressions, the right instrumentation."

In reflecting on the 2007 *Dear Miles* album (see chapter on Blue Note Records), Ron remarked that his quartet is a source of great pride for him. Like Trane had his '60s quartet and Miles had the '60s quintet, Ron too desired to have "a working band" with which he could develop new musical ideas.

That philosophy fueled his decision to document the Quartet in the recording studio as well as to highlight the band in his Carnegie Hall performance in 2007 (see Carnegie Hall chapter). The Quartet closed the show, after Ron's all-star quartet comprised of Herbie Hancock, Wayne Shorter and Billy Cobham performed its set. His Quartet band members appreciate Ron's commitment to train the spotlight on them.

"I was very humbled that he did that," said Payton. "It was his way of showing what he has cultivated."

"It was a stamp of approval," said Stephen. "Sharing the stage with my heroes was one thing. But going on last was quite another. I suspected that Ron would have finished the show with Herbie and those guys. But the order that Ron planned was his way of saying that, yes, I've been known as the bass player in Miles's great band, but I also have my own sound, my own concept, my own bands. I'm not dependent on Herbie or Wayne. Ron wants to be known as Ron Carter. At Carnegie Hall he was saying, this is where I am now."

COLLOQUY

Q&A: The Quartet Questions Ron

At the 2008 North Sea Jazz Festival in Rotterdam, Holland, I organized and moderated a panel that consisted of Ron's quartet members—Stephen, Payton and Rolando—posing questions to their bandleader. In lieu of having Ron be interviewed by a journalist, I figured the musician-to-musician exchange would be a fine change of pace—a welcome departure from a stilted Q&A session where the subject of the audience's interest would be doing his best to stifle his own yawns.

Certainly Stephen, Payton and Rolando have plenty of opportunities to query Ron on all kinds of subjects during their frequent tours in the U.S., Europe and Japan. But I asked them beforehand to go deep, come up with topics that they hadn't previously discussed and to put Ron, as I told the packed crowd in the Volga room a couple hours before they performed, in "the hot seat."

With his cool demeanor and penchant for slipping humor into his philosophical treatises on the bass, Ron relished the opportunity to tell stories. Rolando posed only one question (though he thoroughly enjoyed the panel, often laughing with a high-pitched, sharp chortle), Payton, two, and Stephen, who compiled a list of questions on his handheld texting device, several, including some that he knew the answer to from conversing with Ron but felt the audience should hear. As moderator, I also felt free to slide in a few questions of my own to contribute to the fluidity of the 45-minute session.

The Q&A opened with topics related to Ron's sound, moved on to his Miles days (the bulk of which is included in the Miles chapters), then concluded with Ron's advice to the audience for what to listen for in the quartet's performance that evening.

ROLANDO: *Maestro, in your earlier recordings, I hear you solo with the bow. I still see the pocket on your bass for the bow, but in the last few years I've spent with you, I haven't seen you play with one. So, I'd like to know when did it stop and will it be coming back?*

RON: One of the reasons you haven't seen it in the past two years is I've been wanting to concentrate on the pizzicato bass sound. Plus, the strings I use on my bass now are not the quality of the kind I used to use. The strings are a combination of core that is metal, silk wrapping that is the second layer and the black nylon winding on the third level that you see. These strings are great for playing pizzicato but not for arco. Another factor is that I'm still trying to make the bass sound good when just playing time. If I play pizzicato and arco, something gets lost in the process. I look forward every night to playing time and doing something different to get the guys I'm playing with to do the same. Finally, I've already documented my arco work, so I don't feel like I have to keep doing it.

PAYTON: *On the road, you rarely use your own bass, but instead whatever bass the venue provides for you. But I've noticed that whatever instrument you use, you still get your own sound. So, what adjustments do you make or what elements do you use to get that consistent sound?*

RON: It's really a drag these days for musicians to travel with their instruments. The worst is flying where the airlines charge three times the normal price to bring the bass—charges for excess weight and the oversize. So traveling with the bass is prohibitive because of the cost. The solution is what I call bass du jour—in other words, bass of the day. Like a pianist, I have to make do with whatever is available. There are several problems with this.

First, for me as a tall man, most basses are too short. My options are to get them to make a taller stick for the bass to stand on or to sit to play it. But I always play standing. I'm not comfortable sitting.

Second, all these basses have different strings than my bass in New York. I would never suggest to a bass player to let me put my strings on their bass. Most bass players like their particular strings and don't want anyone fooling around with them. I can appreciate that point of view. Besides it would take an hour to change a set of strings, and we usually arrive in a city and go right to the bandstand so there wouldn't be enough time.

The only thing I bring that's my own that I'm comfortable with is a small pickup. That allows me to try to get my sound into the bass I'm playing.

PAYTON: *But how do you get that sound?*

RON: I like the mystery of not knowing why things are the way they are. I enjoy being able to say to that question, "I don't know how I do that. I can't explain why my sound comes through even when I'm using someone else's bass and someone else's strings." I just try to translate the sound in my ear to this particular bass, to hopefully get that sound that people hear on my records.

A WOMAN FROM THE AUDIENCE: *I think the sound you get, despite using a bass that's not your own, is in your fingers. That's where I feel your sound is. Your unique sound is in your fingers.*

DAN: *Show the audience your fingers, Ron.*

RON: Oh, no, I can't. That's the magic. (He laughs.) I can't show that.

DAN: *Why is using the pickup important?*

RON: The bass was the last jazz instrument to be given the kind of recording attention it deserved rather than just being the sound in the background. It used to be that people would imagine the beat without hearing the definition of the notes, the intonation, the tone quality. Since 1960 or so, time has been spent developing built-in contact microphones for a bass. There are several today that are quite good.

But there's been a wave of players in the last 10 years or so who feel the need to play the bass natural. I think of those players as bass vegetarians. They don't play with meat. Their view is that the bass should not be amplified. But I think that's an awful view. I'd suggest they have someone go two meters away from the bandstand and listen. You wouldn't be able to hear the bass at all. I can't imagine that a bass player would appreciate not being heard by the audience.

Some people use air microphones next to their bass. But the problem is most clubs don't have adequate sound systems, or they're not maintained from night to night. You end up with the bass drum or the piano getting in your way. If they don't use a pickup, bassists pull at their strings so they can be heard in the back of a room.

I can understand why players want that natural sound they used to hear on Miles's Prestige albums. They want to sound like Paul Chambers on *Cookin'* and *Steamin.'* But they don't realize the time and devotion Paul put into getting that sound. He used to go to Rudy Van Gelder's studio in New Jersey every Saturday for four or five weeks and spend hours with Rudy trying to figure out how to record his bass. I don't know of any bassists today who would do that. On those Miles Prestige records, the sound was arranged in a way where Red Garland was way in the background, Philly Joe's drumming was mostly high hats and cymbals, with no real bottom sound, and Miles and Trane were playing pretty high. That left the whole midrange of the bass open to Paul.

So, if a bassist doesn't want to use a pickup, don't come to my house.

STEPHEN: *This leads to my question. In the 20 years of my association with you, I've talked with many bassists like Ray Drummond, Peter Washington and Bob Cranshaw who all say that you changed the sound of the recorded bass. You mentioned Paul Chambers with Rudy Van Gelder, but how is it that your sound has changed through the years,* *from* **My Funny Valentine** *to the sound you had with V.S.O.P. to your sound with McCoy and then your latest recordings for Blue Note?*

RON: During my Miles years, I was using a string setup of golden spiral nylon-wound gut on the D and G and a nylon orchestra string with black winding on A and E. Around 1969, the company that made those strings got sold to another string company, and the quality, I'm sorry to say, took a big drop for the worse. My friend, the guitarist Attila Zoller, was in the process of inventing new guitar strings. He said maybe we should think about doing the same with bass strings. I was curious about the process and I had the time, so for a year we experimented with different material—different sizes of core, different types of core material, silk and nylon wraps. We finally came up with series number 7700, which I use to this day, made by LaBella Strings.

The type of string is important for my bass to be able to function, to make it sound good. When pickups became more evolved and developed, people would call me about the sound. And I would give advice, like it sounds too thin on the G string or it makes the bridge vibrate too much or it's in the wrong location. Those who trusted my judgment would make adjustments. So the pickups have helped to change and determine my sound.

Then there's the studio. I always tell a new sound engineer to come out of his booth and into the studio and stand by the bass. I tell him my job is to make the bass sound this way in the studio, and his job is to make it sound this way when the record gets to his house. Many engineers have never been close enough to an upright bass to know what it sounded like. The best engineers don't get offended by the way I want my bass to sound.

The fact of the matter is when I play a note in the studio, it has to go through four steps before it gets to your house. First, there's the edit; second, the mix; third, the mastering; and fourth, the pressing. The people at each step may have their own view as to how the bass should sound. It's amazing that after all those steps my bass sound can maintain its identity. I'm always hoping that the live studio bass sound can be translated into your house.

STEPHEN: *I hear all that you're saying, but I'm still wondering why the Ron Carter sound is so unique, why your sound on the bass is so personal, whether you're playing on a record with Milt Jackson or Roberta Flack?*

RON: I've always demanded that I have my sound. I tell my students in New York, you can always fix a note, but you can't fix the sound. I try to instill in them the importance of finding the sound that they want to be responsible for and to not settle for anything less. Not all bass players perform with that kind of insistence to make their own personal statements no matter what the bass du jour is.

Too many bass players today get into the solo aspect of the instrument. They just slide around until they get to their solo where they play forcefully, dramatically. That becomes the holy bread while everything else is milquetoast. Your bass sound needs to be consistent no matter what you're doing. You have to commit to that.

STEPHEN: *The Miles rhythm section concept with you, Herbie and Tony was different than the way Paul Chambers worked with Wynton Kelly and Philly Joe Jones. You interacted with a soloist. Why?*

RON: In the rhythm section, we were able to capture a soloist's attention by the notes we played. So you have a G chord—GDBF—and I'm playing B for the first note instead of G. And there was an expectation that Tony would play on 1, but he played on 2, or the soloist would expect Herbie to play on 1, but he wouldn't play until four bars went by. Because of the devices we used in our approach to the music, we'd always force Miles or Wayne to step back for a second. We were always using our rhythmic approaches to play things that the soloist wasn't expecting to hear. In that way, we made Miles and Wayne play better. We put them on notice: Step back because here it comes.

STEPHEN: *As a follow-up, I've heard bootlegs of your concerts, where the band was playing a blues in F with the melody in F. But then all of a sudden, you'd drop down to a D-flat when Miles started to play his first two choruses. It sounds like Miles had no idea that was the new arrangement you decided to do.*

RON: I always hope to get the soloist's attention, to put something in their ear that they weren't expecting. So if a soloist expects the first note in a blues in F to be F, the best thing to do is not play that note. I like doing that. Play G-flat, B, E. All those notes work, but you have to know what they mean. It really can get complicated, but that's part of the fun and can open up a whole new life for the soloist to live. Some people think it's easy. They say, anyone can do that, but they can't. They think it's as simple as falling off a log. Hardly.

PAYTON: *Your work has been documented since you were young. What do you do now that is better or different than what you did in your early days?*

RON: I've always thought that a recording session was like going to school free for me. If I play certain notes, do they sound better if played here on the neck, or there? I listen and maybe the note is a little sharp here, a little flat there. But that's OK. I've come to the belief that you won't get a better take than the first two takes of any song with anybody. I don't care if you do 25 takes or 75 takes. The first two are best. That's what I've learned—to maintain focus to get the best you can out of the first two takes, to not allow the energy, the enthusiasm, the mind-set to dissipate. If it's taken 45 takes to get it right, you've lost the intensity. I try to bring to my record dates a level of commitment to the music that other guys don't always have. I've come to see the studio as a place to make music that can be very special. You won't see me fooling around, making phone calls, eating a sandwich right before recording a track. I learned to bring a different attitude, so that when I arrive everyone else falls into place. I feel the vibe and say, let's not miss this opportunity. Let's jump on the magic carpet and ride.

STEPHEN: *Who is still on your short list of people that you'd like to play some choruses behind?*

RON: Ahmad Jamal. He works as much as I do so I've never had the chance. I've told him that one night when he's in town I'm going to tell his bass player to go home for an hour and watch CNN so I can cover for him.

STEPHEN: *What were three bands you wish you had played with?*

RON: The Duke Ellington Band. The Count Basie Band just to play with Freddie Green. And more time with Oscar Peterson, though I did play with him one night.

STEPHEN: *If you could put together a sextet of people from jazz history, who would be in it?*

RON: Can I have three or four people for each instrument? On guitar, Jim Hall, Freddie Green, Russell Malone. On drums, Connie Kay, Tony Williams, Roy Haynes, Kenny Clarke. Oh, and of course, Payton. On piano, you, Herbie, Cedar Walton, Red Garland. Percussion, Rolando, Ralph MacDonald. My point is that not any one person makes it work for me. They all bring their own sound and their own challenges to me as a bassist. I love having the opportunity to play in a lot of different environments.

STEPHEN: *My last question. Brace yourself. It's political and it's a question that has been asked of Bill Clinton and Barack Obama. Boxers or briefs? (Laughter)*

RON: That's personal and political.

STEPHEN: *Is that what you mean when you said you like catching people off guard?*

RON: Yes.

DAN: *The very last question. Many people in this audience will be seeing your quartet show in a few hours. Can you give them a road map of what to expect when they hear you perform?*

RON: Hopefully they'll leave the show with a melody. This is a very melody-oriented band. We're a group that delivers interesting dynamics—not just loud, but a nice flow of loud, medium loud, pianissimo. We all get involved in the emotion of the dynamics. We also segue from song to song. My job is to make these segues have a smooth enough transition so that you don't realize we're into a new song until after the third chorus goes by. We're asking you to follow our story. There is a new story every night. Hopefully we'll find the right letters, the right punctuation marks, the right sentence structures so that when you leave our performance tonight you'll have heard a great story by four guys who believe in each other.

CHAPTER TWENTY-TWO

The Nonet: The Cello Choir

WHILE EATING DINNER at the bar in between sets on the second night of the Ron Carter Nonet's four-night engagement in March 2008 at Birdland in New York, Kermit Moore, one of the four cellists in the frontline of the chamber jazz ensemble, smiled and said, "Wow, wasn't Ron amazing tonight! He was on fire." The esteemed cellist, conductor and composer—a mainstay of Ron's lush, low-register band whose history dates back to 1976—marveled as if he had never heard the bandleader in better shape.

Indeed, Ron had a good time in that set, playing with a sensibility that was equal parts adventure, humor and unpredictability. He grimaced during some stretches when he was soloing on his piccolo bass, as if each note were fathomed with a newfound sense of meaning. But he also smiled with pleasure as he conducted his cellists who keenly watched for his cues to take the music around more bends.

CELLO JAZZ

THERE IS NO band like this—a jazz quintet expanded into a nine-piece group with a choir of cellos—on the face of the planet. It's a one-of-a-kind dream ensemble for Ron that serves as a bridge to many posts in his past. It's a unique chamber group that works on the threshold of where jazz meets classical music, melding rhythmic depth with inventive counter-melodies in a sonic surge of elegance and fire. But, importantly, the Nonet encompasses Ron's string history, including his early days of playing the cello—his first instrument played in elementary through high school, and, later on such recordings as his debut album, *Where?* in 1961 and Eric Dolphy's *Out There* a year earlier)—as well as his several years playing the piccolo bass in his own quartets and his chronicled renown as upright bassist par excellence.

The Nonet's low-end tones give the music a resonant fullness: the bass, played by Leon "Boots" Maleson, at the bottom; Ron's smaller-sized piccolo bass, tuned one fourth higher than a standard rhythm section bass, on a rung above; and the cellos on top. "I'm in the middle, which allows me to play in a range that I don't get a chance to play in that often," Ron said. "I'm out of the bass range, and because the piccolo bass has thinner strings with a brighter sound, it has more of a cello feel. I can do more things on the piccolo bass than on a bass because of that instrument's physical limitations. With the cellos in the background, I can slip in and out of the music like riding a wave at the beach."

Cellists are a rarity in jazz—Erik Friedlander is one of the few contemporary exceptions—but four cellos in one group as a string quartet of low notes? It's easily a jazz anomaly, which to Ron makes the Nonet the perfect workshop to explore new realms of composition. "I love the sound of the cellos, which are sympathetic to the jazz language," he said. "Whatever the arrangement, the cellos can play anything. Give the cellists the right notes and chords, and the results are mind-boggling. Even if I took out the other instruments' parts, the four cellos could stand on their own."

Ron added, "Violins are bright, and violas can't penetrate other sounds around them. Cellos have the range of the violin, the warmth of the viola and they have the ability to make their presence heard in a reasonably sized ensemble without a lot of miking."

When he initially dreamed of a nonet in the mid-'70s, a classical music friend tried to dissuade him from attempting to form such a group. "This guy told me that you can't write jazz for strings because they can't play it," Ron said. "I said, what? In New York? I was confident I could find cellists who knew about Charlie Parker and Miles Davis and who went to jazz clubs. That convinced me to find the right combination of notes to write and the right combination of players to perform them. I knew we could get this done, and we did."

Ron asked viola player Selwart Clarke, whom he knew from their studio work together in various recording sessions in the '70s, to find him four cellists who would have the flexibility and openness to work in a jazz setting. Kermit Moore was one of the recommendations.

"I knew Ron as a working colleague," said Kermit who has played first cello in a number of orchestras throughout his career. "We were writers and composers who worked on commercial jingles and albums. I knew of Ron from his working with Miles's group, but I didn't know that he had been a cellist. We talked about that. He said he was so busy that he didn't have time to play the cello, but he told me he still had one. I wanted to look at it. So he invited me to his place. Most of us play Italian cellos, but he had an old French cello. I even borrowed it from him once."

Kermit played cello on Ron's *Pastels* Milestone album, recorded in 1976, which featured Sanford Allen as the concertmaster of a full string ensemble of nine violinists, three viola players and three cellists. However, the four-cello-charged group was officially launched with the album *A Song for You*, recorded in June 1978 at Rudy Van Gelder's Englewood Cliffs, New Jersey, studio and named after one of the record's tracks, "Song for You," a melodic gem written and originally recorded by pop star Leon Russell. In Ron's group were four cellists—Kermit as well as Charles McCracken, John

Abramowitz and Richard Locker—Kenny Barron from Ron's Quartet at the time on piano (Leon Pendarvis subbed on one track), Jack DeJohnette on drums and various sidemen including percussionist Ralph MacDonald and guitarist Jay Berliner. Ron played bass and piccolo bass for the sessions.

The album, originally released on Milestone (with the notation "with special thanks to Selwart Clarke and Rudy Van Gelder"), was reissued on a single twofer CD in 2003 paired with Ron's 1980 album *Parfait*, a Quartet date with Boots on bass and Ron on piccolo bass.

NONET PLAUDITS

THE FIRST REAL Nonet date was *Pick 'em*, also recorded at the Van Gelder Studio in December 1978 (it was remastered in 2001 for CD by Milestone as a twofer with Ron's 1981 *Super Strings* album, another recording with a full string section and Allen as concertmaster/musical supervisor). In Eugene Holley Jr.'s liner notes to the reissue, Ron recalled meeting Kermit for the first time when he played in the Black Composers Orchestra—a group comprised of members of the Society of Black Composers that the cellist had founded in 1968 (in 1964 Kermit also founded the Symphony of the New World).

"Someone told me that when you write for string [players], they don't know how to swing," Ron said. "And I guess that may be true in a broad sense if you're talking about the New York Philharmonic string section. But in New York, you have players who can do everything…. So, this early Nonet record was my attempt to see if it was possible to write for a cello quartet and have them be an integral part of the jazz band. I write all their [parts]. I'm responsible for every note they play."

Looking back at *Pick 'em*—featuring the four cellists from *A Song for You* as well as Ron's gigging band mates, including Kenny Barron, Buster Williams, Ben Riley and Ralph MacDonald—Ron told Holley, "This record was a great success for me."

Tunes Ron explored with the cello-charged group on *A Song for You* included "Song for You" and the flamenco-tinged "El Ojo de Dios," both of which are in today's Nonet library. From *Pick 'em*, Miles Davis's blues-steeped "All Blues" and Ron's uptempo "Eight," based on another *Kind of Blue* number, "So What," continue to figure prominently in Ron's Nonet repertory.

In 1988, *The New York Times* critic Jon Pareles weighed in on one of the Nonet's rare performances, a date at Fat Tuesday's, a club on 17th Street and 3rd Avenue in New York. He described the "hushed and somber" tones of the band's music, while at the same time noting that "it luxuriates in the woody, burnt-sienna sound of low strings." As for the cellos, he observed that they played in unison not only to "nudge forward" Ron's solos on piccolo bass, but also to add "ballast—sustained chords in a stately bolero or mock-classical chords—in a piece that toyed with the contrast between straight and swinging time."

Pareles also gave plaudits for Ron's solo showcasing. "Where many jazz bass solos devolve into desultory plunking, Mr. Carter usually maintains suspense and anticipation," he wrote. "He mixes bluesy lines and rich sustained melodies in one of jazz's most songful pizzicatos. While he uses quick triplets and sliding notes along with such extended techniques as a mandolin-like tremolo strumming, he can also state a melody with minimal embellishment...."

Ron revisited the nonet format on disc twice more in the '90s: in 1990 for the Ron Carter Nonet *Eight Plus* album that unfortunately didn't see the light of day in the U.S. until 2003 on Dreyfus Jazz and in 1993 on the Blue Note album *Friends*, with a couple of guests, Hubert Laws on flute and Alison Deane on piano and harpsichord.

The former recording featured the tunes "Eight," "Song for You," "Little Waltz" (another Ron original) and two other tunes that are in today's songbook: the funk-tinged, upbeat "El Rompe Cabeza" (which, translated, means "the brainteaser") and a rendering of the hymn "Just a Closer Walk With Thee." The ensemble consisted of Boots on bass, Ron's current Quartet pianist Stephen Scott, drummer Lewis Nash, percussionist Steve Kroon and cellists Chase Morrison, Carol Buck, Rachel Steuermann and Kermit.

On *Friends*, the cello quartet included Kermit and Carol, plus Caryl Paisner and Marisol Espada. Stephan and Kenny Barron shared piano duties. In addition to two originals, Ron created an arrangement of John Lewis's "Django" as well as several arrangements of classical pieces composed by Sergei Rachmaninoff, Eric Satie, Frederic Chopin and Gabriel Fauré. In the opening to his liner notes, Kermit wrote, "This unique grouping gives Ron Carter the resources with which to mold infinitely variegated scores. The rhythmic and harmonically coloristic variety are the fortuitous results of this formulation."

NONET AT BIRDLAND

"WE'VE CHANGED PERSONNEL in the cello section a lot since we first started," Kermit said. "But we love playing for Ron. He has a great knowledge of classical music and he knows about composition. He's the epitome of serious scholarship. That's why he always has good musicians around him. All the cellists that have played with him appreciate that." Kermit added that Ron's intimate knowledge of the cello is key. "Ron writes uniquely for the cello."

Dorothy Lawson, a member of the hip, eclectic New York string quartet ETHEL, said after one Nonet performance in 2003 at Birdland that she was pleased with the performance. "It's such a great musical experience working with Ron," said Dorothy, who had been a member of the Nonet for five years at that time and is the first call for the band today. On that night she played with Kermit, Carol and Zoe Hassman. "This is an opportunity to sit in with one of the best. Ron has so much integrity. I love the fact that this band is so bass heavy. I love the introspection and the frenzy in the pieces. Musically, this is as satisfying as anything I do."

Dorothy also jokingly said that it was great being prominently placed at the front of the stage. "As cellists, we're usually just the girls in the back."

At that Birdland show, Ron was on the far left of the stage with his piccolo bass, positioned in front of the rhythm section and flanking the cellists who were seated behind their scores in the front row. He conducted the show, signaling on the first piece for the swing part to kick in after a string prelude. The cellists provided color and rhythm; the rhythm section drove the beat, especially on "El Rompe Cabeza." Throughout the evening, with Boots holding down the bottom beat, Ron was free to explore the sonic potential of his piccolo bass, taking lush pizzicato excursions, dialoguing with the bass and bowing up a gritty storm with a rock sensibility. The beauty of the evening was a lush rendering of "Song for You." At the close of the set, Ron beamed.

After that weeklong outing, he explained that little was left to happenstance. "With the Nonet, there's so much going on and I'm responsible for so much more than a quartet. These are all my arrangements. I write them at home, I copy the score for each member, and we actually rehearse. By the second or third night of a gig, the cellists understand that I mean those notes and we start to come together. Basically, I'm responsible for everything they play. It's great having eight people on stage with you. There are more voices, more conversations, more strange things happening."

While there is ample space within the music for improvisation by the rest of the band (the cellists play from the charts), Ron noted that he has built in a sense of routine that he doesn't apply to his smaller groups. The Nonet, he said, requires a different mind-set. For example, he learned by experience to keep the set lists the same each night. "When I first started working with the Nonet, I'd notice that we'd have off nights. It took me awhile to understand you can't change the program and have the cellists feel all right about that. They're used to playing chamber music. They performed much better when they knew the routine. They jumped right into the music then."

Still, Ron admitted that he likes to throw curves. "Everyone in the group has to look to me for the cues," he said. "I may cut choruses in half or extend parts. I keep the players flexible so they can adapt to sudden changes within the score. They get used to the surprises. The more they do this the more the music takes on a different kind of bounce."

Ron talks with the band before each set about what worked the previous night as well as what needs to be done better. "So it's a testament—not just to their career growth but also to their experience in approaching music— of their determination to give this music the sound that's required," he said. "While early in the week, there may be problems, I expect by the last night of the week that everyone is in the zone of the music, with its different rhythms, the cues coming in different places, the arrangements changing every night."

Ron likened the cello choir to a horn section and referenced back to his gigs playing in the Thad Jones–Mel Lewis Orchestra that reigned at the Village Vanguard in the '60s and '70s. "I enjoyed playing in that group," Ron said. "Despite the charts being written in the same physical way, the cues would come in different places and there would be different soloists each night—one night it was the trumpet, the next sax, or maybe even no solos. I loved watching that band flower under Thad's direction. If I could be accused of stealing, it would be from that band." He paused, and added, "I just wish I could have stolen more."

Another wish? That he could be in a better position to hear the band the way the audience hears it. "Unfortunately, I'm a part of the sound, " Ron said. "I'd love to be in a place where I could hear what's taking place as a result of the entire band's labor."

THE NONET AT MERKIN

A WEEK LONG STINT at a club like Birdland is the best-case scenario for the Nonet because of the group's comfort level with the music. But the ensemble also plays one-off dates, which pose a different set of issues. Case in point: the Nonet's performance at Kaufman Center's Merkin Concert Hall in New York on May 7, 2007. The afternoon before the evening show Ron gathered his group—his quintet and cellist choir comprising Kermit, Carol, Zoe and Maxine Neuman subbing for Dorothy—at the hall for a last-minute rehearsal. This proved to be both pleasing as a meeting to get reacquainted with the music as well as stressful when the arrangements weren't working.

At times, the cellists had their pencils out, writing in new notes and pause points. Casually dressed in jeans and wearing a baseball hat, Ron at one point impatiently barked at the group like a surly taskmaster when a run-through of a section was stopped several times because of missed cues or chart adjustments. He emphatically admonished, "Come on everybody, we've got to get this right." Ron was visibly upset. He growled. The hall felt tense. However, by the close of the rehearsal when the group played a spot-on take of "El Rompe Cabeza," Ron smiled, picked up the sheet music and like a matador held it in front of him as if a charging bull were bearing down on him in attack mode. He whisked the sheet away up in the air, successfully dodging the rushing enemy, and then instructed everyone to show up no later than 7:30 p.m.

Problems encountered; hopefully, problems solved.

That evening's show—a one-night deal that required getting the music "right"—proved to be a success. If there were any flubs, they went unnoticed by the audience. Unlike the afternoon rehearsal where Ron was uptight at times and exacting in his surgical fixes to repair broken parts, at Merkin he looked relaxed—not harried, not angry—and appreciative of how the group was finding all the right notes, negotiating all the right turns, filling the hall with a lyrical and mysterious sonority. Sitting on a tall stool and tapping his left foot to the rhythms, Ron, in a stylish gray tuxedo with a white collared dress shirt, led the swing, the glee, the romanticism. He played glissandos, hammer-ons and even played arco on the piccolo bass, a rarity.

At one point as the evening was winding down, Ron introduced the band and proudly told the audience, "I'm hoping that you can see what is a bass player's dream." After an impeccable sway through "All Blues," the show ended with a moving, reverential rendition of the hymn "Just a Closer Walk With Thee," with Boots leading off with a solo, the rhythm section tapping out a march-like beat and the cellists playing the melody. Ron sat it out, taking in the performance as a treat.

NONET AT BIRDLAND, PART 2

AT HIS WEEKLONG Birdland Nonet date in 2008, Ron launched into the first set with the Spanish-tinged and at times avant-gardish "Abide With Me" that segued into a brio take of "El Rompe Cabeza." Next up was the funky "Good Lookin' Out," where Boots and Ron played off each other, trading lines, cracking jokes, making musical allusions that elicited laughter from the audience. "Song for You" made for a lyrical pause and like most Nonet shows proved to be a low-tone highlight. Before finishing the set with the swinging "Eight" and "Just a Closer Walk With Thee," Ron played a solo interpretation of "Willow Weep for Me," which was not on the set list. It was piccolo bass limelight time as Ron strummed the instrument like a down-home country blues guitar in the prelude, then played with a series of surprising leaps and bounds.

Unpredictable was the operative word. Ron said later, "The adventure is what it's all about. You've got to take a risk. Music is all about taking chances."

As for launching a solo while the rest of the band watched, Ron said that during each set he tries to gauge the stress level of the cellists in the frontline. "They're not used to being in the spotlight and feeling this kind of scrutiny," he explained. "They've got drums and percussion playing behind them, and they're not used to playing in a jazz club environment. When I feel they need a break from that ominous pressure, I pause and take it alone to give them a chance to exhale and not worry about the downbeat."

Regarding Boots, who also played cello when he was coming up, Ron said that he can't think of another bass player that he'd rather play duets with. Firstly, since they have played together for so long, they've learned how to stay out of each other's way when playing. "You develop that sense," said Ron. "The sensitivity level gets built up so that it becomes easy to step out of the way of each other. Boots is experienced and sensitive enough that, if we do face the problem of crossing into each other's range, he can make the adjustment."

Ron said that Boots has great phrasing. "I like to step back, then play another phrase or develop what he played," he added. "He hears me play a phrase, then he may add in a different note. That's what's so important in this music: to take it somewhere else."

Boots, who can't recall exactly how he picked up his nickname (he figures it was either from "Yakety Sax" saxophonist Boots Randolph or Boston saxophonist/educator Henry "Boots" Mussulli), said that he came up playing bass in bands that included cellists, so he knew the parameters of range required. "So I knew where to play so I wouldn't cover up the cellos and sometimes where I would need to phrase with the cellos. I always need to listen to Kermit as the leader of the cellists. Then with Ron, I pick notes so as to not conflict with him too. It's a matter of range, register, volume. Sometimes I'm really good at it. Some days I'm not as successful."

The most musically rewarding part of Boots's Nonet playing is when he and Ron play duets. "It's fun and a challenge," he said. "Ron pushes me a little, and though we haven't talked about it, I think I may push him a little too. I play something. Ron picks up on it. You want it to be a conversation, not a mimicking back and forth. I don't really think too much about it when we do it. It just happens."

It's obvious onstage and off how much Ron respects Boots. He appreciates how Boots will be honest in his assessment of what's working or not working with the Nonet. "Sometimes Boots will say to me, 'Do you really feel this note should go here?'" said Ron. "He's trying to figure out the best way to get something right, whether it's at the next rehearsal or in the next tune or in the next chorus. I know I don't have all the answers, so I like how Boots feels so comfortable making suggestions. He's not intimidated by me."

Boots has become so essential to the Nonet, Ron said, that if he's unavailable he doesn't accept a gig for the group. "It's just too much work, and it's not fun. Boots brings so much to the table. He's played with other bass players in sections on Broadway and in chamber groups. Most jazz bass players haven't and therefore aren't attuned to the subtleties of pitch when playing in unison or octaves. In the past when Boots was sick or unavailable, I'd have guys come in and do the Nonet book and sometimes do it well, but never at Boots's level."

Catching the Nonet live is a rarity, even in New York—which brings up one of the main downsides of the ensemble: the lack of opportunity to hone the playing. Like jazz big bands and orchestras, the days of touring a band like the Nonet are largely over. "The cost to travel is prohibitive," Ron said. "There's no budget. Every time we play, the cellists are willing to stop their schedules to work on this music. They probably have four or five jobs every month, on Broadway or in an orchestra. So this is a commitment. In our short time together, we try to address the problems we face in this music—to try to solve these problems with a very short rehearsal or on a cramped bandstand. And on our best nights, we make it sound as if we've been together for more than 20 minutes."

Given the sublimity of performance each time the Nonet takes the stage, it's more like 20 years.

CHAPTER TWENTY-THREE

The Commingling of Jazz and Hip-Hop

THE MOST UNLIKELY recording experience of Ron's exhaustive session work came in 1991 when the pioneering rap group A Tribe Called Quest rang him up. The request? To deliver bass lines on the track "Verses From the Abstract" for its sophomore CD, *The Low End Theory*, the follow-up to its triumphant debut, *People's Instinctive Travels and the Paths of Rhythm*, issued in 1989 on Jive Records.

As it turned out, Ron not only helped to make *The Low End Theory* one of the best hip-hop—and pop—albums of all time, but he also contributed to the ushering in of an era in the early to mid-'90s where jazz and hip-hop, both rooted in the African-American music tradition, commingled in an intriguing and, at times, compelling fusion of rap and swing. A natural teacher in the classroom and on the bandstand, Ron also served to further school Q-Tip—Tribe's co-founder and MC, born Jonathan Davis, whose legal name now is Kamaal Fareed—in the rudiments of making music that expanded beyond beat basics into rhythmic sophistication.

As for Ron's willingness to appear on a hip-hop record at a time when the rap-infused music was entering its second decade of impact (and often controversy) as a pop genre, his son Ron Jr. is not at all surprised. "It's one of the biggest misconceptions about my father that he didn't know anything about hip-hop culture and music," he said. "How could he not? He had two teenaged sons who wanted to be DJs and were hanging out in Harlem in the '70s. He bought my brother Myles and me mixers so that we could learn."

Ron Jr. recalled four essential records that "every wannabe DJ" learned to mix on: "Dance to the Drummer's Beat," "Apache," "Scratchin'" and "Take Me to the Mardi Gras." The two Carter sons played those tunes over and over, so much so that Ron banned them from being spun in the home. "My dad told us to find some new records," Ron Jr. said. "He got tired of listening to those other ones. But he looked on hip-hop as an art form that was getting the young kids into music. He even went to all the top hip-hop clubs where we hung out in Harlem, like the Renaissance Ballroom, Autobahn and Disco Fever, to pick us up."

REQUEST FROM QUEST

STILL, RON WASN'T a hip-hop aficionado by any stretch of the imagination, so that when Tribe Called Quest's management contacted him, he had to do some homework. Who better to ask than Myles, who was living in Paris at the time as a graffiti artist and was steeped in the city's hip-hop culture—which included the French rap group NTM and the Control of Paris artistic movement that Myles co-founded.

"My dad called me up, told me about the request and asked me if he should do it," said Myles. "Well, I knew that Tribe Called Quest was strictly about the music. As it turns out, they were one of the most interesting and innovative hip-hop groups of all time. They had a noncommercial groove. My father has this incredible timing and cadence that can't be duplicated. His sound is so distinctive. So, what could be a better fit?"

In his book, *Check the Technique: Liner Notes for Hip-Hop Junkies*, Brian Coleman singles out *The Low End Theory* as one of the "36 immortal rap albums" and notes that A Tribe Called Quest "added a serious, studious, jazz edge to their supremely innovative productions." Coleman points out that the music of Tribe's first album was, in the words of Q-Tip, "emotions and colors." He then quotes Q-Tip on the second project as striving for a new level of sonic creativity: "I was chopping beats differently than other people were back then. The [second] album was like a project. A show. And everybody was invited to watch. The first album was about color, and *Low End Theory* was more about technique."

Q-Tip told Coleman that the album got its name, *The Low End Theory*, because he wanted to expand the dynamics by stressing the low end, the bottom. It was a no-brainer then for Tip to see if he could snag Ron for a session. As a kid, the rapper was surrounded by music, especially jazz. "My dad was a jazz enthusiast," he said. "He was a hard-bop guy, the grittier and funkier the better. He had albums by Lockjaw Davis, Art Blakey, Lee Morgan, Horace Silver, Jack McDuff. Plus, he had albums by Miles and Duke and Coltrane. My cousins and uncles were into jazz that was more expanded, like the Headhunters. They loved Miles's albums like *In a Silent Way* and *Filles de Kilimanjaro*."

Yet Q-Tip gravitated to Miles's '60s quintet with Ron. "I always come back to the Plugged Nickel stuff and albums like *E.S.P.* and *Nefertiti*. I still listen to them. I could hear Ron being the anchor of everything that was going on. Usually a drummer would keep the beat on the ride cymbal, but Tony moved around a lot and really had a lock-up with Herbie. You'd expect the lock-up between the bassist and drummer. So Ron had to do double duty, to be the percussive force as well as establish the root to develop the harmony.

"In my way of thinking Ron Carter was the seminal bass player of the '60s and '70s," Q-Tip said. "His sound was very precise, concise and rhythmic, and he played harmonically to lay the framework for songs. He's an icon."

With the Carter legacy deeply ingrained in his own musicality, Q-Tip asked the group's management to contact Ron. "It was an honor to get him on the record. I wanted his sound and his musicianship. He's so economical. He never overplays. He's probably the tastiest bass player ever. Some guys go overboard, but every note that Ron plays is there for a good reason."

While Q-Tip thought that his management team contacted Ron's management, Ron says that the request came directly to him. He discussed the offer with Myles, and then signed on to play on a track. "But first I told them that there were stipulations," Ron said. "Cursing wasn't so blatant as it is today, but I said I didn't want to have that on the tune. The trend toward harsh language was certainly going in that direction back then. To play on a tune like that would mean I endorsed it. The second thing I said was no drugs at the session. I never did drugs. If they were there, I'd go home. If not, then we'd get this done and have a great time doing it."

SIX DEGREES OF SEPARATION

Q-TIP RECALLS RON as being very cordial, even though he knew of Ron's reputation as a person who could be prickly. He didn't give Ron any instructions on how to play "Verses From the Abstract." Q-Tip said, "Ron came into the studio by himself, tuned his bass, settled in and got right down to business. He listened to the tune, wrote out some chord changes and then knocked it out. It wasn't complicated. We did a couple of passes, and I think we kept the first take. That was that. I remember it being really easy. He was maybe there for just a couple of hours."

Ron set up in the control room and plugged his pickup into the control board. Q-Tip was in the studio ready to rap the lyrics. "I asked him to rap it before we recorded so that I could hear the commas and the length of the sections," Ron said. "I didn't need to write anything down because I could hear the tune in my head. We did a few takes where I would move my commas around to match the phrasing. I wanted to make the song have some chord changes because what I was hearing was a monotone. I said to myself, geez, how can you listen to this all day without some kind of harmony? So I tried to sneak some chords in to see if that would work."

Ron wasn't sure that what he was proposing would fly. "All they would have had to do was say, 'Mr. Carter, that's not working,' and that would have been OK. I was in their employ. They trust what I do. They can't be afraid to tell me it's not working. That way I can do it differently and make the tune better for them. That's my job." There were no complaints, so Ron left them with one instruction. He laughed when recalling it: "I told them, whatever you do, just make sure the bass sounds good."

Even though Q-Tip recalls that there wasn't a whole lot of interaction, he does remember talking with Ron while he was setting up his bass. "I told Ron that I wanted to play the bass, and he said, play the piano first. That's where everything will begin for you. If you know the piano first and foremost, then you'll be able to play the bass."

Ron remembers the exchange, saying that while he was impressed by how hip-hop artists were adept on the computer—cutting and pasting together music and words—they lacked the musicality to use different chords or use a different tonal center: "Instead of rapping in a drone without harmony or chord changes, they could elevate what they'd be singing by using another way of making lyrics that would be determined by the use of chords and harmony."

Ron added, "That's why I told Q-Tip to play the piano and spend time with someone like Sir Roland Hanna to see how chords and harmony work. I suggested he learn some simple chord changes like I, IV, V, I that would make the lyrics sound different, so the background would not just be boomp-boomp-shish, boomp-boomp-shish. It's a shame rap guys who were really interested in the music and not just the rap didn't learn the basic skills to fully bring what they were doing into fruition."

In the March 2008 issue of *Filter* magazine that celebrated Tribe's legacy, Ron was asked to weigh in on Q-Tip. "I used to say that if rappers ever discovered a major triad, I'd give them a dollar—and I still have the same one," he said. "Q-Tip was aware of the jazz community. I think he would've hired Mingus if he were alive because he was Q-Tip's favorite bass player. But I didn't mind coming second to Charlie. A Tribe Called Quest was on the right track for elevating the musicality of hip-hop."

Called by *All Music Guide* critic John Bush as "one of the closest and most brilliant fusions of jazz atmosphere and hip-hop attitude ever recorded," *The Low End Theory* ranks in the top 10 hip-hop albums of all time by Breakdown FM's highly respected hip-hip culture proponent Davey D and is heralded as "a hip-hop masterpiece" by the *New Rolling Stone Album Guide*. Featuring Ron on the deep-grooved acoustic bass tune, "Verses From the Abstract" is a funky, philosophical autobiography by Q-Tip (a.k.a. The Abstract) who celebrates heroes and colleagues. Rapping such lines as "rapping is my duty" and "I'm hooked on the swing," Q-Tip at the end acknowledges his special guest: "And this one goes out to my man, thanks a lot, Ron Carter on the bass, yes, my man Ron Carter is on the bass, check it out..."

"I was really honored that Ron appeared on the record," Q-Tip said. "People still talk about that song and his association with that record. It was a landmark event." He went on to say that many hip-hop aficionados became curious about jazz. "Countless people who never knew a thing about jazz or Ron started exploring, and that led to Herbie and Miles and other cats like Weather Report and Jaco and Stanley Clarke. It was six degrees of separation."

The CD went gold in 1992 and platinum in 1995.

Brian Coleman notes that in addition to having a strong impact on serious-minded listeners, *The Low End Theory* had a "huge impact on other producers in the way the groups used samples, chopped beats and Ron's instrumentation."

MC SOLAAR STYLING

As a hip-hop fan, Coleman paid attention to Ron's contributions. "I've always been a music nerd, so I looked up who Ron was," he said. "Most fans probably didn't dig that deeply, but this led me to Guru with his Jazzmatazz albums where he used jazz musicians." In Tribe's wake came Branford Marsalis's hip-hop-infused Buckshot LaFonque music and a few years later to the Philadelphia hip-hop group, the Roots, who hired jazz bagpipe player Rufus Harley to record with them. Plus, the jazz-rap connection led to the 1994 two-CD compilation album *Stolen Moments: Red Hot + Cool*, a 16-track hip-hop-meets-jazz CD on Impulse that raised funds to fight AIDS.

Again, Ron was part of the mix, this time collaborating with French hip-hop star MC Solaar (real name Claude M'Barali) on the tune "Un Ange en Danger/An Angel in Danger." Ron brought his harmonic and funky sensibilities to the session, with a great bass solo in the mix.

As he had previously with Tribe, Ron called Myles about participating on the track. "I suggested that he do it not so much because MC Solaar was a great rapper, but because of the goal of the CD, which was to fight AIDS," Myles said. "In France, we called what MC Solaar did nursery rhymes. It was commercially successful, but it wasn't artistically at the same level as the best rappers. It's kind of like comparing Vanilla Ice to the Notorious B.I.G. MC Solaar was kind of cute, but he wasn't in the trenches with us."

Reluctantly, Ron agreed to record the song with MC Solaar. "I didn't know this guy, and I couldn't speak French," he said. "So I said OK as long as I could bring Myles to the date and have him be paid as my translator. I wanted someone on my side for a change so the producer and the engineer wouldn't get too far afield. I told Myles that if there were anything being rapped or said in the studio that I didn't like we'd stop."

The tracking took an hour and a half. And for Ron, it was a fun experience that even turned into a video that was excerpted in Ken Burns's PBS documentary series, *JAZZ*. "I thought what we did was the best meeting of minds between jazz and hip-hop on the *Red Hot + Cool* album," Ron said. "Most of the other acts seemed to be about blending but also showing how individual they were. MC Solaar and I were concerned with how we could match each other's style rather than be independent of each other on the same stage."

Fifteen years after the two had last collaborated, Ron got the opportunity to perform with MC Solaar again in 2008 when a French concert promoter proposed a one-time jazz-hip-hop summit at Châtelet, a 1,100-seat venue in Paris. Also on the bill was trumpeter Roy Hargrove with his funk-infused RH Factor band.

(Years earlier, Roy had played with Ron in a house band assembled for a TV special. During the group's rehearsal, Roy got an upfront glimpse of Ron's measured authority. The trumpeter played a solo, after which the bassist took him aside. "Ron called me out on a note in bar 13 that didn't go with the chord the band was playing," Roy said. "That showed me how deep Ron is.")

Roy opened the sold-out Paris concert with RH Factor, after which he dueted with Ron on "Every Time We Say Goodbye," which the Parisian newspaper *Le Monde* called the concert highlight. The writer then said, "Another great moment: the appearance of MC Solaar, although Ron Carter and his long fingers' supple accuracy sometimes gave the rapper a hard time…" The show ended with a semi-jam session that featured all three headliners.

LITIGATION RAP

TRIBE AND MC Solaar's work with Ron presaged the maturity of rap's fascination with jazz. In the early '90s, hip-hop artists were figuring out that it was cheaper to hire live instrumentalists in lieu of sampling recordings. Why? Primarily because there had been many litigation proceedings initiated by jazz artists who fought to get monetary compensation when their licks were sampled and showed up as major parts of a hip-hop recording. Myles was a source that enabled Ron to know when his bass lines were being ripped off.

"The morsels of excellence from my dad showed that the rappers had good taste," Myles said. "But they don't give thanks for Ron Carter, and that's not right. I'm not mad at them, but on the underside is the fact that some of these rap records sell millions and jazz musicians don't even come close to that."

Myles says that he can identify his dad's bass playing immediately. "I can't explain how I do it," he said, "but it's the way he puts notes down. It's the amount of pressure he applies when he plucks or when he caresses. It can't be duplicated. He has such a distinct sound. Like rap, it's his timing and cadence. Rappers can be pretty clever with their samples, but all it takes is one note of resonance for me to identify something that's my dad's. I tell him when I hear his samples, and then he follows up with his lawyer, I assume. I heard six or seven records with my dad's bass lines sampled."

One such sample was Dr. Dre's hit tune, "A Nigga Witta Gun," from his classic 1992 gangsta rap album *The Chronic*, where the rapper used Ron's bass line that opens organist Johnny Hammond's song "Big Sur Suite" from his 1974 Kudu/CTI album *Higher Ground* that Bob James arranged.

"Myles heard it on the radio and told me Dr. Dre was an up guy," Ron said. "So I bought the album and found the track where he sampled my eight-bar bass line that he used over and over as the backbone of the tune."

Hammond's tune was owned by Creed Taylor's publishing company that subsequently contacted Dre, his publisher and lawyer. They negotiated an agreement. "The album sold about 3 million copies, and I believe our share was in the neighborhood of $70,000," said Alan Bergman, Ron's lawyer. Ron and Johnny split the proceeds.

"It was Johnny's song and my bass line, so the bulk of the royalties went to him," Ron said. "Johnny was in poor health at the time, so it came in handy. While what I received wasn't huge, the settlement served as an announcement to the rappers."

Even so, Ron wishes that he could have interfaced with Dre and his fellow hip-hop musicians. "Of all the music available in the world, how did this track get their attention?" Ron asked. "Plus, if they had called me, I believe I could have found something better for them to use."

As for Ron's legacy to the hip-hop world, the final chapter is yet to be written.

Now primarily a solo artist, even though A Tribe Called Quest has staged reunions, Q-Tip told New York's *Metro* free daily (the October 5–7, 2007 edition), "I exist in the tradition of Stevie Wonder, Duke Ellington, the Beatles, John Coltrane. I'm in a very elite group."

When I talked to Q-Tip, he said that he heeded Ron's advice about learning piano before delving into the bass. He had already started to "noodle" on the keys.

I asked him, do you still have aspirations to play bass?

"Yes, I do," Q-Tip replied.

Do you have a bass?

"I do, an upright and an electric. I have a piano that I've been shedding on for a couple of years, so I get lost in that. So, I'm definitely ready to move on to the bass soon."

When I told him that Ron gives lessons in his house, his ears perked up. I passed on Ron's information to Q-Tip, and the two have been in touch.

COLLOQUY

The *DownBeat* Blindfold Test Live

"It's nice to see you all here," Ron said, as he spoke to a packed hall of some 400 people at the International Association for Jazz Educators in New York in January 2007. The occasion? A live Blindfold Test, sponsored by *DownBeat* magazine that I moderated. "When I read the Blindfold Test in *DownBeat*," Ron continued, "I figure that it takes place in a small room with two chairs, no windows, maybe four or five people, a sound engineer, a speaker that's about so big. I'm happy to see that I was wrong. So, I will treat you today like you're sitting in my living room."

For the next hour, Ron, in essence blindfolded from knowing who the performing artists were, listened carefully to six selections of music—ranging from classic recordings by bass legends Oscar Pettiford and Scott LaFaro to upstart tunes, including a live track from an experimental Christian McBride musical adventure—and thoughtfully reflected on what he was hearing as well as wagering guesses as to the identities of the musicians. He was brutally honest in his assessments, which at one point prompted me to ask him: "Ron, aren't you afraid of hurting someone's feelings?"

Dressed impeccably in a suit and a fancy tie, Ron seemed surprised by the question. "Don't get me wrong. There's something pleasant about all of these tracks because these people are trying to make music," he said. "Anyone in this day and age trying to make a record gets four stars from me just for trying. When you get to my age category, you no longer have that fear of hurting somebody. When you've been listening to music for a very long time as I have, you can make an honest commentary on this music that may be instructive to these people who you are commenting on." He paused and then added, "I didn't just start listening to music in 1995. My history is broad and starts way before 1963."

After a series of tracks that Ron found fault with, I remarked, "I can't seem to play anything you like," to which he responded, "Wait a minute. My job is to be honest, and so far I've been doing that. It's not what I don't like. I appreciate it all. And I'm not assuming a whole CD would sound like the track you played. I'm not only speaking as a player, but also as an analyst, an experienced performer and an old hand at making records."

As a point of historical reference, the Blindfold Test originated in the late 1940s when jazz critic Leonard Feather came up with the idea of interviewing artists about what they most loved to talk about: the music itself. Rather than firing a series a questions at an interview subject, he figured he'd get more insightful responses by playing a recording and asking for a subjective assessment. Feather introduced the concept of blindfolding in *Metronome* magazine, then soon after brought the feature to *DownBeat*, which as jazz critic Gary Giddins noted, "copyrighted it—a sore point for [Leonard]." After parting paths with *DownBeat* several years later, Feather took the concept to *JazzTimes* magazine and renamed it Before/After.

"The significance of the Blindfold Test greatly exceeds its entertainment value," Giddins wrote in an appreciation of Feather's life when he passed away in 1994. "It added a phrase to the language and a new dimension to the issue of critical authority, demonstrating that people often judged a work of art differently when they didn't know who signed it." He pointed out that Feather "embarrassed scores of musicians who thought that race and gender were audible, or that studio men can't improvise, or that big names are invariably identifiable."

Inevitably musician prejudices surface, and in the best cases where bravery of frank opinion trumps static favoritism, candid responses are elicited. Case in point: a Blindfold Test with Miles Davis that Feather administered in 1958. He played the track "The Way You Look Tonight" by Sonny Rollins in the company of Thelonious Monk. Miles's response: "I know that's Sonny Rollins, but I don't see how a record company can record something like that. You know the way Monk plays—he never gives any support to a rhythm section.... I like to hear him play, but I can't stand him in a rhythm section unless it's one of his songs."

Monk himself was in the spotlight of one of the more famous Blindfold Tests where Feather started the 1966 session by playing Andrew Hill's "Flight 19" from his *Point of Departure* album. As Feather noted: "After about two minutes, Monk rises from his seat, starts wandering around the room and looking out the window. When it becomes clear he is not listening, the record is taken off."

Monk then said, "The view here is great, and you have a crazy stereo system."

Feather replied, "Is that all you have to say about that record?"

Monk: "About *any* record," which prompted Feather to "find a few things you'll want to say something about." By default, Feather played Monk several of his own compositions as rendered by other musicians to get the Blindfold ball rolling.

I've been doing live Blindfold Tests since I developed the idea at the Monterey Jazz Festival in 1995. I continue to stage one there, as well as at the North Sea Festival. Before the organization folded, I also used to do live tests at IAJE.

Perhaps my most outrageous IAJE test involved Freddie Hubbard at its 2002 conference in Long Beach, California. My goal is to program the test by offering a variety of music—some the blindfoldee may know, others that will undoubtedly be unfamiliar so as to hopefully generate intriguing conversations about the music. I played Freddie tracks from Sonny Rollins and Booker Little, which he adored. But I also played him young trumpeter Russell Gunn's funky and electronic take on Monk's "Epistrophy" (from *Ethnomusicology, Vol. 2)*, and Lester Bowie Brass Fantasy's "In the Still of the Night" (from *The Odyssey of Funk & Popular Music*).

At the beginning of the Gunn track, Freddie, much to the crowd's delight, made funny faces at the clanging electric guitar rhythm, laughed at the funky bass lines, exaggeratedly opened his eyes wide at the sound of the turntablist, then opened his eyes even wider when Gunn began to play the theme. Then, with his countenance having morphed from glee to anger, Freddie barked, "I don't wanna hear this. Turn it off. Really, I don't wanna hear anymore. And I don't want them," pointing to the audience, "to hear this. If I don't like it, I don't have to hear it, at least not today."

Then he continued his tirade: "See how these record company people come up with some bullshit like this. This sounds like the theme from *Peter Gunn*. It's coming up with this hipness that has nothing to do with Monk's melody. When this kind of shit gets put out there, it makes me mad. It's like not appreciating what Monk did when he wrote this. Putting some funky beat and funny stuff on it, well, this destroys the music. We gotta stop doing that."

Freddie commanded that the track by Bowie also be halted after about a minute and a half. He frowned and said, "Do I have to listen to this? That's it. Take it off. This music sounds like church music to me, like the Salvation Army thing. The Salvation Army band would play something like this, pray, then go out of the church and go back to their KKK meetings. It didn't feel right, like the motive wasn't right in doing this tune. It's like the difference between listening to Barry Manilow or Billy Eckstine. I wouldn't want to be playing music like Barry Manilow."

When told it was Lester Bowie, Freddie calmed down a bit. "I knew Lester. He liked poking fun," he said. "But you've got to be careful with that shit. I love Bowie, but I don't like hearing him play that."

For Ron's IAJE 2007 Blindfold Test, I compiled a set list of several tunes to play him. Tracks that didn't make the cut because of the time factor included The Bad Plus "Smells Like Teen Spirit" remake of the Nirvana pop hit, an Omer Avital solo piece "Bass Introduction," Milt Hinton's "Jon John," Stanley Clarke's take on "Salt Peanuts," Jaco Pastorius' "Donna Lee," Ornette Coleman's "Jordan" and Charlie Haden's Quartet West version of "Alone Together." I also considered a McCoy Tyner tune with bassist Henry Grimes and a Percy Heath number. But time allowed only six songs to be spun. The following is the full transcription of the session that was published in the May 2007 issue of *DownBeat* in truncated (read: edited) form.

OSCAR PETTIFORD

"Why Not? That's What" (from *Montmartre Blues*, Black Lion, via Napster, rec'd 1959) Pettiford, bass; Allan Botschinsky, trumpet; Erik Nordstrom, tenor saxophone; Jan Johansson, piano; Jorn Elniff, drums; Louis Hjulmand, vibes

Oscar Pettiford is my first guess. He was a fabulous player. What I'd like the audience to pay attention to is how in this session the bass is more present and a little louder than it normally is. There's not much bass drum on this record and the piano is mixed far in the back, so that Oscar Pettiford sounds so present—all that with him playing without an amplifier.

Oscar Pettiford is one of my all-time favorites. I wished more bass players would go back and listen to his music. His pitch is perfect, his intonation is always right on. His selection of notes is always excellent. He wasn't just looking for something to do, and he knew the chords. And his sound is more personal than most of the bassists of his era.

At that time, I was listening more to Cecil Payne and J.J. Johnson than other bassists for influences. They were my first two musical heroes. I played with Randy Weston's band and Cecil was playing with him. At the time, there were five major baritone saxophone players: Cecil, Gerry Mulligan, Serge Chaloff, Harry Carney and Leo Parker. They each had their individual style. I figured it was certainly possible for bass players to do the same, to sound more personal.

As for J.J., the first time I saw him live I noticed how he found all the notes so close to the bell. He didn't have to go further. I studied trombone in college for my degree, and so I was amazed at how J.J. found all those arrangements of notes by not going a long way from the bell. I thought, if that's possible on the trombone, it must be possible for the bass—to play across the bass rather than up and down [the neck] to find the same group of notes.

DAVE HOLLAND QUINTET

"The Eyes Have It" (from *Critical Mass*, Dare2, 2006) Holland, bass; Chris Potter, tenor saxophone; Robin Eubanks, trombone; Steve Nelson, vibes; Nate Smith, drums

I'm still pretending that you're here in my living room, so what I'm saying is living-room commentary. To that end, I hope the musicians on these tracks don't come to my address or send me terrible e-mails. That said, this is the kind of song that as a bass player, I hated to play. And I'll tell you why. You're working backwards. The only person who is playing this song's form while the saxophonist is soloing is the bass player. The bass has to stick in a 7/4, 9/4 kind of rhythm. The drummer is free to play whatever he wants and occasionally hits the downbeat and the trombonist plays at will. But all that works if the bass player only plays this line. I was into this mind-set for a very long time—feeling solely responsible for manning the rhythmic integrity of a piece.

On this tune the intro sounded so complicated. Close your eyes and you're lost. I admire people who have the ability to write like that, but there's not a musical connection for me to have any fun playing like that.

(*After several audience members guess Dave Holland*) Well, I feel the same way. Again, I don't like those kinds of tunes. I resented playing them back then, and as I get older, I resent them even more.

CHRISTIAN MCBRIDE

"Mwandishi Outcome Jam" (from *Live at Tonic*, Ropeadope, 2006) McBride, bass; Geoffrey Keezer, keyboards; Ron Blake, saxophones; Terreon Gully, drums; various others

I've always admired musicians who came from the avant-garde school—people like Albert and Donald Ayler, Fred Hopkins, the AACM. I admired bassists who found sounds that had never occurred to me in that environment. Those players made it a point to play music as far removed from their training as possible, so it seemed to me. I enjoyed how the bassists played things that I found interesting.

But there's the other side of the picture. When free players go into the more mainstream music, for lack of a better word, and play changes and chords, it's obvious that the lack of preparation is laid out pretty plain. So you see this kind of music where the bass part says "play it freely," and so the bass player plays three bars of 4/4 and one bar of 3/4. When everyone comes in, there's this expectation that there will be swing—wanting to play the time so that everybody sounds good but without the harmonic base to make it work. So even though playing free means there are no restrictions, it's actually quite limited.

This is all to say that this track points out the limitations in playing this way. When the bass player is fighting to find the common tonality of the horn players, the time gets slower. There's nothing worse than hearing a band slow down. I like listening to this, but I'd like to sit down with the band, play the track and discuss what adjustments would make it work—solving the problem of having no tone center, while expecting to play free.

Do I like it? Would I play this in my living room? If I moved, yes.

But I'd listen to this because it's a lesson to me as to how other people see music. That's still important to me even if I don't play or endorse it. It's important to me to understand other points of view of how people are making music. So, this track might not be in my living room, but close by, maybe in the vestibule or near the kitchen.

(*After the audience guesses Christian McBride*) Again, I'm being honest in my comments. I pride myself in that, while I'm aware of the consequences. Christian has been a friend for a very long time. I would hope he'd go back and listen to this track to find out what I'm talking about.

BILL EVANS TRIO

"Gloria's Step (live, take 2)" (from *Sunday at the Village Vanguard*, OJC, via Napster, rec'd 1961) Evans, piano; Scott LaFaro, bass; Paul Motian, drums

One of the things I look for when I listen to music is what form is being played. Is it AABA, ABC... what is the structure of the song? When I hear this style where no one is committing himself to playing the downbeats or posts that mark the form of the tune, it's hard for me to enjoy the music because I can't tell the beginning from the end. When the bass player is playing this style of bass line with a nonquarter note to the bar kind of timing, he ends up playing notes that I'm not sure I could endorse. I don't know who this is, but they're clearly influenced by the Bill Evans Trio, with Scotty and Paul. I think that if it's not those three guys, then whoever it is didn't learn enough from them and the shortfalls of playing in that style.

I would hope people would pick up on the shortfalls and not add these problems to their style. It's like taking a pair of trousers to the tailor to make a copy. But there's a snag in the pants, so the tailor makes a copy, including the tear. It seems to me that if players adopt this style, they need to understand the things that don't work. Again, I'm interested in listening to this kind of music, to try to figure out why I'm not hearing the form and why I'm not hearing someone take responsibility for maintaining some kind of order. I'll listen to a piece like this several times, wondering where are the bars, where's the bridge. But this kind of tune doesn't allow for that because it's a matter of very comfortable random playing.

It sounds like the Bill Evans Trio because the bassist and drummer aren't playing a specific beat all the time, and the pianist is playing a nonspecific meter. It makes the music more free, but there's no one responsible for playing the beat in every bar. When you have this kind of rhythmic concept, it's hard to listen to all night. I want to hear a song where everyone is committed to saying, "There's going to be a bridge right here" or "This is a C7 chord right here." I don't hear that kind of musical commitment here.

(*After hearing that the tune is Evans*) Well, that's what I mean. One of the things that made this group different was the way Scotty played the bass lines. Ahmad Jamal was doing something like that years earlier, so it wasn't as new as we thought. But I heard Scotty at the Village Vanguard at his last gig. It was quite a night. We all knew there was something different going on, but we weren't quite sure what it was. In New York then, you could hear something new and you weren't sure how long it would last—two choruses or two months. Fortunately for our music, what Scotty was doing is still part of the jazz language.

DIEDRE MURRAY/FRED HOPKINS

"Doo Wop" (from *Stringology*, Black Saint, 1994) Murray, cello; Hopkins, bass; Marvin Sewell, guitar; Newman Baker, drums

One of my concerns with this piece is that no one seems to know what's happening. First, no one seems to know whether there's a bass solo, and secondly, when does it stop? Third, there's no sense of when the cello player is going to play, and fourth, what chords are going to be played and what kind of an arrangement do we have here? It sounds to me like these musicians went into a studio and the producer was so afraid—and I use that term advisedly—to not step on the musicians' creativity. That no matter how awful it sounds, he won't tell them; or that no matter how long the song is, he won't say enough; or that no matter how many takes on the same song get tried, he won't say, "Are you guys kidding?"

So, for fear of stomping on creativity, there are no restrictions. Those things always sound like this. The producer should have said, "Wait a minute, before you play, you need to have this, and here's how you get this, and we need to get this. And if you can't do all three, then, see ya, goodbye." Unfortunately, these players needed some structure. I also didn't understand why the guitar player was used so sparingly here because he could have had an input to the overall picture. It seems to me that the producer was reluctant to make these kinds of commitments.

(*After being told who the players are*) If you go back far enough, before 1960, I think records by people like Don Ellis, Jaki Byard, Beaver Harris and Dave Burrell all have things that are similar to this track. There needs to be a system of organization. This music lacks focus in approach.

DUKE ELLINGTON

"Money Jungle" (from *Money Jungle*, Blue Note, rec'd 1962/2002) Ellington, piano; Charles Mingus, bass; Max Roach, drums

I've heard this record before. It's Duke, Charlie and Max. On this recording, I'm wondering if there was any overdubbing because there's a very discordant sound on Charlie's bass, which is unusual because he always played a good fiddle. But overall, I would call this particular track Charlie Mingus at his contrary best.

One of the first jobs I had in New York was at the place called The Playhouse, on West 4th and 6th Avenue, that's no longer there. Charlie had a band with Doug Watkins, Eric Dolphy and Dannie Richmond. One afternoon Doug wasn't available, so Eric, who I knew from our playing together with Chico Hamilton, recommended that Charlie call me to do the matinee. I played bass and Charlie played piano. When I wasn't playing bass, I listened to him. It was like going to school for free.

But for all of Charlie's greatness, to me he tended to be too contrary sometimes and determined to not make the band sound good. It was almost like he was sabotaging his band to sound awful. I never knew him well enough to ask him about that. When I played Bradley's, he'd come by. He'd get a small booth in the corner, order dinner, listen for a couple of sets, then leave and go home. From that encounter, I felt like he felt that I was on the right track. I think he appreciated me trying to get it right.

When I hear Duke, I'm reminded a lot of Randy Weston. Another one of my first gigs was with Randy and we played in a high school gym in Brooklyn with Freddie Hubbard, Candido on congas and Max Roach on the drums. I treasured those days playing with Max in his prime. It was nice to be thrown into that cauldron of activity and watch how these fabulous musicians played form and changes as well as had their own individual sound based on the history of their instruments.

The next week Ron reflected on his experience being blindfolded, especially in front of an audience. Again, he said that his opinions were based on his many years of listening and playing. "You have to understand that my comments are a little different than what a critic would say in the newspaper. Most of them are half my age and some of their critiques—the most notoriously famous ones—are based on using the kind of vocabulary to express views that hide what they really mean. The critic becomes the focus rather than the CD or the performance."

What Ron wanted to point out to the audience at the BFT session was how the presence of the bass in the recorded music played was "far from the norm and really far from the norm when you hear it live." A stickler for making sure the bass is integral to the sound mix, Ron said that most recordings have the instrument out of sonic proportion to what the rest of the members of a band are playing. "I was listening to a record the other day on the radio in my car," he said. "I've got a decent system in my car. And I was disappointed in hearing the mix where it was almost as if there was no bass on the tune. Only various bass notes would poke out.

But I'm sure that whatever the bassist was playing—the notes he was choosing—were essential to the arrangement. Listening to this on my car stereo was embarrassing for me as a bass player."

Speaking of embarrassment, one of the leaders of a tune played for Ron's assessment at the BFT—Christian McBride—was actually in the audience. "Someone told me later that one of the people I had commented on was there," Ron said. "I certainly hope that I didn't offend him. I just thought it wasn't a good record, and I know this bass player can play much better than that, and I was disappointed—although I understand the need to get 'product' out to the street because without it you can't really work and you can't get better gigs. I guess the urgency to maintain that level of public visibility vis-a-vis gigs overrode the quality of the product. Even so, the sound of the recording wasn't very professional either."

Ron said that he hadn't seen or talked to Christian since the BFT session, but hoped that he didn't feel bad. "Of course, I'd be interested to see him and ask him how he felt about my commentary," he said.

As for Christian, he's had his own share of encounters with Ron over the years—some of them good, some of them unpleasant (see the Christian McBride snapshot). Even so, he crowns Ron the undisputed bass living legend on the planet, given the deaths of Ray Brown and Percy Heath. Like Ron, an active proponent of jazz education, Christian attended the IAJE event and was finished with his activities by noon on Saturday. He wanted to attend the Blindfold Test, which started at three p.m., but because of the conference frenzy, he and his wife Melissa decided to leave early and go home.

"You know how nuts everything can get at IAJE," said Christian. "The more people we talked to slowed us down, and the next thing you know it was three, so I said, 'Let's go see Ron get blindfolded.' Melissa asked me if something of mine would be played, and I replied, 'Yeah, I just feel it.'"

They stood in the back of the hall to be inconspicuous, but in the five minutes before the session started were surrounded by friends and fans. They slipped into the back row. "So, I'm sitting there trying to cover my face," Christian said. "Of course, the guy who comes over to sit next to me is David Wong, a young bass player who studies with Ron. He said hi and I'm thinking, 'Oh, shit.'"

The next thing Christian knew several other friends were in the same row at the moment that Ron made his entrance into the hall. They told Christian not to hang his head. Melissa asked him if he were going to go up to Ron and say hi. "If Ron doesn't know I'm here, that's great," Christian told her. "If he knows I'm here, I don't want him to compromise his thoughts."

"Do you really think he'd do that?" asked Melissa.

"I don't know," replied Christian. "But I'd rather him not know I'm here. So, Ron walked on the stage, and I laid back."

After the Pettiford tune was played, next came the Dave Holland tune, which, Christian said, "Ron shot down relatively quickly."

"Sweetheart, if Ron didn't like Dave Holland," said Melissa while laughing, "I sure hope they don't play something from *Live at Tonic*."

Indeed, the next spin was "Mwandishi Outcome Jam," at which time, Christian recalled, "the last ten rows turned around and looked at me. I kept telling them to turn back around. Melissa was laughing her ass off."

Ron weighed in; Christian breathed out. Later he said, "I go on the record as saying that I absolutely love what he said. Just the fact that Ron was analyzing something that had me on it was a thrill. Hearing him break down the music, whether he liked it or not, was a big thrill. After it was over, I was totally not affected. All I could think of was how cool it was."

Melissa told him, "I don't think Ron liked it."

Christian replied, "I don't think he didn't like it. He was commenting on my playing that was pretty abstract in the middle of the piece. Had he heard the piece in its entirety, he might have said something else, so that's fair."

Later that week Christian received an e-mail from his former manager Mary Ann Topper, who sat a couple of rows in front of him at the BFT. There were two parts to the missive. First she asked Christian if he would be able to play at a gig with vocalist Kurt Elling, who she was managing. Then she wrote that she thought it would be a good idea for him to call Ron.

"Mary Ann wasn't sure that Ron knew I was there," Christian said. "She said that Ron was a little worried that I would be offended by what he said about my record."

"Why would you think I'd be offended?" wrote Christian, who said that Mary Ann nevertheless felt it would best if he called Ron anyway.

Admitting that his next action was "completely mean," Christian wrote back, "Ron would be worried that I'd be upset? Good. I'll let this sit for awhile before I call him."

At last word, Christian had yet to open the communication line, but, he said, "I have every intention of doing so."

Attending the event was *DownBeat* editor Jason Koransky, who said that this live Blindfold Test was "particularly spotless...as Ron, right off the bat, made the audience feel at home by saying that he welcomed them into his living room. He was candid and made astute observations. Some people in this setting have reservations about telling the truth, but Ron certainly didn't. And he criticized without insulting anyone. It was matter of fact. He said here's why I didn't like this—even in his response to Dave Holland's band, which is one of the most rhythmically innovative ensembles out there today. But Ron articulated, this isn't for me."

Jason also noted that if some people might interpret his comments as offensive, they'd be missing the point of the critique, that this kind of honest musical criticism is what's needed in jazz. "There's a lot of music that's not hunky-dory good, which needs to be said," he said. "So what Ron offered is truly invaluable."

Overall, Jason observed that the Blindfold Test opened a window onto Ron's character: "This showed an amazing glimpse into his persona, speaking his mind in the same way that translates into his playing."

PART VI
THE ART AND SCIENCE OF THE BASS

CHAPTER TWENTY-FOUR

The Instrument: The Art and Science of the Bass

BACKSTAGE ON A hot Saturday afternoon at the Playboy Jazz Festival at the Hollywood Bowl in June 2006, Bill Cosby, wearing a T-shirt emblazoned with the pro-Native American slogan: Homeland Security—Fighting Terrorism Since 1492, joked about his little comedic routine while Ron, Russell Malone and Mulgrew Miller were performing their Striker Trio set. He kept sneaking out from the wings and whispering things in the ears of the players, cracking them up.

"My job as the emcee is to make sure everything is all right with the musicians," Cos said. "So, I went up to Ron and asked him if the sound was OK on the monitor, and he said, 'I need more guitar.' I told him, 'I don't think so. He's not good.' So, then I went to Russell and asked him, 'How ya doin'?' He said, 'I'm fine,' and I replied, 'I don't think so because you have very little hair.' Later I walked out to Mulgrew and told him that Ron had called for two tunes to end the set. I said, 'But you've got 16 minutes left on the clock. Are you going to make it?' Mulgrew said, 'Oh, yeah.' I replied, 'You better because I know where you live.'"

A jazz fan who grew up in Philadelphia, one of the hotbeds of the music, Cos has been a jazz proponent and supporter, whether he's slipping into a show at the Village Vanguard or bringing levity to the stage at the Apollo Theater at the annual Jazz Foundation of America fundraiser show. Cos crossed paths with Ron on many occasions over the years. "I have a short, great Ron Carter story," he said. "At the University of Massachusetts, Amherst, in its jazz glory days when Max Roach and Archie Shepp were there as professors, there was a concert that had a bunch of American heroes like Dizzy, Moody, maybe Mary Lou Williams, Ron and others."

A doctoral student in education at U-Mass., Cos invited all the musicians to his home in Greenfield, north of Amherst, for dinner. At one point, he said to Ron, "I've watched bass players file their fingers and some of them have calluses on their hands. I notice that you don't have any. So I wonder, what do you do to keep your fingers like that?"

Ron succinctly replied, "Play correctly."

LESSONS FROM THE TROMBONE

RON HAS SPENT his entire adult life perfecting that "correct" quality of "play" that has been an inspiration to multiple generations of bassists. He has been a stickler for finding the right notes on his instrument by the least taxing means possible, preferring to find those notes playing horizontally across the bass neck versus strenuously seeking out those notes vertically.

Ironically, it wasn't four-string players who influenced Ron in that regard, but the trombonist J.J. Johnson. "When I first moved to New York in 1959, I was stumbling around trying to find my bearings and going to clubs to see what was going on," Ron said. "One Monday night at Birdland, I happened upon a jam session that J.J. was in. I watched him play trombone and was amazed at his technique. Instead of using the entire slide, he was extending the slide only halfway out while still managing to hit all the notes he needed. That got me thinking about my bass and how to get that same effect of covering a lot of territory without a lot of physical effort."

That question had perplexed Ron for years. When he was learning how to play the bass in an orchestra at school, he studied books that showed the best fingerings on the neck. But he thought there must be a better and easier way to get to those same notes. "Watching J.J. on the trombone unlocked that for me," he said.

Intrigued by J.J.'s less-is-more movement, Ron caught the trombonist again, this time at the Half Note in a band with Tommy Flanagan and Nat Adderley. "I watched closely how J.J. managed to play all those notes without using the full slide," he said. "I remember thinking that he must have figured out all the notes available in each position he played in, so that when he wanted to play a note he wouldn't have to push the slide out as far as other trombonists who were putting so much effort into playing."

It was then that Ron transformed his ah-hah moment into action. He recognized that he could do the same on the bass, whose range and sound is similar to a trombone. He began to explore J.J.'s approach, which "opened such a big door for me as a bassist, especially when doing a gig where you're playing three sets a night six days a week. I needed to find a way to make playing not be cumbersome, so that at the end of the evening I'd still have enough energy to get in a car and drive home. That's when I learned how to play horizontally, finding the notes available in the same place on the neck without rabbiting—without having to hop way down the bass neck."

The bass–trombone connection was underscored by *New York Times* music critic Jon Pareles when he reviewed a Ron Carter Quartet date in 1983 at Sweet Basil. After praising Ron's "profusion of different attacks," including "trills and quiet strummed double-stops" on the piccolo bass, Pareles noted that "his long-breathed lines could have come from the world's gentlest trombone."

BASS TRADEMARKS

No MATTER WHAT the instrument, when a musician achieves virtuosity, singularity of voice reigns as the determining factor. On the bass, there's no mistaking Ron, who speaks articulately with a readily identifiable, pulsing authority. Bass aficionados and educators take note.

Writing online for The International Institute of Bassists website (instituteofbass.com), Cliff Engel academically analyzed Ron's approach to bass-line building."

Engel pointed out that Ron may often repeat lines from chorus to chorus as a means of establishing the harmony and uses such techniques as ostinato or repeating motifs. Engel accentuated Ron's mastery at left-hand articulation (signature pull-off skips, glissandos and extended glissandos that may last a full measure or more) and rhythmic embellishments (patented rhythmic drops, skips, ghost skips, slurred skips, triplets and syncopation), all of which are trademarks of his playing.

"Carter's unmistakable tone and the inevitable quality of note choice and phrasing contained within his lines remains unprecedented," Engel wrote. "Carter swings through chord changes, in and out of half and double-time feels, with ease. Always aware of his musical environment, Carter spontaneously interacts both melodically and rhythmically with other members of the group. Within the framework of his solos, Carter demonstrates virtuoso technical facility and utilizes a variety of techniques including double-stops, octaves, pull-offs, hammer-ons, glissandos and melodic horn-like runs. He is a true master of bass-line construction and an icon of the jazz bass tradition."

In 1994 at the Montreal Jazz Festival, Ron opened a window onto his technique and art by playing five evenings as the fest's featured artist-in-residence. Each night at the intimate 400-seat Salle du Gesu, he was showcased in a different instrumental context, including solo, duo, trio, quartet and nonet. His solo set was like a bass clinic.

Ron opened that show with a bluesy melody, plucking his upright's strings as a way of demonstrating how to cruise into a fat, bouncy groove. After noting that one of a bass player's jobs is to play the meter behind the groove, he experimented with different time structures, moving from blues riffs to walking bass lines. He introduced different techniques, from pizzicato runs bubbling into a syncopated rhythm to fingernail scratches conjuring up eerie voicings. Then he showed how beautifully a bass can play a melody by sketching a stunning rendition of the classic "Body and Soul."

SNAKES IN THE GRASS

RON IS ADAMANT that jazz bassists need to pay more attention to the potential of their instrument. "Most bass players have missed the boat," he said. "They've got to set aside the idea that playing time is not an important role of the bass. Bassists play like snakes in the grass during the time sections. But when it's a solo opportunity, it's as if a light goes on over their heads. They get enthusiastic all of a sudden. But after the solo is over, the light goes out and they go back to hiding. Now why is that? I tell students that they're missing out on a lot of fun discovering new melodies to assist the band to play differently. I tell them that one of the greatest pleasures I have on bass is playing notes that will make the saxophonist play a line he wouldn't have thought of if I hadn't sent him in that direction."

Ron also asserts that just waiting for a bass solo spot is a dead end. "I'd rather watch CNN than do that," he said. "If I don't solo for a week, I'm cool. There are plenty of other creative things to do. You can play a counter melody in quarter notes, you can make a tune get tense or show new flavors, you can go from swing to bossa nova to Latin. You can do whatever you want instead of being dormant."

In teaching private lessons at his apartment, Ron stresses the instrument's assets. He speaks highly of Larry Grenadier, who has sought out his wisdom whenever their busy schedules allow them to hook up. "Larry is a fine young bassist," Ron said, "but he's developed some bad habits that take awhile to shed. I've given him pointers on how to hold the bass better so that he doesn't get so tired by the end of an evening. For example, he was playing the bass straight up. I told him to tilt it back 25 degrees so that it can rest on his body."

Ron stressed that more than one session was essential. "The bass is more complicated than that," he said. "Before Larry first came over, I asked him to write down 15 things that he wanted to work on. Then I told him to subtract five. The 10 remaining areas are what we began to focus on." Included in that list was harmony and theory, lead tones, harmonic resolution of notes, and hand coordination.

"Ron is a master," said Larry. "He's an excellent teacher who is able to verbalize the most abstract concepts. His sound, time feel, bass-line construction and overall knowledge of the bass's function in an ensemble have been an inspiration to me since I began playing the instrument. There were so many things I wanted to learn from Ron, but mostly I was intrigued by his overall ease of playing and his ability to put the music first, giving the music exactly what it needed."

Bassists aren't the only jazz musicians who speak highly of Ron. Drummer Lewis Nash, a longtime associate, calls him the Beacon. "That's my nickname for Ron because he stands so tall physically as well as artistically above the field," said Lewis, whose ears were opened to new possibilities while playing with him. "Ron is the type of bass player who doesn't force his view. He listens intently. I'll play a rhythmic figure and he repeats it with a different twist during the course of a walking bass line. That shows me that he's always in the moment, playfully manipulating the pulse of the music. Ron likes to challenge others as well as himself. He's been playing the same tunes for years, but he still finds something fresh. He's always listening, always searching for the right notes."

THE DOMINANT BASS

Ron's primary bass is a three-quarter Juzek bass, made circa 1910. "According to someone who researched it, the parts were made in Czechoslovakia," he said. "They were then shipped to Germany for assembly." He added, "Since 1969, I've been using an extension that goes down to low C. I was one of the first guys to do this."

The bass has two pickups, a Kurmann system built into the soundpost inside (used primarily for recording) and The Realist, jointly designed by Ned Steinberger and David Gage, which is located under the E string side of the bridge (used in live performances). Ron uses LaBella strings (7700 series), which have a steel core wrapped in silk and then black nylon. For small rooms Ron uses a Gallien-Krueger MBE combo amp; for larger venues, he plugs into an Epifani Piccolo 600 amp head and an Epifani D.I.S.T. 112 bass cabinet on a stand five-and-a-half feet tall. He also uses cables made by Lloyd Salisbury at Professional Audio Cable Solutions.

When giving advice to bass players in the *DownBeat* bass roundtable feature (see roundtable colloquy), one of Ron's nuggets of wisdom was the necessity to "make sure your instrument is in shape to play.... A bass needs a tune-up like a car. When you do that, you take it to the best gas station. You do the same with the bass. Take it to the best repairman."

When Ron first arrived in New York in 1959, he went to a bass repairman named Frank Olivero who had a shop on 55th Street and 7th Avenue. "Frank was an old Italian gentleman," Ron said. "I was always curious about how the bass worked physically from a scientific point of view, so I would ask him why he did certain things or why he used these kinds of clamps, and stuff. He asked me why I wanted to know. I told him I wanted to know what happens when I hit a note, how the string and bridge respond, how the bass itself affects how the sound comes out."

Frank suggested that Ron apprentice at his shop to learn, but because of Ron's schedule of gigging and going to school, he opted to stop by a couple of times a week to watch the bass repairman work on the instruments. "I did this for five or six years," Ron said. "I not only learned about how Frank did repairs, but I also found out what he did to a bass that made it sound better than when it had come into the shop."

Several years later Ron hooked up with bassist, luthier and master repairman David Gage, whose shop in the Tribeca neighborhood of New York is frequented by most of the city's bass players. David was even the go-to specialist sought out by bass players whose instruments were ravaged by Hurricane Katrina and the subsequent flooding in New Orleans. David told *Strings* magazine, "I always tell people everything's repairable, but we had one bass that was just full of water, everything that was glued was apart, all the parts were twisted, and the top was in more than two pieces. It was just not repairable."

A bass player since he was 12 and a bass repairman in New York since 1976, he became Ron's bass doctor in the '80s. They have been good friends since that time, even though there were a few rough patches early on.

Inside his shop that has a bassist wall-of-fame picture gallery of autographed photos of his clientele and racks of basses and cellos from the floor to the loft ceiling, David recalls Ron coming in once with his bass and requesting fingerboard work. "By that time, Ron trusted me," he said. "I did the repair, and then, since Ron had been teaching me a lot about music and the bass, not to mention about life, I decided to polish the back of the neck so that it shined. I wanted to make it beautiful for him. Ron walked in and looked at what I had done to the neck. I said, 'Ron, this is for you, no charge.'"

Ron looked at David and frowned. Then he said, "You remind me of a little kid who told his daddy, 'Look what I did for you: I shined your shoes outside and inside.'"

That was a lesson for David: don't do anything without asking. "Ron was very direct and very honest, but he also made a joke out of it. He said after seeing the shine, 'Now I won't be able to find the notes I'm looking for.'"

Ron insists that the lacquered neck was a problem. "It wasn't going to feel right for me," he said. "There's this film between my hand and the neck of the bass. I'd been trying to get rid of that shit for 35 years, and I told David that he had just undone 35 years worth of work. I want to be able to feel the grain of the wood, not its slickness. So I told him he did a great job except for the polish. I said, 'Please take it off and don't do me any of these kinds of favors again.'"

David was a Ron fan long before arriving in New York in 1976 from his hometown and base in Amherst, Massachusetts. (In recalling his first Ron-sighting at a gig he performed at Alice Tulley Hall, David says that back then Ron exemplified bass in the city.) He learned Ron's licks and tried to figure out his technique, such as the extra pull when walking four-to-a-bar on Miles's "Seven Steps to Heaven." David said that he came to understand that there was a reason for everything Ron did. "It's strategic in the best sense of the word. It's like Larry Byrd on the basketball court. You're not only a great player, but you're also constantly thinking and making everyone else around you better."

David added, "Ron's a smart guy and funny. He is the grand master of bass; he's the standard bearer. He's like a yoga Zen master."

Ron returned the compliment by praising David and his crew, recognizing that they take good care of his bass. "What they do is time-consuming and delicate, where even having the right tools doesn't make the job easier. I have the highest regard for David and the other guys who work for him."

David marveled at Ron's upright bass, which he's used since 1959. "Think of what that bass has been through and what kind of sound he gets out of it." David said that it's not a top-of-the-line instrument, noting that it's more like a Chevy Nova than a Lamborghini. "But Ron made this bass great. People play themselves into an instrument after a period of time. His bass doesn't have a high pedigree like a $100,000 model, but he doesn't need that."

David says that as well as Ron maintains his bass it's as if he hadn't touched it since its last visit to the shop. But weather takes its toll— humidity in the summer, dry air in the winter—so there's always work to be done. David recommends bass checkups every six months. "A bass like Ron's requires glue a couple of times a year," he said. "Cracks in the back open up which I fill with hot glue strips."

Ron feels so comfortable at David's shop that he has given master classes, open to the public, in the workshop room. Just as Ron has become friends with his dentist and eye doctor, he's invited David and his wife Judy into his inner circle, which includes his annual New Year's Day party at his apartment with the meal cooked by Ron's son Myles.

ACOUSTIC OR ELECTRIC

WHILE RON HAS a couple of other basses at home—including his French Tyrolean piccolo bass that was once a mainstay in his quartet and now is featured as the front-line instrument in his nonet—he doesn't own an electric bass. However, he says that's a matter of choice, not prejudice.

The way Ron figures it somewhere along the way someone wrote that he was averse to the entire notion of the electric bass guitar, that somehow it was so modern and hip that it was therefore inferior to the acoustic. Perhaps it was based on a misunderstanding of his reaction to the direction of contemporary pop music (i.e., a 1972 *DownBeat* interview with fellow bassist Richard Davis where Ron said he preferred the unique sound of his acoustic, whose sound an electric could never replicate). Plus, there was the assumption that an elegant, well-dressed gent like Ron who continues to probe the standards of yore would frown on such a plugged-in, funky-sounding instrument (obviously such naysayers were oblivious to Ron's CTI days). Even today, in some people's eyes, Ron is viewed as a stuffy old-timer who censures the electric bass.

Not so, says Ron, who notes that in the late '60s and early '70s he played electric bass as a sideman on many albums, as well as his own. He doesn't attribute his leaving Miles's employ to the bandleader's request that he play electric bass on *Filles de Kilimanjaro*, nor does he cringe at his own participation in pop-oriented sessions in subsequent years. Ron's electric days are not a skeleton in his closet.

Ron says that in the '6ps bass players had to own an electric ax to get session work for recording dates or to play radio and television jingles. It was a fact of life for a bass player-for-hire.

"Not only would you see guys walking down the street with their uprights and Fender basses, but also with bass amps which most jingle studios didn't have," he said. "So four or five of us bassists such as Richard

Davis and George Duvivier went in together to buy amps that we left in various studios. We bought Ampeg B-15s that were great."

Ron became familiar with Ampeg amps in his Rochester days. During his senior year at Eastman, he had to borrow one to play electric in organ groups. "Once a week I played with those organ guys in gigs that started at two a.m. and went to six a.m.," he said.

With his session days proliferating in New York, Ron bought an electric. "Doubling was a part of the job then," he said. "So I went down to Manny's Music on West 48th Street and talked to a salesman. I told him my needs and the limitations of my needs. I wanted to get a foothold in the recording industry, so he recommended a Danelectro, which was the first electric I owned."

Ron took the instrument home and "stumbled" through learning how to play it. "I had to figure out the frets and tuning and sound and pickups. It was all a new language to me, but because I needed it to get work, I spent a couple of hours a day working on it so that I could at least have a minimum of knowledge about how it worked."

Soon, the jazz world began to tune in fully to the electric bass. "Chuck Rainey was one of the guys at the top already," Ron said. "Certain jazz acts wanted that sound. I started playing electric more in Creed's CTI sessions." While he learned the fundamentals, Ron never expected to be competitive, just competent.

He explains that he gave up the electric-bass life, not because he was being an old fogy for tradition's sake, but because he realized he had to choose one instrument or the other. Acoustic or electric? The electric bass was a different animal than the acoustic and mastering it would require hours of practice and study—precious hours that Ron didn't have, given his desire to balance his gigging schedule with his family life, not to mention his desire to continue to fathom the mysteries of his upright bass. Once artists such as Larry Graham (with Sly & the Family Stone) and Bootsy Collins came on the scene and began to discover new ways of making the electric bass speak, Ron realized that he had to make a choice. Rather than being merely satisfactory on electric, he laid it to rest.

Did Jaco Pastorius factor into his decision? "By the time Jaco came along, I was well past playing the electric. It wasn't because of him that I gave it up. It was more about guys like Bootsy who were taking the instrument to a new level."

Did he ever deliver slapping funk lines? "No, that was Larry's thing and came along after me too."

So, no disparaging words for electric bass players? "None at all. In fact, I admire those musicians who are taking the instrument to new levels, the same as what I've been doing with the acoustic bass."

Then there's Ron's son, Ron Jr., who lives in Boston and plays an electric bass in a funk, R&B-styled band. Does he have an extra electric bass that he could lend Ron if he needed one? "Oh, yes, he sure does."

COLLOQUY

The Bass Roundtable

In 2004, Ron's Upper West Side apartment became the setting for a roundtable of jazz bassists to talk about their lives and their chosen instrument. The conversations were recorded and transcribed for an article that appeared in *DownBeat*.

The following is the full transcript of the session, which appeared in a truncated version in the magazine. Participants included the host (at the time, age 68), William Parker (53), Scott Colley (41) and Larry Grenadier (39). I moderated. The meeting began with an around-the-horn self-introduction.

After Ron gave a sketch of himself—where he had come from and where he was heading with his current crop of bands—he concluded, "I thought at this age, I'd be doing less. But I'm doing more. I think I need to enroll in a How to Retire 101 class soon."

William was born in the Bronx, studied at the Jazzmobile school in Harlem with such teachers as Paul West, Art Davis and Milt Hinton as well as studied downtown with Jimmy Garrison and Wilbur Ware. He became interested in John Coltrane's avant-garde period and was inspired by "the aesthetic purpose of music to heal and uplift people." He worked with Billy Higgins and Clifford Jordan in the early '70s, hooked up with Don Cherry at the Five Spot in 1975, and played with Cecil Taylor from 1981-'91. Since then he's played with Matthew Shipp and David S. Ware and piloted his own projects, including the founding of the Vision Festival.

Scott and Larry are New York-based native Californians. The former is from Los Angeles, studied at California Institute of Art, toured with Carmen McRae, and later gigged with Art Farmer, Dizzy Gillespie and Clifford Jordan. He performs regularly with Jim Hall and Chris Potter and has his own groups. Larry was born in San Francisco into a musical family, graduated from Stanford University in '89 and moved to New York in '91 where he scored gigs with Joe Henderson, Betty Carter and Tom Harrell. In recent years, he's been the bassist in bands led by Joshua Redman, Pat Metheny and Brad Mehldau and belongs to the collective band Fly with Mark Turner and Jeff Ballard.

The conversation then shifted to how each was drawn to playing the bass.

RON: My circumstances were more political than a musical light going on in my head. The classical orchestras weren't hiring African-American musicians with equivalent talent. I realized I wasn't going to get my share as a qualified and talented cello player. The one bass player in the high school orchestra at Cass Tech in Detroit was graduating, so since I was determined to be a musician, I started bass and they hired me. That was January 1955.

WILLIAM: When I was 5 or 6, my dad played me Duke Ellington music, and then got me a trumpet and trombone. But I didn't understand how the music was affecting me until I began playing the cello in junior high. But I was attracted to the sound of the bass. Plus, it was very close to the size of a human being, which I liked. Eventually I got one in the Bronx for $100, which took me a long time to save. I met Charlie Haden who told me to play along with records, so I did, and I sounded pretty good.

When I was taking classes at Jazzmobile, Paul West showed me the half position, gave me a chart for Fats Waller's "Ain't Misbehavin'" and sent me into the bathroom to practice. That was at 11 a.m. At seven that night, a janitor heard me playing and told me to go home because the school had closed two hours earlier. I wasn't aware of falling in love with the bass. I didn't have bassitis. It was more about the music and the whole experience.

SCOTT: My brother who was six years older was a drummer, so he told me that I had to play bass. We played together a lot. He was better than I was, but the great thing was that he bought me records and pointed me in a certain direction. Very early on I was a jazz purist. When I was 11 to 14 my scope was pretty narrow: Mingus, Paul Chambers, Jimmy Blanton. I was a strange kid. At first playing bass seemed like a lot of work. I even had to pay somebody my lunch money to carry my bass home for me. When I was a little older, I discovered Ornette Coleman and Jaco Pastorius, people I had been ignoring. My ears opened up. The amazing thing is that through the bass, I started connecting to people and ideas—experiences I wouldn't have had otherwise.

LARRY: I had a similar experience to Scott. My older brother played trumpet and my middle brother played guitar. My father thought it'd be a good idea for me to play bass so we could play together. He bought me an electric bass and thought I should take lessons. The second I could play four open strings, I joined a band. We played [pop] covers. Then I heard jazz through my brothers. I loved it and felt I needed to get an acoustic bass because that was the instrument I was hearing on their records. I bought one, took lessons right away and started buying my own records. The second one I bought was a reissue by Ron and Eric Dolphy.

RON: That was called *Magic*.

LARRY: I think I bought it because I liked the cover.

SCOTT: That's how I bought music too. I remember Thelonious Monk's *Underground*.

LARRY: So I played along to learn and fell in love with the bass, but more than that I fell for playing music in general—the social aspect, the idea of the camaraderie of musicians.

Who were early influences that helped you get to the next level?

SCOTT: Initially it was a lot of bass players, but over time it grew to influences playing different instruments. When I was 12, I was into Mingus. There was a lot I enjoyed about his music. I appreciated his strength and sound and the fact that he was a composer.

WILLIAM: I listened to John Lamb, who was the bass player for Ellington's orchestra. I listened to the record *Soul Call,* the cuts like "Africa Flower" and "West Indian Pancake." His bass playing stood out. Every record I got I listened for the bass, like MJQ with Percy Heath, whose sound resonated but was very economical. At school I listened to Coltrane. Every Sunday at home we listened to Herbie's *Maiden Voyage* with Ron. During the week it was Archie Shepp, Ben Webster, Coleman Hawkins. This was during the Civil Rights Movement, and it seemed like every song you listened to was the soundtrack for your life. And everyone had a different way of communicating: a clarity, a touch, a rhythmic concept.

I listened to Ron, Richard Davis, Jimmy Garrison, Reggie Workman. Each had a sound that stood out. I remember going to a show in Brooklyn. Ron, did you play with Reggie and Jimmy there once?

RON: Yes, years ago.

WILLIAM: I remember all three of you played the same bass if I'm not mistaken. And you all sounded different. You were all getting to the center of the music. That's how I realized you couldn't copy a bass line and get it right no matter how much you tried. You've got to find your own bass lines.

LARRY: I'm here partly because of Ron. He's been a huge influence. A lot of records I listened to over and over again when I was a kid had Ron on them. The guy who first caught my ear was Oscar Pettiford and then Ray Brown. I still have a strong affinity to their playing today. Looking back I think it was the clarity of their playing that an 11-year-old could hear. After that I began to investigate bass lines and what makes a good bass line as well as what makes a good bass player. You play gigs and see how hard that actually is.

Ron, when you first picked up the bass, were you drawn to other bass players historically?

RON: Not really. I was coming from a determination to show that I could play classical music as well as any other musician.

But what caught my ear later as a player were Cecil Payne and J.J. Johnson. I played with Cecil when I was working with Randy Weston. He had his own baritone saxophone sound. There was no mistaking it. And I remember watching J.J. play with Tommy Flanagan and seeing that he never went past the bell when he played. It amazed me because the trombone is pretty complicated. It occurred to me that it was possible to find various combinations of playing on string bass and stay within the physical range of the instrument.

What do you think about William's comment about copying a bass line?

RON: The modern trend is for teachers to ask their students to transcribe bass lines, but with little or no guidance. You can transcribe lines of mine or Larry's or Scott's or William's, but they don't tell you what those notes do, what part of the chord the notes function as, and they can't tell you how this one note in this line makes the whole harmony change. So without specific guidance, transcribing is worthless or futile. You need to understand why certain notes do certain things or why a note is a terrible one.

LARRY: I used to transcribe music a lot, but that wasn't doing me much good. I needed to find out what attracted me to the line in the first place and then very specifically what made the line so good.

What's it like to hook up with a good rhythm section?

RON: When you find something that works you get pretty upset.

SCOTT: Why?

RON: Because you wonder why it doesn't work with all bands. I'm interested in working with drummers who know how to tune their drums. I've done several gigs in town where a drummer will come in off the street and just play. He doesn't care how the drum sounds and how the sound is going to affect the bass.

Once a drummer understands the importance of tuning the floor tom or the bass drum—so that there's no A-flat or a real sharp D that can wipe out all the notes below a certain range in the bass—the night's not so long for the bass player. The sound of the drum affects the way you play on bass. You may be forced to play higher than you normally do just to feel the bass hit those right notes. Most drummers can swing, but that's not my primary interest in a drummer. I want the drummer to understand the sonic relationship of the drum and bass.

SCOTT: A drummer also has to be conscious of the room itself. Adjustments need to be made.

WILLIAM: After awhile you end up only playing with a certain drummer. You take yourself off the market as a bass player who does lots of recording dates. I figured I'd be better off playing with a community of musicians—drummers and piano players—and have a relationship where you can all modify how you play.

I also feel strongly about tone. If you can play with a beautiful tone, that's most important. How can you accomplish anything as a musician if your sound isn't working? There's a maturity of sound. It's like when I played with Ed Blackwell or Billy Higgins. They tuned their drums, but they also had the presence of their sound. Sound translates into tone, and inside the tone is where the nutrients of music are.

LARRY: What Ron says about awareness is so vital. Musicians need to get outside of their own instruments and hear how the group sounds.

RON: A bad note is one thing, but if the sound is bad, too, well...

WILLIAM: If you're using amplification and it sounds trebly or too bassy, if it doesn't sound right, the whole night's messed up.

LARRY: It keeps you from being inspired. That's the problem with amplification. It's a modern dilemma. As everyone gets louder and the size of the drum sets get bigger, the bass player has to turn up too and then there's a big mess.

All of you are accompanists as well as leaders. Who has really challenged you as a player in either setting?

SCOTT: Every thing I choose to take on now is a challenge. I just finished a six-week tour with Herbie Hancock, Michael Brecker, Roy Hargrove and Terri Lyne Carrington. We spent the whole time formulating the music in such a way that everyone had input. In that way, I don't think of myself as accompanying or leading. My goal in the music is to not be determined by whether it's my band or not. With my own group, I like to step back and let the other musicians surprise me in ways I hadn't thought about before.

What's it been like playing with Jim Hall?

SCOTT: I've played a lot with Jim in duo and trio in the last 10 years. We've been playing more with no preconceived compositions, but he also weaves a melodic thread through everything that connects it all. He has the amazing ability to hear every note I play. So if I go beyond a chord change, he'll incorporate it somehow into what he plays. With him, every note counts.

RON: My preference is a little different. One of the reasons why the Miles band was able to do what it did is that we played the same library basically for those five years, in the '63-'68 period. We knew the library going into each gig. We'd start with "Autumn Leaves" and end with "So What" or something like that. Working with the type of players in that band night in and night out gave us the opportunity to know what the tunes were all about—what choices are possible, what are the changes, what are the ways to make a tune sound different but still maintain its [essence]. The more you play a song the more you understand it.

Among the five of us in Miles's band, we probably knew a million tunes, but we focused on a select 15 to 20. By Friday of a weeklong gig the songs would have other shapes, the harmonies would have other views, the melodies were played in a different fashion. You could make a mistake one night and fix it the next. One night's seed could be a plant for the following evening.

I've been in bands where everyone knows lots of tunes, so every night is a fight for the library. And you never get the chance to really learn the song.

WILLIAM: What Ron describes is the ultimate situation, and it doesn't have anything to do with style or category of music. It has everything to do with getting to the center of the music. That is really free music—free meaning that you can choose from all that you know. I played with Cecil Taylor for 10 years. We rehearsed every day for five or six hours and we learned his language. Then we'd be free to make sense of that language and take the music into a different direction, like playing a tango, bossa nova, waltz. You were free to go anywhere as a navigator to shape the music.

RON: Mr. Parker, anyone who could make a five-hour rehearsal all those days is stand up to me. I can't do that. Please, don't call me for one of those rehearsals.

Larry, I saw you play last fall with Joshua Redman and Ali Jackson, and you were so deep into the music.

LARRY: I've played with Josh in different contexts over the years, so it's a natural connection. Plus the three of us had just come off the road playing as Kurt Rosenwinkel's band. As for Brad, I've played with him over the last 10 years, and we've been fortunate to play a lot of gigs. We've grown together and come up with more of a collective sound. It's like what you said, Scott, about Jim Hall. Brad is so aware of the function of the bass. Every note I play I hear a reaction in the best sense. Brad is very aware of the space the bass needs. Having a long-term relationship fosters growth.

Do you think the function of the bass is fully understood?

LARRY: I don't think so, especially with how we can alter the sound of the music. It's like the Miles Plugged Nickel sessions. When the boxed set came out, it was as if people were just noticing for the first time how much Ron was affecting the direction of Miles's band. Ron was shaping the music as much as anyone else and at times more so. His bass had rhythmic and harmonic power.

RON: The bassist's role is best defined by the role he wants to play. A bass player is used to milling around in the shadows until the spotlight hits him for a solo and then he plays more aggressively, with more energy. But the bass player can be active all the way through a song without even taking a solo and can even offer the opportunity for someone to play differently. You've got to stand up and be counted. You may not have your face on the cover of a magazine, but you can be there in the fine print.

WILLIAM: The bass player is definitely the navigator. Bass provides the shape and drive of the music. You can have a white canvas and everyone is painting it red. But I come in and paint a yellow dot. It stands out and is the right note and rhythmic inflection. The bass keeps the music moving like blood flowing. Bass players in the '50s were just accompanists, but since then you can hear bassists who are guiding the direction of the music, making a thread that brings everything together.

SCOTT: You look for things in the music at every moment. You're always searching for the right thing to play and it's different for all of us.

WILLIAM: Ron, on your records with Miles, you didn't solo that much, but you're always aware of the bass. A whole line could be like a solo. You can listen to the contour, the balance, the shape that contributes to the whole band.

RON: You play good notes. No one can explain how much fun it is to make a saxophonist play a different order of notes.

When you played with Miles, were there instances when you would surprise him with what you played?

RON: It happened most nights. Miles would always get back to where I was standing on the stage so he could hear. The bass wasn't as audible in those large performance halls then as now. There's more of an awareness with promoters of having the bass be heard in a hall.

Occasionally Miles would ask, what's that note? I'd say, that chord is G7, Miles, and I'm playing B in the bass. Or he'd ask, why are you playing that rhythm here? And I'd say, because Tony [Williams] is playing the same one. Miles never told me what to play. Not one note. He trusted that we all knew where we all wanted to end up. He knew we all possessed the musical ability to find the route to the open door at the end. In that group more than anything else, they all trusted the bass player's input.

What thumbnail advice can you give to aspiring bassists?

LARRY: Study with Ron.

RON: Can't get more thumbnail than that *(laughs)*.

LARRY: Generally, get a good teacher at any point in your career to keep that inquisitiveness about the music and to find new places to go with your instrument. Be open, listen, take advice to heart and practice practice practice. What do you practice? You have to find that out, then put in the time. There's no short or secret way to get from here to there.

RON: Magic, right?

LARRY: Yeah, magic. I'm astounded people think that. It takes work.

SCOTT: I agree with Larry. There aren't any shortcuts. It takes patience. And even then, you can practice 10 hours a day for five years and still not develop your sound. You keep picking and choosing everything you hear to come up with your sound.

WILLIAM: My advice is to learn as much as you can and not be afraid of anything. Don't box yourself in unless you are really obsessed. Some people, all they want to play is the B-flat blues. They feel that's what they were born to do. But I say don't be afraid to play the B blues, the C blues. Stretch it around. Be open. Finding your own voice is like looking for your nose. You look everywhere and it's right there. You take awkward first steps and it may sound bad. But that may be the embryo of what eventually will be your own personality on the instrument.

RON: Off the top of my head, play in many environments. A lot of young bass players are just in one group. You only get a limited view. Second, bass players play awful notes. Your job is to try to play as few of those as possible. When you play in different bands, you can make a terrible sound one night that sounds good with some other band.

Third, make sure your instrument is in good shape to play. I've seen some awful basses with cracks, the pickup wire broken, pegs squeaking. A bass needs a tune-up like a car. Fourth, go hear guys play live. Figure out how they get from point A to point B, what strings and pickups they use, how they hold the bass. You see those things and you can start getting a view of yourself with what works for you. And finally, enjoy playing time. That's how we work.

PART VII
APPENDICES

APPENDIX ONE

In Their Own Words: Anecdotes and Opinions

BUSTER WILLIAMS

On meeting Ron for the first time: "I was on tour with Nancy Wilson, and we stayed at the same hotel as Miles and his band—I believe it was called Gens le Pont—near Antibes on the French Riviera. I met Ron, Herbie, Tony and George. We were there for a week, and I remember a jam session where I first saw Ron play. I thought he was great. He instantly became one of my influences. When you see someone who plays your instrument play the hell out of it, you pay attention—to his technique, his ideas, his composure."

On their common passion for fast cars: "Ron's always been a car guy. It seems as if he gets a new car every six months. He's always trading in for another car. He likes so many cars that he just wants to try them all. When Miles had his Ferrari, I had a Corvette Sting Ray. Miles talked about his Ferrari all the time, but he didn't say much about my Corvette. When I was playing with Ron, I had a 1972 Mercedes 500 sedan. Ron likes to drive fast. One week we played at the Regatta Bar in Boston, and every night after the show Ron jumped in his car and drove back to New York. I went with him. He made the trip in incredible time. But he's a good driver. I never felt in any danger. He was just going fast. Plus, he never got any tickets, which was miraculous."

CHICK COREA

On being influenced by the Miles Davis Quintet: "I felt there was an aura about the group, and I could hear the individuality come shining through on everything that they did. I would have been totally disheartened if no one had carried on the bass tradition in Miles's group after Paul Chambers, as Ron did."

On listening to the group's recordings: "My friends and I were glued to the records they made, like *Four & More*. I remember the first time we heard *Seven Steps to Heaven*. The rhythm section played so transparently. We were just glued onto Tony's drumming. Tony and Herbie could go real free because Ron was pinning the whole thing down with his bass. Ron didn't play in a pedestrian way. He held it all together, and it was easy to tune into what he was playing and see what a creative part of the music he was. It was inspiring."

On crossing paths after both their stints with Miles: "I don't recall playing on Ron's album *Parade* [in 1979]. But I do remember the first time we recorded together. It was Hubert Laws's *Wild Flowers* [1972] with Ron and Richard Davis both playing bass. There I was, new to New York, a starry-eyed guy from Boston making a record in a major studio with all these famous people around me. I was quivering. Then I saw Ron. He was there smoking a pipe and reading a newspaper between takes. When everyone was ready to play, Ron delivered the music. He was relaxed and so much the professional."

On Ron's influence: "I considered Ron my mentor and my hero. I'll always consider Ron a mentor. I'm 66 and I still want my mentors. Ron is one of them, just like Roy Haynes and Herbie and Sonny Rollins. Ron is in that category of amazing trendsetters who set a high level of artistry and creativity in their music."

GONZALO RUBALCABA

On touring in Europe with Ron in support of his album *Diz* [1994]: "I was really young, and Ron was my teacher in every respect. But he never acted like a teacher. His attitude was more to follow us. He was very honorable with the drummer [Julio Barreto] and me. He never imposed. He followed. Each concert we played, he was always doing something different with the tempo, harmony and rhythm. I respect people who, no matter what age, style or tradition, attend to the music. Ron attends to everything."

On Ron's personality: "I don't know why he [projects] being distant or aloof at times. Only he knows why he acts certain ways. That's his own story. He may be taking certain positions just to be safe. I completely understand that. But Ron is such a smart musician and a sweet man. He's a lot more sensitive than he projects. He's a person and a musician who is more open than people think. People see him on the outside as a classy guy, as a gentleman. But he's also really open to new experiences. What keeps him fresh is his ability to think in so many different ways about the music."

IN THEIR OWN WORDS: ANECDOTES & OPINIONS

STANLEY CLARKE

On Ron's influence: "I wouldn't be a bass player today if it hadn't been for Ron Carter. Probably in the last 30 to 40 years, Ron has been the most important bassist in jazz. Even if a kid playing bass today has never heard of Ron, he'll be playing Ron. That's how important he is."

On Ron's bass lines: "Ron wasn't tremendously virtuosic. But he was the true jazz bassist. As a kid in Philadelphia, Charles Fambrough and I would take Ron's bass lines apart to see how he treated chords and made chord changes, to see how he'd weave his bass lines through any changes, whether they were modular or linear."

On Ron being a genius: "The word genius gets thrown around a lot, but it fits Ron. He's my favorite kind of genius. He's really subtle, but heavy. If you listen to him with Miles, it's like hearing 10 players in one. You hear Paul Chambers, then Mingus, but what Ron was playing came at a time when the music was changing. Listen to Ron with Miles on 'Stella by Starlight' from *My Funny Valentine - Miles Davis In Concert*. His choice of notes is so subtle and shows how much thought went into playing them that way. I still listen to this."

On the first time he played with Ron: "We worked together on Deodato's *Prelude* [1972] that resulted in his hit fusion version of Strauss's 'Also Sprach Zarathustra' [better known as "Theme from *2001: A Space Odyssey*"]. I thought Ron would hate me for the rest of my life. I was playing electric bass and the coil cable snapped and nicked his bass. He gave me a look that was like, 'I'm going to kill you.' But Ron was the ultimate professional. Someone came in just then and said, 'Let's record,' and we started."

On the acoustic bass versus the electric: "I never studied how to play electric bass. It's like a hobby. But what I am at heart is an acoustic bassist. And for that, Ron is the guy. He's the foundation. Ron showed the bottom of what can be played on that instrument."

On Ron the person: "I don't think Ron realizes how many people love him. He's stoic. He's a beautiful guy. And he is the bass guy. I don't think he realizes how much I dig him."

ESPERANZA SPALDING

On Ron as an influence: "I was influenced by Slam Stewart, Anders Jormin and Dave Holland—he's a monster. I don't check out bass players that often. I'm more into checking out how players interact. I transcribed every musician's part on some of Herbie Hancock's music. That's when I discovered that Ron is a monster too. I admire him so much. What he does in the mix is unbelievable. His orchestration is incredible."

On Ron at Berklee College of Music [2005]: "Ron handed me my degree. He told me to calm down. I think he picked up that I'm hyper."
On the prospect of taking lessons with him: "I'd like to. I e-mailed him about it, but haven't heard back from him yet. But that's OK, because, after all, I haven't heeded his first piece of advice yet."

CHARLIE HADEN

On Ron's music from two live *DownBeat* Blindfold Tests:

"N.Y. Slick" (from *The Golden Striker*, Blue Note, 2003) Ron Carter, bass; Mulgrew Miller, piano; Russell Malone, guitar

---

"I love the sound that all three musicians get out of their instruments, and I love the way they play together. It reminds me of Oscar Peterson and Ray Brown with either Herb Ellis or Jim Hall. But I have some styling doubts about this being Ray Brown. The way the pianist plays those beautiful voicings with his left hand while he was soloing with his right makes me feel real close to Oscar. Another person who did that was Ray Bryant and, of course, Horace Silver. But the person who really did it was John Lewis, but this isn't Percy Heath.

"I have never heard this song before, and it's not something I would play. I'm an adagio guy, and that's a little too cutesy pie for me. Not that I have anything against that. It reminds me of 'The Surrey With the Fringe on Top.' Every time I hear that song I cringe, especially with the eighth notes played at the end of the phrase. It reminded me of when my parents had a farm. Every morning the chickens woke us up playing 'Surrey.' But it's difficult for me to tell who this is exactly because I don't listen to things like this.

(After audience member guesses) "Yes, that's Mulgrew. I love his left hand. He uses sevenths and thirds in the bass line, which I love. Russell is a great guy with a great sense of humor, and I love Mr. Carter's playing."

—January 2005 (Long Beach, California, IAJE Conference)

"Mr. Bow Tie" (from *Mr. Bow Tie*, Blue Note, 1995) Ron Carter, bass; Gonzalo Rubalcaba, piano; Lewis Nash, drums; Steve Kroon, percussion

---

"Well, first of all, the bass was mixed too loud. It's probably Ron Carter. On piano, that's Gonzalo Rubalcaba. The piece was nice. It sounds like it could have been written by Gonzalo. Maybe it's a Cuban song. I love Gonzalo. He takes a lot of care and listens while he's playing. On this track, he's playing very thoughtfully and with a gentleness and stillness. He has the ability to play with tenderness, then strength, then emotion. That's rare in the '90s when rock and pop keep pushing the volume up and up and up and even jazz is getting louder and louder. Pretty soon we won't be able to hear the humanness in the instruments."

"I'll give this piece five stars. The tune on the whole was nice, but what impressed me was Gonzalo's inspiration and improvisation."

—September 1997 (Monterey Jazz Festival)

DAVE HOLLAND

On Ron in Miles's Quintet: "I listened to Miles's music well before he offered me the fulltime job to replace Ron as the bassist. Whenever a new Quintet album came out, I went to the record store and bought it to check out what was happening that was new. They were doing some interesting things with how the rhythm section functioned. Tony was a great drummer, Herbie was so intuitive in the way he comped harmonically and Ron was the foundation as well as the harmonic director by what notes he chose. He made unorthodox choices. When I played gigs at the time, we emulated what they were doing. It's what you do as a young musician. That's how you pick up new languages. I used to play along with the records from that time. When I was 18, 19, 20, what Miles was doing with the Quintet was setting an example for us of where the music was being taken. I wanted to be a part of that music as a result."

On Ron's bass playing: "I listened to the way Tony tuned his drums so that you could hear Ron's sustain on the bass, his low-end playing. I loved how his E string had a ringing sustain. I also heard Ron playing with Herbie on his Blue Note records. The first time I heard Herbie's *Empyrean Isles* with Ron, Tony and Freddie Hubbard, it was exciting. It was new music, new sounds, new voicings in the rhythms. I remember staying up all night listening to the way those guys played."

On following Ron in Miles's group: "I knew that Ron had come before me, so I tried to not be so tied in to the way he played. It happens with all young players. You think to yourself, how did Ron do it? But I realized that the best thing was to be myself. The first record I was on with Miles was *Filles de Kilimanjaro*, which Ron also played on. Suddenly, I'm the bass player. I was very self-conscious. I knew the Quintet had been together for a long time and the music was working on intuitive levels of connection. There I was a new person coming into that. I was 21 and a slightly shy Englishman. I was just hoping to keep up and make a contribution while trying to read the cues and hear the signals."

GRADY TATE

On first meeting Ron: "After touring with Quincy Jones's big band, I worked in the New York studios. The first day I went, Ron was there. On the first downbeat, he made my blood boil. He had a big, full intonation that was unbelievable. I recognized that he and I had the same feel. Ron always stabilized the tempo. We became studio partners, laying down whatever rhythms were needed. Ron read his butt off and could improvise really well. The arrangers would give us the lead sheets, and we'd put in the sound that we felt was needed. We did that every day and then went our separate ways to our individual gigs at night."

On gigging with Ron: "Ron and I became tight. We were buddies. Before leaving home on a tour, my wife used to ask me who was in the band. I didn't know all the musicians, but I knew Ron was coming. So she would fix two lunches, one for me and one for Ron. He always had an undercurrent of humor and lightness in his playing. It was like, lighten up or die. Ron's time is so good, and mine wasn't bad either. His bass and my bass drum were joined together at the hip. And I felt like my drumming put a punctuation point on his full, round sound. The things we played fit into each of our microwaves. Playing with Ron is one of the great thrills of my life."

JAVON JACKSON

On meeting Ron: "I was working with Art Blakey at Sweet Basil opposite Ron's band with Cedar Walton and Billy Higgins. When I got my first leader date at The Village Vanguard, I hadn't been signed to Blue Note Records yet, so [owner] Lorraine Gordon asked me who I was going to bring with me. She wanted a good band. So I asked Ron if he would play. He said, 'Sure.' I asked him how much it would cost me. He said, 'You can't afford me, so pay me what you can.' After that we became friends. He and Janet invited me over for dinner. I was happy to be a part of their family. Ron encouraged me to go back to school to get my Masters."

On punctuality: "I played a gig with Ron where the starting time was 9:30. I arrived at 9:15 or 9:20. And Ron told me: 'I've been here since 8:45, and I was beginning to have a music concern.' So the next night, I got there at 8:45, but he came at 8:30."

On Ron's musicianship: "Ron has a mystique, like the mystique Miles had when he recorded for Columbia. Ron's a private guy up to a point, but you see him teaching a clinic and he's so accessible. Even though he's already made his contribution to jazz and stands for so much, he's still awake. He's always trying to create for tomorrow."

JOHN PATITUCCI

On Ron's influence: "I started out as a Ron fanatic. He was one of my huge influences, not only because of his feel and sound, but also for his musical mind. He is an architect of the highest order on the bass. I started listening to Ron early, when I was 13. I listened to him over and over on his own records and with Miles and other leaders. People don't realize how deep an effect he has had on bass lines in music. He took the walking tradition to a whole new level with how he outlines the harmony and creates rhythmic interest. He's a bass player who serves as the catalyst running the show on the bottom. If you listen to what he's playing carefully, what he plays on the blues is incredible. The interplay of Miles's group was such that Ron played over forms and stretched while also keeping the band together. Listening to those albums still totally floors me. He showed the ability to compose while keeping the harmony and melody free. That's a huge thing."

On Ron's recordings: "Ron's output as a leader and a session player is staggering. He can play it straight, swing into a groove with elegance or take the music all the way out. The breadth of his studio contributions is huge. His historical footprint is massive. The statements he's made over the decades are phenomenal—that depth of sound, the growl he gets, his rhythmic approach no matter what the setting is, how strong his sound is, yet so pliable."

On meeting Ron: "When I was playing in Chick Corea's band, I would bump into him on the road. When I first met him, I told him how thrilled and excited I was. He asked me why, and I told him I played the bass. I had breakfast with him once in Mexico, and I gave him a copy of my new album, *Heart of the Bass* [1991]. Later he wrote me a letter to let me know that he was listening to my record again and signed it with a smiling face. He may have an intimidating presence, but for him to pay me a compliment like that meant the world to me."

On Ron's impact in his playing in Wayne's quartet today: "If Ron hadn't done what he did when he played in Miles's band with Wayne, I don't know what it would have been like for me. The way Ron played was 100 percent important to me. He widened the boundaries, he opened up a way to be able to give but also stay connected, he threw things out and played like a composer, totally shaping the musical concept. I play the way I do in Wayne's quartet because of Ron."

On teaching at City College: "The school didn't hire me until after Ron left. But it's been a great honor to try to follow in his footsteps there."

JACKY TERRASSON

On hooking up with Ron: "I filled in for Mulgrew on three trio gigs that took place in Europe. I remember sitting in a cab on my way to JFK airport to go to Europe for another performance. Ron called me on my cell phone: 'Jacky, it's Ron Carter.' I thought, wow. I had met Ron before and seen him perform many times, but I had never played with him. He went straight to the point: 'I'm looking for a piano player, no, a great piano player, to do this gig. Are you available?' I told him I was in a taxi and would call him from the airport. Once there, I checked my schedule, called him and told him I could do it."

On bandstand attire: "Ron asked me, 'Do you have a dark suit?' I said, yes, I do. Then he asked, 'And dark shoes?' Yes, again. Then he said, 'OK, you've got it.' When we played, I had the uniform, and Ron brought me three ties, which I assume were the ties he gives to Mulgrew—one for each show. I'm cool with Ron's uniform. I have no problem with musicians dressing up for shows. Ron's the boss, and he wants us to go onstage looking the best we can. He's professional, and meticulous to the point."

On the library: "Ron asked me for my address to send his book. A lot of his arrangements are written out, but there's a lot of room for improvisation. He likes the music to be tight. It's reminiscent of the Modern Jazz Quartet. He told me I'd have to learn the book and learn the notes because it's serious music. I called him a couple of times with questions. Then a week before we left, we had a couple of rehearsals and that was it."

On performing with Ron: "It was a ball. Once we got past the tight arrangements, everything opened up. I love how Ron plays the harmonies. Sometimes I wasn't sure where our playing was going to end up, but like a cat, we always landed on all fours. I love playing that way. It's discovery, getting to a moment where a door opens."

On the traveling: "The only thing Ron told me was to be on time. I wasn't late, but I had heard stories about that. We flew to Europe, and then took overnight bus rides. I remember going to the back of the bus to a bunk bed to sleep. But Ron, I think, stayed up all night in the front, smoking his pipe and watching the road. We arrived at our hotel, and he said, 'OK, gentlemen, sound check is at four.'"

WYNTON MARSALIS

On Miles's Quintet with Ron: "I never heard that band till I was 18. I didn't know the history. In the '70s I was into funk, pop, Stevie Wonder, Marvin Gaye. I was a black kid in my teens, and that's what we listened to in my social circle. My father had some of Miles's records from the '50s, so I heard that. And as a trumpeter I also listened to Freddie Hubbard, Clark Terry, Sweets Edison, Blue Mitchell—the great ones. It wasn't until I was late in high school that I heard Miles's albums like *E.S.P., Circle in the Round, Filles de Kilimanjaro*. The interaction of the band on those albums was really unusual—flexible with form. Then I listened to *My Funny Valentine*, and I started to hear the quality and intelligence in the playing. The different times, different keys."

On getting to know Ron: "I recorded Herbie's album *Quartet* in 1981 with Ron and Tony, and we all went on the road. It was like being in school learning from Ron. I got close to him. I learned how he constructed components of the music and how he studied Bach's chorales as a foundation for playing harmonies. I loved him. He was so soulful. He was never aloof to me. It's as if he treated me and took care of me like a son. I was around the age of his kids. He always talked to me. I didn't get along with Tony so Ron acted as a buffer. We played together in New York, with Branford too. One time Ron and I drove to Cincinnati because he had to get his bass worked on."

On Ron's contributions to his career: "I looked up to Ron. He was very serious and had an unimpeachable integrity about playing. I could play with him, and I knew that he'd always keep the form. For me, going on the road with those guys when I was 20 was an education of the highest order. I didn't know very much. It was good fortune, good luck. It was like winning the lottery."

On Ron's career as a leader: "I haven't really followed it very closely. I did hear him playing those Bach records. He's always doing something new, and he brings excellence to every project. Everything he does, it's all about the music. It's clear that he's brought so much to jazz, like the way he interprets the beat, his harmonic conception that I believe isn't fully appreciated, and the freedom and intelligence he brought to the bottom voice."

JIMMY HEATH

On meeting Ron: "It was in 1962 when we recorded three sessions for Milt Jackson's sextet album *Invitations*, with Tommy Flanagan, Connie Kaye, Kenny Dorham and Ron. Orrin Keepnews produced it for Riverside Records. I met Ron at the first rehearsal. I remember him being a very proper gentleman who took care of serious business but also had a great sense of humor."

On playing with Ron: "He's a talented musician, a complete musician. He can read anything you put in front of him. And he was always on time. I call it Carter's Clock. He would stop in the middle of a set if we were going two or three minutes over. We're supposed to be off? Let's finish the tune. We performed and recorded together over the years, including the Riverside Reunion Tour."

Memorable moment with Ron: "Ron became a great composer over the years. Not too long ago he called me up for some information about a notation program for writing arrangements. When he called, I was washing the dishes. He made a joke about that, like why wasn't my wife doing the dishes? Soon after, I received a package with a beautiful white-with-blue-stripes chef's apron from Ron, with a note saying, 'Man, you stay in the kitchen.' I called him and said, 'Ron, if I was a restaurateur, you'd be the maitre d' at the door.'"

DR. BILLY TAYLOR

On Ron's career: "Ron is one of those guys who I admired, but never had the opportunity to work with. I knew him through Miles's band, and the way he played showed a depth of musical feeling and knowledge. I often played opposite Miles's band, and I was always struck by Ron's musicality. He held down the bass chair in a very personal manner."

On Ron's personality: "Ron's a funny dude. He's one of those guys who tells you a joke that you only get a couple of minutes later. I also remember Ron as one of the players you could depend on. I found that out when I was emceeing concert bills that he appeared on."

Most memorable moment with Ron: "I did a piece on Ron for the *CBS Sunday Morning* show. That's when I learned about a lot of the things Ron was doing, such as his cello group. I admired the fact that he was working with jazz and European classical music. I went to some of his gigs for the show, and then the camera crew went up to the roof of his building and took photos of him up there."

THE DREW SCHIBSTED STORY

MY NEPHEW DREW was in New York for a week, visiting the big city from his small university town of Chico, California. Drew not only attended a show by Ron but also got to meet him.

On June 9, 2006, Ron appeared at the Tribeca Performing Arts Center (borough of Manhattan Community College), as the special guest artist in an evening honoring the music of Oscar Pettiford, who tragically died in 1960 at the age of 37. (TPAC's series of shows that season was celebrating the renowned but long-defunct jazz club, Café Bohemia, where Oscar reigned as the original musical director.)

Ron, who was honored that evening with an award by TPAC at its first Lost Shrines Celebration, performed in a show of Oscar's tunes arranged by pianist Eric Gould and rendered by an all-star band that included tenor saxophonist Don Braden, alto saxophonist Antonio Hart, trombonist Robin Eubanks, trumpeter Sean Jones, bassist Leon Lee Dorsey and drummer Vincent Ector.

During the evening, Ron embellished the tunes by playfully swinging solos full of bluesy motifs, guitar-like runs and thick tonal richness. With thumb-strummed grace, he played lyrical melodies, oblique lead lines, neck slides and fluttered harmonics as well as comped the horn players with single-note runs and strummed chords. Of the two bassists, Ron's volume won out, as the mixing board downplayed Leon's contributions in favor of spotlighting Ron's.

The show came in two parts, separated by an intermission, which is when Drew met Ron.

A few words on Drew: He is a precocious 14-year-old, whose interests run the gamut from computer video games to jazz. He's been a fan of jazz since he was quite young, when he became fascinated with the piano playing of Cyrus Chestnut. Over the years, I've collected autographed photographs for him, including Cyrus, Wynton Marsalis and Ron.

The night before Ron's TPAC show we went to Dizzy's Club at Jazz at Lincoln Center to hear vibraphonist Joe Locke and his band. Even though Locke played a fine set with blurring vibes excursions, Drew was appreciative but not overwhelmed. The next night with Ron in the spotlight was quite different. During the first half of the show, he whispered in his Aunt Yvonne's ear that this was great.

Before continuing with the story of Drew's encounter with Ron, I must bring up the subject of attire. Drew, a teenager from California, hit town decked out in a combination of post-punk/surfer garb. At Dizzy's, he wore a T-shirt with light blue jeans, with rips across his lower thigh just above the knees. He wore sandals and was sockless. He was a little surprised by the attendees at the club, who were dressed for the evening in classier outfits. We told him it was OK. While New York has a cosmopolitan vibe, in the last decade the city has also accepted California casual in the workplace and nightspots.

Still, the next evening Drew insisted on dressing up a bit, borrowing my favorite dark blue dress shirt that fit him perfectly. So, he wore a fine shirt, but still the jeans and sandals. I had told Ron earlier in the week that I'd be introducing him to my young nephew, who was intrigued by jazz.

So, with the first part of the show over, Drew, Yvonne and I went backstage. I asked Drew later to write about his first encounter with Ron.

> **In Drew's words:** "I had been looking forward to my New York excursion for the better part of a year. My Uncle Dan informed me on the phone that I would be meeting Ron Carter, the famous jazz bassist.

I wasn't quite sure what to expect, never having brushed with fame before. Whatever anxiety there was manifested itself in the corridors leading to Ron's dressing room during intermission. If I had the nerve, I would have asked my uncle if we could turn back. However, I knew very well that my uncle was *really* excited about introducing me to this incredible musician. Plus, I didn't have the nerve, and so, under the facade of willing compliance, I trudged on.

"I'm going to be honest; the first thing I saw when I walked in the room was a delicious looking Quiznos sub sitting on a desk. *Well, I suppose they eat all right,* I quietly thought to myself. There were several individuals in the room who all possessed the intangible characteristic that separates artists from other human beings. They were chatting among themselves; I had no idea a dozen people could make so much noise. I finally realized that somewhere in this room was Ron Carter, and I set myself about looking for him.

"Well, I'm not entirely sure if there's anyone more recognizable than Ron Carter. I quickly located him sitting in a chair on the far side of the room, conversing with someone, presumably an assistant. Uncle Dan, Aunt Yvonne and I approached. The tall, impeccably dressed African-American bass player swiveled his chair to meet us, his smile and relaxed body language creating an aura of charisma. Dan introduced me, and Ron firmly shook my hand, still smiling his genuine smile.

"The first thing I remember him saying is this: 'You got any socks, man?' I looked down at my feet. Sure enough, I was not wearing socks with my sandals. I hadn't thought anything of it, and was a bit taken aback.

"'Yes,' I answered.

"He then made it clear to me that I did not in fact possess any socks, and that he was going to personally purchase and mail me a quality pair. Perhaps under different circumstances I would have protested, saying that I *did* have socks; I just wasn't wearing them, but alas, there was no resisting! I honestly can't remember anything past that point. I walked out of the dressing room somewhat stupefied; gaining a pair of socks was not a consequence of the meeting that I expected.

"Somewhere in here I'm supposed to communicate to you my impressions of Ron Carter, so I, as a 'Cool Californian,' will tell you that Ron Carter is indeed a very 'cool' individual, as well as an incredibly talented musician. I can also vouch for his alacrity; my socks arrived in the mail less than two weeks after my trip. With less than 10 minutes of personal experience, I'm going to recommend not only purchasing but also *reading* his new biography. It's sure to interest."

APPENDIX TWO

Infrequently Asked Questions

What make of car do you drive?

An Audi Q4 that has enough space in the back for my bass to fit.

Have you ever driven on a racetrack?

Yes, twice. The first time was with Miles in the '60s. I drove his Maserati at a racetrack in California. I went 90 miles per hour. The second time was more recently, at the Skip Barber Racing School at the Pocono Raceway [in the Pocono Mountains of eastern Pennsylvania], where I took a two-day course on defensive racetrack driving.

Do you still hit golf balls like you used to with Miles?

When I'm home, every Saturday I can, I go down to Chelsea Pier. I like the exercise. I need to do it given the routine of my life. I like being able to hit a golf ball 220 yards.

What kind of pipe do you smoke?

A Dunhill. I smoke a blend of tobacco that is custom-made for me by De La Concha Tobacconist at 56th Street and 6th Avenue in New York. They call it the Ron Carter Blend.

Do you own your apartment on West End Avenue or rent it?

I own it. It's in a co-op building. I bought the apartment in August 1973. [Note from a City College friend: When Ron became a Distinguished Professor, his wife Janet had a party for him at their home and invited all of his colleagues. One of the professors, a classical violinist who lived in a tiny, rent-controlled apartment in Riverdale for years, took one look around and declared that in his next life he wanted to be a jazz musician.]

Being that you're one of the best-dressed jazz musicians, where do you buy your clothes?

In New York, I buy custom suits and shirts at Paul Stuart on Madison Avenue. I also like Ralph Lauren and Frank Stella on Columbus Avenue. In Japan, I buy custom suits at F-One in Osaka.

Since you supply the ties for all your band members, where do you buy them?
At Paul Stuart.

What's your favorite vacation spot?
Turks and Caicos Islands [in the North Atlantic about 575 miles southeast of Miami]. It's quiet, there's no TV, no telephone. And no one knows me there.

How many hours of sleep do you get at night?
When I'm on tour, about three; when I'm home, around six. I may play a show at night, but then I have to get up three times a week at 5:45 a.m., which is when my personal trainer comes.

How many bass-related surgeries have you had?
None. My general view is that if you play the bass right, you won't get hurt. The bass isn't like the violin or piano where players can get carpal tunnel syndrome injuries. If I have an injury, I invite my doctors to come see how I perform so that they can suggest rehabilitation without surgery. My biggest concern is in transporting my bass and amp. So when I first got my personal trainer, I had him carry my bass and amp from my apartment to my car, then asked him to come up with exercises for me so that I could do that regularly without injuring myself.

What kind of non-bass surgeries have you had?
Once I was sitting on a chair with wheels and I flipped and fell onto my back. I had to have surgery to fix that. I've had two shoulder surgeries—one on each shoulder—for arthritis, where calcium deposits were scraping nerves. And I had LASIX eye surgery. I was wearing trifocal glasses at the time, and I was tired of never being able to find my glasses. My friend Victor Bailey said that he got the surgery from this doctor in London, who was world-renowned. So I got it done, and now my eyes are as good as a fighter pilot's.

What kind of books do you like to read?
Mysteries because I can hear the sound of music in the background of the stories. My name has appeared in several novels by writers like Michael Connelly and by Richard Greener in his book *The Ettelbruck Speculation*. [He reads an excerpt where the main character, NYPD Homicide Detective

INFREQUENTLY ASKED QUESTIONS

Ron Tillery, who is a bass player, pretends he's Ron Carter while he's practicing: "... He was Ron Carter—for as long as he could get away with it. He did the best he could with the Fender. It wasn't an upright. But, hey—he quickly reminded himself—*I ain't no Ron Carter either* ... It made him happy. It made him sad. It made him happy to be sad. He was making it—music."]

Who are your favorite authors?
Langston Hughes and any good mystery writer.

What is your favorite color?
Lavender.

What is your favorite sport?
I like them all, but basketball appeals to me the most. I like the idea of the teamwork that's involved even if the team has a big star on it.

What politician during your lifetime do you have the most respect for?
Rep. John Conyers from Detroit. He's the only person I know in a high political office who loves jazz and has made its recognition and preservation one of his political goals. He put into the Congressional Record how important jazz is to the U.S. And I also like John Conyers for the political goals he has.

What entertainer outside of the music world do you have the most respect for?
Curt Flood, the baseball player, for saying that a team cannot own you for life.

What's your favorite hobby?
Going to the beach and doing as little as possible.

But I thought you liked doing crossword puzzles?
Yes, but that's work.

Given that you are such a stickler for being on time, and even early, for gigs, what was your worst experience for being late for a show?
In 1973 I was scheduled to play with the Billy Eckstine Big Band at the Apollo Theater. I had been moving from our uptown apartment to our apartment on West End Avenue. I was doing most of the moving myself. As a result, I was running late. I had to change clothes and drive uptown. I got there just in time for the downbeat. I apologized afterwards to Mr. Eckstine. He said, no problem as long as you're there for the first note.

The other time was with James Brown in 1967. I was performing in a string section around the time he had that hit song, "It's a Man's Man's Man's World." It was a four-night gig at Latin Casino in Camden, New Jersey. Well, I was doing a recording date with Lee Morgan at Rudy Van Gelder's studio, and the session went really late. So I flew down the turnpike and got there just in time for the downbeat. James Brown's band would have to be there an hour before every show. I got there just in time. After the show, I went to James Brown to tell him I was Ron Carter and that I was sorry for being late. He said, "I know who you are, and I know that this was not an act of carelessness." And then he said, "Thanks for the recognition of my music and me."

Was your son, Myles, who was born in 1965 during your tenure with the Miles Davis Quintet, named after Miles?

No, it was my wife Janet's preference. I told Miles that Myles already had two eyes and didn't need another one.

What stereo equipment do you listen to music on?

In my living room I have Tetra Speakers, Model 606, that are also known as Thee Fraboni. I also have the Tetra 500 Subwoofer, also known as Thee Carter 500 because I helped to develop the subwoofer with the company. For the first time ever, I can hear what my bass sounds like in a session. I power my Tetras with Bel Canto electronics. The Bel Canto amplifiers can deliver up to 1,000 watts per channel when necessary. You know, I spend a lot of time in the studio getting the sound of my bass to play with the room's walls. With the Tetras, I can hear all the interactive artifacts of the room. Listening to this system is the closest I've come to actually being there. As Benny Golson says of his Tetras, "They are miracles," and I have to concur.

What is your Desert Island music? (Courtesy of the "Desert Island Jazz" April 2007 interview by Alisa Clancy, host of the daily "A Morning Cup of Jazz" program on KCSM, Jazz 91.1 FM, San Mateo, California)

- Miles Davis, *Kind of Blue*, "All Blues"
- Houston Person and Ron Carter, *Now's the Time*, "Einbahnstrasse"
- The Ron Carter Nonet, *Eight Plus*, "Eight"
- Rosa Passos and Ron Carter, *Entre Amigos*, "Desafinado"
- Ron Carter, *Brandenburg Concerto*, "Brandenburg Concerto No. 3 in G Major"
- Samuel Barber, Adagio from String Quartet No. 1, Op. 11

APPENDIX THREE

Selected Awards & Honors

- The International Society of Bassists Distinguished Achievement Award (June 2009)
- The New York-based Elders Share the Arts organization's Bel Kaufman Flamekeeper Award (Remembering the Past to Inspire the Future), which honors creative legacy (June 18, 2009).
- Jazz Wall of Fame—ASCAP Award (2008)
- The Austrian Cross of Honour for Science and the Arts (Austria's most prestigious artist award)—Previous recipients include Leonard Bernstein, Lionel Hampton, Oscar Peterson, Art Farmer, Ray Brown and Dave Brubeck. The award was presented by the leader of the Austrian Parliament, Mag. Gabi Burgstaller, at the Salzburg Jazz Festival (October 27, 2007).
- Acoustic Bassist of the Year—Jazz Journalists Association (2006)
- Lost Jazz Shrines Celebration Award—Tribeca Performing Arts Center in New York (2006)
- Honorary doctorate of music (DMA)—Berklee College of Music (2005)
- Ron Carter Day—Newark, New Jersey (August 2, 2002)
- Hutchison Medal—The highest honor bestowed by the University of Rochester, parent school of the Eastman School of Music (2002)
- Honorary doctorate of music (DMA)—New England Conservatory of Music (1999)
- NEA Jazz Masters Award (1998)—National Endowment for the Arts
- Honorary doctorate of music (DMA)—Manhattan School of Music (1998)
- Grammy Award—Best Jazz Instrumental Performance, Individual or Group for *A Tribute to Miles* album by Ron Carter, Herbie Hancock, Wallace Roney, Wayne Shorter and Tony Williams (1995)
- Distinguished Professor—The City College of New York (1993–2003)

- Grammy Award—Best Instrumental Composition ("Call Street Blues") from the film *'Round Midnight* (1987)

- *DownBeat* Critics' and Readers' Polls: Acoustic Bassist of the Year—Critics: 1975, '76, '77, '78, '79; Readers: 1973, '74, '75, '76, '77, '78, '79, '80, '81, '82, '83, '85, '86, 2007

APPENDIX FOUR

Selected Discography

It's impossible to know how many sessions Ron appeared on in the studio. Estimates range from 2,000 to 4,000. In lieu of a comprehensive discography, the following diverse sources provide a selected overview of Ron's recording history.

I. SELECTED DISCOGRAPHY AS A LEADER OR CO-LEADER—BASED ON ENCYCLOPEDIA OF POPULAR MUSIC

- *Where?*
- *Uptown Conversation*
- *Alone Together* (with Jim Hall)
- *Blues Farm*
- *All Blues*
- *Spanish Blue*
- *Yellow & Green*
- *Pastels*
- *Piccolo*
- *Third Plane*
- *Peg Leg*
- *A Song for You*
- *1 + 3* (Japan only)
- *Pick 'em*
- *Jazzstars in Concert* (with McCoy Tyner, Sonny Rollins)
- *Parade*
- *New York Slick*
- *Patrao*
- *Parfait*
- *Super Strings*
- *Heart and Soul* (with Cedar Walton)

- *Etudes*
- *Telephone* (with Jim Hall)
- *All Alone*
- *Plays Bach*
- *Panamanhattan* (with Richard Galliano)
- *Carnaval* (with Hank Jones, Sadao Watanabe, Tony Williams)
- *Friends*
- *Live at Village West* (with Jim Hall)
- *Jazz, My Romance*
- *A Tribute to Miles* (with Herbie Hancock, Wallace Roney, Wayne Shorter, Tony Williams)
- *Mr. Bow-Tie*
- *Akioustically Sound* (with Akio Sasaiima)
- *Brandenburg Concerto*
- *The Bass and I*
- *So What*
- *Orfeu*
- *When Skies Are Grey*
- *The Art of Three (Blow It Hard)*—Billy Cobham (with Ron, Kenny Barron)
- *Stardust*
- *4 Generations of Miles* (with George Coleman, Mike Stern, Jimmy Cobb)
- *Dialogues* (with Houston Person)
- *Eight Plus*
- *The Golden Striker*
- *Entre Amigos* (with Rosa Passos)
- *New York Cool: Live at the Blue Note*—Donald Harrison (with Ron, Billy Cobham)
- *Bill Frisell, Ron Carter, Paul Motian*
- *Dear Miles*

II. EMI MUSIC JAPAN DISCOGRAPHY

RELEASE DATES ARE issue years in Japan. Albums with an asterisk reissued in the United States on sister EMI label Blue Note Records.

- *Ron Carter Meets Bach* (1992) *
- *Friends* (1993) *

- *Jazz, My Romance* (1994) *
- *Mr. Bow-Tie* (1995) *
- *Brandenburg Concerto* (1996) *
- *The Bass and I* (1997) *
- *So What* (1998) *
- *Ron Carter Plays Jazz* (1998)
- *Romantic—Ron Carter Meets Classic* (1998)
- *Orefu* (1999) *
- *Sugawa Meets Ron Carter—Air* (2000)
- *When Skies Are Grey* (2000) *
- *Holiday in Rio* (2001)
- *Stardust* (2001) *
- *The Golden Striker* (2003) *
- *Dear Miles* (2006) *
- *It's the Time* (2007)
- *Jazz & Bossa* (2008)

III. RUDY VAN GELDER SESSIONS

IN THE COLLOQUY in the Miles Davis section of the book, famed engineer Rudy Van Gelder said, "[I have] a list from my private files of recordings during the LP period that I made with Ron Carter playing bass. There are 105 entries. I'm really proud of that."

Those recordings are listed below (in alphabetical but not in chronological order) with leader, album title and label:

- Nat Adderley—*Calling Out Loud* (A & M)
- Nat Adderley—*You Baby* (A & M)
- Airto—*Natural Feelings* (Buddha)
- Airto—*Free* (CTI)
- Airto—*Star Jazz* (CTI)
- Gene Ammons—*My Way* (Prestige)
- Roy Ayers—*He's Coming* (Polygram)
- Chet Baker—*She Was Too Good to Me* (CTI)
- George Benson—*Take Five* (CTI)
- George Benson—*Bad Benson* (CTI)
- George Benson—*Body Talk* (CTI)
- George Benson—*California Concert* (CTI)
- George Benson—*White Rabbit* (CTI)

- George Benson—*The Other Side of Abbey Road* (A & M)
- George Benson—*Shape of Things to Come* (A & M)
- George Benson—*Beyond the Blue Horizon* (CTI)
- Kenny Burrell—*God Bless the Child* (CTI)
- Kenny Burrell—*Guitar Forms* (Verve)
- Artie Butler—*Have You Met Miss Jones?* (A & M)
- Jaki Byard—*Here's Jaki* (Prestige)
- Donald Byrd—*Electric Byrd* (Blue Note)
- Ron Carter—*Where?* (Prestige)
- Ron Carter—*Blues Farm* (CTI)
- Ron Carter—*All Blues* (CTI)
- Ron Carter—*Spanish Blue* (CTI)
- Ron Carter—*New York Slick* (Milestone)
- Ron Carter—*Parade* (Milestone)
- Ron Carter—*Pick 'em* (Milestone)
- Ron Carter—*Peg Leg* (Milestone)
- Ron Carter—*Patrao* (Milestone)
- Ron Carter—*Etudes* (Elektra)
- Hank Crawford—*We've Got a Good Thing* (Kudu)
- Hank Crawford—*Don't You Worry 'bout a Thing* (Kudu)
- Hank Crawford—*Help Me Make It Through the Night* (CTI)
- Deodato—*Prelude* (CTI)
- Paul Desmond—*Skylark* (CTI)
- Paul Desmond—*Pure Desmond* (CTI)
- Paul Desmond—*Summertime* (A & M)
- Paul Desmond—*From the Hot Afternoon* (A & M)
- Don Ellis Quintet—*New Ideas* (Prestige)
- Gil Evans—*Out of the Cool* (Verve)
- Gil Evans—*The Individualism of Gil Evans* (Verve)
- Stan Getz—*Voices* (Verve)
- Stan Getz Quartet—*Sweet Rain* (Verve)
- Astrud Gilberto/Stanley Turrentine—*Gilberto With Turrentine* (CTI)
- Johnny Hammond—*Wild Horses Rock Steady* (Kudu)
- Johnny Hammond—*Johnny Hammond The Prophet* (Kudu)
- Johnny Hammond—*Higher Ground* (Kudu)

SELECTED DISCOGRAPHY

- Herbie Hancock—*Speak Like a Child* (Blue Note)
- Coleman Hawkins—*Night Hawk* (Prestige)
- Coleman Hawkins—*The Hawk Relaxes* (Prestige)
- Freddie Hubbard—*Red Clay* (CTI)
- Freddie Hubbard—*Straight Life* (CTI)
- Freddie Hubbard—*Sky Dive* (CTI)
- Freddie Hubbard—*First Light* (CTI)
- Freddie Hubbard—*Keep Your Soul Together* (CTI)
- Jackie & Roy—*Time & Love* (CTI)
- Milt Jackson—*Sunflower* (CTI)
- Milt Jackson—*Olinga* (CTI)
- Milt Jackson—*Goodbye* (CTI)
- Antonio Carlos Jobim—*Wave* (A & M)
- Antonio Carlos Jobim—*Stone Flower* (CTI)
- J.J. Johnson, Kai Winding—*Israel* (A & M)
- J.J. Johnson, Kai Winding—*Betwixt & Between* (A & M)
- Hubert Laws—*The Rite of Spring* (CTI)
- Hubert Laws—*In the Beginning* (CTI)
- Hubert Laws—*Carnegie Hall* (CTI)
- Hubert Laws—*Morning Star* (CTI)
- Hubert Laws—*The Chicago Theme* (CTI)
- Hubert Laws—*Crying Song* (CTI)
- Hubert Laws—*Afro-Classic* (CTI)
- Herbie Mann—*Glory of Love* (A & M)
- Wes Montgomery—*A Day in the Life* (A & M)
- Wes Montgomery—*Down Here on the Ground* (A & M)
- Wes Montgomery—*Tequila* (Verve)
- Lee Morgan—*The Procrastinator* (Blue Note)
- Gerry Mulligan—*Carnegie Hall Concert* (CTI)
- Esther Phillips—*Black-Eyes Blues* (Kudu)
- Yasushi Sawada—*Imagination* (Victor)
- Don Sebesky—*Giant Box* (CTI)
- Don Sickler—*The Music of Kenny Dorham* (Uptown)
- Horace Silver—*Silver 'n Percussion* (Blue Note)
- Horace Silver—*Silver 'n Strings* (Blue Note)
- Horace Silver—*Silver 'n Wood* (Blue Note)

- Horace Silver—*Silver 'n Voices* (Blue Note)
- Horace Silver—*Silver 'n Brass* (Blue Note)
- Horace Silver—*Silver 'n Percussion* (Blue Note)
- Jimmy Smith—*Got My Mojo Workin'* (Verve)
- Gabor Szabo—*Mizrab* (CTI)
- Grady Tate—*She Is My Lady* (Janus)
- Ed Thigpen—*Out of the Storm* (Verve)
- Stanley Turrentine—*Sugar* (CTI)
- Stanley Turrentine—*Cherry* (CTI)
- Stanley Turrentine—*Salt Song* (CTI)
- Stanley Turrentine—*Don't Mess With Mister T* (CTI)
- Stanley Turrentine—*The Sugar Man* (CTI)
- Various Artists (including Herbie Hancock, Freddie Hubbard, Joe Henderson)—*One Night With Blue Note* (Blue Note)
- Various Artists (including Lee Konitz, Lennie Tristano, Billy Bauer, Arnold Press)—*25 Years of Prestige* (Prestige)
- Various Artists (including Freddie Hubbard, Stanley Turrentine, Herbie Hancock)—*In Concert Volume 2* (CTI)
- Grover Washington Jr.—*Soul Box* (Kudu)
- Grover Washington Jr.—*All the King's Horses* (Kudu)
- Grover Washington Jr.—*Inner City Blues* (Kudu)
- Grover Washington Jr.—*Side Star* (Kudu)
- Kai Winding—*The Incredible Kai Winding* (Impulse)

NOTE: Not all RVG sessions Ron appeared on are listed above (for example, Bobby Hutcherson's *Components* on Blue Note)

IV. SIBLEY MUSIC LIBRARY, EASTMAN SCHOOL OF MUSIC

IN DECEMBER 2001, Ron donated more than 700 albums from his personal collection to Eastman School of Music's Sibley Music Library. The collection comprises recordings with Ron as a performer (even if only appearing on a single band or track). Daniel Zager, associate dean and head librarian of Sibley, said that the school started with Ron's albums, "then supplemented that list with searches of our online catalog for Carter recordings held by Sibley Music Library prior to this gift or purchased since receipt of the gift. It is not a comprehensive discography of Ron's recorded work, but it is an extensive one, representing holdings that we are proud to have."

The full collection is available at the Sibley Music Library homepage: www.esm.rochester.edu/sibley. Select "Voyager Catalog," then as an "Author" search type in: Ron Carter Audio Archive and Collection.

SELECTED DISCOGRAPHY

The following is a sampling (80) from the Sibley collection (with titles in alphabetical order):

- McCoy Tyner—*13th House* (Milestone, 1982)
- Flora Purim—*500 Miles High* (Milestone, 1976)
- Michael Longo—*900 Shares of the Blues* (Groove Merchant, 1974)
- Wallace Roney—*According to Mr. Roney* (32 Jazz, 1987/1997)
- Kenny Garrett—*African Exchange Student* (Atlantic Jazz, 1990)
- Jimmy Scott—*All the Way* (Sire, 1992)
- Esther Phillips—*Alone Again, Naturally* (Kudu, 1972)
- Sonny Rollins—*Alternative Rollins* (Paris: RCA, 1981)
- Herbie Mann—*America/Brasil* (Lightyear Entertainment, 1997)
- Kevin Hays—*Andalucia* (Blue Note, 1997)
- Ron Carter—*Bass Phrazes* (Pangaea Recording/Big Fish Audio, 2000)
- Milt Jackson Orchestra—*Big Bags* (Riverside, 1962)
- Gene Ammons—*The Black Cat!* (Prestige, 1971)
- Randy Weston—*Blue Moses* (CTI, 1972)
- Bob Brookmeyer—*Bob Brookmeyer and Friends* (Columbia, 1965)
- Bobby Timmons Trio—*Born to Be Blue* (Riverside, 1963)
- Billy Joel—*The Bridge* (Columbia, 1986)
- Cedar Walton—*Cedar Walton Plays* (Delos, 1987)
- James Williams All-Stars—*Classic Encounters* (DIW/Jasrac, 2000)
- Attila Zoller—*Common Cause* (Enja, 1979)
- Bobby Hutcherson—*Components* (Blue Note, 1965)
- Bob James/Earl Klugh—*Cool* (Warner Bros., 1992)
- Phil Woods Quartet—*Cool Woods* (Somethin' Else, 1999)
- Cyrus Chestnut—*Cyrus Chestnut* (Atlantic, 1998)
- Roy Ayers—*Daddy Bug* (Atlantic, 1969)
- Diana Ross—*Diana Ross Live* (EMI, 1993)
- Bette Midler—*The Divine Miss M.* (Atlantic, 1972)
- Don Heckman/Ed Summerlin—*The Don Heckman-Ed Summerlin Improvisational Jazz Workshop* (Ictus Records, 1967)
- Joey Baron—*Down Home* (Intuition, 1997)
- Kevin Eubanks—*Face to Face* (GRP, 1986)
- Hank Mobley—*Far Away Lands* (Blue Note, 1984)
- Eric Dolphy—*Far Cry* (New Jazz/Prestige, 1961)

- Prince Lasha—*Firebirds Live at Berkeley Jazz Festival, Vol. II* (Birdseye, 1975)
- Roberta Flack—*First Take* (Atlantic, 1969)
- Tony Williams—*Foreign Intrigue* (Blue Note, 1985)
- Sam Rivers—*Fuchsia Swing Song* (Blue Note, 1965)
- Gato Babieri—*Gato Barbieri's Finest Hour* (Verve, 2000)
- Herbie Hancock—*Gershwin's World* (Verve, 1998)
- Eddie Harris—*Greater Than the Sum of His Parts* (32 Jazz, 1998)
- Hank Jones—*Hanky Panky* (East Wind, 1975)
- Harry Connick Jr.—*Harry Connick* (Columbia, 1997)
- Shirley Horn—*I Remember Miles* (Verve, 1998)
- Martin Mull—*I'm Everyone I've Ever Loved* (ABC Records, 1979)
- Eric Gale—*In a Jazz Tradition* (EmArcy, 1988)
- Cindy Blackman—*In the Now* (HighNote, 1998)
- Randy Brecker—*In the Idiom* (Denon, 1997)
- Tony Bennett—*Jazz* (Columbia, 1987)
- Benny Green—*Kaleidoscope* (Blue Note, 1997)
- Dexter Gordon—*Landslide* (Liberty/United/Blue Note, 1962)
- Michel Legrand—*Legrand "Live" Jazz* (BMG, 1991)
- Lou Donaldson—*Lush Life* (Blue Note, 1986)
- Pete Hamill—*Massacre at My Lai* (Flying Dutchman, 1970)
- Kronos Quartet—*Monk Suite* (Landmark, 1985)
- Jane Monheit—*Never Never Land* (N-Coded Music/Warlock, 2000)
- Charles Earland—*Odyssey Island* (Mercury, 1976)
- Charles Lloyd—*Of Course, Of Course* (Columbia, 1965)
- Shirley Scott—*On a Clear Day* (Impulse, 1972)
- Benny Golson—*One Day, Forever* (Arkadia Jazz, 2001)
- Booker Little—*Out Front* (Candid, 1961)
- Marc Whitfield—*Patrice* (Warner Bros., 1991)
- Billy Cobham—*Picture This* (GRP, 1987)
- Tommy Flanagan—*Positive Intensity* (CBS/Sony, 1977)
- Renee Rosnes—*Renee Rosnes* (Blue Note, 1990)
- Gil Scott-Heron—*The Revolution Will Not Be Televised* (Flying Dutchman, 1974)
- Ithamara Koorax—*Rio Vermelho* (Imagem, 1995)
- Ruth Brown—*Ruth Brown* (Cobblestone, 1972)

- Benny Goodman—*Seven Come Eleven* (Columbia, 1982)
- Stephane Grappelli—*So Easy to Remember* (Omega, 1993)
- Helen Merrill—*Something Special* (Inner City, 1978)
- Oliver Nelson—*Sound Pieces* (Impulse, 1966)
- Russell Malone—*Sweet Georgia Peach* (Impulse, 1998)
- Yusef Lateef—*This Is Yusef Lateef* (Riverside, 1960)
- Michael Wolff—*The Tic Code* (Razor & Tie, 2000)
- Michael Franks—*Tiger in the Rain* (Warner Bros., 1979)
- Toshiko Akiyoshi Quintet—*Toshiko at Top of the Gate* (Columbia, 1969)
- Geri Allen—*Twenty One* (Blue Note, 1994)
- Manhattan Transfer—*Vocalese* (Atlantic, 1985)
- Abbey Lincoln—*World Is Falling Down* (Verve, 1990)
- Chet Baker—*You Can't Go Home Again* (A & M, 1977)
- Sunbirds—*Zagara* (Finger Records/Polydor, 1973)

V. ETHAN IVERSON SELECTED

I AM A devout fan. Ever since I was 14 or so, the name Ron Carter on a record has significantly increased the chances of my purchasing it. As a discography, the following list is severely incomplete. It's just a selection of the Ron Carter albums I own or have heard over the years. To avoid duplication, box sets aren't considered; only the first issued titles are given.

I have starred the discs I think are particularly good examples of prime Ron Carter. Naturally, albums documenting crucial relationships with Miles Davis, Herbie Hancock, Wayne Shorter, Joe Henderson and Hank Jones are all "prime." Other albums are starred because of a particular drummer: A favorite hobby of many musicians is comparing how Tony Williams, Elvin Jones, Jack DeJohnette, Billy Higgins, Roy Haynes, Al Foster and everybody else sound next to Ron Carter. It's always a significant relationship. Ron Carter makes everyone pay attention.

—ETHAN IVERSON,
pianist of the jazz trio The Bad Plus

- Pepper Adams—*Encounter!** (with Zoot Sims)
- Geri Allen—*Twenty One*
- Chet Baker—*Once Upon a Summertime*
- Joey Baron—*Down Home*
- Kenny Barron—*One + One + One**
- Bob Brookmeyer—*With Friends*

- Jaki Byard—*Here's Jaki*; *Hi-Fly*
- Ron Carter—*Etudes**; *Uptown Conversation**; *Patrao*; *Where?*; *Third Plane*; *New York Slick*; *Anything Goes*; *Parade**; *Blues Farm*; *All Blues**
- Miles Davis—*Seven Steps to Heaven**; *Live in Europe**; *Four and More**; *My Funny Valentine**; *E.S.P.**; *Sorcerer**; *Miles Smiles**; *Nefertiti**; *Live in Berlin**; *No Blues**; *Live in Toyko**; *The Greatest Concert Ever**; *Water Babies**; *Filles de Kilimanjaro**; *Live at the Plugged Nickel**
- Deodato—*Deodato*
- Paul Desmond—*From the Hot Afternoon*
- Eric Dolphy—*Out There*; *Far Cry**
- Roberta Flack—*First Take**
- Tommy Flanagan—*The Ultimate Trio**; *Positive Intensity*
- Bill Frisell—*Bill Frisell, Ron Carter and Paul Motian*
- Red Garland—*Crossings*
- Stan Getz—*Stan Getz and Bill Evans*
- Benny Golson—*Free**
- Dexter Gordon—*'Round Midnight* (soundtrack); *The Other Side of 'Round Midnight*
- The Great Quartet (with Freddie Hubbard, McCoy Tyner and Elvin Jones)—*Live at the Playboy Jazz Festival*
- Johnny Griffin—*The Kerry Dancers*
- Jim Hall—*Live at Village West**; *Alone Together*; *Concierto*
- Herbie Hancock (also V.S.O.P.)—*Empyrean Isles**; *Maiden Voyage**; *Speak Like a Child**; *V.S.O.P.** (California); *V.S.O.P.** (New York); *The Tempest in the Colosseum*; *Trio* (Japan); *Quartet**
- Barry Harris—*Magnificent**
- Eddie Harris—*The In Sound*
- Coleman Hawkins—*Night Hawk*
- Joe Henderson—*Mode for Joe**; *Tetragon**; *The Kicker**; *Power to the People**; *State of the Tenor Vol. 1**; *State of the Tenor Vol. 2**
- Andrew Hill—*Grass Roots*; *Lift Every Voice*
- Johnny Hodges—*Three Shades of Blue**
- Shirley Horn—*I Remember Miles*
- Lena Horne—*Lena and Michel* (with Michel Legrand)
- Freddie Hubbard—*Red Clay*; *Super Blue**; *Sky Dive*; *Stardust* (with Benny Golson)

SELECTED DISCOGRAPHY

- Bobby Hutcherson—*Components*
- Milt Jackson—*Invitation; Sunflower**
- Hank Jones (also The Great Jazz Trio)—*Kindness, Joy, Love, and Happiness*; Hanky Panky*; Milestones*; Live at the Village Vanguard Vol. 1*; Live at the Village Vanguard Vol. 2*; The Great Tokyo Meeting*; Live Under the Sky*
- Antonio Carlos Jobim—*Stone Flower; Wave**
- Steve Kuhn—*Life's Magic**
- Mel Lewis—*And Friends*
- Branford Marsalis—*Scenes in the City; Royal Garden Blues**
- Wynton Marsalis—*Hot House Flowers*; Black Codes (From the Underground)*
- Mulgrew Miller—*The Countdown*
- Wes Montgomery—*Down Here on the Ground*; A Day in the Life; Tequila*
- Frank Morgan—*Yardbird Suite*
- Lee Morgan—*The Procrastinator**
- David Newman—*Newmanism*
- Hermeto Pascoal—*Hermeto*
- Sam Rivers—*Fuchsia Swing Song; Contours*
- Sonny Rollins—*Now's the Time*; Milestone Jazzstars* (with McCoy Tyner and Al Foster)
- Wayne Shorter—*Speak No Evil*; The All-Seeing Eye*; Schizophrenia*; The Soothsayer**
- James Spaulding—*Brilliant Corners*
- Bobby Timmons—*Born to Be Blue; In Person*
- Charles Tolliver—*Paper Man**
- Stanley Turrentine—*On a Clear Day; Sugar; More Than a Mood*
- McCoy Tyner—*The Real McCoy*; Extentions; Supertrios*; Triden; Fly With the Wind; Passion Dance; It's About That Time* (with Jackie McLean)
- Cedar Walton (also Sweet Basil Trio)—*Heart and Soul*; Cedar Walton - Ron Carter - Jack DeJohnette; Cedar Walton Plays; Saint Thomas; My Funny Valentine*
- Tony Williams—*Foreign Intrigue; Life Time*
- Nancy Wilson—*But Beautiful*

Acknowledgments

TOP-OF-THE-LINE ACKNOWLEDGMENT GOES to the dean of jazz bassists: Mr. Ron Carter—a.k.a. Checkpoint Charlie, the Beacon, Jazz Master, Pops—who allowed full candid access into his life during our many interviews. Ron also provided copious material, including magazines, clips, photos and recordings that he and his mother Willie collected over the years. Thanks also go to Ron's family members, friends, band mates (present and past), students and colleagues whom I interviewed about his life and music.

High fives go to the ArtistShare team, specifically Brian Camelio, whose vision and encouragement made this book possible, and Andrew Hadro, whose attention to detail aided mightily in getting the production of the book off the ground. And because of ArtistShare's unique model of participation, I want to sincerely thank all the people who supported the project.

Huge thanks go to Professor Barbara Hanning of the Music Department at The City College of New York. From day one, she has helped with the project, reading each chapter and editing. Her copyediting catches and insightful edits— helping me find the right words—proved to be invaluable. A jazz-journalism colleague and an amazing book designer, Forrest Dylan Bryant was responsible for taking all my word documents and transforming them into the finished product. He too has been a major source of encouragement and inspiration.

It's said that you can't judge a book by its cover. But in my way of thinking, you can't have a book without an aesthetically pleasing cover. A standing ovation goes to Carol Friedman for both her superb portrait of Ron and meticulous cover design.

As my friend Stuart Brinin always reminds me, the photographer is an unsung hero when it comes to making the written word come to life. Not only is Stu a great friend, but he's also a damn good photographer. Check out his shots of Ron in the galleries. Special thanks also go to Claire Hoeffler who contributed wonderful shots of Ron from his college days taken by her late husband, the esteemed photographer Paul Hoeffler. Kudos also to Ron's sister Sandy for early photos of her brother, as well as Arthur Lieb, who contributed pictures from Ron's high school days at Cass Tech, and Jack Vartoogian for his intimate photo of Ron at rest on the bass. I am grateful to Spike Sugiyama at EMI Japan and Cem Kurosman at Blue Note

Records for getting me access to the photos of Ron's EMI Records album covers; likewise, to Nick Phillips and Larissa Collins of the Concord Music Group for doing the same from Ron's catalog there.

In the course of my research, several people were integral to helping me unearth hundreds of articles on Ron's career. Special thanks go to Terri Hinte, who, shortly before she left Fantasy Records (now owned by the Concord Music Group) as its longtime publicist, photocopied Ron's entire clip file that she had collected throughout his career with Milestone Records. Jason Koransky, editor of *DownBeat*, was another invaluable resource. He combed the magazine's archives to photocopy all the coverage Ron received there throughout his career. Speaking of *DownBeat*, in addition to Jason, whose support and encouragement were immense throughout the book-writing project, thanks are also due to publisher Frank Alkyer, who helped to publicize the project while the biography was being written.

Special thanks go to Nat Hentoff for writing the Foreword, Ethan Iverson for contributing to the discography and Drew Schibsted for his written appreciation of Ron in the "In Their Own Words" appendix. Thanks also to Rudy Van Gelder for his discography information as well as Douglas Lowry, dean of Eastman School of Music, and Daniel Zager, associate dean and head librarian at Eastman's Sibley Music Library, for their help with Ron's discography.

I also extend my appreciation to String Letter Press for permission to reprint a sidebar I wrote on Ron's teaching ("Tackling Improvisation") from my May 2004 cover story on Ron for *Strings* magazine, and to *Bass Player* magazine and writer Brigid Bergen for permission to use her sidebar ("Ron Carter's 5 Tips for Players") from her September 2003 article. Both sidebars appear in the chapter on Ron's teaching career.

Also thank you to Verena M. Pfister, one of Ron's biggest European fans and a participant on this project. Special thanks go to Madeleine Crouch, general manager at the International Society of Bassists, who from the very beginning of the book project was a great supporter who offered enthusiastic encouragement.

Other thank you's go to Don Lucoff (DL Media); Michael Bürgi (*Mediaweek*); Rob Hayes; Wendy Oxenhorn; Quintell Williams; Alisa Clancy and Melanie Berzon for letting me sit in on their interviews with Ron on KCSM, Jazz 91, in San Mateo, California; Michelle Kuypers at the North Sea Jazz Festival for allowing me to set up a Q&A session with Ron's quartet members, who interviewed him in front of an audience; and for the hospitality at the clubs and performance venues where Ron performed during the course of the project—in New York: Birdland, the Blue Note, Merkin Concert Hall at Kaufman Center, the Tribeca Performing Arts Center; in California: Yoshi's in Oakland and the Hollywood Bowl (Playboy Jazz Festival).

A big round of applause also goes to cable network BETJ for its support of the project. Thank you especially Paxton Baker and Tony Wheelock.

Finally, on a personal level, thankyouthankyouthankyou to friends and siblings who cheered me on. Eternal appreciation goes to my parents—Flip (for his spirit of independence which gave me the fortitude to take on such a challenging and rewarding project), and Shirl (a painter who has been a fan of my artistic endeavors ever since I started writing as a kid and continues to read all my *DownBeat* articles). Last, but certainly not least, hugs and kisses to my significant other, Evantheia Schibsted, who has been the biggest support through the many peaks and valleys I traveled while writing this book. Your patience and wisdom and faith sustained me.

Index of Names

A

Abdul-Jabbar, Kareem 31
Adderley, Cannonball 74, 81–82
Adderley, Nat 75, 172, 195, 378, 417
Alexander, Eric 81, 201
Allen, Geri 15, 56, 196, 228, 229, 238, 423
Allen, Sanford 60, 70, 169, 256, 348
Altman, Robert 228–230, 231, 239, 318
Altschul, Barry 110
Austin, Patti 163, 218

B

Bach, Johann Sebastian 53, 55, 159, 175, 252–257, 265, 270, 294, 297, 301, 405, 416
Bailey, Victor 241, 259, 288, 410
Baker, Chet 157, 160, 166, 171, 172, 182, 228, 294, 307, 417, 423
Baron, Joey 196, 214–217, 421, 423
Barretto, Ray 83, 179
Kenny Barron 164, 165, 169, 171, 177, 182, 232, 256, 316, 319, 321, 328, 330, 333, 336, 349, 350, 416, 423
Beatles, The 109, 135, 154, 362
Begian, Harry 52
Belafonte, Harry 229, 238
Belden, Bob 12, 99, 104, 141, 256
Benson, George 111, 158, 304, 417, 418
Bergman, Alan 167, 362
Blakey, Art 64, 77, 80, 81, 123, 235, 329, 335, 357, 402
Brecker, Michael 26, 145, 163, 284, 390
Brown, James 67, 108, 412
Brown, Ray 67, 71, 85, 223, 234, 235, 237, 241, 262, 268, 319, 372, 388, 400, 413
Brubeck, Dave 55, 67, 74, 75, 77, 100, 108, 183, 413
Burrell, Kenny 55, 56, 74, 77, 79, 87, 158, 196, 201, 215, 235, 305, 418
Byard, Jaki 75, 78, 87, 214, 370, 418, 423
Byrd, Donald 54, 56, 104, 240, 418

C

Campbell, Jeff 70
Carter, Benny 294, 297, 298
Carter, Betty 74, 234, 235, 335, 386
Carter, Janet Hasbrouck 15–16, 31, 68–69, 72–73, 75, 87, 103, 116, 134, 177–179, 310, 402, 409, 412
Carter, Lutheran 38–44, 72
Carter, Myles 16, 31, 48, 87, 134, 162, 177, 179, 356, 357, 358, 360, 361, 362, 383, 412
Carter, Ron Jr. 16, 31, 48, 72, 87, 117, 134, 136, 177, 179, 356, 385
Carter, Willie 38–44, 47–48, 426
Chambers, Paul 53–54, 56, 71, 76, 79, 84, 88, 100, 102, 114, 118, 130, 148, 149, 156, 232, 241, 262, 268, 334, 342, 344, 387, 397, 399
Chapin, Simeon 272–273

Clarke, Stanley 127, 259, 359, 366, 398–399
Cobb, Jimmy 88, 102, 142, 197, 416
Cobham, Billy 19, 138, 146, 159, 161, 162, 171, 205, 321, 339, 416, 422
Cohen, Noal 58, 60, 63, 67
Coleman, George 13, 103, 105, 115, 116, 123, 125, 142, 416
Colley, Scott 386–394
Coltrane, John 6, 22, 66, 70, 74, 100, 130, 153, 183, 199, 210, 263, 266, 357, 362, 386, 388
Corea, Chick 106, 111, 134, 171, 198, 232, 322, 332, 397–398, 403
Corman, Ned 61–62, 90
Cosby, Bill 262, 377
Crossley, Payton 30, 183, 247, 327, 341, 337
Cuscuna, Michael 106, 110, 147, 176, 200

D

Davis, Art 70, 386
Davis, Miles 3, 5–6, 9, 10, 11, 12, 13, 22, 23, 25, 26, 28–30, 31, 32, 53, 74, 75, 86, 88, 99–146, 148, 149, 156, 160, 162, 163, 171, 172, 175, 176, 177, 180, 182–184, 195, 196, 197, 200, 202, 207, 210, 213, 214, 215, 218, 225, 231, 232, 233, 244, 250, 263, 265, 267, 268, 274, 294, 295, 302, 304, 309, 319, 320, 321, 322, 326, 327, 329, 331, 338, 339, 340, 342, 343, 344, 348, 349, 357, 359, 364, 383, 384, 391, 392, 393, 397, 398, 399, 401, 402, 403, 404, 406, 409, 412, 413, 416, 417, 421, 422, 423, 424
Davis, Richard 79, 114, 215, 219, 269, 270, 304, 383, 384, 388, 398
DeJohnette, Jack 26, 122, 144, 159, 160, 170, 171, 182, 208, 284, 349, 423, 425
Desmond, Paul 4, 55, 155, 157, 160, 195, 199, 307, 418, 424
Deutsch, Didier 154, 155, 161, 164–166
Dolphy, Eric 75, 78, 85, 196, 347, 370, 387, 421, 424
Dorsey, Leon "Lee" 269–270, 407
Duvivier, George 75, 78, 79, 84, 85, 218, 384

E

Early, Gerald 108
Eastwood, Clint 202, 223, 224
Eckstine, Billy 365, 411
Edwards, Esmond 85
Ellington, Duke 4, 64, 71, 74, 75, 144, 157, 256, 265, 345, 362, 370, 387, 388
Ellis, Don 75, 78, 122, 214, 370, 418
Ellis, Herb 67, 177, 316, 319, 400
Ellis, Pee Wee 57, 58, 65, 66, 158
Evans, Bill 74, 81, 138, 167, 174, 195, 302, 369, 424
Evans, Gil 79, 88, 104, 153, 183, 244, 326, 418

F

Farber, Seth 262
Farmer, Art 65, 80, 88, 101, 102, 116, 138, 171, 174, 302, 321, 386, 413
Farnsworth, Joe 81, 201
Feldman, Victor 82, 103, 105
Flack, Roberta 195, 202, 214, 343, 422, 424
Flanagan, Tommy 75, 199, 305, 336, 378, 389, 405, 422, 424
Foster, Al 168, 172, 176, 206, 207, 423, 425
Franklin, Aretha 195, 201
Freedman, Robert 249, 321
Frisell, Bill 196, 209, 212, 213–217, 247, 416, 424

INDEX

G

Gage, David 12, 381, 382
Garland, Red 101, 130, 172, 232, 295, 342, 345, 424
Garrett, Kenny 200, 421
Getz, Stan 55, 154, 195, 198, 214, 242, 418, 424
Gibson, Peter 68
Golson, Benny 65, 72, 80, 88, 181, 199, 201, 249, 265, 267, 412, 422, 424
Goodman, Benny 22, 198, 266, 423
Gordon, Dexter 227, 422, 424
Green, Benny 200, 234, 319, 335, 422
Grenadier, Larry 259, 380, 386–394

H

Haden, Charlie 200, 366, 387, 400–401
Hall, Jim 19, 26, 88, 157, 167, 174, 196, 198, 214, 224, 302, 303, 308, 318, 325, 345, 386, 391, 392, 400, 415, 416, 424
Hamilton, Chico 13, 72, 74, 75, 100, 304, 370
Hancock, Herbie 9, 10, 14, 19, 25–30, 86, 100, 104, 106, 109, 110, 111, 113, 114, 116, 117, 118–123, 124, 126, 127, 128, 129, 131, 132, 133, 134, 135, 137, 138, 139–141, 142, 144, 145, 146, 159, 161, 171, 173, 175, 196, 200, 202, 215, 228, 246, 283, 284, 295, 299, 321, 329, 339, 344, 345, 357, 359, 388, 390, 397, 398, 399, 401, 405, 413, 416, 419, 420, 421, 422, 423, 424, 431, 432
Hanna, Roland 56, 60, 138, 157, 162, 181, 235, 268, 294, 307, 329, 333, 336, 359
Hanning, Barbara 33, 263–267, 271, 426
Harrison, Donald 205–206, 416
Harris, Stefon 256

Hayes, Louis 55, 82
Haynes, Roy 77, 78, 85, 87, 269, 345, 398, 423
Heath, Albert "Tootie" 81, 82, 84
Heath, Jimmy 84, 105, 405–406
Heath, Percy 84, 303, 321, 366, 372, 388, 400
Heckman, Don 78, 171, 197, 229, 255, 337, 421
Henderson, Joe 84, 127, 155, 162, 165, 167, 176, 195, 210, 246, 255, 320, 322, 386, 420, 423, 424
Higgins, Billy 228, 234, 236, 273, 316, 336, 386, 390, 402, 423
Hinton, Milt 43, 54, 76, 79, 117, 184, 267, 366, 386
Hochkeppel, Zach 176
Holland, Dave 23, 25, 111, 124, 134, 144, 284, 367, 372, 373, 374, 399, 401
Horne, Lena 85, 203, 424
Hubbard, Freddie 77, 79, 81, 137, 139, 155, 156, 159, 173, 175, 176, 195, 196, 228, 234, 303, 365, 371, 401, 404, 419, 420, 424
Hutcherson, Bobby 84, 127, 228, 420, 421, 424

I

Iverson, Ethan 137, 423–425, 427

J

Jackson, Javon 177, 250, 402
Jamal, Ahmad 23, 337, 345, 369
Jobim, Antonio Carlos 158, 180, 195, 214, 242, 243, 244–245, 246, 248, 249, 251, 419, 425
Johnson, J.J. 4, 75, 102, 171, 195, 321, 366, 378, 389, 419
Jones, Hank 83, 87, 138, 172, 215, 336, 416, 422, 423, 425
Jones, Philly Joe 101, 104, 130, 172,

232, 303, 344
Jones, Sam 61, 82, 84

K

Keepnews, Orrin 73, 82, 83, 84, 130, 167, 168, 169, 170, 171, 172, 173, 174, 195, 212, 253, 302, 303, 320, 405
Kelly, Wynton 82, 88, 102, 103, 336, 344
Koenigswarter, Pannonica "Nica" de 83
Korman, Clifford 267
Kronos Quartet 253, 422
Kroon, Steve 177, 227, 247, 335, 336, 350, 400
Kuhn, Steve 78, 206–208, 425

L

LaFaro, Scott 71, 363, 368
Larios, Sergio 278–282
Lateef, Yusef 55, 77, 79, 329, 423
Laws, Hubert 137, 138, 159, 171, 218, 255, 321, 350, 398, 419
Legrand, Michel 203, 422, 424
Lewis, John 24, 27, 76, 77, 161, 255, 263, 318, 350, 400
Lieb, Arthur 51, 426
Locke, Joe 181, 182, 284, 407
Lovano, Joe 308
Lundvall, Bruce 175

M

Mabern, Harold 81, 103, 201
Maleson, Leon "Boots" 171, 235, 332–334, 335, 347, 349, 350, 351, 353, 354, 355
Malone, Russell 20, 47, 228, 240, 294, 304, 313, 315–326, 345, 377, 400, 423
Mangione, Chuck 63–65, 67, 101
Mangione, Gap 57, 63–65
Mann, Herbie 161, 329, 419, 421
Marsalis, Wynton 25, 140, 175, 252, 321, 404–405, 407, 425, 437
Mason, Harvey 166, 169, 177, 202, 246, 337
McBride, Christian 228, 231–241, 308, 363, 367–368, 371–372
McCurdy, Roy 57, 65
Melnick, Dan 23
Miller, Mulgrew 20, 23, 24, 26, 27, 28, 47, 84, 128, 240, 246, 313, 315–326, 336, 377, 400, 403, 404, 425
Mingus, Charles 4, 22, 74, 326, 333, 359, 370, 387, 388, 399
Monk, Thelonious 22, 66, 83, 164, 174, 182, 213, 215, 228, 240, 253, 258, 307, 329, 330, 332, 336, 364, 365, 382, 388, 422
Montgomery, Wes 83, 154, 156, 158, 167, 179, 195, 196, 304, 419, 425
Moore, Kermit 169, 254, 347
Moors, Jerry 63
Morales-Matos, Rolando 30, 250, 327, 338, 340
Motian, Paul 147, 196, 213, 215, 368, 416, 424

N

Nash, Lewis 12, 177, 227, 235, 241, 256, 308, 319, 333, 350, 381, 400

O

Obama, Barack 13, 345

P

Parker, William 386–394
Passos, Rosa 247–249, 412, 416
Patitucci, John 9, 402–403
Payne, Cecil 76, 79, 366, 389
Persip, Charlie 77, 78, 79, 81, 87

Person, Houston 203–205, 247, 297–298, 412, 416
Peterson, Oscar 5, 67, 234, 299, 319, 326, 345, 400, 413
Pettiford, Oscar 71, 85, 154, 181, 274, 307, 311, 324, 326, 330, 333, 363, 366, 388, 406
Phillips, Esther 67, 158, 419, 421

Q

Q-Tip 356–362

R

Reed, Waymon 66, 67
Ribot, Marc 209, 211
Riley, Ben 138, 164, 232, 235, 311, 328, 330, 349
Rivers, Sam 111, 123, 175, 196, 422, 425
Roach, Max 50, 55, 61, 64, 79, 103, 127, 283, 370, 371, 377
Rollins, Sonny 23, 28, 64, 65, 67, 130, 158, 167, 172, 173, 196, 272, 306, 312, 326, 330, 364, 365, 398, 415, 421, 425
Roney, Wallace 117, 127, 128, 136, 141, 197, 283, 413, 416, 421
Rubalcaba, Gonzalo 144, 177, 200, 246, 398, 400

S

Santana, Carlos 127, 202
Schibsted, Drew 406–408, 427
Scott, Stephen 30, 177, 183, 227, 235, 247, 327, 335–336, 342–345, 350
Sebesky, Don 156, 157, 165, 169, 215, 224, 307, 419
Shorter, Wayne 19, 25, 26, 28, 29, 30, 32, 81, 100, 105, 108, 109, 110, 111, 112, 114, 119, 120, 122, 123–126, 127, 128, 131, 132, 133, 134, 135, 137, 138, 139, 140, 141, 144, 146, 158, 173, 174, 175, 196, 202, 210, 228, 241, 269, 283, 337, 339, 344, 403, 413, 416, 423, 425
Snyder, John 166, 208
Spalding, Esperanza 399–400
Squitero, Roger 183, 338
Stern, Mike 142, 416
Stokowski, Leopold 69
Strozier, Frank 103
Summerlin, Ed 77, 263, 421

T

Tate, Grady 11, 180, 198, 215, 218, 326, 401–402, 420
Taylor, Arthur 199
Taylor, Billy 77, 198, 204, 240, 406
Taylor, Creed 148, 150, 153–154, 155, 156, 157, 158, 160, 161, 164, 165, 199, 211, 242, 244, 303, 362, 384
Terrasson, Jacky 403–404
Timmons, Bobby 74, 81, 82, 84, 85, 165, 337, 421, 425
Topper, Mary Ann 41, 237, 238, 246, 308, 373
Tribe Called Quest, A 196, 356–362
Trucks, Derek 208–209, 284
Turrentine, Stanley 137, 158, 195, 319, 418, 420, 425
Tyner, McCoy 167, 168, 172, 175, 183, 196, 208–212, 273, 284, 320, 330, 331, 342, 366, 415, 421, 424, 425

V

Van Gelder, Rudy 78, 85, 122, 130, 147–150, 153, 176, 253, 307, 330, 342, 348, 349, 412, 417–420, 427
V.S.O.P. 139–141, 146, 173, 176, 183, 233, 342, 424

W

Waldron, Mal 85

Walton, Cedar 80, 174, 228, 234, 236, 307, 316, 322, 336, 345, 402, 415, 421, 425
Weston, Randy 74, 76, 86, 102, 265, 366, 371, 389, 421
White, Lenny 155, 181, 198, 318
Wilkins, Ernie 77, 84
Williams, Buster 114, 129, 144, 232, 328, 349, 397
Williams, Colleen 127
Williams, Tony 10, 14, 86, 100, 104, 105, 106, 109, 111, 112, 113, 114, 116, 117, 119, 120, 121, 122, 123, 126–130, 131, 132, 133, 134, 135, 137, 138, 139, 140, 141, 142, 171, 172, 173, 174, 175, 196, 197, 198, 202, 210, 215, 216, 228, 232, 237, 246, 267, 283, 320, 321, 322, 344, 345, 357, 393, 397, 398, 401, 405, 413, 416, 422, 423, 425, 427
Wilson, Nancy 32, 397, 425
Wong, David 268–269, 372

Z

Zain, Saadi 271–272
Zimmerman, Oscar 60

About the Author

FOR MORE THAN two and a half decades, Dan Ouellette has been covering music for numerous publications—reviewing and critiquing albums and shows, commenting on the evolving state of the recording industry, and profiling artists ranging from Dizzy Gillespie and Astor Piazzolla to Frank Zappa and Norah Jones. His passion for writing about jazz and popular music has taken him throughout the world, including Africa, Australia, Europe, China and Turkey.

A regular contributor to *DownBeat* since 1987, Dan regularly writes cover stories as well as the bimonthly "The Question Is..." column. He also contributes frequently to *DB*'s "Blindfold Test" page, each year moderating live tests before audiences at the North Sea Jazz Festival in the Netherlands and at the Monterey Jazz Festival.

As the Jazz Notes columnist for *Billboard* for five years (2003–'08), Dan profiled new and veteran artists, broke news on record companies, and weighed in on various subjects ranging from the post-Katrina rebuilding in New Orleans to Wynton Marsalis's standing in the music world.

Dan has been a contributing editor at *Stereophile* for several years and the jazz consultant/jazz radio programmer for Napster since 2005. His writing has appeared in numerous national and international publications, including *Salon*, *Pulse!*, *The New Yorker* (special sections), abcnews.com, *Acoustic Guitar*, *Strings*, *Vibe*, *Playboy* (Japan), *Mediaweek*, *Edutopia*, *San Francisco Chronicle*, *San Francisco Examiner*, *Oakland Tribune* and *San Francisco Bay Guardian*. He is a longstanding member of the Jazz Journalists Association.

Dan also served as the music editor of several Schwann publications, including *Schwann Spectrum* and *Schwann Inside*, the monthly jazz and classical magazine.

In 1999, Dan moved from San Francisco, where he covered the Bay Area music scene extensively, to New York, where he is now based. He splits his time between two very different islands: Manhattan, where he's stimulated by the lively jazz scene, and Shelter Island, where he finds the quiet and relaxed country/beach atmosphere conducive to writing.

www.ingramcontent.com/pod-product-compliance
Lightning Source LLC
Chambersburg PA
CBHW071851290426
44110CB00013B/1103